THE ART OF WAR
WATERLOO TO MONS

The Art of War Waterloo to Mons

William McElwee

Indiana University Press
Bloomington / London

First published in the United States by Indiana University Press

Copyright © 1974 by William McElwee

Manufactured in the United States of America

Library of Congress Cataloging in Publication Data

McElwee, William Lloyd, 1907–
    The art of war: Waterloo to Mons.
    Includes bibliographical references.
    1. Military art and science—History. 2. Military
history, Modern—19th century. I. Title.
U41.M3   355'.009034   74-17459   ISBN 0-253-31075-0

2 3 4 5 6 82 81 80 79 78

Contents

Maps

1 The Legacy of Napoleon

The Crimean War was a political watershed. From one point of view it was the end of an era. For the first time for almost forty years European Great Powers had found themselves at war with one another on issues which might decisively alter the map of the world and imperil that balance of power so carefully established and safeguarded by Metternich and his dancing satellites at the Vienna Congress in 1815. It thus impinged upon a world in which statesmen and soldiers alike had grown up in the belief that the fundamentals, both diplomatic and military, were safe from change. There were, of course, innumerable crises. There had been at least one temporarily successful revolutionary outbreak in every European capital save London; and the growing clamour of newly self-conscious Balkan nations for emancipation from Turkish rule was a ceaselessly boiling pot. Great Britain and France were engaged in laying the foundations of empires overseas whose significance was only to be apparent much later, and which threatened the interests of no other Great Power. The only non-European Great Power, the USA, comfortably isolated within the Monroe Doctrine, was exclusively occupied with the absorption of vast Indian territories in the far west.

Thus, for forty years, none of the world's great armies had faced each other in what French writers call *La Grande Guerre*. The Russians had had a taste of it when they attacked the Turks, both in the Balkans and in the Caucasus, in 1828, but were never faced with any serious necessity for military rethinking. In Italy, too, the business of suppressing periodical revolutionary outbreaks did twice bring the Austrians up against the properly equipped and trained Piedmontese regular army, in 1821 and 1848. But

1

the Italians, outnumbered, inexperienced and never very well-
led, did little more than give Field-Marshal Radetzky a run for
his money. He trained in the process a whole generation of
Austrian officers to whom the Lombard landscape and the tactics
suited to it became as familiar as those of Salisbury Plain were to
be to later generations of British soldiers. Their campaigns were
like a well-rehearsed play given by a repertory company in its
own theatre. If the Italians were caught west of Milan they were
defeated generally at Novara. If they escaped that and pushed
towards the fortresses of the Quadrilateral they met disaster at
Custoza. Benedek, who had served as Radetzky's Chief-of-Staff
and had fought again over the same ground as a Corps Commander in 1859, underlined the fact when in 1866, at the last
moment, Francis Joseph transferred him to the chief command in
Bohemia. 'In Italy', he said sadly to the Emperor, 'I know every
tree on the road to Milan.' In 1856, when the Congress of Paris
brought the Crimean War to an end, the same sad observation
could have been made by almost every serving officer in continental Europe of the stones in the streets of his own capital.
Almost every army in Europe – even the smallest – had seen some
form of active service. But it had all been street-fighting, in 1820,
1830, or 1848, when the Liberal intellectuals had turned out the
mobs to hack up the cobbles of their streets for barricades and man
the windows and cellars of their still-medieval, tortuous streets. It
was all, beyond doubt, murderous fighting and, as such, valuable
military experience. But it did not prepare the minds of commanders, junior officers, or soldiers for the problems of *La
Grande Guerre* any more than did the organisation of punitive
columns in the Khyber Pass or the foothills of the Atlas. Ironically, the Crimean War, though it was the first great struggle
fought out for years between the regular armies and navies of
three Great Powers and two lesser ones, did strikingly little to
correct the imbalance of this military inexperience. The commanders were far too much of the old school to learn anything
before disease or exhaustion carried them off. St Arnaud, the first
Commander-in-Chief and, so *Larousse* proudly assures us, '*Le
vainqueur des Russes à la bataille de l'Alma*', had only been an
obscure, fifty-year-old Brigadier-General in North Africa when,

in 1851, alone among senior French officers, he had consented to organise the military *coup d'état* which destroyed the Second Republic and paved the way for the Second Empire. This he did quite brilliantly; and he may, indeed, have had the 'condottiere spirit'.[1] But nothing in his experience fitted him for the command of a large allied army in a major pitched battle. His frontal assault across the Alma river and up the heights beyond proved the splendid fighting spirit of the British infantry, and particularly of the Brigade of Guards and the Highland Brigade. But it did not promise well for future operations and it was probably just as well that he died almost immediately of disease. Of the succeeding generals, Pélissier had been born in 1794 and served under Napoleon I. Lord Raglan had fought as a subaltern at Waterloo; and his successor, General Simpson, had only frontier experience to guide him in the impossible task of maintaining an army in the field in the teeth of the incompetence of the authorities in London. For the Russian commander, Prince Menschikoff, the Crimea represented the inept climax of a disastrous career, diplomatic and military, which stretched nearly back to the Congress of Vienna.

In the circumstances the lessons learnt were not of any great importance in the following period to any of the participants concerned. The French, who had done less badly than any of the other armies concerned, cashed in on what glory was going; their faith in their military machine and its higher command was, if anything, strengthened; and the glittering triumph of the Congress of Paris assuaged the lingering sense of humiliation inherited from Waterloo and the Vienna settlement. The Russians were shocked by defeat into a vast, long-overdue, but also overambitious programme of social and legal reform, but did little to bring their military arrangements up to date. The almost total breakdown of their War Office administration, particularly on the medical side, had compelled the British to urgent and immediate reforms. But they, too, were slow to rethink their tactical doctrine and to remedy the shortcomings of their obsolescent equipment.

Looking backwards, then, the Crimean War was just a belated epilogue to the age of Napoleon. Only a very few statesmen and soldiers perceived that it might also be the curtain-raiser for a

3

A*

very different sort of drama. The forty years during which there had been no major disturbance of the peace were followed by fifteen which would see the whole shape of the world altered and its future determined by five wars, and which, we can now perceive, set the stage for the great, world-wide struggles of the twentieth century. By the end of them two new Great Powers, the German Empire and the Kingdom of Italy, had appeared on the European map; and the pattern of the future development of the United States of America had been decisively settled by four years of bitter civil war. The careful balance of power established at Vienna had been destroyed for ever. Europe was to settle into two massively armed camps; and their hostilities would in the end bring all human civilisation to the brink of ruin. This was the ultimate achievement of the generals of the age of Moltke.

Moreover, these generals were given no time to digest any lessons, tactical or technical, to be learnt from the Crimea. In 1859, within three years of the Congress of Paris, the French with their Italian allies were engaged in a major war against the Austrian Empire on the plains of Lombardy. The Americans found themselves locked in a great civil war in 1861. Three years after that Austria and Prussia together were to extinguish for ever the over-swollen nationalistic ambitions of the Danish monarchy; and in 1866 Prussians and Austrians were to meet at Königgrätz – a battle more decisive for the world's future than even Waterloo. By 1871 the high drama was over. The French Empire had gone and the German was in being. To guide them the commanders had only the experiences of the Napoleonic campaigns fifty years before, rationalised and annotated by Clausewitz; and their tools were still the tools of Napoleon I, Schwarzenberg, Blücher, and Wellington, last exercised in the grand manner in Belgium in 1815. The admirals were even worse off. They had to guess wildly at the modifications to the 'Nelson Touch' needed as a result of half a century of bewilderingly rapid technological advance. On the Mississippi and in the Adriatic they would have to learn the hard way the limitations and capabilities of the steam-driven, ironclad battleship, with the fates of nations at stake on the issue.

All this gave to the military history of the age of Moltke a unique urgency. Genuinely decisive battles, as those historians who have tried to chronicle them have found, are, at any rate in modern times, rare in the history of mankind. The local effects of many were, of course, immediate and catastrophic. Jena and Auerstädt demolished, at what was virtually a single blow, the whole military achievement of the Great Elector and Frederick of Prussia. But a far more effective machine had been rebuilt by Scharnhorst and Gneisenau within eight years. Trafalgar, dramatic and splendid though it was, merely set the seal on an English naval predominance which was already absolute; and, though writers understandably love to delve in the forbidden territory of the 'ifs' of history, a Napoleonic victory at Waterloo would not have made the Hundred Days more than the forlorn hope they always were. Yet the structure and nature of the German state which were to plunge the twentieth century into two devastating world wars were settled in the battle of wits between Moltke and Benedek between dawn and dusk of 3 July 1866, and in a week of manoeuvering in and around Sedan five years later. The Kaiser and Hitler were the heirs of that inheritance, just as Mussolini, *Mare Nostrum*, and the Abyssinian War all sprang from the battlefields of Magenta and Solferino. There was never an age in which the soldiers did more to determine the future of mankind.

It was, also, an age in which the world was dominated largely by military autocracies, so that the course of history depended on the intellectual clarity and the decisions of comparatively few men. It was in the minds of statesmen and soldiers, as the special trains rolled the sovereigns and plenipotentiaries away from Paris in 1856, that the future of mankind would be settled. In this situation the soldiers, of course, came second. They could only play the game the politicians made for them. It is, therefore, very important to the historian of the age of Moltke that this, unlike 1914–18, was a period when the statesmen still controlled the generals. Bismarck and Cavour, the two men who most deliberately moulded the framework of the modern world, both used war as a calculated instrument of policy. Bismarck particularly, both in 1866 and in 1870, kept the Prussian generals on a very tight rein. By the end of both campaigns he was, in consequence, scarcely on speaking terms with his two oldest friends, Moltke, Chief of the General Staff, and von Roon, the Minister of War, or, indeed, with his King, William I, the titular Commander-in-Chief, who showed no gratitude for the process which was transforming him into a German Emperor.

The Emperor of the French, Napoleon III, also provoked and sought to use war to further his policies: to shore up the always precarious prestige of his dynasty at home, or to further his cloudier international ambitions. His heredity alone forced him to assume responsibility for both political and military decisions. But in his military decisions he was just as much circumscribed and hampered by political considerations as were the Prussian generals. In this respect the only essential difference between him and Bismarck was that he was, in the end, unsuccessful. Even the Austrian commanders, though they held their appointments from an Emperor whose authority was, in theory, absolute, could never make a military decision untrammelled and unconfused by overriding political considerations. There were always far-reaching diplomatic complications in Germany or Italy, and internal rumblings of discontent in Hungary, Bohemia, or Croatia, or in Austria itself, to limit their freedom of action. At one point in 1859 they even had to send two Army Corps home from the front because the political situation in their homelands made their loyalty independable. At no period in the world's history have military developments been so controlled and contained by politicians of one kind or another; and the historian who does not give full weight to the intentions and dilemmas of the statesmen can make no sense at all of the course of the wars and the characteristics of the armies which fought them.

This, then, was the handicap which the future was to impose on the military thinkers and leaders of the age of Moltke. The burden of the past they would find almost equally difficult to shake off. In every army forty years of hypnotic peace had taken their toll. Staff officers had occasionally to think out new techniques and even to consider changes of equipment and of long-established methods of supply and maintenance to meet the demands of remote desert, mountain, or jungle warfare. Regimental commanders had been required to give their juniors a few hurried hints on the dangers and difficulties of fighting a civilian population in its own narrow, obscure streets, where the solid cobblestones made perfect material for an artillery-proof barricade and every window would conceal a sniper. But the army organisations had remained unchanged. The grand mobilisation schemes and the hypothetical plans of campaign stayed in their pigeonholes. New ideas and new inventions alike were dismissed with polite scepticism. Each year ageing senior officers, whose longevity was the despair of their juniors, squeezed themselves more painfully into increasingly expensive uniforms to superintend the stereo-typed evolutions of their troops on the *Manöverplatz*, with a pause for a daily picnic lunch, and a Gargantuan dinner to round off. Nothing changed in the armies except the uniforms, which were constantly altered at the whims of minor royalties or wealthy colonels. There was no time and little disposition to digest the lessons of the Crimea. In every country and at all levels, officers entered the period of revolutionary, and sometimes catastrophic warfare which opened in 1859 with a mental equipment and troops and weapons which they themselves or their fathers handled, nearly fifty years before, in the campaign of Waterloo. To understand their actions during the next fifteen years, both on land and sea, it is thus essential to have a clear grasp of two things: the problems and plans of the statesmen; and the inheritance, intellectual and material, of the leading soldiers.

In 1856 the areas within which decisions could be taken which would decisively influence the world's history were only two : the continents of Europe and America. The future of two thirds of the world's population, in India, in Africa, and in far-eastern Asia would be determined immediately and for the next fifty years in Downing Street and the Quai D'Orsay, the Wilhelmstrasse and the Ballhausplatz and, more remotely, in Washington and St Petersburg. Of the diplomats who would make these historic decisions only two were in that year effectively in power: Napoleon III in Paris, intent on any adventure which would break up the Vienna pattern, liberate France from her standing role as the bad boy of Europe, and further the interests of his dynasty; and, in Turin, Count Cavour, busily engaged in transforming the archaic kingdom of Piedmont and Sardinia into a modern state and making his Sovereign, Victor Emmanuel II, King of all Italy. Abraham Lincoln was not elected on the Abolition of Slavery ticket until 1860. Bismarck, universally regarded as a mere firebrand, would have to wait for his chance until 1861, and in 1859 was despatched

by a hesitant Prussian government to the Embassy at St Petersburg, to prevent him from influencing current policy and, in his
own phrase, to 'cool him down'. A new liberal-minded Tsar was
wholly absorbed in the problems bequeathed to him by that autocratic martinet, Nicholas i; and in London Lord Palmerston,
excluded from the Foreign Office by the hostility of the Queen,
concentrated, as Prime Minister, on frustrating the Liberal intentions of Mr Gladstone at home and the Prince Consort abroad.
Thus the soldiers had to function largely in an intellectual
vacuum. None of the generals anywhere had any clear idea of
what their political masters were at. In Vienna where for a
hundred years a repeated miracle had provided the Empire with
a man of genius to administer its foreign policy, it was for twenty
years at the mercy of second-rate civil servants and soldiers, and
Vienna had ceased to give Europe a lead.

Napoleon iii was the stormy petrel of European diplomacy. Intent only on smashing up the delicate balance of power established
by Metternich, Castlereagh, and Talleyrand, he wanted a war, provided that he was reasonably certain of winning it and it was near
enough at hand to enable him to take command of his own armies
and prove that he was a proper offspring of the Napoleonic
Legend. The tragedy, both for France and for his dynasty, was
that he was inefficient. When, in due course, Cavour and
Bismarck took a hand he found himself playing, in the modern
phrase, 'out of his League'. Nor was he well served. Himself an
upstart and an adventurer, he depended on the glittering façade
of success to keep himself in power and compensate the French
for the loss of all their political liberties. It was thus a regime
which attracted to it ambitious careerists and speculators, and
which had continually to advertise its authentic Bonapartist traditions. Men like Walewski, the great Emperor's illegitimate son, or
who, like Oudinot, had good 'Napoleonic' names, had a sure
passport to an eminence far beyond their abilities. Furthermore,
since the Emperor himself exploited his inside knowledge to enlarge his private fortune on the Paris Exchange, it is not surprising that his administration became at all levels corrupt as well as
incompetent.

Such a man, so situated, inevitably handled foreign affairs
themselves as though they were an elaborate speculative venture.

Obsessed by the dangerous *idée fixe* that the nationalistic passions engendered by the French Revolution were in the long run an irresistible force, he was to abandon the centuries-old French policy which had regarded any move towards unity in Germany or Italy as an inherent threat. Instead, he proposed to assist the nationalist drives on both sides of the Alps in the belief that he could control them and at the same time secure such an enlarged power for France as would enable her still to dominate the European political scene. At the base of all this reasoning there lay two fatal delusions. One was that in the political sphere he had to deal with benevolent National-Liberal intellectuals and idealists; the other was the belief that the French army was still the best in Europe. Deceived by Cavour's wholly realistic and, in the circumstances, unavoidable preference for representative, parliamentary government, he thought him a relatively powerless and well-intentioned simpleton who would gratefully accept the beneficent results of French patronage. Similarly he would accept, until far too late, Bismarck's bluff pose as the old-fashioned, straightforward, Prussian country gentleman who had neither the patience nor the wit to grasp the subtleties of French diplomacy. In consequence, in 1859, when he and Cavour deliberately forced an unwanted war on Austria, he lost all control of the situation and in the end only just saved his face. Not until 1940, when Mussolini played jackal to Hitler's Germany, would France have to pay the full price for this delusory victory which laid the foundations for a new Great Power on her Alpine frontier.

It is worth dwelling at some length on this 1859 situation because the French miscalculations, military and political, during those months lie at the root of all Europe's disasters ever since. In the long run Napoleon's military miscalculations were probably even more important than his political blunders. He won Magenta and Solferino, the two great battles of that war, but only with great difficulty and at appalling cost. His belief that the French army was unquestionably the best in the world was thus confirmed. He was also convinced that the Austrians were very nearly as good. These delusions were shared by almost all the European military commanders. Only Moltke and a handful of his General Staff colleagues, comparatively junior officers in the Prussian military hierarchy, reached the correct conclusion : that two great armies, wholly antiquated both tactically and logistically, had blundered their way through a campaign which, in the last analysis, proved only that both could be comfortably defeated by a more modern conception of the potentialities of fire and movement. Moltke's perception of the truth was to transform the map and the whole future of Europe. It is, however, at this stage important to remember that, but for Bismarck, he would never have had the chance. Equally Napoleon in 1866 would never have played his cards as he did had he not reckoned that the Austrian army was more than a match for the Prussians.

If Napoleon's miscalculations were important, the more scientifically accurate conclusions of Cavour and Bismarck were even more so. From the soldier's point of view what was important was that all three of these statesmen were perfectly prepared to use war deliberately as an instrument of policy. With the morality of such an outlook the historian of the art of warfare is not directly concerned. He can only record that politics consist of the acquisition and use of power and that throughout human history problems which have defied solution by negotiation have had to be solved by force. These three were not in the modern, pejorative sense warmongers. After 1859 Napoleon said, and certainly with truth, that he hated war. His publicly stated reason was that it was 'too uncertain'; but he was also deeply shocked at Magenta and Solferino by more than his own inability to control the events of a great pitched battle. The mangled civilian corpses with which St Arnaud had strewn the streets of Paris in 1851 to achieve his *coup d'état* had left him unmoved, since he was not required to contemplate them. At Magenta on 5 June 1859, he could no longer ignore the stench of war under an Italian midsummer sun, the appalling casualties of a hard-fought 'soldiers' battle', and the sufferings of the wounded from heat, dust, thirst and the swarms of flies – sufferings so frightful, incidentally, that they inspired the foundation of the Red Cross. He would never again thenceforward willingly involve himself personally in the conduct of military operations. Nevertheless his career – his Star – required that other people should fight wars; and he was prepared to encourage them.

No such personal difficulties clouded the vision of Count Camillo Cavour, who had enjoyed effectively supreme power in

Piedmont since 1852. Short, tubby, and bespectacled, he was physically unimpressive, but behind his twinkling charm there was a brilliant brain, an iron will, and a complete lack of political scruples. Though he has come down in history with Mazzini and Garibaldi as one of the great Liberal triumvirate who freed and united Italy, he was never doctrinaire. Thus his preference for constitutional monarchy was as calculated as everything else about him. He had studied British political institutions on the spot and admired them. But – much more important – the cause of constitutional monarchy could rally the support of moderate opinion throughout the country, whether conservative or liberal, and would have the further advantage of gaining the active good-will of France and Great Britain. All these he must have not merely for the ultimate welding of the infinitely disparate Italian population into a single nation, but even more for the essential preliminary task of ousting Austria from the Peninsula. Austria had made it abundantly clear that in all circumstances she would fight to preserve her protectorate over Central and Southern Italy and her direct rule of Lombardy and Venetia – the richest provinces of all. War was therefore for Cavour not merely, in the disapproving phrase of the League of Nations Covenant, 'an instrument of policy'. It was the very object of all his policy. Bismarck was to use the word *Realpolitik* to describe his own methods; but Cavour was at least as ruthless an exponent of political realism – perhaps the most cynical and successful the world has yet seen. 'If we did for ourselves', he once remarked roguishly to d'Azeglio, 'what we are doing for Italy, what shocking rascals we should be.'

Cavour, in fact, had already placed his stakes on the table when he persuaded his cabinet to send 17,000 Piedmontese troops to join the Allies in the trenches before Sebastapol. On the face of it this was a lunatic decision. His tiny kingdom had no interest in the maintenance of the integrity of the Ottoman Empire, and even the maintenance of this small force placed a severe strain on its resources. It was, none the less, a brilliant coup. One of his soldiers was to remark to a grumbling companion : 'Out of this mud Italy will be made'; and this was true. Great Britain and France were placed under an obligation to allow him to present the Italian problem to the Congress of Paris as an international problem, and not just a matter of Austrian internal politics, and so clearly suggest to Napoleon where the field for his next international adventure lay. Moreover this army of 17,000 was a by no means contemptible contribution to the Allied effort at a moment when disease, frostbite, and administrative incompetence had reduced the number of effectives in the British front line to a mere 11,000. At the battle of the Tchernaya, General La Marmora and his troops had done very well indeed. For a major war in northern Italy Piedmont would be able to muster about 75,000 men—an army which Austria could easily outnumber by four to one and still retain a striking force in reserve for use elsewhere. But Austria's hedging policy throughout the Crimean War left her without a friend in Europe; and Cavour had at least proved that, if he could find an ally among the great powers, the Piedmontese army would be a force to be reckoned with.

When Cavour pulled off this first great coup Bismarck had still seven years to wait before he could take over the guidance of Prussian policy. But he was already wholly preoccupied with the not dissimilar problem of achieving German national unity without damage to the Prussian state and to the monarchy which he served. For him, too, the central difficulty was the entrenched hegemony of Austria, expressly designed by Metternich to preserve for ever an ineffectual German Confederation which frustrated equally the ideals of the National-Liberals and the ambitions of Prussia. He was a responsible statesman and he would gladly have avoided war if he could. But he, too, knew that the Habsburg monarchy was compelled by the circumstance always to fight rather than surrender power or provinces. For him, as for Cavour, the final solution of his problem was bound to be a military one.

Thus, if the Congress of Paris be taken as the opening of a new age – the age of Moltke – it left all Europe save Great Britain and Russia already committed to policies which must lead to war. For different reasons Napoleon III, Bismarck and Cavour were all intent on destroying the balance of power so carefully established in Vienna in 1815. For forty years this had been preserved by the sheer diplomatic genius of Prince Metternich, since Austria's own survival depended on it. If once the principle of national self-determination were accepted, the polyglot Habsburg Empire would disintegrate. Only the dynasty, the army, and the bureaucracy transcended the linguistic frontiers and held the whole ramshackle structure together. For more than two centuries the army had rendered imcomparable service to the dynasty. Though seldom spectacularly successful, it had more than held its own since the days of Prince Eugene and, though outlying provinces had been lost, others had been added, and the Empire, against all reason and probability, had survived. There was no collapse in Austria after the defeat at Austerlitz in 1805 comparable to that of the apparently much more cohesive army and state in Prussia after Jena and Auerstädt a year later. But the army had always been able to count on powerful allies to sustain them in their struggle to preserve an anachronism. By 1856 this was no longer true. The stupidity and overconfidence of Count Buol had thrown away the whole of this priceless diplomatic inheritance. Austria had bitterly alienated both sides in the Crimean War and emerged from the Congress of Paris without a friend. Her diplomats had failed her, and her soldiers would have to face the looming series of crises alone.

Thus, for the three years which elapsed between the end of the Crimean War and the opening of the Italian campaign of 1859 the politicians and soldiers of every government in Europe faced the certainty of not one, but several wars. The Spaniards might hope to remain isolated beyond the Pyrenees and the Belgians could shelter behind their guaranteed neutrality. But, from the Vistula to the English Channel, every power, great or small, was involved in calculating the chances and risks of a dimly foreseeable future. Danish nationalist ambitions in Schleswig-Holstein directly involved Scandinavia. Any stirring of the European melting-pot would arouse dangerous passions and ambitions in the Balkans. Even Great Britain and Russia, though they would remain uncommitted militarily, were inevitably to see their vital interests at stake in the reconstruction of the European state system which impended.

Yet, remarkably, the commanders and general staffs on whom the ultimate decisions would rest, remained intellectually undisturbed. This was partly because statesmen, though they may sometimes foresee the course of events, can seldom predict the pace at which they will develop. But it was far more the consequence of the forty-year general peace. Like any other professional, the soldier can only progress in his art by practising it; and this practice, during a prolonged era of peace, he is absolutely denied. However seriously he may study the lessons of the past, the social and economic changes which are taking place around him, and the scientific and technological advances which are being achieved by his civilian contemporaries, he cannot know the answer in advance. In a peace-time world the consequences of a new invention can be easily and immediately tested. The less dramatic, though equally decisive changes brought about by social and educational reform can be, over the years, measured and assessed. The warrior, on the other hand, has no such experience on which to base his highly speculative conclusions. Not even the most militarist of modern societies, so far as is known, has allowed a field-firing exercise in which troops actually kill each other, or in which warships and aircraft deliberately batter each other to pieces.[2] Even the commander of genius can only speculate in his study and tentatively verify his conclusions in the artificial, mock-battle conditions of an annual manoeuvre. He can only guess at the actual impact of a new weapon, or at the changes in the morale and discipline of the troops he may have to command resulting from an industrial revolution or a far-sweeping Education Act.

The nineteenth century, largely billed in the history books as the era of the genesis of modern, total war, in fact gave the world two of the longest periods of general peace in the recorded history of humanity: 1815–56, and 1871–1914. The revolutionary tactical thinking of Epaminondas, of Philip of Macedonia and Alexander the Great, of Gustavus Adolphus, Frederick the Great, and Napoleon was based on recent and personal experience. The generals and admirals of 1859 and 1914 had no such luck. However intelligent, they could not know, until they had learnt in practice, the impact of the armour-piercing shell upon armour plate, or the devastating effect of the breech-loading rifle and the machine gun on infantry and cavalry tactics. The lessons to be drawn from the 'fringe' warfare of the intervening periods were often downright misleading; and none of them had first-hand experience of handling large formations in a theatre of war which could cover a continent.

The men of 1859 were under a further and particular handicap. Every important army in Europe had emerged from the campaigns of 1812–15 with legitimate reasons for self-congratulation. The strategical genius of Napoleon had shown that the army organisation and the tactics, hectically evolved by Carnot when the crisis of war broke over the Revolutionary government of 1792, could smash the great, tradition-based armies of the old monarchies. French armies had dictated peace in every capital in Europe save London and Moscow; and it could fairly be argued that Nelson's fleet and the Russian winter were factors beyond the capacity of the best tactical system in the world. Excuses could easily be found for the final, decisive defeat at Waterloo. The Emperor was not at the height of his powers, or in good health. Grouchy had blundered, unforgivably. Blücher, still more unforgivably, had broken all the rules by not retiring, as he should have, to the north-east: and so Wellington's bovine tactics on the ridge of St Jean had gained a wholly deceptive and undeserved victory.

France's enemies could find similar causes for satisfaction. Austria, shattered at Ulm and Austerlitz in 1805, had all but revenged herself triumphantly on a Napoleon still at the height of his powers four years later, when the Archduke Charles had brilliantly defeated him at Aspern-Esslingen and come within an ace of decisive victory at Wagram.[3] In the final campaign she had put 250,000 troops into the field under the command of Prince Schwarzenberg, to play a decisive part in the campaign which liberated Germany and ended at Paris. The army reforms of the Archduke Charles were vindicated and, therefore, unchallengeable. Similarly the wholesale reorganisation of state and army in Prussia after the disastrous humiliation of Jena and Auerstädt in 1806 had enabled old Blücher to play his spectacular part in the advance on Paris in 1814 and by his timely arrival at La Belle Alliance on Wellington's left a year later to set the seal on the victory of Waterloo. The doctrines of Clausewitz and the reforms of Scharnhorst and Gneisenau became as unchangeable as scripture. The Russian leaders, equally, saw no reason for dissatisfaction with the performance of their armies in the Napoleonic era. Eylau, Friedland, and Borodino had been the Emperor's hardest fought and most costly victories; and it had been unquestionably they who had finally turned the tide against him in 1812. Apart from the defensive value of the Russian winter, mere numbers and the infinite capacity of Russian soldiers for dogged endurance and self-sacrifice made them always formidable. Nicholas I, who succeeded his brother, Alexander, in 1828 was not, in any case, a man much given to innovation. Himself educated on the drill square, he was entirely content to have, even in peace time, a million men permanently under arms : highly drilled automata who would suffer and die for him without fear or question. Neither he nor his generals felt any need for new weapons or tactical reform. Even in Britain, where the early industrial revolution offered unique opportunities for technological advance, the soldiers were very slow to adapt themselves to a changing world. The Duke of Wellington remained Commander-in-Chief until 1828, and again from 1842 onwards; and he presented an insuperable barrier to progress or modernisation. He was justifiably well satisfied with the army which he had forged in the Peninsula, which had fought its way from Lisbon to Toulouse without a single major defeat, and had triumphantly held the ridge at Waterloo. He saw no reason to tinker with a machine which had served him so well; and he lived until 1852. Moreover, he bequeathed to the army a body of senior officers who had grown grey under his tutelage, sublimely uncritical of a system which had governed their lives for half a century. Only in Prussia was there any discernible creative impulse within the military machine. But, until the appointment, in October 1857, of the Freiherr von Moltke as Chief of the General Staff, that, too, was frustrated and partially defeated by the confused thought of the Prussian politicians.

The armies of the lesser European states offered no exception. Each, according to its historical political affiliations, conformed to the military system and doctrine of one or the other of the Great Powers. Thus the governments launched themselves into one of the most dramatic and decisive periods in the history of warfare with military machines geared and carefully nursed for a resumption of the Napoleonic wars. Napoleon III, moreover, had staged in France a deliberate and self-conscious attempt to revive not only the glories, but the very institutions of the earlier Empire. This circumstance, too, had an almost hypnotic effect on the military thinking of the period. It had already become an ingrained habit to think of the French army, its tactical doctrines and its leadership, as lying at the core of all the problems of the European general staffs. The contemporary situation did nothing to correct this habit of mind. Like his uncle, Napoleon III was an adventurer. He was equally and avowedly dedicated to the disruption of the European state system and the radical alteration of the existing territorial balance of power. Inevitably the capacities and intentions of the French military machine became the central factor in the calculations of all the politicials and soldiers.

Between 1792 and 1815 French military theory and practice had been an improvisation imposed by two men of genius. Neither Carnot nor Napoleon had very much choice in the matter. When the Committee of Public Safety – the government of a new French Republic which had renounced war as a means of aggrandisement – found itself threatened all along the frontier from the Channel to the Alps by three of the European Great Powers, the old army of the French Monarchy had virtually disintegrated. The vast majority of the predominantly aristocratic officers were in exile or in prison. There was scarcely a regiment which had not mutinied at least once, and none was well enough drilled or disciplined to face even the harassingly counter-marched troops of the Good Old Duke of York, let alone the ordered ranks of the Prussians and Austrians. The enemy armies, composed largely of illiterate, conscripted peasants, uninspired by patriotism and sublimely unconscious of their own national identity, but hammered by years of brutally ruthless discipline on the drill-square, had been brought to a state where it was virtually impossible for them to disobey an order, even in the suicidal conditions of a close fire-fight on an eighteenth-century battlefield. Carnot had neither the instructors nor, above all, the time to match such troops at their own game. What he had – and his opponents had not – was a mass of volunteers and equally enthusiastic conscripts produced by the *Levée-en-Masse*. They would lay down their lives unthinkingly and gloriously for the Revolution, or for France, but the essence of the Revolution, as they understood it, was a rejection of authority and of old-fashioned discipline. He had also an incomparable body of warrant officers, to whom the abolition of privilege had suddenly opened the avenues of promotion, and out of whom were to be found the senior officers of the new army.

Of this political and social situation was born the column which was to smash the lines of the ancient monarchies. The best trained survivors of the old army were pulled out to form *voltigeur* companies: marksmen, sometimes armed with a rifled carbine, and trained in the use of cover, they were thrown out in front in skirmishing order to harass and confuse the enemy. In attack the rest of the infantry followed this screen in densely packed columns which varied in strength from battalions to – in exceptional cases – whole divisions. The basic conception was of a battalion formed in columns of companies on a frontage of 50–75 yards at one yard per man, and to a depth, varying obviously in proportion to the front, of 15 to 25 yards. A gap of at least 150 yards was allowed between each column, whatever its size, in order to allow the skirmishing screen to withdraw at the moment of contact to form a reserve or move to protect a vulnerable flank.

At first sight such a tactical system, in an age when battles had come to be dominated by fire power, might appear to be both crude and retrogressive. At a sober, walking pace the column would advance perhaps a thousand yards, the senior officers and the standards in front, with the drums beating out the step, while the excitement in the rear ranks steadily mounted. Then, at something under three hundred paces from the enemy line the officers' swords would leap from their scabbards, the drums would break into the *pas-de-charge,* those who could see anything to fire at would loose off their muskets and the rest would hoist their shakos on their bayonets, and the whole solid, cheering, excited mass would fling itself across the narrow, critical gap which lay between the front rank and the enemy. A handful of bayonets and the crude weight of a mass of human bodies were flung against the carefully drilled volley fire of the professional armies, covered only by the smoke and confusion created by the skirmishers and such artillery fire as could be brought to bear. Even the Greek phalanx, charging against a far less formidable fire, had been able, by progressively lengthening the pikes carried in successive ranks, to produce three or four times the number of steel points directed at the enemy at the moment of impact.

As a method of assault it was, of course, crude and long out of date; and neither Wellington nor the Archduke had any difficulty in thinking out effective answers. But it had many advantages. It exploited to the fullest possible extent the enthusiasm and courage of the French recruit and it eliminated the need for elaborate drill and prolonged training. The rawest newcomer could have little difficulty in keeping his place in so closely packed a mass; and only if things went wrong, if the front ranks wavered and momentum was lost, would the column fall into confusion and utter disaster.[4] Up to the moment of the assault, moreover, it provided unit and formation commanders with a wonderfully flexible tactical instrument. It could move across broken country without falling into confusion. It could change direction and alignment with bewildering rapidity in a way quite impossible to the ordered lines of Frederick the Great; and so long as the basic sub-unit column remained undisturbed, formations could be shaken out into innumerable different patterns to suit changes of ground or situation. The French commanders learnt to exploit these possibilities with brilliant skill. General Morand, during his long, fighting advance at Auerstädt, regrouped his division no less than four times before the final triumphant assault. It was this which gave the French the tactical mastery on the battlefield itself so spectacularly completing the defeat of an enemy already out-manoeuvred and outmarched. So long as the column, at the critical moment of the assault, could break through the inflexible, over-drilled enemy line, the French armies remained virtually invincible.

Surprisingly this tactical system, essentially a hasty improvisation designed in the midst of a major national crisis to meet a particular set of political and social circumstances, survived unmodified to the final débâcle of the Imperial army at Waterloo in 1815. For this there were two main reasons. In the first place Napoleon himself paid very little attention to unit and sub-unit tactics. His own peculiar genius lay in the swift co-ordinated movement of large masses of troops, so as to pin an enemy down and force him to fight in circumstances wholly disadvantageous. The instrument which he had found ready to hand for his first, breath-taking campaigns in northern Italy had proved itself perfectly adequate to his needs, and he seems never to have called into question its fundamental weaknesses. Circumstances combined to blind him to the fact that his opponents were slowly evolving effective methods of dealing with the column. He never saw a Wellingtonian army in action until Waterloo, and was able to attribute an unbroken series of defeats in the Spanish Peninsula to the incompetence of subordinates; and his own tactical genius extricated him from near-defeat in the Aspern-Wagram campaign of 1809 without noticing that it was the tactical superiority of some of the Austrian formations which had brought him so close to disaster. But perhaps more important was the fact that he never had the time or opportunity to carry through a fundamental retraining of his army on more sophisticated lines.

For Napoleon's *Grande Armée* – those 400,000 incomparable fighting soldiers who in three years were to overrun all Europe to the banks of the Niemen – was itself every bit as much of a gigantic improvisation as the hasty levies of the armies of the First Republic. In manpower, equipment, and supplies it represented the maximum which the rickety French economy could support and maintain; and it was deliberately designed to win a war in a single, annihilating campaign. All the strength was in the front line. There was no army of reserve in the homeland to hold the frontiers in case of a setback and to furnish drafts to replace the casualties inevitable even in victory. There were no bulging arsenals from which expenditure and losses of essential supplies could be made good; and even if there had been there was no transport system which could have brought them to the remote, hard-marched troops. The regimental depots were not centres where raw conscripts could be drilled and taught to use their weapons, but supply dumps where the recruit could draw the essential minimum to cross the Rhine and conquer a continent: a uniform, his weapons, a single pair of shoes, some ammunition, and a bread ration. By the system known as 'amalgamation', he would be posted straight into a unit to learn all his skills the hard way, in action, from such veteran soldiers as survived. 'Conscripts need not spend more than eight days in training camp' was Napoleon's dictum.[5] Accustomed to easy and spectacular victory, the troops of the *Grande Armée* subsisted in between battles on loot and dispensed with drill and discipline out of the line. So long as the troops had learnt to manoeuvre in column, to charge with the *élan* inherited from the revolutionary armies and to form square if threatened by cavalry, nothing more was thought necessary.

At one moment, in 1804, when the reorganisation of the Imperial army was complete, when the majority of officers and men had seen some active service, and the remainder had had plenty of time to become absorbed into battalions, there were signs that a more sophisticated system, combining fire-power with shock tactics, was being evolved. A regiment would deploy one of its two battalions in close support of the *Voltigeurs* to carry the fire-fight to within striking distance of the enemy, when the second battalion would pass through in column to settle the issue with the bayonet. But after 1805, as the casualties mounted along with the victories, the raw recruits began to outnumber the veterans, and most regimental commanders found themselves unable to man even one battalion well-enough trained to advance to the attack in extended order.

The French became more dependent than ever on massive shock tactics, and nowhere more decisively than at Waterloo.[6] By then the French generals had come to rely on the massed artillery for covering fire, to dispense with preliminary skirmishing and fire-fighting, and leave all to the sacrificial courage and patriotism of their troops. If employed in sufficient mass, the bayonets of the infantry or the sabres of the cavalry would do the job alone. The more advanced tactical theorists toyed with plans for getting the best of both worlds: of exploiting the flexibility of the column until it was within assaulting distance, and then deploying units and sub-units into line. In practice, from Austerlitz onwards, mounting casualties and the increasing proportion of untrained recruits in the line regiments made such a manoeuvre unthinkable. For field commanders the drill manual of 1791 still reigned supreme in 1815.

This, then, was the inheritance of military thinking bequeathed to the Second French Empire by the First. The Bourbon and Orléanist Monarchies left Napoleon's military machine more or less undisturbed. Some units which had perished in the Revolution, such as the *Gardes du Corps* and the Swiss Guard, reappeared for a time, and the uniforms changed with the regimes.

But there were no drastic reforms of doctrine or organisation. There was perforce innovation and improvisation among the 'Colonial' generals, as they wrestled with the novel problems set by their elusive enemies in the vast spaces of North Africa. The metropolitan army lived peaceably in its provincial garrison towns gossiping and reminiscing, and wistfully awaiting the advent of another great military leader, its routine only disturbed by the annual manoeuvres in the classic battlefield areas between Châlons and Nancy and the occasional eruptions of the volatile Paris mob. General Jomini rather easily gained a European reputation with his tactical essays[7] which became prescribed reading for ambitious young officers in all the military academies. But there was no new thinking in these. They were little more than an elaboration and systematisation of the combinations of tactical manoeuvre in column first evolved on the battlefield by Napoleon's generals. The fire-fight continued to be regarded as only the essential pre-liminary to the assault with the *arme blanche*; and at the decisive moment shock tactics were to settle the issue. Thanks to the genius of the Russian General Todleben, the Crimean War had become primarily an exercise in siege warfare in conditions reminiscent of the great Vauban, which inevitably imposed the same basic tactical pattern : a bombardment and an assault. Since they triumphed at the Malakoff redoubt when the British failed before the Redan, French generals saw no need for fresh thinking. Their medical and supply arrangements clearly needed drastic overhaul. Their tactical doctrines appeared to have been wholly vindicated.

Inevitably all military thinking in Europe was dominated until 1856 by that of the French. This was partly due to the colossal, and posthumously somewhat inflated prestige of Napoleon himself. It was also largely a consequence of the Vienna settlement. To the mind of 1815, haunted by the memory of nearly twenty-five years of defensive warfare, France was *par excellence* the aggressor. All Europe's diplomatic and military arrangements rested on the assumption that their primary aim was to contain France within the frontiers imposed on her by the peace settlement. The only notable exception was the small, but virile Kingdom of Piedmont and Savoy, whose ambitions could only be furthered by the total disruption of the Vienna state system. But the armies of northern Italy had been virtually incorporated by the French during the Napoleonic era. For Cavour France was the necessary ally, and General La Marmora's tactical theories prudently conformed to those of his French colleagues. Russia, preoccupied with Balkan and Far Eastern projects, was a law unto herself. The remaining Great Powers formulated their theory of *La Grande Guerre* on the assumption that France would be the main enemy and that their essential task was to prepare to defeat the French.

In consequence, in Great Britain, Austria, and Prussia, the natural conservative inertia engendered by a long era of peace was strengthened by the French conservatism itself. Their generals reckoned that they or their predecessors had worked out methods of defeating the column which had served perfectly well, and saw no reason to start tinkering with systems which had once already brought them decisive victory. The British were not in fact going to have to test their theories on continental battlefields, though the traditional view that the integrity of the Ottoman Empire was a vital British interest would bring them to the brink more than once. Not until 1914 would they find themselves op-posed by a powerful, well-equipped modern army; and some-thing of the spirit of the Duke of Wellington still haunted their manuals of drill and tactics even then. It must be remembered, furthermore, that the tactical modifications which enabled the Duke to win all his Peninsular battles were not revolutionary but, in essence, reactionary. He parried the threat of the French column not by abolishing the old, rigid eighteenth-century line, but by improving it. By making it standard practice to form it into two ranks instead of three he brought the whole devastating fire-power of every unit to bear at the moment of impact.[8] He trained it to select positions where a low ridge protected it from the massive fire which covered the initial stages of the advance, and only to move up to the ridge itself at the moment when the launching of the enemy assault inevitably masked their covering fire; and he liked to rest his flanks on obstacles impenetrable to a charging column. Finally, he drilled and disciplined it ruthlessly to hold its fire until, quite literally, the troops could see the whites of the enemies' eyes. At that range the inaccuracy of the old musket ceased to matter. The impact of the first massive volley devastated and disintegrated the column and deprived it of the weight and momentum on which it relied for victory. As always, fire-power, intelligently applied, proved itself superior to shock tactics, however massive, and however sacrificial the *élan* of the attackers.

Wellington's tactical reforms were thus, in essence, a perfecting of the methods of Frederick the Great and the Duke of Cumberland. Even the apparently revolutionary reforms in Light Infantry drill and discipline and tactics which Sir John Moore carried through in his famous camp at Shorncliffe looked not forwards, but back to the ideals and experiments of French and Prussian generals fifty years before, and to the experiences of British and Colonial officers in the backwoods of North America. Thus, by the time of the Duke's death British thinking on drill and tactics had become embedded not merely in the Napoleonic era, but in the methods evolved by eighteenth-century commanders to meet the limitations of their dull-witted peasant conscripts. Indeed, much of the ceremonial drill still practised by the British army of today is derived from the same source. In the course of time there were inevitable modifications to meet the possibilities of the new weapons produced by the technological advances of the industrial revolution, such as the Gatling gun, and the breech-loading rifle with its vastly increased accuracy, range, and rate of fire. With them Wellington's double line of infantry ceased to have meaning. On the frontiers of Empire forward-looking commanders could brilliantly adapt uniforms and weapons to the needs of a local campaign. Placed in command of a sizeable force of all arms large enough to be described as an army, British generals reverted to the old basic formulas. The carefully dressed, scarlet-coated line of infantry in close order remained the fundamental concept of their tactical thought, until their innate and conservative complacency was at last destroyed at the turn of the century by the marksmanship and skill in fieldcraft of a handful of Boer farmers. At its worst it could lead an upright, conscientious, well-trained officer like Lord Chelmsford to throw away a well-balanced, well-equipped force to Zulus armed only with assegais. But even the best showed the same old-fashioned rigidity. Had the Duke been privileged to watch the operations of Sir Garnet Wolseley and Sir Herbert Kitchener in Egypt and the Sudan, he would have seen the desert sands 'red with the blood of a square that broke', and have benevolently observed Winston Churchill participating enthusiastically in the classic charge of the 21st Lancers at Omdurman.

The tactical theories of the Austrian generals were as deeply rooted in the Napoleonic and eighteenth-century past as were the British. They too had a single dominating figure able, like the Duke, to frustrate all reform and all creative thought with an imperturbable conservatism. Nor could they claim, as Wellington and the British army could, an unbroken row of successes against the French between 1809 and 1815. But their senior generals matched the British in longevity. Their grand old man, Radetzky, was three years older than Wellington. Appointed Chief-of-Staff after Wagram in 1809, he had served in that capacity under Schwarzenberg in the campaigns of 1813–14, and had won his last victory as Commander-in-Chief in Italy at the age of eighty-three, when he defeated King Charles Albert of Piedmont at Novara in 1849. Like Wellington, he was essentially a figure of the eighteenth century and lived *en grand seigneur*, with a charming Italian mistress who presented him in his eightieth year with his fourth illegitimate child. In the closing years of his life he went spectacularly bankrupt for the third time and was once again compelled to appeal to the Imperial government to pay off his astronomical debts. It is revealing that, when the Finance Minister protested to the Crown Council that this would seriously affect an already unbalanced budget, he was immediately over-ruled by his young, but commonsensical Emperor. 'It is cheaper', Francis Joseph said, 'than a lost war.' Radetzky survived, still in the saddle, until 1858. Had he managed to live for one more year, he would have fought his last battle at the age of ninety-three and very likely have won it. Even then he bequeathed to the army his Chief-of-Staff, Lieutenant-General Baron von Hess, a sprightly septuagenarian and the most popular officer in the army, who was to become the Emperor's chief adviser in mid-campaign exactly fifty years after his baptism of fire at Aspern. And even the most able of the younger generals, the Archduke Albrecht, as the son of the great Archduke Charles,

was steeped in the Napoleonic tradition. The Austrians, moreover, could counter English Peninsular boasts with the undoubted
fact that they alone had defeated the great man himself when still
in the heyday of his career and before the *Grande Armée* had been
destroyed by the Russian winter.

It was in 1801, the year that Sir John Moore established his
camp at Shorncliffe, that the Archduke Charles set himself to find
a tactical answer to the apparent invincibility of the French
column. In the one which he found there was, as in Wellington's,
an eighteenth-century element. Austrian field-marshals had spent
so long trying to counter the *blitzkrieg* methods of Frederick the
Great that they had become incurably defensive-minded. Intelligent though he was, the Archduke could not altogether escape
from this prevailing climate. His tactical manual, which remained
in use until his death in 1847, insisted so strongly on the need for
substantial reserves at every level and covering forces on all flanks
that conscientious commanders were apt to find at the critical
moment they had less than half their men in actual contact with
the enemy. But the basic infantry tactics were revolutionary. The
line disappeared altogether. Battalions were to fight subdivided
into three 'divisions',[9] each of two companies, one behind the
other, and each independent. Divisions were to be drawn up in
clumps, with a recommended interval of about fifty-four paces
between them; and they were to send forward from a quarter to a
third of their men to thicken up the skirmishing screen provided
by the specialist Jaeger battalions and conduct the opening, or
fire-fight phase of the battle. These as the moment of contact
approached, were to fall back and rejoin their companies for the
shock phase. In defence divisional clumps were to be sited with a
view to giving the maximum field of fire, and all were to fire
continuously at the charging enemy column if they were not the
direct object of attack and, if opportunity arose, charge into it
from the flank. In attack they were not required to keep a rigid
alignment, but were to charge straight upon the enemy with their
bayonets. The Austrian battalion thus presented the enemy with
no vulnerable line to be broken. Only one division would normally be at risk since the column, depending as it did for success on
its solidity, weight, and speed, could not weave a serpentine,
follow-my-leader course about the battlefield overrunning each in

turn. Meanwhile it was itself exposed to a withering fire from both sides and presented two open flanks to a counter-assault. There was the disadvantage in the attack that a divisional charge could not match the weight and impact of the French; but there was the compensating fact that it presented no single, concentrated target to the enemy's defensive fire.

This was a thoroughly modern conception of infantry tactics – more modern, indeed, than any of the ideas current among the general staffs of 1914. But it demanded a complete re-orientation of infantry training, with a much greater emphasis on musketry and an encouragement of the sort of initiative and self-reliance in battle which cannot be achieved by harsh discipline on the drill square. Particularly it would be much more exacting in its demands on junior officers both as instructors, and on the battlefield where every small isolated group would have to act independently. But the Archduke believed it could be done, though he stipulated a breathing space of nine years of peace so that on mobilisation every man returning from the reserve would have absorbed the same basic training. This he was never allowed, thanks to the muddle-headedness of his brother, the Emperor Francis, and 'the mad, destructive obstinacy' of Baron Thugut, his Foreign Minister. Within a year of his getting fairly started came the disastrous campaign of Ulm and Austerlitz; and four years later, when he was fairly on the way to success, that of Aspern and Wagram. Even so, the second time he came very near to success, and Napoleon was caught napping by an opponent he had thought he could afford to despise.

The Emperor's jealousy of his more gifted brothers prevented the Archduke from ever again being entrusted with supreme command. In the campaign of 1813–14 the army which he had created was never given a chance to show its quality, thanks to the ineptitude of Prince Schwarzenberg, who was by profession a diplomat rather than a soldier. But his system had become the official doctrine of the Austrian army and the Austrians had ended up on the winning side. Like the French and the British, the Austrian generals saw no need to tinker with what had proved itself in action and had stood up very well to the demands of the Italian campaigns and the revolutions of 1848. Moreover the men who commanded the army during the long Metternichian calm were not creative military thinkers. Radetzky was essentially a field commander, with a superb *coup d'oeil* for a battle situation and a disregard for danger which endeared him to his troops. Prince Windischgrätz, apart from being the greatest snob in Europe, was distinguished only for the ruthless brutality with which he blew the mobs off the streets of Vienna and Prague in 1848. General Haynau enjoyed a certain prestige in Austria as the conqueror of Hungary in 1849; but most of the work was in fact done by his colleagues, the brilliant and charming Russian General Pashkiewitz, and the Croat 'Iron General', Jellaçic. Outside Austria he gained only a wholly deserved notoriety for having had a whole convent of Hungarian nuns publicly flogged. So the Austrian military faith remained pinned to the doctrine of the superiority of fire-power and the tactics of the small group. Statesmen and generals alike launched themselves blithely into the war of 1859, complacently certain that the army which had ultimately triumphed over the First French Empire would make short work of the Second. Among the officers the only regret was that Hess, who was beginning to show his age, had not been immediately appointed Commander-in-Chief to pick up the thread of his Napoleonic warfare.

There were factors in the military situation of Prussia which made it, in fact, far more promising than that of any other Great Power. But these were not apparent on the surface. The Prussian army was just as much hampered by the longevity of its generals as the others. Though two of the three grand old men of the Napoleonic era, Gneisenau and Clausewitz, died of cholera while preparing a campaign against the Polish revolutionaries in 1831, this merely left the field open to less able but longer-lived senior officers; commands in the field were dictated by a rigid protocol based on seniority; and the same rule which had given King Frederick William III von Mollendorf as his principal adviser for the disastrous Jena campaign was to land Moltke, when he conducted his first campaign as Chief of the General Staff against Denmark in 1864, with von Wrangel in chief command – a dotard so garrulous that Bismarck habitually gave him false information in confidence in order to get it spread convincingly in foreign capitals. Thus Moltke had to fume impotently in Berlin while Wrangel pointedly ignored his frenzied telegraphic directives. Gneisenau never commanded in the field the army which he had largely created and trained; and it was sheer luck for Prussia and her allies that the system threw up the septuagenarian Blücher to lead the Prussian armies from 1813–15.

After years of selfish isolation, Prussia had taken on Napoleon single-handed in 1806 and had suffered defeats more spectacular and a collapse of morale such as the apparently decadent Austrian Empire never experienced. With French garrisons in Berlin and all the principal fortresses, the nation of Frederick the Great all but disintegrated. Equally spectacular was the recovery during the following six years, staged on the civilian side by Stein and on the military by Scharnhorst and Gneisenau. Essentially their work was imitative, based on the profound studies of Carl von Clausewitz into the system and methods which had enabled Napoleon almost to subjugate the whole of Europe. It was from this that the concept of the nation at war was evolved, requiring not merely a new kind of army, but a new kind of nation altogether. A Frederician army of arbitrarily conscripted and illiterate peasants, many of them mercenaries, could never outmarch the French, or match their self-sacrificing heroism on the battlefield. If the whole resources of the nation were to be mobilised, the obligation for military service must of course be – as it always in effect had been – universal. But henceforward the men called to the colours were to be inspired by an informed patriotism which must not be destroyed by the rigid drill and brutal punishments of the old army. Something of the iron discipline which had held together the armies of the great Frederick would always remain in the Prussian system, and this was to give the Prussians a certain advantage over the French throughout the coming century. Combined with the effects of the abolition of serfdom and a system of universal elementary education, it would provide the commanders with a soldier whose dogged courage and unshakable loyalty would outmatch the *élan* and enthusiasm of the French; and this was one very important element in Moltke's military inheritance.

Tactically speaking that inheritance was less enviable. Rigidly determined on a slavish imitation of the French, the Prussian generals evolved nothing so progressive as the system which the Archduke bequeathed to the Austrians. They modelled their battle practice precisely on that of the French and concentrated only on doing the same things better. In this they were not immediately successful. More than six years were needed to complete so comprehensive a national renaissance; and between 1812 and 1815 Blücher must, in consequence, have suffered more tactical reverses than any other victorious general in history. The immense resilience of the new-type Prussian soldier enabled him, nevertheless, to return continuously to the attack; and Blücher's final re-appearance at La Belle Alliance after the last of his defeats at Ligny in time to turn the dogged defence of Waterloo into decisive victory silenced all Prussian self-criticism. The shortcomings of the column as an exclusive method of attack passed unnoticed. Clausewitz and his disciples, like their master, Napoleon, were predominantly concerned with grand strategy and the manoeuvring of large formations. They, too, underestimated the importance of sub-unit tactics, so that the system evolved by Carnot and the early revolutionary generals in France to meet a particular social and political crisis became as deeply embedded in the Prussian army as in the French. It formed another and less desirable part of Moltke's inheritance, and one whose significance even he failed to notice throughout his first two victorious campaigns. Only the horrifying casualties inflicted by the new French rifle in the opening battles of the war of 1870 forced him to appreciate the limitations of shock tactics in the attack and to modify the doctrine of the Prussian army in mid-campaign. To the outward eye, in fact, the Prussian army in 1859 was as clumsy and antiquated an instrument as any of the others.

This impression had been confirmed by the events of 1848–50 and the belated and abortive mobilisation of 1859 in support of Austria. Though the Prussian army had proved itself perfectly competent to blow the mobs from the barricades in the German capitals, its administrative machinery had broken down badly when it attempted a full-scale mobilisation against Denmark and, when faced by the threat of war with the still-shaken Austrian Empire, the Prussian generals had lost their nerve altogether. Even in 1859, when Moltke had already been in the saddle for two years, the mobilisation had been behind schedule and had produced far short of the total number of front-line troops theoretically available. All this helped to obscure from the general view of the very real advantages which the Prussians did in fact possess as a result of the reforms of 1806–16. The complete lack of any proper staff organisation and of any school for the training of potential staff officers had been a major cause of the disasters at Jena and Auerstädt. Clausewitz may have been neglectful of sub-unit tactics, but he bequeathed to his successors a reformed and unique Great General Staff which was to bring a wholly new technique into the conduct of large-scale military manoeuvre. Unseen by the rest of the world, the young officers who qualified for the coveted crimson trouser-stripe and shoulder flashes of the Staff worked with a quasi-monastic dedication at the problems of mobilising and employing the whole strength of the nation in any foreseeable war; and both Moltke and his friend, von Roon, the Minister of War, were products of this school. Though still hampered and frustrated by their seniors in 1859, they would very soon come into their own and would astonish the world.

Moreover, with her territories divided and scattered from the east coast of the Baltic to the Rhineland, Prussia almost inevitably took the lead in the development of railways and ultimately laid down the pattern for all the other thirty-eight states which made up the rest of Germany; and since war was, in fact as well as jest 'Prussia's national industry', that pattern followed in the first place the needs of any army which might have in a hurry to mobilise on any one of a dozen threatened fronts. A final advantage – again largely overlooked by contemporary statesmen and generals – was the possession of a breech-loading rifle as the standard weapon of the Prussian infantry. The British had begun training their infantry to use the Minié rifle from 1851 onwards; and most of the units sent to the Crimea were equipped with it, though the Grenadier Guards were only trying it out for the first time on the Malta ranges on their way out.[10] It was, moreover, already being replaced by the Enfield. It had a much greater range and accuracy than the old smooth-bore, and it is doubtful if without it the 93rd Highlanders, the 'thin red streak topped with a line of steel',[11] could have halted and dispersed the charge of 1,500 Russian horse at Balaclava. But these rifles did not have the greatly accelerated rate of fire which was the decisive advantage of the breech-loader. The Prussians had begun experimenting with their Needle Gun in 1842 and had started issuing it to their infantry in 1848. But the old guard among their generals hotly opposed this step and fought hard for the Minié. Not until they had watched the progress of the 1859 campaign in Italy were the Prussian High Command at last convinced of the overwhelming importance of fire-power in modern warfare; and by 1864 the whole of their army was equipped with a weapon which would fire at five times the rate of the old muzzle-loader, at far greater range, and with much greater accuracy. This alone was to give Moltke an advantage in his opening campaigns which he was never wholly to lose, though there was very little tactical adjustment to meet the potentialities of the new weapon; and its importance was largely unperceived outside Prussia.

In spite of these reforms, the Prussian leaders, from the tactical point of view, lived almost as much in the past as their contemporaries elsewhere. In Europe, at any rate, the generals were launched in 1859 into fifteen years of intensive warfare with armies trained to fight the battles of an era which had come to an end on the ridge of Mont St Jean forty years before. The admirals were slightly better off, in that the advent of the ironclad, steam-driven battleship forced them to take more account of technological advances unprecedented in history. The generals unmoved by the consequences of industrial revolution, continued to plan for another round of the Napoleonic wars.

2 War as an Instrument of Policy: The Armies of the Continental Powers

Before the Congress of Paris broke up Napoleon III had already declared what his next adventure was to be: he had assured Cavour that he regarded war between France and Austria as inevitable. Later he was to define his object as the freeing of Italy 'from the Alps to the Adriatic'. He had in mind a nicely limited campaign in northern Italy which, with Piedmontese help, he was reasonably certain he would win, and which seemed unlikely to provoke interference from any other major power. Even pacifist opinion in England would approve of such a cause. Prussia had already shown her hostility to Austria in Germany; and Russia would not lift a finger to save an ungrateful Austria to whom she largely owed her defeat in the Crimea. For the occupation of the Danubian principalities by a theoretically neutral Austrian army 300,000 strong[1] had pinned down on the Balkan frontier some 321 Russian battalions – twice the number they had in the Crimea – and had made it impossible to reinforce Prince Menschikoff after his defeat on the Alma. Moreover, in return for the acquisition of Lombardy and Venetia, the Sardinian Monarchy could reasonably be asked to cede to France – subject, of course, to a plebiscite – the predominantly French-speaking provinces of Savoy and Nice, thereby gratifying the French people with one more of the long-covered *frontières naturelles* and a further instalment of the foreign glory for which they were always ready to sacrifice, for a time at least, their political liberties. The plan rested on a grave political miscalculation. For the Prussian government would not in practice be able to resist the clamour of German public opinion for help to Austria in her struggle with the hereditary enemy. This was all the more dangerous because the plan also rested on a still graver military miscalculation.

It is not surprising to the historian that governments contemplating war frequently underestimate the strength of their opponents. But it is astonishing how often they have overrated the forces at their own disposal. When Cavour got his war in 1859 both French and Austrian Emperors very quickly found that they had been grossly misled as to the number of troops available to them. Even the Prince Regent of Prussia, whose army, for political reasons, only mobilised too late to exercise any decisive influence on the course of events, had cause for bitter disappointment. The numbers of his regular army fell short of expectation; and the territorial reserve – the *Landwehr* – turned out when it was assembled to be obviously unfit for active service without radical retraining.

With its long Algerian experience and its record in the Crimea, the French army in 1859 was already rated the best in the world. But, except for its tactics, there was nothing about it which was reminiscent of the First Empire. Indeed, the structure, organisation and methods of recruitment were based on a conscious denial of all that the Revolutionary and Napoleonic armies had stood for. Neither the restored Bourbons nor the Orléanists had wished ever again to unkennel the mob. The *Appel au Peuple*, the *Levée-en-Masse* and, indeed, the whole concept of the Nation at War had no place in their cautious defensive foreign policies and represented in their minds an inherent threat to internal stability. Both regimes had rested on the support of the propertied classes : the rich industrialists, the provincial bourgeoisie, and a landowning peasantry; and the leaders of the Second Republic, though they had called the masses to the barricades to gain power, were drawn from the same comfortable class. In the end, when property itself was threatened, they too needed an army which was absolutely dependable and quite uncontaminated by revolutionary principles. In any case a people's army, representing the true strength of France, would have meant an intolerable increase in taxation.

All this Napoleon III had to accept as part of the price to be paid for reviving the Empire at all. Bourgeoisie and peasantry, frightened by the excesses of the Revolution, had seen in him the saviour of law and order. To win their votes he had even had to assure them that 'the Empire means Peace'. He therefore had to accept the military system of his predecessors as it stood and make the best of it. The Napoleonic glories had somehow to be revived without the Napoleonic army. He could recreate the Imperial Guard, revive the Imperial uniforms, and give the whole a superficial glitter and *panache*. But it remained in essence the old, small, professional, long-service army, cut off from the rest of the nation and immune from subversive revolutionary influences. The Corps Législatif continued to fix the total strength at the number for which it was prepared to pay; the old system was perpetuated by which the army annually selected by lot from each age-group the numbers required to bring it up to strength, and which made a farce of the theoretically universal obligation to military service; and the wealthy continued to spare their sons the inconveniences of military training by buying substitutes, so depriving the army of the services of all but a handful of the better born and better educated elements in the nation. It was a system, moreover, which also deprived the army of any effective trained reserve in the event of a major war. It would not have been so bad if the majority of conscripts had retired into civilian life when they had completed their seven years' service.[2] But after such a period of segregated and dedicated service most felt wholly cut off from their contemporaries and hopelessly unfitted for retraining in civilian jobs. They tended, therefore, to sign on for a further period of service; and this suited the politicians admirably, since the longer a man served the less likely he was to be corrupted by dangerous civilian influence. But in a crisis it also deprived them of a potential reserve of trained men of over twenty-seven, most of whom might be expected to remain fit enough for active service for another few years. These would at least have tided the army over the first dangerous months of war while the so-called 'second portion' – those who had drawn lucky numbers, but who remained legally liable for service – were organised and trained.

In states where the front-line strength on mobilisation

35

depended on large numbers of reserves recalled from civilian life
there was always some justifiable uncertainty as to how many
would actually respond to the call. As the Prussian staff found to
its cost in 1859, it was also impossible to know in advance how fit
and ready for active service the reserve would be. It was inexcusable that the French Ministry of War, with only the serving
regular army to reckon, should have produced most shockingly
variable estimates of the actual strength at their disposal. In 1859
they cannot have had much more than 300,000 men, of whom
200,000 were committed in advance to the Army of Italy. The
safety minimum in Algeria, even at a time of national crisis, was
50,000. Something over 6,000 were pinned down in Rome under-
propping the Papal government and ensuring essential Clerical
votes for the Empire. On paper, and according to the official
account, the Emperor left behind him when he set off for Italy
eleven infantry and five cavalry divisions: Marshal de Castellane
had two infantry divisions and a cavalry division at Lyons and an
infantry division at Besançon; Marshal Magnan had four infantry divisions, two in Paris and one each at Lille and Mézières;
Marshal Pélissier, Duc de Malakoff, held the vital frontier with
four infantry and four cavalry divisions distributed between the
fortresses of Châlons, Metz, Lunéville and Strasburg. But these
were not the formidable force suggested by a paper strength
almost exactly the same as that of the Army of Italy. They were
merely the essential garrison troops of the fortresses, the depot
maintenance parties, the minimum needed to keep public order,
and the odd, non-combatant units which made up the army's
administrative tail. Not one of these divisions could have taken
the field had Prussia moved more quickly to Austria's help. If
Francis Joseph had decided to fight the campaign to a finish, the
Second Empire would have come to a much earlier inglorious
end.

In 1859 Napoleon III's faith in his star was undimmed and,
by the narrowest of margins and for the last time, the gamble
came off. The overall shortage of numbers had decisive diplomatic and political effects as the tide of nationalist feeling rose in
Prussia and throughout Germany and the fundamental weakness
of his situation was fully revealed to the Emperor; but it did not
directly affect the course of the campaign. The Army of Italy

duly arrived in the theatre of war at the agreed strength and, thanks to the dilatoriness of the Austrians, in time to save the Piedmontese army from annihilation. The battles were won, though very chancily, and not at all in the Napoleonic manner; and France's military pre-eminence was confirmed. The small professional army had justified the faith of its protagonists. It had defeated the Russians and the Austrians and had outclassed the British in the Crimea; and the Prussians by themselves presented no serious threat. By signing the precipitate armistice of Villa-franca when total victory seemed to be within his grasp Napoleon had saved his face and concealed from the world in general and the French public in particular the grave dangers involved in the army's lack of reserves. More important still, in the excitement of victory, as the fashionable world paraded in the new colours of magenta and solferino, everybody, including the Emperor and his advisers, tended to overlook the other and still graver defects in the French military system revealed by the campaign.

The advocates of the existing French army based their case on the undoubted fact that the experienced, campaign-hardened French soldier was more than a match, man for man, for any other soldier in Europe. But this superiority could only make itself felt if the troops were already organised for war, efficiently led, and properly equipped and supplied. The army must be capable either of a swift offensive, or of a defence of the frontiers pro-longed enough to give time to organise into effective armies the large reserves represented by the 'second portion'. The mobilisa-tion of 1859, the move into Italy, and events in the course of the campaign showed all too clearly that none of these conditions was fulfilled. Ironically, the very needs and duties of the peace-time army on which the excellence of the individual soldier was founded worked actively against the construction of an efficient war machine for a European theatre of operations; and the haunting fear of the revolutionary masses in Paris and in the great industrial cities dominated the minds of politicians to the exclu-sion of all else. In consequence the army, whether at home or abroad, was organised in garrisons whose strength and composi-tion varied according to local needs, but never conformed to the standard pattern of a European army. There were no Army Corps, Divisions, or Brigades, and therefore no commanders or

37

staffs accustomed to handle such formations. There were only Garrison Commands, under generals of appropriate rank, and staffed by officers trained to organise at lightning speed self-sufficient columns of all arms perfectly adapted to their own local needs in the deserts and mountains of Algeria, the jungles and paddy fields of Indo-China, or the barricaded streets of a French city. Nothing in their experience prepared them for the Napoleonic concept of *La Grande Guerre*.[3]

Thus the much vaunted professionalism of the French was to prove as much a handicap as an asset on the congested roads and railways of continental Europe. Algerian regiments arrived at Genoa in 1859, and again at Marseilles in 1870, fully equipped for the only sort of campaign they understood. In addition to a seventy pound pack of bivouac and other necessary equipment, every man carried enough rations and ammunition to make him self-sufficient for several days; and behind each regiment there moved a second column of mules and pack-horses with further reserves. All this had to be dumped or parked before going into action, and in a moving battle was never seen again. Divisional Commanders could not lose the habit of closing up their formations each night when they were on the march into what amounted to a fortified camp. For his retreat on Metz in 1870 Bazaine adopted a caterpillar-like method laid down by Marshal Bugeaud for a desert column withdrawing through a defile in hostile country, first deploying tomorrow's rearguard on the objective of the day's march, and mounting covering forces along both flanks before moving the main body of the Corps.[4] The troops, in consequence, were under arms or on the march for twenty-four hours at a stretch and the rate of movement for the Corps as a whole was one kilometre an hour.

Professionalism, moreover, was confined to the lower levels of the army, and the real troubles began at the top of the tree. The military education of the Emperor himself was limited to a brief youthful experience in the artillery of the Swiss Militia and to a faint whiff of active service when he took part in 1831 in a Carbonarist march on Rome. For his further military education he had carefully read M. Thiers's monumental *History of the Consulate and the Empire* and the summary of the art of warfare published by General Jomini in 1837; and he had written a

treatise on artillery. The day after the signature of the Treaty of
Paris, in April 1856, he had assured Cavour that France would
soon join him in a war against Austria; and this was to be fulfil-
ment of a pipe-dream in which he commanded his own army and
showed the world what a Napoleon could do. In the summer of
1857, to get his hand in for this exacting task, he brought the
Imperial Guard to the training area of Châlons and personally
conducted in the grand manner, *à la Louis XIV*, manoeuvres
against an imaginary enemy to a programme meticulously laid
down in advance. Each day ended with dinner for the senior
officers at the Emperor's headquarters, after which the Minister
of War, Marshal Vaillant, read aloud accounts of the more spectacular victories of Napoleon 1 taken from M. Thiers's great
work. Apart from the creation in 1858 of five, static Army Commands at Paris, Lyons, Nancy, Tours, and Toulouse, which had
no operational significance whatever, nothing was done to prepare the army for a major campaign during the three years which
elapsed between the decision to fight it and the actual outbreak of
war. Absorbed in his dreams, the Emperor took the whole army
and, more dangerously, the Ministry of War, on trust; and this
was almost certainly why he had embarked on his Italian adventure in the belief that he left behind him an adequately garrisoned
France. He would never face facts until they were forced on
him.

The Ministry of War deserved no such sublime trust. Marshal
Vaillant was an obese seventy-year-old, incapable of sitting a
horse except at a walk, whose military ideas were infantile, but
who was designated *ex officio* to become the Major-General and
so the Emperor's Chief-of-Staff on the outbreak of war. Apart
from the bureaucrats responsible for the day-to-day administration of the garrisons, the staff – the only General Staff which
France possessed – was an esoteric clique, largely drawn from
officers who had been able to afford an expensive though quite
inadequate military education at St Cyr, Metz or Saumur. They
manipulated senior appointments and cut a dash in Paris society;
but they made no attempt to study the elements of their profession. In the three years which preceded the outbreak of a war
which all Europe knew to be impending there was no attempt to
draw up plans of campaign or movement orders for the concen-

tration of a field army of 200,000 men and all its impedimenta across the Alps or by sea to Genoa. There was no study of the intricate problems involved in the movement of large masses of troops and material by rail. Worst of all, the composition of Corps, Divisions and Brigades, and the appointment of their commanders and staffs were left undecided until the actual day of mobilisation.

The results of this *fainéantisme* were as ludicrous as might have been expected, though serious for the troops concerned. As early as 10 March 1859, as a result of rumours of Austrian concentrations on the Piedmontese frontier, the War Ministry was instructed to form at Briançon an advance-guard division under General Bourbaki ready to move at twenty-four hours' notice to Turin. The order did not go out to Marshal de Castellane at Lyons until 17 April; and only then was it realised that Bourbaki was still, in sublime ignorance of his future, commanding his garrison at Besançon, while his two designated Brigade Commanders, Generals Ducrot and Trochu, were similarly employed at Orléans and Paris. The Austrian three-day ultimatum which precipitated the war left Vienna on 19 April. Only on the 21st did Napoleon formally order the creation of the five Army Corps which, with the Guard, were to form the Army of Italy. Two days after that Marshal Canrobert arrived at Lyons at ten o'clock at night to take over command both of his own III Corps and Niel's IV Corps for the passage of the Alps by the Mt Cenis and Mt Genèvre passes. He found an order awaiting him to cross the frontier forthwith, but received almost immediately a telegram from Bourbaki, his advance-guard commander, which ran: 'The troops of my division are without blankets. It is cold. We have neither tents nor water-bottles, nor camp equipment, nor cartridges. There is no hay. Absolutely nothing necessary for the organisation of a division has been sent here.'[5] The only answer Canrobert could get to his own protests to the War Ministry was a terse telegram from the Emperor himself: 'I repeat my order that the frontier is to be crossed forthwith.'

On 26 April the harassed Marshal, who had since been ordered to proceed at once to Turin with General Niel to co-ordinate movements with the King of Sardinia, sent a telegram to the War Ministry which summed up all the frustrations and grievances of his brother generals: 'They have forgotten to provide for my Army Corps operational staff, Q staffs, provost, medical services, artillery, and engineers. . . .'[6] The only satisfaction he got was a postscript to a personal letter from the Minister of War transmitting the Emperor's orders for his preliminary movements on arrival in Italy: 'I note with distress', Marshall Vaillant wrote, 'that your troops are not organised for war. You will be putting this right.'[7]

The pattern was everywhere the same. The army arrived in Italy well ahead of all the equipment and supplies needed for a campaign which had already begun – 'the opposite', as the Emperor telegraphed to Marshal Randon, the new Minister of War, 'of what we should have done'. He added that he held the Ministry 'very much to blame'.[8] But he himself shared with his ministers and officials the cheerful French belief that somehow things would sort themselves out. When he gave out his first orders, for the general advance of the Allied Army, and Marshal Baraguay-d'Hilliers protested that neither i nor ii Corps had yet got their artillery, he shrugged the matter off: '*On s'organisera en route.*'[9] That might have stood as the motto of the whole supply service, the *Intendance*. The ammunition and rations piled up at Genoa because there were no officers with the experience or energy to get such large masses of material moving on the largely one-track railway lines. By local purchase or requisition, and with the help of a hastily organised civilian transport column,[10] the army was somehow fed and kept on the move, though at the cost of great hardship to the troops. Worst of all, on the day of the final battle at Solferino, where the horrible sufferings of the wounded precipitated the foundation of the Red Cross, the French medical supplies were still piled up on the docks. The much-vaunted professionalism justified itself in that the French troops outfought the Austrians and by the narrowest of margins won both the great battles for their Emperor. The commanders and staffs were saved from total discredit only by the French genius for improvisation and the still greater incompetence of the Austrians. It was only to save face, and for entirely political and diplomatic reasons, that Francis Joseph conceded peace terms which allowed Bonapartist propaganda to present to the world a gloriously victorious campaign. Documents tending to discredit the official account were prudently removed from the archives of the Ministry of War.[11] During the next six years nothing was done to remedy the alarming faults which 1859 had revealed in the French military system.

The Emperor himself was certainly uneasily aware both of his own military shortcomings and of the peril to which he had exposed France when the Prussian mobilisation found him without a second army to defend the Rhine. But, once again, the adventure had come off. His belief in his destiny was confirmed; and the only prudent decision he took was to launch the next adventure in Mexico, as he thought, well out of harm's way. Revolution there had threatened ruin to large numbers of French, British, and Spanish investors. So in 1861 a joint expedition set sail, to which France contributed a naval squadron and six thousand troops under General Lorencez. This was already a dangerous commitment for an army so over-stretched in Europe and Algeria. A year later it became even more so. The British and Spaniards pulled out; but Lorencez was heavily defeated in the attempt to capture the city of La Puebla and French pride demanded revenge. Instead of cutting his losses, Napoleon had to send out an Army Corps under General Forey; and for four long years another 30,000 of the precious regular army were pinned down in an unspectacular, unrewarding campaign against an elusive enemy and in conditions even worse than those of the Sahara. Then, in 1866, a sudden European crisis, combined with the ending of the American Civil War, compelled a humiliating withdrawal; and the puppet Emperor Maximilian was left to face a firing-squad at Queretaro.

The Mexican campaign, which always seemed to be on the edge of success, earned Marshal's batons for Forey and Bazaine. But it brought irretrievable ruin both for the Empire and for the French army. When, in 1866, Napoleon III encouraged the Italians to join with Prussia in a joint attack on Austria's remaining supremacy in Germany and Italy, he was counting on a long drawn-out war between roughly equally-balanced opponents, during which he would have plenty of time to replenish the arsenals drained by Mexico, draw in what could safely be brought from Algeria and Rome, and re-incorporate Bazaine's over-swollen Army Corps into the army. He would then appear on the Rhine at the head of 250,000 men as an armed mediator and dictate to both sides terms of peace acceptable to France. The Rhine frontier might at last be won without even having to fight for it.

Prussia's swift mobilisation in unexpected strength, brilliant staff work, and the Needle Gun, achieved a decisive victory within seven weeks and caught the French completely unprepared. Far from armed mediation, France was not even in a position to demand compensation for Prussia's great accession of strength in North Germany. Clearly the small professional army no longer provided security on the cheap. Seven years too late, and in a political climate far less favourable than that of 1859, Marshal Niel was instructed to produce a project for raising the strength of the French army on mobilisation from the estimated 288,000 of 1866 to at least a million. Napoleon reckoned, reasonably correctly, that nothing less would meet the threat posed by a new and enlarged Prussia. The many schemes produced during the next eighteen months, including the one finally passed in January 1868 by an increasingly intransigent Corps Législatif, aimed at a front-line army on mobilisation of some 800,000 men, with a trained National Guard of at least 400,000 in reserve. Honestly implemented, this would have more than met Napoleon's requirement. By 1875 France would have had a regular army of 800,000 on mobilisation, consisting of men who had served five years with the colours and four on permanent leave. This part of the programme, which would entail no increase of the annual contingent, was running with complete success when the war came – five years too soon – in 1870. The strength of the regular army on mobilisation, as reported by Marshal Leboeuf to the Council of Ministers, precisely confirmed Niel's estimates: a total of 662,000 men which, though inadequate, was more than double what had been available four years earlier. When the Algerian and Roman garrisons had been subtracted and the necessary allowances made for fortresses, garrisons, and the rest, there remained 370,000 available to face the Prussians on the Rhine.

Swiftly mobilised and competently led, this might well have sufficed to hold off the initial enemy onslaught and gain time for the organisation of the 400,000 *Gardes Mobiles*. Niel had intended to enrol in this revised version of the National Guard all those who for one reason or another escaped the call-up. They were to serve for five years and to have three weeks' training a year. The niggling economies and deep-rooted prejudices of the Corps Législatif made a travesty of even this modest programme. Deputies of the Left were reluctant to put further military power at the disposal of a dictator; and the Right was haunted by the old fear of arming the mob; and all were agreed that it would be far too expensive to provide uniforms, arms and equipment. What materialised in 1870 was an untrained, mutinous rabble which cluttered up the already over-burdened railways and could only subsist on its way to the base camps by looting. When they ultimately arrived they created insoluble problems for harassed commanders whose time and staff were fully occupied in imposing order on their newly created formations. They, too, had neither rations, uniforms, nor equipment for this unforseen invasion. All they could do was to telegraph to the Government demanding that they should all be sent home. In total effect the *Garde Mobile* was a liability; and it remained largely on unreliable nuisance even when Gambetta and his friends had really roused the nation and were improvising the armies which prolonged the war through the winter after the bulk of the professional army had fallen into German hands at Metz or Sedan.

Shaken out of their complacency by the shock of the overwhelming Prussian victory in 1866, Napoleon and his military advisers had appreciated clearly enough the obvious lessons to be learnt from it; and by 1870 they reckoned that they had found the answers. They had given the French infantryman the Chassepot, a breech-loading rifle in every way superior to the Needle Gun; and they hoped to supplement this superiority of fire-power with batteries of Mitrailleuses capable of firing 150 rounds a minute. They had failed to match the total numbers of the Prussian field army. But the superiority of the French soldier man for man was not a myth, and, properly led, 370,000 of them should have been enough to hold the Prussians on that narrow frontier for long enough to sort out and train the *Garde Mobile*. What they had failed to learn – and this was the main cause of the débâcle of the Imperial army in 1870 – were the lessons of their own campaign in 1859. In the first place there was still no planned organisation for a field army. The distribution of the troops destined for the Army of the Rhine was only settled at the moment of mobilisation. Once again commanders and staffs had hastily to be detailed and assembled at the last moment; and only then were regiments informed of their Concentration Areas and to whom they had to report. All authorities, political as well as military, were agreed that the best chance for France and for the Imperial regime lay in a swift offensive to disrupt the ponderous German mobilisation, undermine the wavering loyalty of the South Germans, and bring the Austrians in on the French side. But the only plan in existence was one drawn up by the ex-Sapper, General Frossard, in 1863, for a static defence of the frontier by two armies in previously prepared positions while the reservists and *Mobiles* were gathered and organised; and this, *faute de mieux*, was adopted. Marshals Bazaine and MacMahon became titularly and temporarily Army Commanders, though they continued to command their own Corps and were given no extra staff. Indeed, their wretchedly overworked staffs were only further burdened by the allocation of a third Division to each Corps to give the Commanders additional prestige.

Worst of all the unremedied faults, however, was the slowness and confusion of the mobilisation itself. The declining popularity of the Empire had made it unwise to alter the old system whereby regiments were normally quartered in garrisons as remote as possible from their depots and recruiting areas lest the troops be contaminated by local political feeling. The double journey which every regiment had to make, first to the depot to embody reserves and draw war equipment and then to the Concentration Area, placed an intolerable burden on an already overstrained railway system. This more than anything else had slowed up the move into Italy in 1859 and put the whole Piedmontese army in jeopardy. By sending regiments directly to their Corps Assembly Areas in 1870 the War Ministry did at least get France's metro-politian army concentrated in good time on the frontier, but only at its peacetime strength and largely without its war equipment. The reservists were still either at their depots awaiting equipment which had not yet arrived from the central magazines or making their way in small, forlorn parties, subsisting as best they could, on interminable railway journeys in search of units which had already begun to move forward to the frontier. Equipment and supplies were generally either still in the arsenals or stranded somewhere on a chaotically blocked railway system. In the circumstances the civilian railway officials did extremely well. But there was no army staff to advise them or co-ordinate their decisions; and every local commander ordered and counter-manded special trains as he thought fit. Moreover – again for political reasons – the whole railway layout was inconvenient for the movement of large masses to Châlons, Metz, and Strasburg, since it was designed rather to bring troops from the provinces to Paris in the event of revolution. Cross-country journeys were often virtually impossible, and troops and material piled up in indescribable congestion and confusion in the Paris stations and at the larger junctions.

When, on 6 August, the twenty-third day of mobilisation, the French army fought its first defensive battles at Spicheren and Wörth it numbered only 270,000 against 462,000 Germans. Half the reserves were not yet in; and every one of the six army corps was seriously deficient in equipment and supplies. Once again, the medical services came off worst : all their stores were still at the Invalides in Paris, awaiting transport. Behind this thin screen there was not even an unorganised and untrained Army of Reserve. No plans had been made for providing it with officers, uniforms, weapons, or supplies. Only in the Department of the Seine were regiments actually formed; and these proved so mutinous and intractable that, for safety, they were transferred from Paris to Châlons, where they constituted the last straw for Marshal Canrobert as he desperately tried to hammer into some sort of military shape the partially trained units haphazardly thrown together which made up his VI Army Corps. Leboeuf was not wrong when he said, in a phrase which was to hang like a millstone round his neck, that the French army in 1870 was ready 'to the last gaiter-button'. The troops and the reservists were there in the numbers which he had forecast; and the arsenals and magazines were filled with all the stocks needed for the opening campaign.[12] But neither he nor any of his colleagues had visual-ised or attempted to solve the problems involved in mobilising and deploying them, though all of them had been experienced in a lesser degree eleven years before. The Ministry of War was per-fectly capable of supplying the needs of colonial armies and small expeditionary forces. It was quite unequipped intellectually for the organisation of *La Grande Guerre*.

The Austrian army which Napoleon challenged so light-heartedly in 1859 was in many ways better organised for European warfare than the French, though it suffered from many very similar disabilities. Its main trouble was that in its perpetual struggle to preserve the *status quo* it was permanently committed in too many different theatres, each separated from the others by long distances and formidable mountain ranges, and linked only tenuously by an inadequate railway system. It was not difficult for the Austrian statesmen and generals in 1856 to know where to expect trouble in the years ahead. They had merely to glance at their own recent military history. In 1848 and 1849 it had been only by hard fighting that the army had restored order in the Emperor's hereditary lands. In those same years Radetzky had fought two pitched battles to save the Austrian hegemony in Italy; and in 1850 the whole strength of the Empire had been mobilised to foil Prussian ambitions in Germany. In 1852 it had needed a partial mobilisation in Croatia to save the Montenegrins from extermination by the Turks; and two years later the Russians had only been prevented from making havoc in the Balkans by a full-scale mobilisation which had brought the government to the verge of bankruptcy and the desperate expedient of a Forced Loan.[18] All the cards were on the table. The peace-time distribution of the Austrian army showed that the government understood clearly enough the dangers which threatened it. It was divided into four Army Commands. Strongest in numbers was 2nd Army in northern Italy and in the coastal areas around the Adriatic. It was fully organised into five Army Corps – the v, vi, vii, viii and ix – in all some 125,000 fighting men. When allowance was made for skeleton garrisons in the fortresses of the Quadrilateral and in the Dalmatian ports this would give the Commander-in-Chief in Milan a field army of about 100,000 effectives immediately available as a striking force. But, unless reinforced from beyond the Alps, he would not have very much more for an offensive campaign even when mobilisation was complete. Most of the reserves called to the colours were needed to bring the garrisons up to strength, protect the ports and lines of communication, and provide a small reserve in

case of trouble in Tuscany, Parma, or Modena. In 1859, when
the Austrian government plunged so rashly into war with France
and Piedmont without waiting for mobilisation to be completed,
Count Gyulai crossed the Ticino to open the campaign with
110,000, which represented the maximum effort of 2nd Army
when acting on its own. North of the Alps, stationed in German
Austria, Bohemia and Moravia, were the I, II, III and IV Corps
composing 1st Army. This meant a peace-time strength of about
90,000 and on paper should have provided the Empire, when it
was fully mobilised, with a mobile field army of 120,000 available
for service on any front provided that it was not already
committed in Germany. Here again, however, the figures were
delusive. Apart from garrison commitments in Federal German
fortresses and the need to protect the cities of western Austria,
substantial forces were pinned down in their homeland by the
fear of renewed revolutionary outbreaks in Vienna and Prague.
3rd Army, stationed in Hungary, and roughly the same strength
as 1st – X, XI, and XII Corps and a Cavalry Corps, the XIII –
was even more heavily tied down. Until 1867, when their ancient
Parliament and semi-independent status were restored to them,
all politically articulate Hungarians were irreconcilably opposed
to the centralised bureaucracy of Vienna; and the situation in
neighbouring Croatia was little better. Thus not much more than
half of 3rd Army could safely be drawn off for operations further
afield than the Hungarian frontier. It ought to have been possible
to supplement some of these deficiencies by forming another
Corps from 4th Army, approximately 30,000 strong, stationed in
Galicia. But once Buol's futile policy during the Crimean War
had made an embittered enemy of Russia it was no longer permissible to strip that frontier; and another 50,000 were immobilised
in Croatia and along the so-called 'Military Frontier' in the
Balkans. Nevertheless, the mere existence of the Armies, with
their thirteen Army Corps already formed and brigaded, gave the
Austrians an immense potential advantage over the French, had
they known how to exploit it. While Canrobert and MacMahon
had to fumble their way into a working relationship with their
Divisional and Brigade Commanders, and even their own
personal staffs, Benedek led out into battle a formation with
which he had been working daily for years. Even the reservists, if

by good fortune they rejoined the colours in time to be included in the campaign, found themselves serving not only with old comrades in the ranks, but under commanders at all levels who were already familiar figures. This was all the more important when, thanks to the close-order tactics which dominated the battlefield until 1870, the Army Corps was the basic tactical, as well as administrative, formation of an army. Seldom deployed on a front of much more than 3,000 yards, it could be led as well as commanded by an energetic general on a good horse. Indeed, after 1859, the Austrians dispensed altogether with Divisional Commanders and let Corps Commanders deal direct with four Brigadiers. The lesson was underlined, and the staff of Prince Frederick Charles's Prussian 1st Army was to pay dearly for it, when he suppressed Infantry Corps Headquarters in the Bohemian campaign of 1866, so that his orders had to be copied out for ten infantry divisions, a cavalry corps, the reserve artillery, and various supply trains.

Above all, the Austrians failed to exploit the existence of their standing Army Commands, already in peacetime tactically organised. Gyulai, as the Commander of 2nd Army in North Italy in 1859, automatically led it into action and made a sad hash of the opening phase of the war. The Austrian army, withdrawn into the shelter of the Quadrilateral fortresses, was then reinforced and reorganised. The Emperor, advised by Hess, but with a staff drawn almost entirely from his own Military Cabinet, took supreme command. Count Schlick, another of the veterans, who had fought, always with distinction, at Aspern and Wagram and off and on ever since, superseded Gyulai; and 1st Army was brought down from Vienna complete with its headquarters and its woeful Commander, Feldzeugmeister Count Wimpffen. No more disastrous combination could have been forged. Hess, accustomed as Chief of Staff to issue orders direct to all the Corps Commanders of the Austrian Army, could not break himself of the habit. His orders of 22 June 1859 for the crossing of the Mincio, which led two days later to the encounter battle of Solferino, detailed all movements and dispositions to eight Army Corps and all the cavalry divisions, leaving the Army Commanders with nothing to do save ride round to see that they were being carried out. And the Army Commanders themselves were an ill-assorted pair : Schlick, hard-fighting and outspoken, and adored by his troops; Wimpffen, who owed his rank entirely to his wealth and social status, one of those Austrian generals who, in Suvaroff's malicious phrase, 'had the ineradicable habit of being defeated'. Thanks to his helplessness and his deplorable seat on a horse he was known throughout the army as 'the Begging Friar'. The totally unnecessary defeat which resulted from the unfortunate combination disillusioned the Austrians with the whole idea of subordinate Army Commands, with disastrous results in 1866. Then, while Moltke co-ordinated the movements of vast masses of roops by dint of short Directives to his three Army Commanders, Benedek's overworked staff had to produce written orders for thirteen different formations, for Corps and Army troops, and for the supply columns of the entire army. This was one reason why the Commander-in-Chief's orders seldom went out – and never arrived – on time. Furthermore, if the army had to be subdivided for a particular operation, the luckless staff officers of one of the Corps Commanders were bound to find themselves, like those of Bazaine and MacMahon in 1870, trying to draft orders both for their own Corps and for the rest of the Army.

There were other and more intractable reasons for the failure of the Austrians to exploit the full potential of what was, on paper, a very formidable standing army. Thirteen Army Corps, with the Galician army and the garrison of the 'Military Frontier', made up a peace establishment of 350,000 men. This was more than enough to hold in check all the forces which normally threatened the unity and stability of the Empire. If it could ever have been united in one theatre it could by itself have faced any European power in a major war. But there were never enough reserves available on mobilisation both to replace the permanent frontier and fortress garrisons and to take over from the armies the preservation of order throughout the Empire. A crisis north of the Alps was the greatest threat. Both Radetzky and Hess reckoned that, even when the troops in Istria and Dalmatia had been replaced by reserve formations, not more than one Corps and one division could safely be drawn off from 2nd Army in Italy. 3rd Army, in Hungary, could normally spare only the cavalry corps and a single infantry division. A new Reserve

Corps could be formed by combing out the younger age groups from the permanent garrisons and replacing them with older reservists; and another could be hastily formed from 4th Army in Galicia, provided Russian benevolent neutrality was assured. Even so, Austria could only produce for the opening phase of a possible war with Prussia in Bohemia an army of 180,000 men, which might be outnumbered by two to one. When war actually came in 1859 it was in Italy which, with its standing garrison of five Army Corps, was far the most favourable theatre. But for various reasons the number of trained reservists available fell far short of what had been expected. At the height of the war there were never more than 220,000 men in Lombardy, Istria, and Dalmatia. The combined French and Piedmontese fleets were more than a match for the Austrian squadron at Trieste, and the Austrians were unaware that, having no troop transports with them, the enemy were incapable of an amphibious operation. Far from drawing on the garrisons of Venice, Trieste, and Fiume to reinforce the field army, the government had thus to divert much needed reserves to coastal defence. This was why Francis Joseph had to fight the decisive battle of Solferino with only 120,000 men. Clearly Austria's failure to preserve her pre-eminence in Italy and Germany sprang largely from the breakdown of her army organisation and her recruiting system.

In Austria, as in France, there was no universal obligation of military service. Almost all professional men were exempt and, indeed, all who had received a secondary or higher education : and anyone could buy himself out for 1,000 Gulden. The government's perpetual financial difficulties further restricted the numbers which could be called up; and in practice, out of a population of 35 million, only 83,000 young men aged twenty joined the colours each year. Once sworn-in they were obliged to remain in the regular army for eight years and in the Reserve for another two. On paper Austria should therefore have had a standing army in peace-time of well over 600,000 men and a reserve of trained troops immediately available on mobilisation of 120,000, all long-service soldiers. If it had ever been realised, this would, indeed, have been impressive; and journalists, diplomats, and the more light-hearted politicians and soldiers, loved to talk of the army of three-quarters of a million men on which the

Emperor could count in a crisis. But most of the senior soldiers, at least, must have been very well aware that these figures bore little relation to the truth. As always in Austria, financial stringency imposed its restrictions. An infantryman rarely served more than three years, and often as little as a year and a half, before being sent home. Gunners and Sappers served on average four to six years; and only the cavalry stayed with the colours for the full eight. This was the factor which reduced the standing army from a theoretical 660,000 to 350,000 : enough to deal with the army's normal peace-time commitments, but leaving a dangerously small surplus available for use as a field army in a crisis.

Men who were thus sent home remained, of course, serving soldiers until they were twenty-eight. They were technically on permanent leave; and there was no need for a mobilisation decree to recall them. On the figures alone, therefore, optimists could reckon on an immediate reinforcement of 300,000 trained soldiers, and, on mobilisation, on a further 160,000. In practice at least 2 per cent, and generally 25 per cent, had immediately to be written off : men who had died, fallen sick or been injured; and a large number who had simply vanished without trace. Nearly as many more were lost through sheer maladministration. Lists got mislaid or were not kept up to date, and changes of address were not noted; and a 100 per cent response to an Imperial Proclamation of mobilisation could scarcely be expected from a multilingual, largely illiterate, and frequently discontented population. In 1859 the War Ministry sustained an even worse shock. Only on mobilisation was it discovered that for some years past the officers of most of the infantry regiments had been in the habit of sending each new intake of recruits straight home as soon as they had been enrolled and making up numbers by keeping on the already trained older age groups, who should have been on permanent leave. They thus saved themselves the tedium of supervising elementary instruction on drill and musketry and at the same time ensured an impressive performance on parades, manoeuvres, and inspections. Of the 375,000 infantry recalled to the colours for the war in Italy, 255,000 were found to be totally untrained and incapable of loading a musket.[14] This shocking discovery did not, however, prevent the government from sending a premature ultimatum to Piedmont which precipitated a war which they should have tried to avoid, or, at least, postpone.

Frantic efforts were made in the years following 1859 to remedy this discrepancy between the paper figures and the numbers of trained men actually available; and the figures for the next general mobilisation, in 1866, did show a considerable improvement. In fact for the war against Italy and Prussia in that year Austria put into the field a larger force than any she had been able to raise since the record year of Aspern and Wagram. Even so, the figures were extremely disappointing. When mobilisation was complete the total number of men with the colours, apart from the garrisons of the Military Frontier, who were locally recruited, was found to be only 528,000; more than half the number of reservists normally to be expected had somehow slipped through the War Ministry's fingers. There were, moreover, further deductions to be made. When men found to be unfit and those in essential government employment had been sent home, and the necessary number set aside as craftsmen, officers' servants, bandsmen, and the like, there were only, in round figures, 460,000 combatant troops available for the two field armies: 400,000 infantry, 29,000 cavalry, 24,000 artillerymen and 10,000 sappers and pioneers. Moreover, even though the Empire was fighting for its historic German and Italian supremacy, twenty-two battalions had still to be left behind in Hungary and six in Vienna for fear of internal disturbances; and the fortress garrisons on both fronts absorbed another 94,000 men. So the Archduke Albrecht and his imperturbable Chief-of-Staff, Major-General John, could only be given three Army Corps and a scratch infantry division – some 74,000 men, and a handful of cavalry to defend Venetia and the Quadrilateral against more than double that number of Italians. Benedek in Bohemia had seven Army Corps and five cavalry divisions, a total of 238,000. Only with the help of a Saxon Army Corps 23,000 strong could he meet the Prussians on roughly equal terms.

It is a favourite habit of senior soldiers to lay the blame for any shortcomings in their armies on the niggardliness of their governments: and the Austrian generals of the later nineteenth century certainly had plenty of justified grievances against the men who mismanaged the Empire's finances. But undoubtedly it was very largely their own fault that Austria failed so dismally to deploy her full strength in 1859 and 1866. The administrative branches of the Ministry of War had become infected with all the vices of the highly centralised German-Austrian bureaucracy with which Francis Joseph set out to govern his heterogeneous dominions after the troubles of 1848–9. The rank and file of the officials were dull plodders, unimaginative and uninspired; and the staff work of many of their seniors was of the same stamp. General Krismaniç, Benedek's Chief of Staff in the Bohemian campaign, was typical of this school: slow, methodical, competent, and painstaking, he worked rigidly by the book and was incapable of modifying a plan or a judgement to meet unforeseen accidents or unexpected enemy moves. No more unsuitable man could have been found to deal with the fast-moving Prussians or, indeed, with the mercurial temperament of Benedek. The other school consisted of the high-born officers, drawn from the six hundred families who shared most of the Empire's wealth and stepped into high office as of right, without much bothering to acquire the necessary skills. Often very intelligent, and nearly always extremely good company, these were disinclined to work hard at intractable problems, light-heartedly prepared to leave everything to chance, and rendered sublimely self-confident by the knowledge that their birth made them practically immune from the penalties normally attached to negligence and failure. The total result was that difficult decisions were postponed and, when finally taken, often not implemented. Regimental depots were neither sufficiently staffed or sufficiently provided to deal with the mere numbers involved in a general mobilisation. There was no time in a crisis to cope with complex problems which should have been carefully considered and solved in the years of peace; and in war the penalties of failure are severe.

It is only fair to add that many of the difficulties connected with the mobilisation and administration of the Austrian army sprang from causes quite outside the control of the General Staff. It was not their fault that the policy of centralised autocracy inaugurated after 1848–9 roused bitter resentment. The German Austrians resented having no say in their own government. The other nationalities hated being governed by German Austrians. Above all, Hungary would remain sullenly resentful until her ancient rights were restored; and there this resentment of intruding, German-speaking administrators was not confined to the educated and politically conscious classes. It had spread to the rank and file of the Hungarian regiments, many of which had fought as complete units in the Hungarian national army and against the Emperor in 1849. In 1859 the Hungarian regiments in Count Clam-Gallas's 1 Corps ran away both at Magenta and Solferino, and the Corps had to be sent back to Vienna, though this may have been partly a lack of leadership since the same Corps, under the same general, disintegrated at the Battle of Jitschin seven years later. Benedek, who alone among the Corps Commanders could speak to Hungarians in their own language, got brilliant results from them at Solferino; but at Königgrätz even he could not induce a Hungarian battalion to counter-attack the key position of Chlum, though he offered to lead them in person. In 1859 the War Ministry had tentatively tried the remedy of mixing all nationalities in each battalion. But, great though the assimilative power of the Austrian army had always been, the remedy proved worse than the disease. It caused indescribable linguistic and administrative confusion within battalions and was quickly abandoned after the war. It remained a precautionary rule, however, that troops should never be stationed in peacetime in their own homelands, lest they be infected by local feeling. This, combined with the slow development of the Empire's railways, added weeks to the time it took to mobilise. What sounded a simple enough operation – the recall of some 250,000 men from leave – needing only a stroke of the pen at the Ministry – posed a fearful travel problem for the Czech peasant whose regimental headquarters were in southern Hungary, or the Transylvanian who had to get from the Carpathian foothills to Milan. Since an Army Corps might then have a long distance to travel to its Concentration Area over railway lines, many of them still single-tracked, the temptation to set the machine in motion without waiting for all the reserves to come in was great.

The inherent inability of the Austrian army to mobilise quickly was as widely known outside Austria as it was to her own soldiers and statesmen. It was, indeed, a vital factor in the calculations of all the men who were planning the great wars which were to transform the map of Europe. Moltke defined the situation in terms of a war in Bohemia with icy precision in a conversation

with Roon in the spring of 1866. 'We have', he said, 'the inestimable advantage of being able to carry our Field Army of 285,000
men over five railway lines, and of virtually concentrating them
in twenty-five days on the frontiers of Saxony and Bohemia.
Austria has only one line of rail, and it will take her forty-five
days to assemble 200,000 men.' Yet twice within seven years the
Austrian government allowed itself to be stampeded by the deliberate provocations of Cavour and Bismarck into precipitating
wars which it was her vital interest to avoid, or at least postpone;
with the double disadvantage that she was made to appear the
aggressor when she was, in fact, far less prepared for war than her
opponents. The Austrian General Staff could not, of course, be
blamed for the lack of railways, nor for the clumsy organisation
which resulted from the disaffection of the subject peoples of the
Empire; and it was natural that they should clamour in a crisis
for a premature mobilisation, whatever its diplomatic effects, in
the hope of making up some of the time which their opponents
would inevitably gain on them. Yet in 1859 the three-day ultimatum demanding an immediate Piedmontese disarmament,
though it had been approved by the Crown Council,[15] was despatched from the Emperor's Military Chancery when Austrian
mobilisation had hardly even begun. Cavour, at his wits' end to
fulfil his promise to Napoleon III to provoke a war with Austria
within six months,[16] rose to his feet when he had read it with a
shout of 'God save the King!' The five Army Corps of the
Austrian 2nd Army crossed the Ticino still on their peacetime
establishment, and the war came to an end before Austria had
even completed her mobilisation. Clearly the generals carried a
large share of the blame for their defeat; and the root cause of
their behaviour, as light-headed as it was light-hearted, lay in the
so-called New Reform of 1853 which had reconstituted the
relationship between the three departments which made up the
High Command in Vienna.

   This New Reform was in itself ill-conceived. It reduced the
War Ministry to a mere administrative machine which had no
share in the making of policy. It left the Quartermaster General
as Chief of the General Staff and his department as, virtually, the
Operations Branch of the War Office. But the Chief-of-Staff was
not master in his own house. It was the Adjutant General who

presided over the Emperor's Military Chancery, and so became the most influential of the Emperor's advisers on military affairs, though he bore no responsibility for the conduct of the operations which might result from his advice. The personalities involved in 1853 made this an even more disastrous arrangement than it need have been. Francis Joseph was only nineteen when he took over his bankrupt and badly shaken Empire from the more or less half-witted Ferdinand 1 and substituted centralised absolutism for the haphazard, semi-feudal regime which had collapsed in 1848. Though he was one of the more intelligent rulers thrown up by the Habsburg dynasty during its six hundred years of suzerainty, he could not easily stick to a decision once made, and frequently allowed himself to be talked into unfortunate changes of policy at critical moments. Not unnaturally he found the younger genera-tion of senior soldiers more congenial than the veterans of Aspern and Leipzig. Count Grünne, a conceited, ambitious man who had not seen action, even in 1848–9, became Adjutant General and his most trusted military adviser. His intrigues were largely responsible for the New Reform which gave him control of the Emperor's Military Chancery, and so of all senior appointments in the army. He made Count Gyulai, another general who had seen no active service and who was one of his few friends, Minister of War; and Gyulai was only too thankful to avoid difficult decisions. Hess, the Quartermaster-General, a first-class Chief-of-Staff so long as he had a clear-headed, forceful com-mander like Radetzky, was too retiring and diffident to assert himself. Grünne's influence with the Emperor was decisive; and it took the disasters of 1859 to convince Francis Joseph that it was a bad appointment.

But no changes of appointments at the top and no jockeying about of army corps from frontier to frontier would make up for Austria's greatest deficiency of all: like France, she lacked any form of territorial army. A *Landwehr* had, in fact, been formed in the crisis year of Wagram and had given a very good account of itself. But the Emperor Francis thought it a dangerously demo-cratic institution and abolished it as soon as he could. There was thus no reservoir of trained and organised reserves to relieve front-line troops on the frontier and in provincial garrisons, to replace casualties, and to give the field army something to fall back on if heavily defeated. All through the fifties the government dithered with plans for forming a fourth battalion in each regiment from the men most recently released from the regular reserve. In the end fourth battalions were constituted for all the regiments stationed in the German Austrian lands and on the 'Military Frontier'. From the warlike population of the 'Military Frontier' they were even able in 1866 to raise fifth and sixth battalions for all regiments, so making the whole of the permanent garrison of 50,000 available at need to the Army Commander in Hungary in case of disturbance, and setting free another regular Army Corps for the field army. But outside the 'Military Frontier' collecting up the fourth battalions from their remote homelands, organising them, and despatching them to sometimes equally remote fortresses to relieve regular garrisons was time-consuming. In 1866, when the reluctance of the King of Prussia to declare war gave the Austrians more time than they had given themselves in 1859, the fourth battalions of the regiments in Austria, Bohemia and Moravia did, in fact, get there in time to set 90,000 fortress troops free for active service. Freiherr von Henikstein, who had succeeded Hess as Quartermaster-General and had constantly agitated for the organisation in advance of a Reserve Army, then made a desperate attempt to create one by calling up 80,000 of the young men who had escaped being conscripted. With these he proposed to form fifth battalions to relieve in turn the fourth battalions in the fortresses, where the newcomers could be trained in safety. The fourth battalions would then give him his Reserve Army 90,000 strong. But by then it was too late. The Assembly Area assigned to the fifth battalions turned out to be right in the line of the Prussian advance in Bohemia, which was only slightly confused by the wanderings of large bodies of untrained enemy soldiers. The whole of Austria's strength remained in her two field armies, which was, no doubt, what Moltke had in mind when he reassured his anxious King at Königgrätz. 'Today', he said, 'Your Majesty will win not merely the battle, but the campaign.'

Five years earlier Moltke would scarcely, in similar circumstances, have been able to speak with such imperturbable self-confidence. In 1860 he had given it as his own opinion that the Prussian army could reasonably hope to fight a successful defensive war against Austria. He added that he was opposed to such a war in any case since, whoever won it, the only real gainer would be France: 'Germany', he wrote, 'would pay for her eventual unity by the loss of provinces both in east and west.'[17] He based his judgement on the weaknesses in the Prussian military system revealed in 1850 when she had surrendered to Austria rather than fight, and in 1859 when she had started to mobilise too late to help Austria in Italy. King William I equally disliked the thought of what he considered a civil war. He only consented to it in the end when Bismarck had convinced him that his cause was just and that the honour of his House demanded that he should fight. He was also vividly aware of the revealed weaknesses in his army organisation and determined that they should be remedied; and it was only because of this that Bismarck ever got the opportunity to put his ideas and policies into practice. He alone was prepared to take office and push through Roon's Military reform of 1861 in the teeth of a Prussian Parliament which refused to enact the necessary budget.

It had been the intention in 1816, when the decrees governing Prussian conscription had been issued, that Prussia at war should fulfil the Clausewitzian conception of the nation in arms, as she had in 1812. Out of a total population of ten million Prussia had then mobilised an armed force of some 500,000 men. In future 40,000 young men aged twenty were to be called to the colours to serve three years in the regular army, two years in the Reserve, liable for immediate recall, and thereafter fifteen years in the *Landwehr*. Those who were lucky enough to escape the call-up served the full twenty years in the *Landwehr*. This gave Prussia a standing army of 200,000 and a fully trained territorial reserve which worked out in practice at something under 300,000: a powerful defensive force and enough to maintain her status as a great power, but too weak in striking power to attack any of her three formidable neighbours. The permanent military aspect of citizenship was further emphasised by the territorial organisation of both standing army and reserve. The kingdom was divided into military 'Circles' (*Kreise*). In each *Circle* the most important city became the permanent headquarters of an Army Corps and its lesser neighbours housed divisional commanders and their staffs, regimental headquarters and depots, barracks, stores, magazines, and remount stables. The army was permanently and geographically

c

in being; and no conscript recruit had more than an easy day's journey from his home territorial unit, officered by men of substance in the district, but also integrated into the command structure of the local Corps. Thus Scharnhorst sought to perpetuate the Clausewitz ideal of war as an integral part of civilian life.

It was a system which was to give Moltke priceless assets in an age when speed of mobilisation became a vital war-winning factor. It enabled the decentralisation of the whole complicated business of mobilising and equipping troops and reserves to formation commanders who already had all the machinery under their hands. Commanders, moreover, went into action with staffs and units whom they had themselves trained and who were accustomed to work together. But it was not as efficient in practice as it looked on paper. *Landwehr* units inevitably contained a high proportion of fathers of families and of men whose civilian occupations had rendered them quite unfit for active service; and they therefore could not be used either in reserve formations in the regular army or as replacement units for the casualties of the opening battles. For these purposes the Austrian fourth battalions, though slow to mobilise and relatively small in numbers, were much better suited. Above all no allowance had been made for the rapid growth of Prussia's population. By 1850 it had risen from ten to eighteen millions, but the 1816 Decrees had never been amended. Each year, as the lots fell, ten thousand young men went free, save for token service in the *Landwehr*, while their contemporaries were close-harnessed to the military machine until their fortieth birthdays.

The revolutions of 1848–9 and the abortive mobilisation against Austria revealed that the *Landwehr* was permeated with Liberal ideas and no longer reliable as an instrument for internal security. The efficiency of its units was impaired by the presence of a high proportion of officers and men who had done no regular service and by the selection of officers on the basis of local and social standing; and most men and officers were physically unfit for any form of active service. All these faults were underlined during the belated mobilisation in support of Austria in 1859. But the more intelligent generals were already fully aware of them; and so was the Prince Regent who was shortly to succeed his unstable

brother as King William I. Prince William had seen service under
Blücher and was deeply rooted in the Prussian military tradition.
He regarded himself essentially as the heir of Frederick the Great
and, above all other things, responsible to his People for the army
which had largely created and now protected the state and the
nation. Within the narrow limits of his field of vision he thought
very clearly. He had no wish to become a German Emperor. But
he did feel very strongly that, if Prussia were to be required to
pull the chestnuts out of the fire for Austria every time she ran into
trouble in Italy or the Balkans, the least Francis Joseph could do
was to concede him the permanent right to command all German
troops north of the Alps in the event of a general war. It was, in
fact, the Austrian refusal to make this concession which had made
Prussia delay so long before mobilising in 1859. William had no
wish to fight Austria, but it was intolerable to him that Prussia
should be so weak militarily that she should have to submit
tamely to Austrian bullying, as she had in 1850. He therefore
accepted, when it was put forward by Roon, his Minister of War,
a project for military reform which would redress the balance of
power; and the consequences of his decision were to be a decisive
factor in the history of Europe and the world for generations to
come.

Roon's proposal was straightforward and comprehensive.
Henceforward 63,000 young men would be called up each year
to serve for seven years, three in the standing army, and four in
the first line reserve, which was to be automatically recalled on
mobilisation. This would produce a slightly smaller peacetime
army – 180,000 as against 200,000 – but a field army on mobilisation, allowing for the usual 20 per cent wastage, of 355,000. To
compensate for the lengthened period of front-line service, the
obligation to serve in the *Landwehr* was reduced. This had in
1816 been divided into two periods: seven years in the first call-
up seven in the second. The second, consisting entirely of men
over the age of thirty-two, had been regarded as something of a
last ditch reserve, only to be called on when the country was in
danger. Now, to compensate for the increased obligation with the
regular army, the periods of *Landwehr* service were shortened. A
man was to serve only until the age of thirty-one in the first call-
up and to be released altogether at thirty-six. The youngest age

group of the first call-up – the twenty-five year olds – was to be incorporated, if needed, in the field army. From the remainder could be found both a replacement pool for casualties and reserve formations for use on lines of communication or as occupation troops. The second call-up would take over all garrison duties and the maintenance of order in the homeland. The total result of the reform, when the new system was first tried out in practice in 1866, was to give Prussia an immediately available army of 370,000 men. When the necessary deductions had been made for maintenance units, sappers, pioneers, and transport personnel, 48,000 men set aside to deal with the South German states, and another 9,000 to garrison Upper Silesia, Moltke was able to bring some 278,000 fighting troops on to the field at Königgrätz against about 271,000 Austrians. Austria had, of course, heavier commitments elsewhere, including 75,000 men with the Archduke Albrecht in Italy. But it must be remembered that the Emperor of Austria had nearly twice as many subjects as the King of Prussia.

The political crisis arose when, in 1861, Roon had to ask the Lower House of the Prussian Parliament, for an extra nine and a half million Thalers – roughly £1½ million in then values – to pay for forty-nine new regiments needed to accommodate the larger intake of recruits. The National-Liberal majority were happy enough, as good Prussians, to see an increase in Prussia's fighting strength. But as good Liberals they objected as strongly as any English seventeenth-century Parliament to giving an autocratic sovereign a powerful regular army which, as 1848 had shown, could be used to blow a Liberal revolution off its barricades. As a condition of voting the extra money they stipulated that the period of service with the colours should be shortened from three years to two, so that the bulk of the increase should go to the *Landwehr* and the iron Prussian military discipline be less indelibly stamped on the nation's young men.

King William agreed that it was perfectly possible to teach a man all the necessary military skills in two years. 'But,' he said, 'three would be needed to make a real soldier of him.' Furthermore, he was determined that the *Landwehr* should lose its territorial independence and come under the direct control of the local Army commanders. On this point they reached a deadlock in 1861, when the Liberal majority refused to vote the budget unless its wishes were met. The King, driven nearly to the point of despair and abdication, at last listened to Roon's advice and called on Bismarck to take over the government; and Bismarck, treating the crisis as an unconstitutional interference with the royal prerogative, simply raised the taxes without bothering about a vote and left Roon and Moltke to raise and train the army they wanted. Within four years two successful wars and an impressive aggrandisement of Prussian power had cut the ground from under the feet of the National-Liberals; and in 1868 the Assembly formally indemnified the government for seven years of illegal taxation. To them it seemed that the eventual unification of Germany under Prussian leadership would more than compensate for any loss of civil liberty.

Moltke husbanded these large reserves which Bismarck and Roon had suddenly made available with admirable restraint. He was not, of course, beset by racial and geographical problems, as Henikstein was. Nevertheless Prussia had her difficulties. Until the opening victories roused national pride, the war of 1866 was everywhere unpopular; and in the populous Rhine Provinces, acquired from Austria in 1815 and not yet completely assimilated, there was active discontent. They were also cut off from the rest of Prussia by the Kingdom of Hanover, which had allied itself with Austria, so that their forces could not easily be concentrated. Wisely, therefore, Moltke decided not to risk rousing further opposition by calling out the older age-group in the Rhineland. The territorial battalions in Silesia, Posen, and parts of Pomerania and Westphalia were fully mobilised to their war strength of 806, as were those of the Guards' regiments. Elsewhere only 500 men were embodied in each battalion, so that the fathers of families could be as far as possible exempt. This gave him a replacement pool of 129,000 trained men. In addition he incorporated the Guards' and one other *Landwehr* Division in the field army and formed an Army Corps 24,000 strong to cover Berlin against a possible thrust from Saxony. This Corps, when things began to go well, was moved up behind the army in Bohemia and used to hold key points in occupied territory, such as the city of Prague. Since he then had all he could usefully employ in an offensive war, he left the rest at home. They still remained, however, an enormous asset. Had Napoleon fulfilled his original intention of an armed mediation backed by 250,000 men on the Rhine, Moltke could, so he assured Parliament after the war, have raised a total force of 600,000 men, 400,000 of them fighting troops. Less than half would have sufficed to contain the dispirited Austrians rallying along the Danube under the Archduke Albrecht. Intervention by the hereditary enemy would have roused German national feeling to fever pitch and Napoleon would probably have anticipated his final ruin by four years. It was a classic lesson in the economy of manpower. It was, indeed, France who had been defeated at Königgrätz.

It is easy to see how the geographical distribution of the standing army and *Landwehr* speeded up the Prussian mobilisation. With all reserves living almost on the doorsteps of their depots, it only took a day or two to bring units to full war-strength. Each Army Corps could assemble in the area of its own headquarters without cluttering up the main railway lines needed for the move to the Army Concentration Areas on the frontier. Actually Moltke reckoned after 1866 that he had wasted a good deal of time by assembling each Corps before moving it. It only had to be dispersed again for the railway journey and reassembled in the Concentration Area. In 1870 he merged the two processes, moving units straight to the Concentration Area as soon as they were ready and letting the Corps assemble there. So closely did he cut his timings in his anxiety to forestall a French invasion of the Rhineland that most Corps only completed their assembly the day before moving forward to the frontier, and some moved off on the great *Aufmarsch* – the deployment of the armies along the frontier – leaving second-line transport and administrative units to catch them up on the march straight from the homeland. 1 Corps, from East Prussia, was only to entrain at Königsberg on the morning of 5 August and to join the Corps Headquarters at Neunkirchen the following morning as the advanced guards of the army felt their way across the Saar and into France. The light-hearted commander of its 4th Light Battery, Captain Schmidt, provided an even more spectacular example of the ability of the Railway Section of the Staff to move units great distances right on to the battlefield. Hearing on arrival at Neunkirchen that fighting had broken out south of Saarbrücken, he ordered his train on to St Johann on the extreme opposite flank of 1st Army, off-loaded his guns there, and was in action on the Spicheren heights that evening, just thirty-six hours after leaving Königsberg.[18] It was the great advantage of the system of territorial decentralisation that the whole machinery of mobilisation could be left to the Corps Staffs, leaving the General Staff free for the Concentration and the *Aufmarsch* which were, in Moltke's mind, a paramount factor in planning victory.

The Prussian Corps organisation was, of course, extended to the whole of North Germany after 1866 and finally to the whole of the Empire. As with the Austrians, the Army Corps was the most important link in the Prussian chain of command. It was organised on standard lines, with two divisions of two brigades each, and two infantry regiments of three battalions to the brigade. Since all formations were regionally based and permanently established in peace as in war, it could be given a pattern uniquely rigid and mathematically precise. In 1 Corps there would always be found 1 and 2 Divisons, and Brigades were similarly numbered consecutively throughout the army. Only the historic and traditional titles of the regiments added a touch of diversity. The Corps was as self-contained in the field as in its own Province, with its own supply column, medical and engineer detachments, a cavalry regiment, a Jaeger battalion, and six or more batteries of Corps Artillery. Inevitably it became as important tactically as it was in the Austrian army, although the Prussians retained throughout their divisional organisation. By instinct and training their formation commanders moved instantly to the very forefront of the battle the moment any troops under their command came into action, and this had its dangers as well as its advantages. Both were most clearly demonstrated in the hard-fought battles against the French in the opening month of the 1870 war. At Spicheren, one of the classic encounter-battles of military history, muddled staff-work brought the leading troops of two divisions into action with the French south of Saarbrücken during the morning of 6 August. Since these divisions belonged to different Army Corps and, moreover, straddled the boundary between two Armies and since flank formations, obedient to their training, wheeled inwards to the sound of the guns, by 3 p.m. there were, in the thick of the battle and inextricably entangled, units from four divisions drawn from three different Army Corps and two Armies. The serious fighting began at about noon; and by 4.30 there were no less than three Corps Commanders and four Divisional Commanders conducting a confused infantry dog-fight on a front of less than three miles of thickly wooded hills and valleys. Certainly these high-ranking generals gave their hard-fought infantry battalions magnificent leadership, but the overall direction of the battle was in the hands of the septuagenarian Lieutenant-General von Zastrow, last to arrive on the Saarbrücken Heights and already worn out by the ardours of the *Aufmarsch,* who was content to leave to his junior colleagues the conduct of what became a 'soldiers' battle'. Luck, the superiority of the Prussian artillery and the ineptitudes of the French high command gave the Prussians a shockingly costly but spectacular victory. It also showed the extent to which the course of a battle depended on the whims and abilities of Corps Commanders.

On the other hand ten days later, at the battle of Vionville – Mars-la-Tour, one of those same Corps Commanders, Constantin von Alvensleben, deliberately flung his III Corps into pitched battle with the main strength of Bazaine's army on the high road from Metz to Verdun between Vionville and Mars-la-Tour. With remarkable clarity of mind he decided early in the day, when his leading troops gained a precarious foothold across the road, that he was not engaged in a mere rearguard action, but that he had cut the main escape route towards Paris of the finest army France possessed. With a cool courage perhaps even more remarkable he concluded that it was worth staking the possible annihilation of III Corps against the chance of presenting his Commander-in-Chief with an opening for overwhelming victory. His left flank was in the air, protected by only a cavalry division; and in front he was outnumbered by more than three to one. But he hung on grimly, himself under fire, directing his leading troops from an observation post on the road near Vionville, while further back his Chief-of-Staff hammered away at the business of convincing his neighbouring Corps and the Army Commander of the urgency of the situation. It took all day to get the true facts across to Prince Frederick Charles; and the enormous opportunity thus created only dawned on Moltke as he read the belated reports which reached him during the night. If the French Higher Command had been even reasonably competent this deliberately accepted gamble would not have come off, III Corps would have been annihilated, and the whole German advance thrown into confusion. As it was, the day's fighting cost the Prussians some 16,000 casualties; but the decisive result was the victory at Gravelotte two days later and the ultimate capitulation in Metz of nearly 200,000 of France's best soldiers.

When critics later suggested that it was wrong for a Lieutenant-General thus to expose himself in the forefront of the battle, Alvensleben answered : 'At the crisis of an illness the place of the doctor is by the bedside of the sick man. In this case the sick man was the road from Vionville to Mars-la-Tour.'[19] And in the event he was, of course, fully justified. But his very success helped to perpetuate a dangerous tradition of independence, amounting at times to self-willed obstinacy, among the subordinate German commanders of a later age. It was to bring von Bülow and von Klück to disaster at the Marne in 1914, when Moltke's nephew was struggling to control a much more cumbersome military machine against more competent opposition.

The final factor which gave the Prussians their immense superiority in 1866 and 1870 was the Great General Staff. The products of Clausewitz's *Kriegsakademie,* when Molke took charge in 1857, already constituted a unique body of dedicated professionals, ceaselessly preoccupied with the problems which might confront them on the outbreak of war. The particular contribution of Moltke's genius was to direct their studies to the practical problems of the future, such as the difficulties of moving large bodies of troops and quantities of war-supplies by rail. More important still, he personally trained a selected dozen of them each year in war-games and staff-rides. These men strategically dispersed among the staffs of the higher formations, disseminated his ideas and a common doctrine throughout the army, so that when it came to the push only the most wayward of Commanders, such as General von Steinmetz, could deviate far from the accepted practice. Though the doctrine was sometimes faulty, this was a priceless asset when pitched against the blundering commanders and staffs of the Austrian and French armies.

These, then, were the great armies which, between 1856 and 1872, were to decide the fate of Europe and the future of much of

c*

the rest of the world. Two other nations were to be involved on the fringes, as it were, of these campaigns. The Danish army, some 40,000 strong, put up a heroic resistance in 1864 against overwhelming Austrian and Prussian forces, acting in the name of the otherwise powerless Diet of the German Confederation. It had been modelled on and closely associated with the old Prussian army – Moltke himself had begun his education at the Copenhagen Cadet School. But it was unreformed and it had no Needle Gun. The most it could do was to stand on its fortified lines for long enough for the politicians to become convinced that neither Great Britain nor France was coming to their rescue. As soon as the incompetent von Wrangel had been replaced by Prince Frederick Charles of Prussia, with Moltke as his Chief-of-Staff, the campaign was quickly finished.

The army of Piedmont which, within a very few years of its return from the Crimea, was to expand into the army of Italy, was a more serious proposition. La Marmora, brother of the commander of the Crimean Expeditionary Force who, albeit in somewhat undistinguished company, had earned a great reputation on the Tchernaya, was Cavour's very able Minister of War and responsible for a complete reorganisation after the disasters of 1849. His framework was territorially based, like that of Prussia : the country was divided into five military districts and two sub-districts, providing headquarters and training cadres for five infantry and one cavalry division. The peace-time strength of an infantry division was 8,400, which would be increased on the recall of reservists to about 12,000. There was also provision for cadres of officers and NCOs for units in which it was hoped to recruit volunteers from Lombardy and central Italy. Some 15,000 of these were in fact enrolled in 1859. They brought the total of the King of Sardinia's army for the campaign of Magenta and Solferino to approximately 87,000; and in both battles it gave a good account of itself.

For Italy the results of that abortive campaign were out of all proportion to its military achievement, and far greater than anything Napoleon III had envisaged. Thanks to Cavour's diplomacy and the brilliant guerilla campaign of Garibaldi and his Thousand in Sicily and Naples, the number of King Victor Emmanuel's subjects grew in less than two years from five to twenty-one millions. Such a rapid expansion inevitably placed almost unbearable strains on the administrative machine of the original Kingdom, and most of all, perhaps, on the army, which had to make itself immediately ready for a final round of its long struggle with the Austrians. La Marmora, who, after Cavour's death in 1861, had also taken over as Prime Minister, did remarkably well. The fight for Venetia, the last unredeemed Province, came seven years after Solferino; and by then the Italian army had five Army Corps, each of four divisions. Italian divisions, like the Prussian and Austrian, numbered at full war-strength, approximately 12,000 men, so that their corps, more than double the size of the Austrians', were extremely cumbersome. In 1866 this was less important than it might have been, since financial stringency forced the government to mobilise only 8,400 men per division. Even so it was more than the inexperienced Italian Corps Commanders could manage. In the only battle of that short campaign, Custoza where the Italians were defeated for the last time – the troops fought very well and were well-led by their divisional commanders. It was the high command which panicked and lost all control of the battle.

The Danish army would not again be a factor of importance in European military history; and after 1871 the four great armies of continental Europe would be vastly enlarged as the population explosion produced annually more conscripts for military service, and the spreading industrial revolution equipped them with more sophisticated weapons. But, even though the French had to abandon the tradition of a small, long-service professional army, all of them retained to 1914 the essential characteristics of the dramatic and formative years which followed the end of the Crimean War, the same strengths and the same weaknesses. In the same period, though in widely different theatres, and for different reasons, the nations outside the narrow cockpit of Europe were also forming the military patterns which would stamp their activities in the first World War.

3 War as a Means of Imperial Expansion

At the eastern and western extremities of Europe Great Britain and Russia pursued throughout the latter half of the nineteenth century policies of imperial expansion whose problems differed widely from those of their Continental neighbours. Both, it is true, were still preoccupied with the maintenance of a reasonable balance of power in Europe. This did not mean that they would actively oppose the schemes of Bismarck, Napoleon III and Cavour, all of which were variously designed to destroy the balance established by the 1815 Vienna Settlement. They would limit their activity to diplomatic pressure so long as the struggle for mastery in Europe did not threaten to produce a single overwhelming Power which might interfere with their designs elsewhere. Napoleonic ambition had compelled both to a massive military intervention in Europe in the period before 1815. The Kaiser was to do the same in 1914. But until the very end of the age of Moltke their General Staffs were spared the anxious and incessant calculations of the manpower and speed of mobilisation of their Continental neighbours and free to concentrate on the diverse though equally intractable problems presented by the frontiers of vast empires.

This, however, was nearly all that the two great empires had in common. Both, of course, faced the problem of controlling and developing newly subject and comparatively primitive peoples. But Russia's problems were spread along the thousands of miles of Continental frontier to the west, south, and east; Great Britain's were scattered in multiple units, large and small, over the entire globe. The naval and military solutions devised by both after the Crimean War thus differed sharply, not only from the pattern imposed on the Continental powers, but also from each other. Moreover, there were areas where their developing interests could bring them into direct conflict, as the Crimean War had shown.

The new age in the art of warfare heralded by the guns of Magenta found Great Britain suffering from a triple shock. The first – the Crimean shock – was purely military and more important than the startling revelations of chaos and administrative incompetence which could, after all, be remedied comparatively quickly and easily. It was the realisation forced suddenly upon statesmen, soldiers, and the general public that, in order to maintain a mere expeditionary force of 25,000 men in the Crimea, the nation had been forced not only to draw heavily on its colonial garrisons, but to leave the British Isles themselves defenceless on land save for an unserviceable Militia and the units of the Brigade of Guards retained for ceremonial duties. This was made all the more serious by the discovery that the easy assumption that Britannia ruled the waves as she had in the days of Lord Howe and Lord Nelson was no longer tenable. The joint operations with the French in the Black Sea had convinced the senior sailors that in quantity and quality our navy was probably inferior to the French, and scarcely a match for the combined fleets of the Russians.[1] Then, in 1857, the Indian Mutiny dealt the last blow at the complacency in which Britain had basked since Trafalgar and Waterloo. Not only did it impose a further strain on the already overstretched regular army; it brought home the fact that it was no longer possible to leave the East India Company to roll in its rich dividends while at the same time administering a haphazardly expanding empire whose difficulties might at any moment involve Britain in a major war.

India was Great Britain's major military commitment, and on a much larger scale than has generally been recognised either by historians or by Continental soldiers and statesmen, who had both tended to dismiss her militarily as a 'contemptible' Power. It is true that Britain could not at short notice produce an effective army even half the size of that fielded by the Kingdom of Sardinia in 1859 for Continental warfare. The paper strength of the regular army units stationed in the United Kingdom was 70,000. But that included not only a large number who were making their tedious way home from distant colonial stations, but also numbers of recruits and young soldiers not yet developed enough physically to be sent on foreign service and older men who would never be fit again. Even with the units scattered over the globe the total establishment of the regular army fell short of the peace-time strength maintained by Prussia from a population of ten millions. But it was only in Europe that Britain appeared scarcely to rate as a military power at all. In the East Indies there were, with the native troops and the regiments raised in England for service under the Company, some 280,000 men permanently on a war footing and immediately available for active service: and the regular army in the colonies was being increasingly supplemented by locally raised units. All in all the Queen of England disposed of nearly as large a standing army in the time of peace as did the Emperor of Austria. But in a national emergency she was even worse off than he was for reserves. The Militia, almost defunct in 1852, had been revived to supply reinforcements for the 25,000 troops of the regular army in the Crimean period, but was less fit for active service at home than even the Prussian *Landwehr* of 1859. It was legally still only liable for home defence, and even for that was quite inadequate; and behind it there were only the remnants of the regiments nominally earmarked for home service, already milked dry of every officer and man fit for active service to supply field reinforcements for the army overseas. If casualties overseas were heavy there was no replacement at all.

As this situation became clear the British public was justifiably alarmed; but Whitehall reacted with characteristic leisureliness. The Navy had, of course, its separate problems; and the arguments over the conclusions to be drawn from the clash of ironclad ships on the Mississippi and the battle between the Austrian and Italian fleets at Lissa in 1866 were still re-echoing half a century later. The War Office was thus first off the mark with a Royal Commission under the presidency of General Peel, the Secretary of State, whose reforming zeal was seriously handicapped by the presence of the Commander-in-Chief, HRH Prince George, Duke of Cambridge, first cousin to the Queen. On him had descended the mantle of Wellington and Hardinge, and as such he constituted a rallying point for that powerful minority in high places who were prepared to fight to the last ditch for every anomalous scandal and injustice which had been perpetuated by the forty years of inert peace which had followed Waterloo. Worse still, he was almost the last of the typically Hanoverian characters thrown up by the English ruling dynasty and derived his ideas on drill and discipline from Butcher Cumberland and the Prussian school of Frederick the Great. Largely thanks to him it was to take nearly a quarter of a century to get flogging abolished as a standard punishment in the British Army; and an almost continuous series of Royal Commissions was to hammer away at the intractable problems of the recruitment and organisation of an Imperial Army for nearly thirty years. By 1893 the reformers reckoned that they had achieved all their main objectives;[2] and within six years the outbreak of the second South African War was to demonstrate how inadequate that achievement had been.

But in Peel's Commission of 1858 the obstructive force was not actually the Duke of Cambridge. He, for once, was on the side of reform; and the opposition centred in the powerful bloc which represented, on behalf of the newly constituted Government of India, all the vested interests and time-honoured abuses of the defunct East India Company. In four years the whole centre of public preoccupation, political and military had shifted abruptly from the Crimea and the Near East to India. In the autumn of 1854 the 93rd Highlanders had heard the voice of their commanding general as he cantered along what has been immortalised as 'The thin red streak topped with a line of steel',[3] calling to the over-excited young soldiers: '93rd. 93rd. Damn all that eagerness.' In November of 1858, translated from the icy cold of the trenches before Sebastapol to the torrid head of central India, they were to hear it again as Sir Colin Campbell, by then Lord Clyde and Commander-in-Chief in India, characteristically appeared ahead of their pipers to lead them to the final relief of Lucknow, exhorting them to 'Remember Balaclava'. The episode was symbolic of the change of outlook which was to put India at the centre of all British military thinking for the next half century. For India was not only an enormous military commitment in itself; it was also a far better base than Britain for the continuous minor wars and punitive expeditions involved in the reluctant expansion of an already scattered empire. There was plenty of room to quarter and exercise a much larger army than the British public, inveterately hostile to the maintenance of an adequate standing army in time of peace, would have found acceptable in its own country. More important still, the major expense of it all did not fall on the British taxpayer, but on the Government of India. Finally, it was far more accessible to the area, stretching from Shanghai to New Zealand and the Persian Gulf to South Africa, within which took place the vast majority of the fifty small wars in which the army was involved between the end of the Mutiny and the outbreak of the second South African War.[4]

Peel's Commission took four years to reach its conclusions; but it must be remembered that for the first two of them its debates were overshadowed by the still continuing Mutiny, and further complicated by the curious and little publicised 'White Mutiny' of 1859. This slightly ridiculous episode arose out of a genuinely serious issue which was to bedevil the debates of the Royal Commission for over two years. Since 1781 the East India Company had recruited and maintained a number of European regiments alongside their locally raised native battalions. Until 1799 these were composed, according to a contemporary, 'of the scourings of almost every European nation, kidnapped or wheedled on board ships by crimps'.[5] Thereafter the British Government took over responsibility for recruitment and virtually sold what was needed to the Company, which was allowed to train 1,000 men in peacetime and 2,000 in time of war at its own depot at Warley in Essex. This meant in practice that the Indian Government provided in 1856 about a quarter of the European troops stationed in India: nine infantry battalions, all the artillery, all the sappers and most of the gunners being Europeans. They were distributed among the three Presidencies and at the absolute disposal of their separate Commanders-in-Chief, though C-in-C, Bengal enjoyed the advantage over his colleagues in Bombay and Madras that he alone disposed of the four Cavalry Regiments and the twenty-two infantry battalions which made up what were known as the 'Queen's Troops'.

Unfortunately, in spite of improved recruitment and training, the Company's European units were of very poor quality. A lifetime's service in a progressively debilitating climate, the monotony of garrison life, and the absence of any outside stimulus sapped their morale and produced deplorable standards of drill and discipline; and they were poorly officered. Partly this was because many of the more adventurous young officers preferred to serve with the native regiments; partly because of the absolute rule, jealously resented by regular officers of the Indian Army, that the many lucrative and challenging appointments at the government's disposal, and outside the ordinary stream of regimental life, were exclusively reserved for officers directly in the Company's service. The most able and ambitious officers of the Indian Army were thus creamed off, to form, indeed, that brilliant and dedicated generation of men who served India selflessly and whole-heartedly, and who all but made a success of the British Raj; but it often deprived their regiments of the leadership they so badly needed. When the Mutiny broke out the Company's European units were in such poor shape that the government scarcely dared to use any of them in its suppression.

The Indian lobby was strongly represented on the Royal Commission and, fighting to the last ditch, produced a powerful minority report in 1862 advocating the retention of a strong military force wholly at the disposal of the government in India and not available to the War Office for posting elsewhere to deal with some extraneous Imperial crisis. These men were not entirely motivated by the understandable desire to keep within their own charmed circle the large and lucrative range of extra-regimental postings in India. They were strongly supported by all the higher authorities in India, including Lord Clyde, and the new and enlightened Governor General, Lord Canning, on purely disinterested grounds. It was all very well for the Prince Consort, in a memorandum stating the Queen's view that all her troops in India must be under the overall authority of the Commander-in-Chief in Whitehall, to write that 'no government, in any circumstances, would ever venture to withdraw from India the troops necessary for its defence'. It was the view of many senior soldiers and colonial administrators that, harassed by the clamour for economy and a perpetual shortage of recruits, British governments did sometimes take leave of their senses; and Lord Canning was uneasily aware that at that very moment, with the embers of the Mutiny still to be stamped out and trouble looming among his European troops, three reliable Punjabi infantry battalions, two of his crack Irregular Cavalry Regiments, Fane's and Probyn's Horse, and the Madras Sappers were inextricably engaged 4,000 sailing miles away in the Third Chinese War.[6] With this in mind, and partly perhaps to present the British Government with a *fait accompli*, three regiments of European cavalry had been raised for service with the Company. The luckless victims of this experiment were deliberately recruited from undersized men who would not over-weight the light Indian horses and who were universally known throughout their brief existence as 'The Dumpies'. Not unnaturally they were among the first to join in the refusal of the entire body of the Company's European troops to accept an arbitrary transfer to the British regular army when they had contracted exclusively for service in India. This was the so-called White Mutiny which, in fact, fizzled ingloriously out when the Law Officers of the Crown ruled, somewhat smoothly, that the men had, in law, shouldered this much wider obligation; and even the revered Lord Clyde declared decisively against them.

The results of the Commission's conclusions, implemented in 1862, fell far short of their hopes. In the first place, thanks to the Government's chronic inability to recruit enough men to keep the regular army up to establishment, it took more than ten years to bring the total strength of the regular garrison in India up to the total of 69,000 of all arms they believed necessary. In 1867 it had sunk to 55,000, and even by 1871 it was only 61,000. After the Cardwell reforms things improved; and in 1886 it was possible to increase the total to nine regiments of cavalry, eighty-eight batteries or companies of Royal Artillery, and fifty-three battalions of infantry – a grand total of 72,648. With the native Indian and Gurkha regiments added, it made up a formidable body of professional soldiers. But, under the increasing demands of a steadily expanding Empire, it was not more than just enough. For, without this powerful and central military base the whole structure of what still tenuously survives as the British Commonwealth of Nations could never have been built at all.

From 1860 onwards every expedition mounted east of Suez depended almost wholly for logistical support and largely for its fighting troops on the resources of the Army in India. The enormous administrative demands of Napier's brilliant, 400-mile-march into the heart of Abyssinia in 1868 were almost entirely met from his own Bombay Command. Whitehall contributed his most scientific modern equipment: two batteries of 7-pounder mountain guns, a battery of rifled, breech-loading Armstrong 12 pounders, four of the new 'rocket machines', four thousand of the new Snyder-Enfield, breech-loading rifles for his European troops, a company of Sappers, a host of specialist officers, a brand-new telegraph unit, three hospital ships, and a number of sailing vessels specially equipped for animal transport. The Indian Vice-regal Government grudgingly sent an infantry battalion, two regiments of Lancers, a European Battery from Bengal, and 400 of the Madras Sappers, who were an essential element in any Far-Eastern campaign. Two thirds of the 13,000 fighting troops were provided from Bombay, as were the 44 elephants, 1,000 draught bullocks, innumerable horses and pack-ponies, the bulk of the 15,000-odd men of the administrative tail, and the engines, rolling-stock, and material required for the railway from Zula to Koomalyi.[7] In 1882, in Wolseley's Tel-el-Kebir campaign when, once again, the main problems were administrative rather than tactical, more than a fifth of his force was drawn from India.[8]

From the purely military point of view, therefore, the solutions evolved by the Royal Commission of 1858 were brilliantly successful; and they contributed handsomely to the rapid enlargement of British territory, wealth, and prestige during the following fifty years. The ultimate social and political effects in India itself were in general disastrous. It had been the devoutly expressed belief of the Commission that the breaking of the Company's monopoly of lucrative and influential employment under the Government of India, with 'all the advantages attending it', would open up to the Governor-General 'a much larger field for the selection of able and useful officers'.[9] This was undoubtedly true. But the new men, drawn from the British Army which very soon in its turn almost monopolised such appointments, had been reared in an alien, rigid social tradition already a little out of date, even in Victorian England. Together with a newly formed Indian Civil Service, highly selective, devoted, and extremely efficient, they gave India for the better part of a century some of the best government the world has seen. But the development of hot-weather hill stations and a summer capital at Simla vastly improved conditions for European families;[10] and rapid steam transport made it easy for wives to join their husbands. This superimposed on an already caste-ridden India a new and irrelevant social hierarchy with, in due course, a top-heavy Viceregal Court at the summit. Such a world could never throw up men of the calibre of the Lawrences and Nicholsons, the Skinners and Probyns and Fanes and the many less-known men, often born and bred among the people whom they loved and understood and led and governed and bullied, in the easy-going, often corrupt Company's world, tolerant even of mixed marriages and mixed parentage – a world which perished in the Mutiny.

It took another twenty years of Royal Commissions and ceaseless tinkering with reform by Secretaries of State before the other problems savagely thrust on the British Government by the Crimean War and the Mutiny were satisfactorily solved. The only swift and immediate success was that of the Volunteer Movement launched in 1859. Encouraged by the Poet Laureate's urge to : 'Form, Form, Riflemen, Form,' the public flocked to join local battalions and, later, Artillery and Engineer units; while the already existing County Yeomanry regiments provided the cavalry. Thus the Movement within a few years had provided Great Britain with 150,000 enthusiastic and partially trained troops as a third-line defence in the event of invasion. In practice it became the Second Line. For, until the era of Haldane in the years preceding the First World War, no government was able to produce a coherent system of recruitment for the Militia or a proper organisation for the regular army reserves, and the integration of the two with what was to become the Territorial Army.

The fundamental problem which kept the Royal Commissions debating for twenty years was the difficulty of recruiting sufficient numbers for a professional army and a semi-professional Militia in a nation which had set its face against conscription and regarded with deep suspicion any increase in the military budget. The main blame, however, lay with the unimaginative approach of the War Department itself. Two faults, apparently in-built, since they largely persist to the present day, hampered its efforts to attract men into the army. One was the innate and lethargic conservatism of senior officers too-long cut off from the needs of active service and the problems of the regimental soldier; reformers were disturbers of the peace, and it was simpler to accept as immutable the palpably self-defeating cheeseparings of the Treasury. The other was an inherent tendency to prefer administrative simplicity to fighting efficiency : to put the convenience of clerks before the interests of the serving soldier. All the difficulties which haunted the army until 1868 can be traced to one or other of these shortcomings. Then the genius of Cardwell, Secretary of State for War for an unprecedented five years, solved most of the fundamental problems of the regular army for the next fifty years and laid the foundations for the equally decisive Haldane reforms of the territorial reserves in 1908.

There were, of course, many factors which contributed to the Army's inability to recruit the numbers urgently needed for a steadily expanding Empire between 1815 and 1868. One was a barbarously harsh disciplinary system long since abandoned in the more enlightened Continental armies. Another was the rigid determination among senior officers to preserve on active service and in infinitely varying climates the uniform and equipment designed to produce maximum smartness on the drill squares of London and Aldershot. Lord Palmerston had, with his usual clarity and commonsense, put his finger on the crucial point in his evidence to the Finance Committee as early as 1828; and his long service as Secretary at War entitled him to speak with authority :

I believe [he said] there is a great disinclination on the part of the lower orders to enlist for general service; they like to know that they are to be in a certain regiment, connected, perhaps, with their own county, and their own friends, and with officers who have established a connection with that district. There is a preference frequently on the part of the people for one regiment as compared with another, and I should think there would be found a great disinclination in men to enlist for general service, and to be liable to be drafted and sent to any corps or station.

It took the army authorities forty years to accept this fundamental fact and, incidentally, less than sixty to forget it again.

When it was necessary to bring a unit up to full strength drafts of men were suddenly cross-posted into an alien world where the very dialect of their new comrades was often nearly incomprehensible, and so were deprived of the familiarity and friendship which alone compensated for the hardships and poverty of the military life. Thus, when Cape Colony was handed back to the Dutch in 1820, the 91st Argyllshire Highlanders, due to return home, were so heavily milked to bring up to strength the battalions of the garrison destined for India that they numbered scarcely half their proper establishment when they reached England. The knowledge that they might thus abruptly be cut off from their friends and background and condemned to another long spell of tropical discomfort inevitably damaged morale and discouraged recruitment. Yet in 1866 the military witnesses at the Royal Commission of Enquiry into the continuing failure to recruit the numbers required one after another insisted that the army could not be administered on any basis but that of general enlistment; and a year later Parliament endorsed their view. The historian, Clode, writing in 1869, charitably ascribes the opinion of the generals to 'probable forgetfulness or possible disregard of previous experience in this matter'. It is a sad thought that a hundred years later he might well have passed the same judgement, though with greater asperity, on the generals of 1969.

The other great handicap to adequate recruitment sprang from the obstinate preference of all the War Departments for long-service enlistments. Engagements 'for life' had first become the universal rule in 1783. Even in periods of great industrial depression, this was too awesome a commitment for many young men, however attractive the Bounty offered. The army was never less than 20,000 short of establishment; and, still worse, a very large proportion of the serving troops were ageing men quite unfit for active service. In 1806, Wyndham, faced by the need to find an army large enough and fit enough for large-scale intervention on the Continent, reintroduced the Limited Engagement, whereby infantrymen could enlist for seven years, cavalrymen for ten, and gunners and sappers for twelve, with the option, of course, of re-engaging at the end of those periods. This scheme, slightly modified by Castlereagh in 1808, did not wholly solve the problem, and the army remained chronically short of the numbers authorised by Parliament; but it gave Moore and Wellington the armies they needed to play a decisive part in the downfall of Napoleon.

This system lasted until 1829, when the same lunatic Parliament which rejected Palmerston's plea for local, as opposed to general enlistment, abolished it and restored the compulsory and discouraging life engagement. During the long Metternichian peace this did not matter much in practice, since the demand for fit and active young men for service was small; but Chartism at home and the general threat of revolution throughout Europe forced a change of heart in 1847 and the short-service enlistment was restored. By then, however, it was too late. There was, indeed, a welcome influx of short-term engagers. But British officers, like their Austrian contemporaries, naturally preferred parading and manoeuvring troops with long years of drill, discipline, and training behind them to the tedious business of instructing raw recruits, so that they put tremendous pressure on the younger men to re-engage for another term, or even for life. At the same time the soldiers, like the French conscripts, after seven years of segregated military existence, felt themselves quite out of touch with civilian life and were quite untrained for any occupation other than soldiering. So the situation remained unremedied until the Crimean War revealed all its deficiencies; and even then seven years of almost continuous Commissions and Enquiries failed to deal with any of the major problems.

This, then, was the appallingly dangerous situation when Cardwell took over as Secretary of State for War in 1868. He and Haldane, who followed him forty years later and rounded off his work, were perhaps the only two men of genius ever to preside over that great Department. His achievement in his six years of office was remarkable; and but for these two it is doubtful if the nation could have survived the crisis of 1914 without total disaster. Cardwell started with wholesale reorganisation at the centre. All the ramifying and often mutually hostile branches of the army administration were brought together under one roof and made responsible to the Secretary of State; and this included not only the reserve proper, but the hitherto separately administered Militia, Yeomanry, and Volunteers. One benefit of this obviously sensible measure which might well be envied by many modern would-be reformers was the reduction by 1872 of the Department's official correspondence from a daily average of 1,500 letters to 900.[11] Purchase of commissions, with all its attendant evils of vested financial interests, was abolished in 1871 and the way laid open for an intelligent, mathematically graded promotion system, so that more promising seniors could be given responsible postings before they were too old to be valuable and younger officers were no longer left to stagnate for years as subalterns – an evil which was again to haunt the army in the years between the two world wars.[12] It was to take ten years to get all the implications of these decisions worked out in practice. But by 1881 Cardwell's successors had completed the tasks he had set: there were compulsory retirement ages for all ranks; and a proper proportion of ranks in all corps ensured that promotion should not be unduly impeded. These and a host of minor reforms, administrative and humanitarian, did much to make army life more attractive to the potential recruit. An Order of 1871, for example, abolished the barbarous practice of marking for life the bodies of men convicted of desertion or bad conduct with a D or B C, thought the abolition of flogging, already obsolete in most Continental armies by the time of the Peninsular War, had to be postponed to 1881, so powerful was the rearguard action put up by senior soldiers convinced that without it they could not maintain discipline. But the two most important measures, which transformed the structure and the very nature of the British Army, were the Enlistment Act of 1870 and the Localisation Scheme laid before Parliament by HRH the Commander-in-Chief in February, 1872.

The Enlistment Act at last put an end to the 'army of old men', most of them unfit for arduous or active service overseas. Under the new law no recruit could engage for more than twelve years. The permissible minimum was left to the discretion of the Secretary of State, having regard to the exigencies of the service and the differing requirements of the various arms and branches. Clearly a recruit had to be a fully trained and efficient soldier before he could be allowed to leave the colours. Subject to that he was given complete freedom of choice in allocating his service between the colours and the reserve. He could engage for the full twelve years with the colours, or for any combination he pleased which made up the full twelve years. To his opponents in Parliament who argued that the whole system was wasted endeavour, since men only joined the army for the sake of the pension, Cardwell retorted in another of his vigorous speeches that they and he were talking of 'different persons'. They were thinking of the existing system. He was considering the young man who, he hoped, would join the army in the future and who would welcome a few years of serious training before marrying and settling down, perhaps to some trade he had learnt while soldiering. During his reserve service his military skills could be prevented from rusting by evening drills similar to those of the Volunteers; and he would be at any time available to bring a home unit up to strength for war service, or to reinforce a unit anywhere in the world.

The almost complete success of this imaginative reform can best be measured by the table of 'terms of engagement' submitted to Parliament in 1892. This shows that out of a round total of 200,000 serving British troops nearly 160,000 were on short-term engagements. The 'army of old men' had disappeared; and behind the new one stood a substantial regular army reserve, young, fit, and instantly mobilisable. The double object of Cardwell's Enlistment Act had thus been fully achieved. But this, though in itself eminently desirable, was in Cardwell's mind only a stepping stone to his supreme achievement: the Localisation Scheme of 1872. It was a highly complex scheme, and it took more than ten years to work out. But broadly it had three aims. Firstly the regimental system was to be reorganised so that every cavalry, infantry, and artillery regiment had a recognised territorial area in which it would have a Regimental Depot and from which it would draw the bulk of its recruits. Secondly every infantry regiment was to consist of two linked battalions, one normally stationed abroad, the other at home; and reinforcements for the overseas battalion would normally be drawn from the home battalion. Finally all regular reserves, Militia and Volunteer units were to be affiliated to the regiments whose areas they inhabited and to be brought under a unified, regular army command.

The Conservative victory in the election of 1874 deprived Cardwell of office long before his complex and grandiose reform was complete. Fortunately his successors faithfully pursued all his plans to their logical conclusion; and he himself had done so much to clear the ground that only time was needed to finish his work. By far the most intractable problem was the linking of battalions in pairs, one overseas and one at home. There was nothing new about such a scheme. Pitt and the Duke of York had successfully operated it in the early years of the Napoleonic Wars and had only had to abandon it because of its unpopularity, due to bad and inequitable administration, and because it was not combined with short-term enlistment. Since then, however, two new difficulties had arisen. The more important was that the needs of an expanding empire had absorbed into permanent service abroad considerably more than half the available battalions. The other, more easily remediable, was that overseas battalions were based on an establishment of twelve companies, whereas those at home maintained only ten; and this, of course, was the reason for the large drafts required from other regiments by a battalion warned for service abroad.

The second problem was solved simply by placing home and overseas battalions on the same establishment, so that the home units retained the structure and cadre needed for foreign service. It was acceptable that the companies at home would always be well below full strength, since their prime duty was to supply the annual drafts needed to replace time-expired men and casualties in the sister battalion overseas. In an emergency the home battalions could be brought up to full strength within a week, by calling up the trained, regular reserves, so providing the nation both with a regular force sufficient for home defence and a strategic reserve. Cardwell settled his other problem by a drastic reduction of the garrisons permanently maintained abroad. Most of these consisted of small bodies of infantry and artillery which had long lost their military usefulness and stagnated, often in insalubrious climates, with no opportunity for sophisticated training, and no stimulus to effort. The emergent self-governing Dominions such as Canada, Australia, and New Zealand had no longer any need of regular British forces and could easily meet their normal military needs from their own resources; and there were many other garrisons which had ceased to fulfill any intelligible strategical purpose.

The first essential to the implementation of the Cardwell system was thus a drastic reduction of the colonial garrisons. By 1870 he had already abolished all garrisons in self-governing colonies except those in the Citadel at Cape Town and in the fortress of Halifax. Otherwise he left only small forces in some twelve small dependencies such as Gibraltar, Malta, Cyprus, Santa Lucia and Hong Kong which were regarded as vital coaling stations or as essential naval or military bases in the event of war. He was thus able to bring home eight battalions – a total of over 26,000 men. So, at a single stroke, he achieved the balance of home and overseas units which he needed, but it still took over ten years to work out the details, particularly in the case of the infantry, which were at the core of his problem. In the case of the twenty-five senior numbered regiments of the line the task was comparatively easy, since all were already two-battalion regiments. It was only necessary to allot to each a territorial area and a new territorial designation and construct a reasonably accessible Depot which would become the home of the regiment and the hub of its activities. One battalion could then serve at home, one abroad, replacing each other at regular intervals and reinforcing each other as necessary.

The case of the remaining one-battalion regiments inevitably involved the uprooting and fusion of units from different recruiting areas and with widely different backgrounds and traditions. Inevitably there were strange bedfellows. Thus the 81st Foot, the Loyal Lincoln Volunteers, were joined to the 47th Lancashire Regiment to become the 2nd Battalion of the Loyal North Lancashire Regiment, with a Depot at Lancaster. The fusion of the 91st Argyllshire and the 93rd Sutherland Highlanders into the Argyll and Sutherland Highlanders brought together men with backgrounds and traditions as remote from each other geographically and historically as Highlanders could well be; and they were given a Depot at Stirling Castle, outside both counties, and a recruiting area based on the Lowland cities and the industrialised valley of the Forth. But great pains were taken to enshrine the old regimental names in the new titles and to provide some element of kinship. Thus the 42nd and 53rd Light Infantry were blood brothers, both stemming from Sir John Moore's famous Peninsular Light Division, and settled down very smoothly as the Oxfordshire and Buckinghamshire Light Infantry, with a brand new castellated Depot in the Victorian prison style at Cowley. So the amalgamations went through with surprisingly little friction. By 1882 the process was complete and the new regiments were fast developing that happy family atmosphere, which has been the essence and the strength of British fighting troops ever since, in which a man posted from one battalion to another merely found himself among other friends in an equally familiar background. It is one measure of Cardwell's success that by 1893 more than a quarter of the serving infantry had been born in the territorial areas allotted to their regiments.[13]

Home battalions were not, of course, ever stationed at their Depots but were quartered in large agglomerations of all arms in barracks and camps at centres like Aldershot and Strensall within easy reach of training areas large enough to permit extended combined exercises in brigades and divisions, so that they could at very short notice be mobilised either as an army for home defence or as an Expeditionary Force. But, apart from acting as home bases and clearing centres for the service battalions the Depots also performed an invaluable function in co-ordinating the activities of all the miscellaneous Militia and Volunteer units within their regimental areas, which became directly attached to their parent regiments and frequently adjusted their uniform, drill and customs accordingly. All this made it much easier for Haldane to complete Cardwell's work in 1908 by reforming them all into a formidable Territorial Army. The Militia were reconstituted on paper as the third Battalions of their regiments, but with no operational function save that of replacing the battle casualties of the regular battalions at the first impact of a campaign. The Volunteers were regrouped as territorial battalions of their parent regiments, numbering from 4 onwards, totally assimilated in all respects to them, and drawing some regular officers and NCOs from them. Most were trained to a very high standard indeed, and organised into formations with permanent staffs. The result was that Haldane was able to create a separate Territorial Army of fourteen divisions and fourteen cavalry brigades ready, not merely as a second line of defence, but to take its place almost immediately beside the seven divisions – six infantry and one cavalry – which he had extracted from the Cardwell system as the

Expeditionary Force in the event of renewed major war in Europe.

But by then the Age of Moltke had ended. The important point for that period is that Cardwell gave the British Empire exactly what Moltke and Roon gave the German Empire: a flexible system, almost precisely suited to its peculiar needs, capable of fighting campaigns, sometimes simultaneously, in remote parts of the globe. It would be quite untrue to say that the vast British imperial expansion of the latter half of the nineteenth century was a deliberate policy of which the army was the instrument. The restless, perhaps superabundant, energies of missionaries and traders, mineral prospectors and financiers, all most liable to find themselves in conflict with the vested interests of primitive peoples, gradually involved reluctant, and often inept statesmen in commitments which, in the long run, only the army could fulfil and maintain. This was the process which was to involve Britain, by protectorates or outright annexation, in vast accessions of territory in southern Africa. At the same time the collapse of the nominal Turkish suzerainty in North Africa combined with the bankruptcy of the Egyptian Khedive and the absolute need, in a steamship age, of safeguarding the Suez Canal forced the British first to assume an ill-defined 'Condominium' over Egypt, and ultimately to conquer and virtually to annex Nubia and the Sudan. It was Cardwell's achievement that he gave the government an army sufficiently powerful and flexible to meet all these needs in spite of frequently incompetent leadership. It was to emerge ultimately triumphant from major campaigns in Egypt and the Sudan and even to fight its way to final victory in something near a major war against the unexpectedly formidable force of the Boer farmers of South Africa. It was Haldane's contribution to supplement all this by adding a home-based force capable of intervening in a major European war.

Russian political and strategic ambitions had been concentrated since the Middle Ages on imperialist expansion; but it was not until the latter half of the eighteenth century that they brought them into direct conflict with those of Great Britain. From then onwards this conflict became steadily more acute. Russia, of course, could offer no direct challenge to the steady acquisition by Britain of commercially valuable overseas dependencies whose retention rested ultimately on the fact that Britannia still ruled the waves in fact as well as in song. The generals in St Petersburg therefore faced problems vastly different from those which plagued the military authorities in Whitehall. They had to concentrate on the expansion of a land-mass already enormous until they reached the point where British colonial supremacy could be threatened both at sea and by the intervention in India and Africa of overwhelmingly powerful land forces. In the pursuit of these ambitions they were, in spite of occasional reverses, until 1900 remarkably successful.

The essential preliminary to any naval action was the acquisition of a harbour which, unlike their Baltic bases, was ice-free all the year round. They had, of course, their Black Sea ports, except for the brief period from 1856 to 1870 when Britain was able to enforce their neutralisation. But these were useless unless the army could also get control of the Bospnorus and the Dardanelles. Otherwise they must push far enough south along the Pacific coast to give their admirals what they needed. A military threat to Britain was also limited to two areas : a breakthrough between the Black Sea and the Caspian would open up a land bridge into India and Africa. Alternatively an advance through Turkestan and Afghanistan might bring them face to face with the British on the Khyber Pass. All four of these objectives were simultaneously and remorselessly pursued by the Russian government throughout the nineteenth century and right up to 1914. The needs of all four of these widely separated theatres had to be taken into consideration by the Russian General Staff; and only if they are constantly borne in mind can the reforms of the Russian army in the post-Crimean period, which culminated in the Imperial Ukase of 1874, be properly understood. They had taken eighteen years to achieve. But at least they were able to get their new army into action in a major and highly successful campaign in 1877; and they had faced far more formidable problems than Cardwell's when he undertook his great overhaul of the antiquated British military forces.

The eastward advance of the Russian Empire from the Urals to the Pacific had been a continuous process since the sixteenth century, scarcely even interrupted when the Imperial armies were heavily involved in major wars along their western European frontier or southwards against the declining Turkish Empire. As with the British, the soldier generally followed the merchant; and, as trading posts grew into new towns, the army steadily conquered or absorbed primitive Khanates or Principalities the more important of which would in due course add one more strangely accoutred regiment to the already picturesquely diversified Imperial Army. By 1697 they had secured the whole peninsula of Kamchakta on the Bering Sea and were ranged along a 2,000-mile frontier on the northern edge of the old Chinese Empire. From 1851 onwards they overran the territory stretching down to the Amur River and formally constituted it as a new Province in 1858; and two years later they were established in Vladivostock with yet another Province facing, across only a hundred miles of sea, northern Japan. In the same period, at the western end of that long frontier they had acquired the bulk of Turkestan and were threatening to cut the great ancient trade route of the Golden Road to Samarkand.

By 1860, however, the period which had lasted for three centuries, when Russia could, without putting any special strain on her huge regular standing army, progressively move into the political void of northern Asia was drawing to a close. The standing armies of Alexander 1 and Nicholas 1 were immense by European standards, though their effective strength probably fell far short of the million men hysterically attributed to them by western diplomats; and they were perfectly capable of meeting all the demands normally made on them. But, as the Austrian mobilisation in the Carpathians during the Crimean War had shown, the mere threat of intervention by a major power stretched them to the limit of their capacity.[14] There were still some cheap gains to be picked up on the three eastern prongs of their fourfold advance. From 1864 to 1870 they fairly easily completed their domination of the Transcaucasian area between the Black Sea and the Caspian and confronted Turkey along her Armenian frontier. Beyond the Caspian their gains were even more spectacular. Between 1853 and 1859 they had overrun the vast area of southern Turkestan. In 1868 they occupied Bokhara. By 1873 they had acquired Khiva and were half way down the far coast of the Caspian; and in 1876 they seized Samarkand. In 1883 the new Province of the Transcaspian District gave them the whole eastern coast of the Caspian; and the capture of Merv in 1884 brought them on to the northern frontier of Afghanistan.

In the same period, however, the British had also been active. Between 1877 and 1883 they had secured the further exits of the Bolan Pass by occupying Quetta and the southernmost corner of Afghanistan and reinforced their gain by the occupation of Baluchistan. Lord Roberts of Khandahar had handsomely revenged the humiliation of Kabul in 1844 and had made it clear to the Emir that, while Britain had no desire whatever to take over the government of Afghanistan, she would certainly not tolerate any penetration by the Russians; and by astutely playing off one great power against the other, the Emirs were able to preserve their precarious independence. The Russians, meanwhile, had declared the northern half of Persia, including Teheran, an exclusive sphere of influence, which made the Caspian virtually a Russian lake; and the British had countered with a sphere of influence in south-east Persia which secured control of the entrance to the Persian Gulf. So Russia's advance was brought to a halt along the northern frontiers of Persia and Afghanistan, unless she was prepared to undertake another major war with Britain. She did venture one stage further south to annex the Pamirs in 1895. But in the same year Britain occupied Chitral; and the two Empires for the first time confronted each other face to face along two hundred miles of ill-defined frontier. It was a situation of deadlock in which the only flourishing activities were intrigue and espionage.[15] In the meantime the Far-Eastern advance had also been brought to a halt. The Russians did venture in 1875 to seize Sakhalin, off their Pacific coast and most dangerously close to the northern island of the Japanese mainland. The emergence of Japan from isolationist feudal mediaevalism into the status of a great modern power within thirty years took the whole world by surprise. But the Russians had an inkling of it when Japanese settlements began to appear on the Korean coast in the 1870s and 1880s. They did not move south from Vladivostock and contented themselves with declaring Outer Mongolia another exclusive sphere of interest. They got their ice-free harbour at last in 1898 at Port Arthur but, significantly, only on lease from China, to whom the Japanese had recently restored it. So by 1900 it had become clear on both far-eastern fronts that the happy days of easy and progressive annexations were over, and that there could be no further gains save at the expense of a major war.

This had been true for a century on the two nearer, European fronts at the opposite ends of the Black Sea. Both Great Britain and Austria, though for very different reasons, had long since declared their vested interests in maintaining the integrity of the Ottoman Empire. Any Russian advance into the Balkans or Asia Minor, therefore, invited the almost certain intervention of one or more of the European Great Powers. Until the Crimean War the overwhelming preponderance of the Russian army, at least in numbers, seemed sufficient to ward off interference and to permit occasional adventures such as those of 1828 and 1854. But Roon's reforms and Moltke's victories had radically altered the situation. The old regular army could no longer hope to meet its increasingly remote commitments in the east, fight the Turks on two fronts, and still find a sufficient reserve to hold off the great conscript armies of Austria or Germany; and this was the contingency which the Tsar's military advisers had to bear in mind when they sat down in 1871 to work out the great reform which was finally promulgated by the Imperial Ukase of 1 January 1874.

The system which they evolved borrowed features from all the European armies and added a great many more which sprang from the unique peculiarities of the Russian social pattern. The populations of the Provinces were infinitely diverse in language, race, and social customs, and varied greatly in density. The whole nation, moreover, was in the throes of a social upheaval as a result of the recent emancipation of the serfs, tentative experiments in self-government, and the all-too-belated emergence of an educated middle class. It was industrially backward; its administration was incompetent and corrupt; and the government was in perpetual financial difficulty. As a result of all these factors the published Regulations were immensely long and immensely complex. There was scarcely a rule to which there were not at least a dozen exceptions; and the whole volume ran to 224 articles, divided into fourteen chapters.[16] But two overriding limitations dictated the final result and prevented anything like a full mobilisation of Russia's almost unlimited manpower : shortage of cash; and a grave shortage of potential officers. So, though

D

the principle was firmly laid down that all males 'without distinction of class' became liable for military service at the age of twenty and remained so until they were forty, the government took what it needed by an annual ballot, the results of which were final and irrevocable. No exemptions by purchase or substitution were allowed, but those with certificates of even primary education could avoid the ballot by volunteering on considerably more advantageous terms than the rest. Those who were lucky in the ballot were enrolled in the militia and remained liable to be called up in an emergency, though they received no training. Only civil servants were completely exempt. Terms of service varied considerably, especially in the remoter Provinces and frontier Districts. But the norm was a total of fifteen years, six with the colours and nine in the Reserve.

In round figures the government aimed to produce a standing peace-time field army of 600,000 men, trained and brigaded and available for immediate service in any theatre, supplemented by 150,000 Local Troops, who served in their own homelands as fortress and frontier garrisons and, in the case of some recently acquired territories, for the preservation of internal law and order. Behind this there was to be a reserve of trained soldiers on permanent leave of over a million men which was to be used for three main purposes. It had firstly to bring the field army up to an approximate strength of a million men and the Local Troops to their war establishment of 325,000. It had then to furnish a reserve army of half a million, organised into divisions and, if necessary, army corps, which was to be a quite separate entity and in no case to be drawn on to replace casualties in the field army. Finally there were to be 235,000 men held unbrigaded in their various Military Circumscriptions as a casualty replacement pool for both field and reserve armies – which most nations in imitation of the Germans and Austrians were beginning to call the *Ersatz* – and as gaps occurred in the *Ersatz* they were to be filled by progressive call-ups of the Militia, starting with the youngest age groups. On paper, therefore, Russia would be able when mobilisation was complete to throw into the field an army of a million men with over 200,000 trained reservists to replace its casualties and could at the same time rapidly organise a reserve army of 500,000 fully trained troops.

In practice, of course, this was never, before 1914, more than an idle daydream. It made insufficient provision for the inevitable wastage of death and disease among both regular and trained reservists. The primitive transport system made it impossible to concentrate such numbers on any battlefield and for the supply services to maintain them there; and a backward industry could not provide arms, equipment, and sufficient ammunition for such vast deployments. But the 1874 planners could fairly claim to have done a workmanlike and even, from some aspects, an imaginative job. It was not their fault that their system was first put to a major test only three years after they had launched it, when there were only three classes of trained reservists instead of the nine for which they had planned; nor can they fairly be held responsible for disasters thirty years later in Manchuria. Their scheme did at least enable the Russian high command to maintain on the Balkan front a fighting force of some 250,000 which fought its way to almost within artillery range of Constantinople and another, some 65,000 strong, sufficient to storm the great fortress of Kars. Moreover they held intact the army of 200,000 trained reservists which could, by milking the fortress and frontier garrisons, have been brought up to 300,000 to meet the constant threat of Austrian intervention. This was probably a correct policy; but its cost in casualties was appalling, since there remained no trained *Ersatz*. Against a Turkish army, always at its most formidable in a dogged defence, the Russians had many regiments virtually annihilated in the prolonged fighting around Plevna; and their ranks were made up by drafts of Militiamen, wholly inexperienced and mostly illiterate, hastily assembled at their depots, clothed and equipped and given a week of drill, and rushed into battle to learn the art of warfare as best they could from the handful of surviving veterans in their battalions. It was a reversion to the era of the first Napoleon and equally disastrous in its results. But for that the planners of 1874 could not be held to blame.

They can, on the other hand, be given special credit for conserving, and even enlarging the role of the Cossack cavalry regiments in the Imperial Army. These were probably the only really efficient horsed cavalry employed by any army in the world between 1870 and 1940. The crack mounted regiments of the great armies forgot the butchery at Wörth of two whole Brigades of the finest cavalry in Europe without inflicting a single casualty on the Prussian infantry and the equally ineffective gallantry of de Gallifet's Division at Sedan. They remembered only the solitary and improbable success of von Bredow's death ride at Mars-la-Tour, and obstinately refused to learn the mounted infantry tactics which could alone make them useful in a modern battle. Cossacks on the other hand never thought of themselves as shock troops. Born horsemen and marksmen, they had their horses trained to lie down so that they could fire over them, or to stand quietly, unguarded and unpicketed, behind the lines until they were again wanted. The only mounted action they undertook was the pursuit of broken infantry formations, when they sabred the fugitives with a merciless ferocity. Officially they were listed as Irregular Cavalry. But a Cossack regiment was attached to every regular cavalry brigade in peacetime, making a total of 42,000 which was increased to 143,000 on mobilisation.[17]

The Cossacks of the Caucasus lived traditionally in large, self-governing Communes conducted on a system not wholly dissimilar from that of the early Anglo-Saxon settlements in England. With rare wisdom, the Russian government had the sense to leave them undisturbed by bureaucratic interference, merely appointing the Tsarevitch as their chief Headman. They remained immune from taxation and all the regulations for conscription and furnished in return and free of charge the contingents demanded by the War Ministry, under their own arrangements, and on semi-feudal terms. The Cossack trooper furnished his own horse, saddle, uniform, and equipment and served without pay. From the government he drew only his arms and ammunition and an allowance for rations and forage which he spent as he pleased on the open market. On active service, when free purchase became impossible, they all put their allowances in the hands of the Commanding Officer, who bought what was needed from the *Intendance*. The Cossacks were, in fact, a unique survival of a much earlier age, and yet uniquely successful in a world of increasingly technical modern warfare. They certainly formed an important element in the Russian army which was to find itself involved in two of the four major wars which may be regarded as the curtain-raisers for 1914 or, more correctly, as the aftermath of the great age of Moltke.

The British and the Russians were not, of course, the only powers to indulge in imperial expansion during the last twenty years of the nineteenth century, when it suddenly dawned on the civilised world that there was in the central hinterland of Africa a vast, largely unexplored area which was both rich in unexploited raw materials, and especially minerals, and potentially an extremely profitable market for the commercial products of western Europe. Britain, with her long commercial and industrial lead, in the end acquired the most valuable territories but, measured in square miles, France secured by far the largest share. Moreover, whereas the British army only moved in reluctantly to safeguard the gains of missionaries, merchants, and industrialists, the French army was the spearhead and essential instrument of imperial expansion. After Sedan, as after Waterloo, the French thirst for military glory was diverted from dreams of European hegemony to easier conquests overseas where Arab and Berber and Tuareg tribesmen offered, for the time being, a less formidable opposition than the massed armies of Bismarck's German Empire. Thus the spectacular French territorial expansion was essentially a military undertaking: the settlers and traders and missionaries moved, where it was profitable to move at all, in the wake of the small flying columns which pushed steadily inland, marking the progress of French sovereignty with little, castellated forts, each flying its *tricouleur*. The initial advance south from Algeria was slow. A reluctant government had first to annex Tunisia to prevent the chaos which had resulted from the collapse of the Turkish government from spreading into Algeria; and the primary task of the picturesque Zouaves and Spahis and the legendary Foreign Legion was to establish a defensive screen for the prosperous Mediterranean coastal belt. But by 1873 they were well into the Sahara at El Golea; and in 1899 and 1900 they established posts 300 miles to the south in the heart of the desert at Insala and Tuat. Finally, in 1911, Marshal Lyautey in a single brilliant campaign conquered Morocco, though he never wholly subdued one of the most mixed and turbulent populations in the world.

It was in the south that the more profitable and the more

grandiose geographical gains were made. Between 1881 and 1914 France first forged her scattered coastal territories in Senegal, Gambia, Guinea, and along the Ivory Coast into a single whole, leaving the Portuguese with a bare 20,000 square miles in Guinea, penning the Liberian Republic into its narrow coastal strip, and blocking any northward expansion of the British colony of Sierra Leone. At the same time French Equatorial Africa was steadily extended from the mouth of the Congo northwards along the west bank of that great river until that, too, had reached the fringes of the great desert. The second phase was a rapid extension of these gains northwards and eastwards. The vast, ill-defined area of Mauritania was annexed in 1893. A year later French troops hoisted their flag in Timbuktu and Chad; and once these two had been linked they had effectively sealed off the hinterland of the rest of the British West African territories and the newly acquired German colonies in Cameroon and Togoland. In the great vacuum of the Sahara, which nobody else coveted, it was not difficult to link up the southern and northern gains and so establish on the map an empire which stretched more than 2,000 miles north from the Congo mouth to the Mediterranean and westwards to Cape Verde.

It was the avowed dream of the forward school of French colonial soldiers and administrators to push on eastwards to the Nile and ultimately to the Red Sea. But they were unlucky in their timings. When Colonel Marchand with the typical small flying column which the French had learnt to organise and handle so well arrived at the Nile in September, 1898, after an arduous and brilliantly conducted desert march, and hoisted the French flag at Fashoda, he was a few weeks too late. General Kitchener had just brought his army and his gunboats successfully past the Nile rapids and was about to revenge General Gordon by destroying the Dervish army at Omdurman and seizing Khartoum. The British were determined to put an end to their troubles in the Sudan by taking over the whole of that turgid area as an Anglo-Egyptian Condominium, which meant in effect that it was to become a British colony. Colonel Marchand was peremptorily ordered out; and war fever in France, stimulated by a particularly tactless Punch cartoon, rose to a dangerous pitch. After a year of crisis, however, tempers cooled and a demarcation line was agreed defining the rival 'spheres of interest', and so effectively halting any further expansion of the French Empire to the east. Northwards they still made some progress in the Tenere Desert and the arid mountains of Aïr, and in the Tibesti. But there, too, they were brought to a halt in 1912 by the frontier of the newly established Italian colony of Tripolitania.

France's other considerable African gain during this period was the large offshore island of Madagascar in the Indian Ocean, where there had long been French trading posts. It was occupied and annexed in 1886 without much trouble to the army and became, so Larousse complacently assured the world in 1925, a colony which 'grew more prosperous every day'. Even more prosperous, and far more fateful for the future of the civilised world, were the French conquests on the far side of the Indian Ocean in Indo-China in 1861. Napoleon III, disillusioned by his Italian experiences of 1859, and eagerly seeking opportunities for military prestige without the risk of encountering professional European armies, invaded and conquered the southern provinces of the Annamese Emperor, forming out of them the colony, immensely rich in its rice production, of Cochin China, with its capital at Saigon. In 1863 this base was extended to the borders of Siam by the establishment of a Protectorate over Cambodia, whose little King was left with his court and his picturesque splendour, but provided with a French administration and garrison. These were gains which were both commercially profitable and without any immediate serious military risk.

The dangers, however, became excessive when the Second Republic picked up the threads of this modestly imperialist policy and at the same time revived an ancient French ambition dating back to Louis XVI to open up trade with the southern provinces of China by gaining control of the Red River basin at Tonkin. Indo-China, as its name indicates, was and is the ancient historic battleground of two rival cultures and empires. In 1872 the decaying Chinese Empire still retained a nominal suzerainty over the Emperor of Annam and remained obstinately determined to shut out foreign traders from its territory; and when, in 1873, the explorer and adventurer, François Garnier, who had with some government assistance made himself master of the Red River Delta, was killed in an ambush, the French prudently decided to withdraw. A treaty in 1874 restored his stolen territories to the Emperor of Annam in return for some minor commercial concessions from the Chinese. Ten years later, however, when another adventurer, Henri Rivière, revived the same ambitions and was killed in precisely the same fashion, the French rashly reversed their decision. Failure to implement the 1874 treaty was made the excuse for sending troops to capture Hanoi and subdue the whole province of Tonkin and this led in due course to open war with China. A French fleet bombarded Foochow, blockaded Formosa, and seized the Pescadores Islands; and the Tonkin army was ordered to invade Kwang Si Province by way of Lang-Son. Fortunately for France Admiral Courbet's activities sufficed to bring China to terms. For the only distinction recorded of the army – and it was a sinister portent for the future – was that at Tuyen-Quan, a hundred miles short of the frontier, it 'defended itself gloriously'. The Annamese Emperor accepted French Protectorate on the same terms as the King of Cambodia, and Tonkin became yet another rich and profitable French colony. Finally the occupation of Laos in 1893 and some slight extensions of Cambodian territory in 1904 and 1907 rounded off one of the most successful nineteenth-century exercises of military power as a means of imperial expansion.

Italy's entry into what was called the grab for Africa in the early 1880s was at first in no way a military enterprise, nor did it have government backing, or even approval. Italian official territorial ambitions were centred on the Trentino and South Tyrol. But speculative Italian merchants and adventurous small traders found an opening along the southern shore of the Red Sea between the French at Djibouti and the Sudanese frontier. At the same time a periodically insolvent company under the patronage of a royal duke whose hobby was the study of tropical agriculture established extensive plantations of bananas and other fruits far to the south, between the Juba River and the Indian Ocean. For reasons of national prestige the government in due course found itself obliged to subsidise both and to provide a degree of military protection against hostile and untamed tribesmen. Some sort of inland frontier had to be defined and held; and in Somaliland security considerations compelled a steady advance northwards, mostly by protectorate treaties with the coastal Emirs.

Thus in 1896, in one of the periodical auctions at which the Powers assigned each other 'spheres of influence', Italy found herself inadvertently in possession of two remote colonies: the narrow, 700-mile strip of Eritrea on the Red Sea, and Italian Somaliland which stretched from the Juba River to the Gulf of Aden. At the same time she rashly accepted an extremely ill-defined Protectorate over the Empire of Abyssinia. Unfortunately for her that same year saw the accession of the savagely aggressive Menelik II to the throne of Ethiopia. He not only rejected out-right any Italian pretensions to a Protectorate, but roundly denounced these two new colonies which, so he claimed, cut off the traditional and only access of his subjects to the Red Sea and the Indian Ocean. Along frontiers peopled by pastoral nomads who recognised no boundaries to their wandering search for graz-ing and water wells and were ceaselessly involved in tribal battles for possession of some coveted area, any one of which could easily be magnified into an international incident, the utmost patience and restraint was needed to keep the peace. It was thus not difficult for Menelik to provoke the Italians into rash and large-scale military action.

The substantial army which left Eritrea in 1896 was intended to emulate Napier's epic 400-mile march of 1868 and to exact from the Emperor at Addis Ababa an apology and reparation for the alleged damage suffered by Somali tribesmen who were now Italian subjects. But it entirely lacked the sophisticated equip-ment, the military and administrative expertise, and the accumu-lated experience of such expeditions among both officers and men which had alone made possible the spectacular British success. Commanders and troops were mostly unacclimatised and all without any knowledge of the type of warfare in which they were engaged; and the army had barely crossed the frontier when it was virtually annihilated in the savage battle of Adowa. Stimu-lated by wild, though possibly true stories of Abyssinian atrocities and of the mutilation of wounded and dead, the humiliating memory of this disaster was to ferment in Italian memories for forty years until Mussolini's air force and the ruthless use of mustard gas enabled him to exact his revenge and to set his somewhat embarrassed sovereign temporarily on the throne of the Negus.

D•

Italy's third and largest colonial acquisition was, by contrast, emphatically military. The French occupation of Tunis had been bitterly resented in renascent Italy, which regarded the North African coast as a sphere of influence morally due to the heirs of ancient Rome. She had in consequence long cast covetous eyes on the surviving Turkish *Vilayet* of Tripoli which still nominally controlled the only 800 miles of Mediterranean coast not already held by France, Britain, and Spain; and the European Powers had reluctantly agreed that an Italian annexation of this area was inevitable when the long awaited collapse of the Turkish Empire finally took place. The chance of realising this dream came in 1911 when the French decided to seize Morocco. The diplomatic uproar which followed this alleged destruction of 'the Balance of Power in Africa' made it impossible for any of the Powers to protest when Italy took the law into her own hands, declared war on Turkey, and briskly invaded Tripolitania. Had the Turks been able to deploy their full military strength the Italian army might have been in difficulties. But Italy's luck held. The whole Turkish military effort was suddenly diverted into two chaotic Balkan Wars and their sparse garrisons in the *Vilayet* could only put up a feeble resistance. So pride was satisfied, though there was little economic reward for this new conquest. In Cyrenaica at the eastern end there was cultivable land where farming emigrants could do something to relieve Italy's perpetual problem of over-population. The rest was mainly barren desert running nearly 1,000 miles south to the French frontier and nominally including the doubtful privilege of suzerainty over the fanatically puritan Senussi tribes around Kufra. But the army had at least won for Italy a reasonable 'place in the sun'.

None of the remaining Powers had the capacity to enlarge their territories by military aggression. Among the oldest imperialist European nations an exception might, perhaps, be made of the Dutch. It is true that there was no question of expanding their surviving Far Eastern Empire, but rather of con-solidating and maintaining control over it. Since, however, there were still large jungle areas which were not only unpoliced and unexploited, but largely unexplored, their task did involve an element of expansion. Faced with military problems not dissimilar from those of the British, they adopted a radically different solution and created two entirely separate armies. One consisted entirely of volunteers recruited solely and exclusively for service overseas. The other, for home service only, was part conscript, part volunteer and was the minimum deemed necessary to guard the frontier with Germany and give the government a margin of reserve behind the police for the maintenance of law and order. They forfeited thus the flexibility of the British system, since neither force was available to reinforce the other in an emergency; but they saved themselves the expense of annually transporting large bodies of troops to and fro across the seas half way round the world. The government, moreover, had no intention of getting involved in European power politics and there was little danger of civil commotion in that orderly population. So the system served them very well.

The other two survivors of an earlier age of colonisation, Spain and Portugal, also had no intention of getting involved in European power politics and equally lacked the capacity for aggressive military action overseas. At home their armies sat uneasily on the still smouldering embers of civil war and revolution. Abroad the Spaniards did, it is true, indulge in sporadic attempts to push southward the frontier of their narrow strip of Morocco across the Straits of Gibraltar; and they were, of course, involved along with the French and British in the brief foray into Mexico on behalf of the bankers in 1861. In Cuba and the Philippines they sat dourly and formidably on the defensive amidst a rising tide of guerilla republicanism. The Portuguese army in Africa, ill-equipped, ill-drilled, ill-disciplined, and ill-led, was solely concerned to preserve order, if necessary by brutal punitive exercises, in the remnants of their imperial inheritance in Guinea, Angola, and Mozambique. Yet in the general surge into central Africa after 1881 Portugal did remarkably well. By 1895 her West African territory of Angola had trebled in size; and on the opposite coast Mozambique had made large advances up the Zambesi and been pushed forward to the shores of Lake Nyasa. But this was no military conquest. Zealous missionaries and enterprising traders pushed forward into vast areas where there were no fighting tribes like the Zulus to oppose their advance, and the army was only concerned to hold and police their gains; and in this task, against all expectation and in the teeth of universal international disapproval, it has until very recently been doggedly successful.

There was even a moment when the Portuguese seemed likely to extend their gains over the vast and potentially extremely profitable area of the Upper Congo basin. But here they were halted; first by the Anglo-Portuguese Treaty of 1882, which safeguarded for Protestantism and British free trade areas first explored and evangelised by Dr Livingstone; and finally by the Berlin Congo Conference of 1884–5 which created an inchoate Congo State where trade was free for all and nobody had any political or social responsibility whatever. The final and improbable result was that in 1908 King Leopold II of the Belgians, after nearly a lifetime of financial intrigue, acquired enough banking and mining support to buy the whole area, rather as Rhodes's Chartered Company had bought Rhodesia. It became the Belgian Congo; and Belgians were able to boast for years of their solitary colony whose annual profits paid off the charge of their National Debt. The Belgian army was not required to conquer the Congo, but merely to protect the valuable mining centres and larger trading depots. Its main commitment remained as always, the maintenance at home of a force sufficient to defend the nation's neutrality, as stipulated by the Guarantee Treaties; and for this it relied on the construction of great fortresses such as Liège, Namur, and Antwerp, which were to prove in the event and in two World Wars a costly and valueless investment.

The large German acquisitions of territory in East and West Africa were similarly in no way a military achievement and, by contrast, economically a dead loss. Bismarck's colonial policy was conceived entirely in the context of the European balance of power. He encouraged France's colonial ambitions, partly to divert French minds from thoughts of revenge and the recovery of Alsace-Lorraine, partly to foster Anglo-French bickering which might lead to permanent estrangement. The demand for colonies was designed to provoke a convincing quarrel with Britain which would show the French that they must come to terms with the new Germany as their only sincere friend.[18] The unexpected acquiescence of Britain defeated his object and brought consequences – hysterical imperialist enthusiasm in Germany and the clamour for a large fleet to protect the new trade routes – which he found wholly deplorable; and the army chiefs, as haunted as he was by the fear of a war on two fronts, never spared more for the colonies than the minimum necessary to discipline periodically resentful African tribes.

With the end of the Boer and Russo-Japanese Wars the grab of the Powers for overseas dominions came temporarily to an end and all politics were centred once again in Europe. In this context the remaining European armies scarcely counted. The Danes, disillusioned by their experiences of 1864, began the gradual process of disarmament which was ultimately to lead to the total dissolution of their army save for an enlarged police force and a colourful Royal Guard for ceremonial occasions, the safety of their frontiers being entrusted entirely to the benevolence and efficiency of the League of Nations. The Swedish army was so bedevilled by political dissensions that it defied description or analysis.[19] Norway even forty years before it broke away to form a separate kingdom maintained a separate and more coherent system – a modification of the German – but on no considerable scale. There remained only Switzerland.

The Swiss army had never since the time of Napoleon been a factor which statesmen and soldiers needed to take into account whether they calculated their chances of aggrandisement in Europe or overseas. But the Swiss military arrangements, which conformed to none of the established patterns, were nevertheless to become a matter of intense preoccupation to all the general staffs in the uneasy years leading up to the outbreak of the First World War. The German generals' obsession with the need for a quick victory in the west so as to have sufficient forces to counter the slow-moving but apparently very powerful Russian threat in the east had long brought them to accept the necessity of turning the strongly fortified French defensive line from Verdun to Belfort by crossing neutral territory north or south of it. The obvious diplomatic risks involved in the famous Schlieffen Plan of a great sweep through Holland and Belgium so unnerved his successors that they began seriously to consider an invasion of Switzerland, which would certainly provoke an international outcry, but would not involve any power in immediate treaty obligations.

The Swiss army was the only one in the world to be organised on a purely militia basis. Its only regular soldiers were the instructors responsible for training the annual intake of 15,000 young men aged nineteen who made up the front line army, known as the *élite*. These represented only half the annually available manpower, and the system of election, also unique, was based on a series of educational tests. Furthermore, for the advancement of the general standard of education throughout the country, the 15,000 who failed were sent back to school for the duration of the recruit course. Thereafter there were biennial 'repetitive courses', varying in length for the different arms, punctuated by range practice which, for the Swiss, was no hardship since, from the time of William Tell until the advent of the ski, target shooting remained the Swiss national sport. The training exercises were conducted at divisional level and supervised by highly competent regular instructors; and all able-bodied men remained liable for service until the age of forty-four. The total result was a front-line *élite* about 120,000 strong, with a territorial *Landwehr* of 80,000 as a first line reserve and the *Landsturm*, a last ditch Home Guard reserve of 262,000. There were 288 guns in Field or Mountain Batteries with the *élite* and 88 in the *Landwehr*.

Over the centuries the Swiss, fighting in their own mountainous valleys and passes, had more than once shown themselves a match for the finest armies in Europe; and their confidence in their ability to do so was still undiminished in the years before 1914. When the Kaiser paid them a State visit, accompanied by a swollen entourage of generals who were virtually no more than highly placed spies, the world's press openly took the view that his real purpose was to investigate the possibility of turning the French frontier at the southern end. One Swiss newspaper even published a mocking cartoon depicting the Emperor congratulating the winner of a Schützenfest – the rifle match which was the annual sporting highlight in every Swiss Commune – 'And how many of you are there', the Kaiser asked in the caption, 'who can shoot like that?' 'A hundred thousand, Sire', was the answer. 'And supposing I send two hundred thousand against you?' said the Kaiser. 'We would all fire twice, Sire,' replied the prize-winner. It is probable that it was the mountains rather than this sublime over-simplification of the art of modern war which caused the Great General Staff to decide that an invasion of Switzerland would be too slow and costly for their purpose. Though it was never put to the test, it nevertheless seems likely than the Swiss amateur army would have given a very good account of itself; and it certainly became a major factor in the calculations of all the Great Powers.

4 The Impact of Technological Advances on Strategy and Tactics

In any examination of the impact of the Industrial Revolution, and the extremely rapid technological advances which followed it, on the evolution and achievements of the world's armies in the Age of Moltke, there are always two major factors to be taken into account. One, of course, was the varying pace of technical progress in different countries which, thanks to new inventions and their industrial exploitation, might give any one of the Great Powers a temporarily matchless potential superiority over all its neighbours. The other rested on the ability of the military authorities to perceive such an opportunity when it occurred and turn it to practical account strategically or tactically. This was essentially a new problem, and one which has persisted with increasing urgency ever since, imposing on commanders and general staffs considerations and calculations which would have been entirely irrelevant to Frederick the Great or Napoleon, and equally so to de Suffren and Nelson.

One of the first and most spectacularly successful exploitations of industrial advance for military purposes was the influence Prussia's General Staff was able to exercise on the planning of the state railway system. In comparison with Britain the industrial revolution in Prussia's Rhineland States was a late starter. But its progress was rapid, and particularly so in the sphere of railway development. For the scattered territories which were Prussia's legacy from the Congress of Vienna rapid and easy communication with the centre was a political, economic, and social priority; and in that highly centralised state the railway system was not left to develop, as in Britain, according to the hazards of commercial opportunism, nor was it frustrated by the desire of great landlords to preserve the amenities of their estates and their hunting from the obtrusion of railway lines. The Prussian generals were quick to perceive the opportunities which a planned railway system offered for speeding up the mobilisation and concentration of their forces; and their influence was strong enough to ensure that the Prussian railways – and ultimately those of the whole German Empire – were constructed primarily to meet the needs of the army, even at the expense of commercial and civilian convenience. This, like the Needle Gun, was one of the built-in advantages which Moltke inherited when he took over the direction of the Great General Staff. But it was his personal genius which brilliantly exploited this great potential advantage with such spectacular results in 1866 and in 1870.

His first important contribution was the immediate creation of the special railway *Abteilung* of the General Staff which would for the rest of the century devote its time and energies to the study of timetables, movement graphs, and loading schedules for every foreseeable military contingency. It was not, of course, invariably efficient. Both in 1866 and 1870, and again in 1914, there were serious and avoidable breakdowns in the supply systems of the fighting armies. But it absolutely ensured the smooth and rapid movement of the Prussian, and later the German armies to the chosen concentration areas; and it never allowed the paralysing accumulation of vital material in depots and railway sidings which so often hampered the operations of its enemies. Moltke's second, and by far his more important contribution to the great Prussian victories was his imperturbable acceptance of the risks involved by exploiting to the very limits of strategic safety the advantage thus conferred on him by the time gained in the speed of his mobilisation and concentration. The decision in 1866 to disperse his troops among three armies widely separated along the four hundred miles of the Bohemian frontier caused the utmost alarm not only to his three Army Commanders, but to his own Commander-in-Chief, the King of Prussia, offering as it did the maximum opportunity to the Austrians to exploit their inherent advantage of operating on interior lines; and military historians have sought ever since to demonstrate how Benedek might, by clearer thinking, have snatched a great victory in the teeth of the Prussian needle gun. Moltke himself never admitted that he was not at all times in complete control of his operations and free to choose the moment of decisive confrontation; and the hard fact remains that he did, though by the narrowest of time margins, bring his three armies together at Königgrätz and, as he had promised his King, win not only the battle, but the war. Similarly in 1870 his swift concentration in the Saar and Rhineland frustrated the French hope of dislocating the German mobilisation by a thrust into southern Germany which might have undermined the wavering loyalty of the South German States and brought the Austrians actively into the war to revenge the defeats of 1866.

Yet it cannot be disputed that in this matter of railway control, as in so many others, Moltke's very successes contained the seeds of future dangers, and even disasters. Rigid though he was in the standards of efficiency which he demanded from his staff, he himself never allowed his mind to become rigid or to be dominated by systems, even if they were of his own invention. He was essentially an innovator and an improviser who belonged by training and by temperament to the school of Scharnhorst and Gneisenau and the men who had fabricated the Army of Liberation out of the débris of Auerstädt and Jena. 'Not *one* method, *one* means, *one* makeshift, but many' was the great Schlieffen's summary of the legacy of Moltke's military philosophy[1] but even Schlieffen could not prevent a gradual intellectual ossification as the General Staff concentrated more and more exclusively on the methods which had succeeded so brilliantly in 1866 and 1870 and on pushing them to a logical extreme which left no room for original thought. The immensely efficient military control over the new Empire's railways well illustrated this. By 1914 a single order from Imperial Headquarters could cancel all existing time-tables and substitute a minutely elaborate alternative which subordinated everything to the mobilisation programme. When the great day came the troop and supply trains rolled for a fortnight every ten minutes across the Hohenzollern Bridge at Cologne with a remorseless punctuality which only German Staff work could have achieved. But its very efficiency made it inflexible. The machine took charge of the generals and robbed them of all initiative until it had completed its operation. There was a moment when Sir Edward Grey's passionate struggle for peace might conceivably have succeeded if all the Powers had halted their mobilisation. The Kaiser, already aghast at the course of events which his own thoughtlessness had so largely provoked, asked the younger Moltke to stop the movement of all troop trains to the frontiers. The horrified Field-Marshal protested that this was absolutely impossible without total chaos: only when mobilisation had been fully completed could demobilisation begin. 'Your Uncle', the Kaiser said sadly, 'would have given me a different answer'; and Moltke relates that an hour or so later the mere thought of such a suggestion brought him near to nervous collapse.

Admittedly the German determination to extract the utmost strategic advantage from their railway system was not entirely inspired by reverence for the genius who had first perceived the possibilities in 1866 and 1870. Swift mobilisation was for them a sheer necessity. Bismarck once confessed that he used sometimes to wake in the night 'sweating with fear' at the thought of a war on two fronts such as had all but destroyed Frederick the Great. Until 1890 he was able by sheer diplomatic expertise to keep France isolated and to prevent the inherent opposition of Russian and Austrian policies in the Balkans from developing into open hostility. In 1891, within a year of his dismissal by the young Kaiser, his nightmare became a reality. Russia and France united in the Dual Alliance, so dividing Europe into two hostile armed camps and filling all good Germans with the haunting fear of 'Encirclement'. The German railways had to be able to concentrate a large enough force in the west to inflict an immediate and massive defeat on the French; and they must then be ready to rush the armies back more than five hundred miles to the north-east to meet the more ponderously moving Russian army, formidable if only by its overwhelming numbers.

The German staff was, of course, not the only one to devote much time and study to Moltke's great campaigns and to perceive the overwhelming importance of adequate railway communications in an age when the internal combustion engine was still insufficiently developed to supply a workable alternative. For three of the six Great Powers likely to become involved in a European conflagration there was no need to supervise and adapt the development and layout of their railway lines to specifically military needs. Political, social, and commercial considerations had already dictated a pattern which admirably suited their military needs. The Italian programme of railway construction, for example, was launched from Piedmont by Cavour long before he could contrive a practicable policy for extending his King's dominions over the whole of Italy by military conquest. 'Railways', he said, were to be 'the seams which would stitch together the boot of Italy.' Since the whole central line of her northern frontier was blocked by the neutral mountain massif of Switzerland, Italy's commercial access to northern Europe was inevitably by the Brenner Pass into Austria or through the Mont Cenis tunnel, opened in 1871, into France. These perforce became the terminal points of her great trunk railways and this suited her General Staff equally well, since these were the only two areas where Italy might be involved in European warfare.

For Francis Joseph a sophisticated and complex railway system, as soon as his backward economy permitted its construction, was equally essential if he was to hold together the huge, scattered polyglot Empire which still remained to him. Vienna had to be linked to the other ancient capitals of Buda-Pest and Prague and the whole Danube basin linked up with the world's markets through the great port of Trieste. The result suited the Austrian General Staff very well, since it made it reasonably easy to shift their forces to any of their three threatened frontiers: to Galicia, to meet a Russian invasion; over the Brenner into the Trentino, which the Italians were already calling 'Italia Irridenta'; and to the southern frontiers of Hungary and Croatia. Britain, until the advent of Lord Haldane, had no General Staff. But she had also no great transport problem, since her railways were already geared to carry a growing volume of commercial and tourist traffic through the Channel ports which must be the route for any intervention on the Continent.

The French, largely by their own fault, were less happily placed. Their generals had, indeed, learnt something from the breakdown of their transport service in 1870; and cross-country railway lines had been built which made it no longer necessary for everything destined for the German frontier to pass through Paris. But, ironically, their very success involved them in dangers even greater than those of 1870. Between 1870 and 1914 the *École de Guerre* became even more obsessed with the details of Moltke's campaigns than the *Generalstab*; and the best brains in the French army devoted their talents to long and painstaking analyses designed to show how better generalship and staffwork could have defeated the Prussians at Spicheren and Wörth, Mars-la-Tour and Gravelotte. When they thought of the future at all it was only to seek remedies for the mistakes of Napoleon III and Bazaine. Accordingly their improved railway system made possible the rapid and efficient concentration of the whole front line strength of the French army in the classic theatre, between Verdun and Belfort, as demanded by the notorious Plan XIV, and poised for the immediate offensive into South Germany for which Schlieffen had prayed. But they were not designed to provide the wretched Joffre with desperately needed lateral communications when he found himself struggling to extricate his armies and extend his flank progressively north-westwards as the full scope of the German sweep through Belgium revealed itself. Galliéni's dramatic commandeering of all the Paris taxis to convey a division of Manouri's newly formed 6th Army northwards to threaten von Klück's exposed right flank was neither the vital factor in breaking the nerve of the German Army Commanders and High Command, nor the chaotic farce represented by some modern historians. It made its modest contribution to the partial, yet ultimately decisive Allied victory on the Marne. But it also revealed the superannuated, ill-dressed, eccentric Governor of Paris as the only one of the generals on either side – the last heirs of the Age of Moltke – who had the sort of mind Moltke himself would have valued : restlessly determined to adapt new means and modern methods to the unchanging fundamental principles of Napoleonic warfare.

As far as railway construction was concerned the Russians drew from Moltke's successes conclusions quite opposite from those of the other European powers. They had their first object lesson in the military importance of railway communications in so vast an Empire when the melting snows in the spring of 1855 revealed the long lines of whitening bones of men and animals which marked out the march routes of the army to the Crimea. But in the general political and social upheaval which followed the accession of a new zealously reforming, but muddle-headed Tsar industrial progress was slow. In spite of this limitation, the Russian government did succeed by the turn of the century in providing the Empire with a railway system adequate to its needs both economically and strategically, though the single-track Trans-Siberian line – itself a remarkable achievement – was to prove in 1904 an insufficient supply line for a campaign in Manchuria, more than four thousand miles from St Petersburg, against a well-equipped modern army. But on their north-western frontier the Russians applied Moltke's lessons in reverse. For them the essential front in the west was Galicia, where the Austrians barred their way to the great prize of Constantinople. The Austro-German Alliance of 1879, which Bismarck intended to be so permanent that he tried to have it incorporated as a fundamental article in the constitutions of both Empires, made it, however, clear that any Balkan adventure would bring down upon them the increasingly formidable German army in the north.

Along their German frontier, therefore, the Russians adopted their ancient policy of selling ground to gain time. A great tract of territory was left deliberately waste, without any modern means of transport, so that the swiftly concentrated German army would have to march dreary miles across sandy wastes and through swamps and forests to get to grips with its slower moving enemy, and then only with intolerably difficult lines of supply and reinforcement behind it. For some fifteen years after 1891, when the French could still be counted on to take the brunt of the initial German effort, this was a highly intelligent policy : a frustrating defensive in the north and an offensive in the south which could count on active support from the assiduously cultivated, newly emancipated Slav states in the Balkan peninsula. But it became highly dangerous as the growing population and wealth of Germany and the obstinately static birthrate in France made it increasingly clear that Russia must mount a relieving offensive as quickly as possible if the French were to survive the first shock of the German attack and not be left alone and exposed to the military might of Germany and Austria. The sands and marshes of Poland became an obstacle instead of an asset; and the whole railway policy had to be reversed. This in turn became a vital factor in precipitating the outbreak of war in 1914. For the knowledge that the elaborate system of strategic railways in Poland designed to bring the Russian masses quickly within striking distance of Berlin was due for completion at the latest by 1916 powerfully influenced the German generals to insist that the Austro-Serbian dispute must be used to provoke a war which they regarded, anyway, as inevitable.

The varying success with which the European Powers adapted the invention of the railway to their military needs inevitably bulks most largely in the pages of history because it so often determined the fates and futures not only of those directly involved, but of the whole world. If, however, in Olympic terms, a gold medal were on offer to the army which most quickly appreciated and successfully applied the military possibilities of railway transport, it would unquestionably go to the British. In 1866 Moltke and the railway *Abteilung* of his Great General Staff brilliantly exploited the opportunities offered by the five double-tracked railway lines leading to the Bohemian frontier. But he could not then, or ever, within the highly efficient army which he and Roon had jointly created have found officers and men with the administrative experience, expert knowledge and technical skills to assemble in Bombay, only a year later, in 1867, the materials needed to build five miles of railway, transport it all, together with engines and rolling stock, across the Indian Ocean to the Gulf of Aden; and build and operate successfully a railway line which kept the scanty jetties of the tiny port of Zula clear of the clutter with which the French all but immobilised the great ports of Genoa and Marseilles in 1859 and 1870. They set a standard which was to be worthily upheld by the two Railway Companies of the Royal Engineers permanently stationed at Woolwich and Chatham, backed by a fully trained reserve of men who had found peacetime employment on the railways; and behind them again there was a Volunteer Battalion consisting almost entirely of highly trained technological experts. They perished partly, along with much else which was unique and irreplaceable, when the old British army became involved in 1914 in the one sort of war in which its specialised capacities had little value; and finally when progressive motorisation made them entirely redundant. But until then, though their activities made no great history, they frequently proved themselves invaluable not only to the army, but for the relief of the distresses of scattered populations all over the world. Their mute memorial can still be seen at Longmoor Camp in Hampshire, where the permanent way on which they used to practise still remains, its signals – all down – kept beautifully repainted, along with the notices warning motorists of no longer existent level crossings.

Finally, if the British came top of the table in the enterprising exploitation of the possibilities of the railway, the army of the United States of America came, oddly enough and by a very wide margin, at the bottom, in spite of the fact that their Civil War generals had been the first to explore them. As late as 1898, in an age when the great trans-continental railroads were the spearhead opening up the whole American continent from the Atlantic to the Pacific to the amenities of modern civilisation, and the so-called Railway Kings were making incalculable fortunes out of their internecine 'wars', the US army staff staged at Tampa Bay in Florida scenes of transportation chaos beside which the French confusion at Genoa and Marseilles in 1859 and 1870 paled into insignificance. There, while the senior commanders sat in their rocking chairs on the balcony of the Tampa Bay Hotel swapping reminiscences of a thirty-year-old Civil War in which many of them had fought on opposite sides, the thousands of enthusiastic volunteers who had flocked to the colours to liberate the Cubans from Spanish oppression suffered the tortures of the damned; and the inadequacy and misuse of the railway was the root cause of their miseries.

It was on 26 May 1898 that orders to load 25,000 men and their equipment on to the transports already assembled in Tampa Bay reached General William R. Shafter, a gouty veteran of the Civil War so obese that when he sat on two biscuit boxes to preside over operational conferences his belly hung down below his knees. Four days later a cipher telegram informed him that he was to capture Santiago on the south coast of Cuba where the Spanish fleet was reported to be bottled up by a US naval blockade. He was also to arm and organise local rebels for eventual collaboration with the main American army which was being held back in Florida until the autumn for an attack on Havana when the danger season for Yellow Fever was over. Shafter was no military genius and most of his fighting experience had been gained in frontier wars with Red Indians. But he was tough and forceful and had moral as well as physical courage, which was as well for his troops. For by the end of May the ineptitude of the US War Department had jammed every railway line and siding round Tampa with freight cars loaded with guns, horses, corn, ammunition, and supplies of all kinds for which, however, the invoices and bills of lading had been irretrievably lost. Shafter's harassed administrative staff had to unpack more than three hundred loads to find which contained clothing, grain, balloon material, horse equipments, ammunition, siege guns, or food; and when the guns and shells had been located it took further weeks to discover the breech mechanisms and the shell fuses, both of which had been separately packed in bulk.

All this was bad enough. But it was only the beginning of the purgatory which awaited both the supply staffs and the troops. For the sole embarkation point was nine miles further down the bay at Port Tampa. The whole Tampa Bay development had been planned by an enterprising promoter, Morton F. Plant, as a pleasure resort and a springboard for tourist cruises and small steamer traffic to Cuba and to the comfortable half-way stopping point at the island harbour of Key West, which had already become the base for the US Navy and its attendant newspaper correspondents. For this Plant had built two piers at Port Tampa and dredged a narrow channel capable of accommodating two sizeable ships at a time; and these were connected to Tampa itself only by an nine-mile track of single-line railway. Only two transports could berth at a time; and the outer channel could only hold six more waiting to load. In the two months available to it the army's railway staff had constructed sidings and extra lines running from the station to the piers. But every load had still to be carried across fifty feet of sand and up a steep ramp by sweating stevedores who normally slept their exhausted nights scattered about the piers. There were, moreover, no double-track points at which trains could pass each other in opposite directions, so that for half the available time the line was blocked by returning empties. The enterprising Mr Plant extended the delays by continuing to run his normal commercial traffic, to which he added special excursion trains for sightseers; and no extra rolling stock was sent up by the War Department to supplement what was left over locally for army use.

To his eternal credit Shafter took over personal control as soon as the magnitude of the crisis was revealed, sitting on his biscuit boxes on the pier with a packing case for a desk; and he did sort some sort of order out of the chaos. But not Moltke himself and the whole railway *Abteilung* of the Great General Staff could have overcome or circumvented the obstacles of those nine miles of single track and two inadequate piers. The stores designed to last the army for six months had to be cut by two-thirds; and the troops themselves suffered abominably. On 6 June the congestion on the line was such that between 10 p.m. and daybreak not one train got through. The Rough Riders, an enthusiastic body of volunteers, dismounted for the campaign, paraded at 6 p.m. and spent most of the night marching and counter-marching, first to the Tampa Bay hotel where each trooper drew the meagre and largely irrelevant two dollars and ten cents due to him, and then to various points on the railway until they at last boarded a train of coal freight-cars which got them, somewhat begrimed, to the port. There, thanks to the initiative of their enterprising commanding officer, Lieutenant-Colonel Theodore Roosevelt, who had transformed himself, pince-nez and all, from the office of Assistant Secretary to the Navy to become a dashing cavalry colonel, they stole a transport earmarked for two other regiments, one of which had to spend the next two days and nights, unrationed, on a train. So comparatively they fared well. The 6th US Infantry struck their tents at 9 p.m. that night and waited, scrounging what food they could, until 2 p.m. the next day, when they boarded and stood for four hours in a stock train ankle deep in wet cow dung.[2] The Negro troopers of the 10th Cavalry travelled in luxury coaches which even had ice in the water-coolers. But they spent the next forty-eight hours without rations. Their commanding Officer tried to buy them a supper at his own expense at a restaurant on the pier, but was frustrated by a lady who feared that she would get a bad name if she admitted coloured soldiers to her dining room.

General Shafter's reputation suffered irretrievably from these events, over which he never had any real control. Men like Roosevelt spent much of their leisure writing critical and thoroughly disloyal letters to their political cronies in Washington about all their senior commanders, and particularly about Shafter. He did himself perhaps even more harm by remorselessly leaving the newspaper men, to their dismayed fury, to take the same chances as the troops amidst the discomforts of the Port Tampa railway. The War Department, meanwhile, showed not the slightest understanding of the problems. 'Twenty thousand men', the Secretary of State telegraphed angrily on 31 May, 'ought to unload any number of cars and assort contents. There is much criticism about delay of expedition.'³ A week later, by the remarkable efforts of all concerned, Shafter had actually got afloat and ready to sail by far the largest armament the United States had ever despatched overseas. He had embarked 819 officers, 15,058 enlisted men, 30 civilian clerks, 272 teamsters and packers, 107 stevedores, 2,295 horses and mules complete with harness, 81 wagons, 16 light guns, four 7-inch howitzers, four 5-inch siege guns, one Hotchkiss revolving cannon, one pneumatic dynamite gun, eight 3.6 field mortars, and four Gatling guns. His only major shortage was ambulances, of which he had only seven; but he hoped to be able to help them out with transport wagons. At that point, on 8 June, the whole operation was abruptly halted by telegraph for four days while the Navy made sure that it had really located the Spanish fleet. For this, too, Shafter had to take the blame. There were angry letters from Roosevelt describing his troops 'jammed together under the tropical sun on these crowded ships . . . in a sewer; a canal which is festering as if it were Havana harbor.'⁴ Shafter used the four days methodically loading essential extra medical supplies, redistributing his animals and replenishing the water supplies in his transports. Then, at last, on 12 June he was allowed to sail. None of the chaotic discomfort had really been his fault. The plain fact was that the men responsible for the army of the nation which was fast becoming the most technologically advanced in the world failed miserably to apprehend, among other things, the importance of railway lines in any large-scale military enterprise.

It was not difficult to discern the importance of railway development and its exploitation for military purposes. Even in the early 1830s, when the new invention was still in its infancy, strategists both amateur and professional were already exploring its obvious possibilities.[5] French professors could easily perceive the vital necessity for a trunk line linking Paris with Strasbourg, and the British were immediately preoccupied with the provision of adequate communications to Dover and Folkestone. The reasons for the predominance established by Prussia and successfully maintained later by the German Empire were threefold. Germany's central position in Europe, hitherto her greatest weakness, since it exposed vulnerable frontiers simultaneously on every side, suddenly became her greatest asset: railways operating on interior lines would enable her to switch her massive forces from front to front far more rapidly than any of her neighbours. Secondly, the inborn academic thoroughness of the German mind ensured the meticulous study of all the possibilities inherent in the new situation. The French, for example, were far too late in perceiving that, while they needed indeed to connect Paris with Strasbourg, they had also to link cities like Marseilles, Bordeaux, and Lyons directly not only with Strasbourg, but with Metz, Châlons, Verdun, Belfort, and Nancy. Finally, and probably most important, was the predominant influence exercised by the German military authorities in national affairs, so that their needs would always prevail over commercial and civilian interests. Moltke deserved all the credit he had been give for his use of his opportunities. But he played from a far stronger hand than Leboeuf and his colleagues.

The other new invention which was developed more or less simultaneously with the railways and which similarly revolutionised the conduct of military operations was, of course, that of the electric telegraph. Without it the co-ordination of the rapid movement of increasingly massive armies would not have been possible. In this case development was far more evenly distributed, and no particular general staff was able to snatch any important advantage over its rivals. By the middle of the century most civilised parts of the globe possessed adequate telegraphic communications, though some backward areas were still pretty thinly provided. By the time of the Crimean War the trans-Balkan line had got no further than Belgrade; and in the Bohemian theatre in 1866 both Moltke and Benedek had frequently to fall back on mounted officers to carry some of their most important despatches, even over considerable distances.[6] On the battlefield itself, though Bazaine did make a ponderous attempt to direct the movements of his divisions at Spicheren from the telegraph office at St Avold, far behind the firing line, the older-fashioned method was naturally still the norm. It remained so, too, for the British in their more remote campaigns, though towards the end of the century the fact that they generally fought in the sunnier parts of the world enabled them to exploit the invention of the heliograph as a limited and somewhat clumsy substitute for the telegraph.

The other technical factors which revolutionised the conduct of warfare between the Crimea and 1914 were, of course, the long overdue engineering advances which at last made practicable the development of efficient breech-loading artillery and of a range of small arms for the infantry which were jointly to open up entirely new tactical perspectives. Though the two are strictly quite separate subjects of study, they are for the historian indissolubly linked. In any case the engineering problem for both arms was precisely the same : the provision of some form of breech-loading mechanism which would effectively seal the propellant charge against the escape of gases which not only seriously reduced the power and range of the weapon, but by the consequent erosion of the metal of the working parts rapidly made it altogether unserviceable. Moreover the tactical achievements and short-comings of both arms reacted so directly upon each other in battle that it is historically impossible to discuss them independently of each other. In both these spheres, too, Moltke snatched great initial advantages; first by his inheritance of an infantry already equipped with the Dreyse Needle-Gun; secondly by the speed and efficiency with which he remedied the nearly disastrous inferiority of the Prussian artillery in 1866. But here it could be argued that he owed more to luck and to the ineptitudes of his opponents than either he or his many admirers have ever been prepared to admit.

It has become a commonplace of history that the Prussian arming of their infantry with the needle gun was the decisive factor in the defeat of the Danes in 1864 and in the far more important victory over the Austrians at Königgrätz, and much praise has been lavished on Moltke for his deduction from the Franco-Austrian campaign in Italy in 1859 that infantry fire-power was the battle-winner of the future and his consequent adaptation of Prussian infantry tactics to this conclusion. Before 1864 he did, indeed, spend much time and thought to the proper exploitation of the weapon with which his predecessors had endowed him. He had great difficulty in making up his mind which quality of his weapon to exploit by his infantry tactics : whether to hold them back until their greater range had dominated the fire-fight and enabled them to move in comparatively unscathed to the final assault; or whether to move quickly in to close quarters where their vastly superior rate of fire and the fact that they could load lying down might produce a more rapid and devastating victory.

There is reason to suppose that he had not finally made up his mind in 1864; and he did not, of course, have any opportunity of observing the effects of the Needle Gun or of controlling its use until the latest stages of the Danish war. But by then the defects of the weapon itself had settled the matter for him. Experiments with breech-loading guns had been going on for centuries. Even Henry viii had several; and in the eighteenth century all the military powers had tried out various methods by which sharp-shooters and skirmishers could be given a weapon which could be loaded lying down. One of the most nearly successful had been the Ferguson rifle which the Royal Americans – ancestors of the King's Royal Rifle Corps – had used with some success in the Seven Years' War. Conservative military opinion had always opposed all such innovations on three main grounds. One was that the increased rate of fire of such weapons would exhaust the ammunition supply. This was proved in practice to be quite unfounded. A higher muzzle velocity made possible a bullet of smaller calibre and a much lighter cartridge, so increasing the number of rounds which could be carried into the front line. For the rest all that was needed was an improved supply system.[7] The other was that formulated years later by Lord Wavell and in another context, that 'There is no room in war for delicate machinery.'[8] Grit and mud and the wear and tear of active service put strains on intricate mechanisms from which the old muzzle-loader was happily immune. Finally there was the still unsolved problem of sealing the breech efficiently against escaping gases.

In spite of its great reputation and staggering successes, the Dreyse rifle was seriously open to both the latter criticisms. The needle from which it took its name had to pierce the whole length of the cardboard cartridge to reach the detonating charge and was of necessity long and thin, easily bent, or even broken. This was not by itself a frequent enough occurrence to outweigh its overwhelming advantages. The shortcomings of its breech mechanism were far more important. After the first half-dozen rounds the imperfect closure of the bolthead allowed not only the escape of gases, but of fragments of burning powder which frequently inflicted painful burns on the faces of the firers, and sometimes even blinded them. In the face of this risk even the best trained and most self-sacrificing infantryman in the world could not be brought to hold his cheek close against the butt of his rifle to take a careful aim. He flinched away from the discharge; and by the end of the war of 1870 most of them preferred to fire the weapon from the hip. Thus, whether Moltke liked it or not, the Needle Gun became quite inevitably a weapon for cloes-quarter figthing. Although sighted up to six hundred yards, it was virtually useless at any range over two hundred; fired from the hip it could not become seriously effective except at really close quarters. Nevertheless, in a straight infantry fight on reasonably open ground against an enemy armed with even the most efficient muzzle-loading rifle, it made the Prussians invincible unless overwhelmingly outnumbered. On the attack even opponents well dispersed and firing from cover could not load fast enough to stop them from getting to the close quarters at which their fire would be murderously destructive. In defence they could merely stay lying down and let the enemy rush on to his own destruction.

When, at two in the afternoon of the battle of Königgrätz the Prussian Crown Prince's advance guards broke almost unopposed into the key positions on the Austrian right flank and Benedek's army disintegrated in panic flight across the Elbe, Moltke had duly fulfilled his phlegmatic promise to his King to win not only the battle but the war. As the details of casualties and the magnitude of the disaster filtered through, *The Times* correspondent, echoing the views of every general staff in Europe, announced

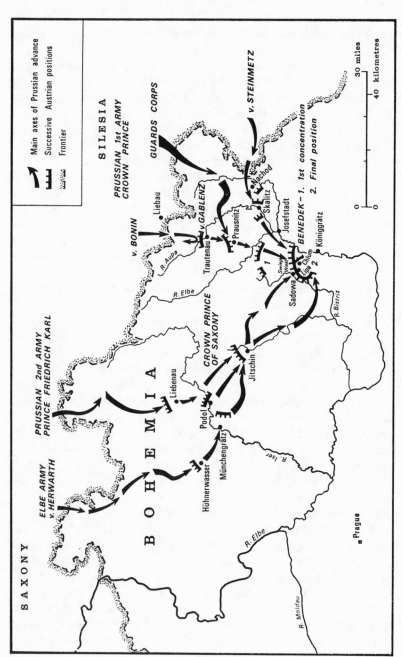

Map 1. The Bohemian Campaign

that 'The Needle Gun is King'; and his judgement has been re-echoed by historians ever since. Yet this was, in fact, an over-simplification. Four years later, after Sedan, the same authorities were loudly proclaiming that the artillery had become the unquestioned 'Queen of the Battlefield'. Ironically enough, this second conclusion might have been drawn by a really shrewd observer of the battle of Königgrätz. For one of the most fascinating aspects of all the great battles of the mid-nineteenth century which reshaped the map of Europe was that they were not only contests between armies, but between rival arms of the service. There were many and various reasons why Benedek was defeated – and was bound to be defeated – in 1866. But before the insubordination of two of his most aristocratic Corps Commanders had brought about the complete collapse of the right wing of his army at two in the afternoon on that 3 July he had demonstrated beyond all doubt that intelligent handling of a superior artillery could, in the conditions of nineteenth-century warfare, completely dominate a battle in the teeth of a better trained and better armed enemy infantry.

This important fact got overlooked in the general excitement over the spectacular triumph of the Needle Gun by everybody except the Prussian high command. Moltke had his little vanities and was at all times reluctant to admit that he was not continuously in control of each situation as it arose. But he had the supreme intellectual virtue of being able to subject his own mistakes to the same ruthless analysis and criticism as he brought to bear on those of others – a habit which he also strongly encouraged among his own staff officers. He had closely followed the Italian campaign of 1859 and, as far as infantry tactics were concerned, reached the perfectly correct conclusion that intensive fire-power was the key to all future success. Since he already had to hand the Needle Gun which then appeared to be the perfect instrument for this, he staked everything on the exploitation of that and altogether overlooked the part played in the French victories by their artillery.

The Austrian generals made the opposite mistake. More correctly than Moltke they attributed their tactical defeats in 1859 to two factors, of which the first and more important was the close and intelligent support given to the French infantry by their gunners and the greatly superior quality of their guns. Gunnery was one of the things about which Napoleon III really did know something and one of his first reforms was to re-equip the whole of his artillery with up-to-date rifled guns. The Austrians had only smooth-bores, virtually unchanged in pattern and performance for a century past. Heavily outranged and wildly inaccurate, their batteries seldom ventured far enough forward to give their infantry the close support they so badly needed. The French tactics of 1859 were in fact those of Waterloo brought to a pitch of near perfection. The *Chasseurs* and *Voltigeurs* in the skirmishing line had lost none of their skill and *élan* in exploiting every advantage the ground would give them in harassing the enemy by fire and movement and clouding the battlefield with their smoke. The artillery, encouraged by its dominance of the enemy's guns and the greatly increased effectiveness of its fire moved up to dangerously close ranges to subdue enemy activity while the massive infantry columns advanced to a striking distance from which their sheer weight of numbers would settle the issue. At Magenta, for example, the Austrians held their own all day all along the line and Napoleon had already retired to his tent and sent a non-committal telegram to the Empress Eugénie in Paris that, after a hard day's fighting, the army was reorganising to resume the battle the next morning. Then, at last light, came the news that MacMahon, by thrusting his gunners into the thick of the fight had enabled his infantry to storm the bridge at Magenta; and Napoleon was able to send an amended despatch to his Empress which said simply: *'Grande bataille, Grande victoire.'*

In consequence of this, and of the dislocation of Wimpffen's two futile and half-hearted attempts to get his army formed up for the vital attack on the left wing at Solferino, the Austrians during the next seven years completely re-equipped their artillery with rifled, though still muzzle-loading, 8-pounder guns. They also retrained their gunners to an aggressiveness and a capacity for self-sacrifice which far eclipsed anything which Moltke could achieve in the Prussian army in the same period. It is true that Moltke did gain in this sphere one fortuitous advantage; but it came too late for him to make any effective use of it in 1866. The designers of artillery weapons had throughout faced precisely the same problem as those who were seeking to perfect a breech-loading rifle; that of effectively sealing the breech. The naval powers were the first to be forced to face the problem seriously when it became clear that the steam-driven ship of the future would be built of iron instead of wood; and in 1847 a Chief Constructor of the British Royal Navy gave it his considered opinion that inventors would never succeed in producing a breech-loading cannon capable of launching at sufficient range a projectile which would do any serious damage to an ironclad ship. If the whole piece, barrel and breech, could be cast in steel, which was not liable to corrosion by powder gases, the problem would be solved immediately. But it was not until the early 1860s that Herr Krupp perfected a method of cooling a steel barrel without producing flaws which would cause it to burst the moment it was fired. Both French and Austrians stuck until then to the traditional bronze or brass, both dangerously liable to corrosion. The British, however, had by 1860 developed a wrought-iron gun bound with exterior steel coils which enabled Armstrong's to supply the Horse Artillery with ten batteries of breech-loading 9- and 12-pounder guns and the Field Artillery with twenty-five 12-pounder batteries and one 6-pounder battery for New Zealand. These innovations were, of course, regarded at the War Office with grave mistrust. Moltke on the other hand leapt at the new idea; but he had only time to equip a few of his batteries with the new Krupp gun. The rest of his artillery in 1866 consisted of the old, pre-1859 smooth-bore guns.

The other factor in their 1859 defeats which the Austrian generals, like Moltke, correctly observed was the inability of their infantry to stand up to the French in the open at the moment of impact, when the artillery had perforce to cease fire for fear of hitting their own troops. They were, however, entirely wrong in attributing this to the faultiness of the tactical doctrine inherited from the Archduke Charles. The real causes were the idleness and incompetence of their junior officers who had failed either to prepare themselves or train their troops for the tasks demanded of them and the laxness of senior commanders who were satisfied, during the long years of Metternichian peace, if the standards of ceremonial drill were adequately maintained. It was this mistake which was the prime cause of the astronomical casualty figures of the Austrian army in 1866 and of the inflation of the reputation of the Needle Gun far beyond its very real merits.

In point of fact, in 1859, the Austrian infantry and gunners, in spite of their obvious shortcomings, did not do all that badly. When competently handled and carefully disposed by commanders who understood both their qualities and their limitations they could be, at least in a purely defensive battle, well nigh invincible. Ensconced behind the Ticino, even the incompetent Gyulai's army had been victorious all along the line throughout a long Italian summer day at Magenta; and even the loss of the bridge could, in the opinion of Schlick and all the best fighting generals, have been made good if Gyulai's nerve had held. At Solferino Count Stadion, charged with a rigidly defensive role in the centre which was to be the hinge for an enveloping advance of both wings, perfectly fulfilled his function from sunrise until two in the afternoon when, as a result of Wimpffen's collapse on his left, he was ordered to withdraw. In and around the great walled cemetery and surrounding buildings of Solferino village he so disposed his infantry and guns that they suffered little damage from the superior enemy artillery and, when the French came to grips with their famed *furia francese*, repulsed them decisively and without serious loss. As a last resort Napoleon flung in his carefully husbanded Imperial Guard; and Stadion repulsed that, too, before withdrawing in perfect order, leaving behind him an enemy so badly mauled that there was no interference either with his movement, or with the more flamboyant withdrawal of Benedek's victorious Corps from the right wing, which came down the same road behind him with bands playing, colours flying, and bringing with it all its wounded and prisoners.

In terms of infantry tactics the only answer to the Dreyse was, of course, the adoption of a weapon equally efficient, or even, like the Chassepot adopted by the French in 1866–7, superior to it. But until 1864 nobody save a handful of Prussian staff officers could know the immense potentialities of the Needle Gun; and even then they were not obvious. Given that limitation, the right Austrian answer to their failures of 1859 was undoubtedly to arm their infantry with the best available muzzle-loading rifle and concentrate on perfecting the tactical conceptions of the Archduke Charles. Combined with their very great superiority in artillery these might conceivably have given them in 1866 a tactical advantage over the Prussians, Needle Gun and all. The decision to revert to the Napoleonic tradition and slavishly to imitate the French tactical system of 1859 was the worst they could have made. The bayonet charge by troops massed in columns presented the Needle Gun with the perfect target in the only conditions in which it could be devastatingly effective.

The campaign of 1859 was not the only one which led the European general staffs astray. Von Gablenz, who commanded the Austrian half of the Allied army against the Danes in 1864, was a soldier of the school of Count Stadion, though far more able. Fully aware of the limitations of the training and tactics of his own troops, he husbanded them carefully and most skilfully exploited their better qualities. Thanks to the inept failure of von Wrangel to make effective use of the Prussian infantry and their new weapon, he helped to confirm the general impression that the Austrian army was at least the second best in Europe and that the Prussians were not a force to be reckoned with. But, apart from Moltke, he alone among the senior generals had seen the Needle Gun in action and appreciated the threat it represented.

Gablenz was probably the man who ought to have been given supreme command in the Bohemian theatre. He had a much more solid, down-to-earth temperament than the mercurial Benedek and he had not, like Benedek, spent a lifetime absorbing the solitary tactical principle of the great Radetzky that an army should always attack. He knew far more about the Prussian army than any of his colleagues, and he had the unique distinction of being the only general in that campaign to win a battle against them. At Trautenau on 27 June his x Corps had the task of blocking the outlet from the most northern of the only three narrow defiles by which the Prussian Crown Prince could move his army across the mountain range of the Riesengebirge from Silesia into Bohemia. By skilful use of his superior artillery and a well-executed flanking movement – the only occasion, incidentally, when the Austrians used this simple manoeuvre – he held the somewhat inexperienced Prussian General von Bonin to a standstill; and in the end the sheer courage and determination with which the Austrians renewed their massive bayonet charges destroyed the morale of the Prussian infantry. They broke and fled up the pass and by midnight Bonin found himself on the far side of the crest, back on Prussian soil.

Gablenz did not let this spectacular success go to his head. By the end of the day three vital facts had impinged on his mind. He had learnt that not only were the Prussian guns inferior to his own, but that their officers still lived in a past when the loss of their guns was as dishonourable a disaster as the loss of its colours would have been to an infantry regiment. They had failed to realise that if artillery was to be effective in battle it must be put at risk; and they were extremely reluctant to move far enough forward to give their infantry proper support. He had also observed that not once in the whole course of the battle had an Austrian bayonet charge actually come to grips with the enemy: the *arme blanche* had, in fact, not killed or wounded a single Prussian soldier. Finally he knew that he had paid very dearly for his victory: in killed, wounded, and missing he had lost 183 officers and 4,231 men. He could not know until the Prussian figures were published after the war that they had lost less than half that number; but he did know that the balance was heavily against him. His immediate reaction after his victory was to order a complete abandonment of the massed bayonet charge in his x Corps and a reversion to the old tactic of keeping the infantry dispersed in small groups and making the best possible use of their rifles.

The casualty figures, not only of Trautenau, but still more those of the other four battles fought by detachments of his army in the last days of June, all defeats in which the Austrian losses were not merely double, but treble those of the enemy, forced Benedek, though more reluctantly, to the same conclusion; and the same tactical instruction went out to the whole army. But it was not possible in five days to put the whole training system of the past six years into reverse. The bulk of the Austrian infantry had been trained to nothing but the use of the bayonet, even in defence. Very few of them had had any musketry practice; and many of them did not even know how to load a rifle, let alone fire it. Benedek certainly still cherished a pipe dream of an Austrian infantry advancing by fire and movement in dispersed groups to overwhelm a Prussian army already disorganised and demoralised by the fire of his artillery. It is unlikely that Gablenz shared this illusion. He fully understood that the effect of the new tactical order, confirmed as it was by the careful dispositions Benedek made for Königgrätz, was to eliminate the Austrian infantry altogether as a decisive factor in the battle. Since the inferiority of its guns and the unadventurous incompetence of its leaders similarly eliminated the Prussian artillery, Königgrätz thus became a straight fight between the Austrian guns and the Prussian rifles, each supreme in their own tactical sphere.

This is what makes 1866 from the technological standpoint a turning point in the history of the art of warfare. For centuries the great armies of Europe had faced each other with weapons of roughly equal performance, and victory had depended on the ability of the generals and the morale and training of the troops they commanded. Now, for the first time, the outcome of battles came to depend on the performance of new weapons, designed by men who would never have to use them, and whose practical capabilities were unforeseeable either by the men who used them or their opponents. This situation has persisted ever since; and it entails for the historian of technical military developments at least a cursory study of the technical dispositions of commanders and the subsequent course of events to determine whether it was the better general, the better army or the better weapon which won. From this point of view events at Königgrätz were as decisive in military as in diplomatic history.

Whatever wistful dreams Benedek may have cherished of an eventual counter-attack, his dispositions for the battle of Königgrätz precisely conformed to the Austrian tradition of the previous century, when staff officers had spent the intervals of peace riding round the Empire selecting promising defensive positions and marking them on their maps with ungainly rings. It was a system known to the more irreverent junior staff officers as 'Sausage Strategy'. His chosen battleground exactly conformed to this definition. His centre was based on the forward slopes of the high ground some five miles west of the Elbe, where his artillery had a field of fire of some 2,000 yards over open stone slopes unbroken by any cover which might be used by advancing infantry, running down to the narrow, wooded and enclosed valley of the little River Bistritz and the village of Sadowa. His refused right flank, stretching right back to the banks of the Elbe, had a shorter but equally clear field of fire in front of it. His left flank looked on the map less secure, since it was thrust further forward on to lower, heavily forested ground. But it had orders to fight only as long a delaying action as possible in the thick woods before falling back up the hills to positions where its artillery was already dug in with equally clear fields of fire. Benedek had started his army life as a gunner but it was his outstandingly able artillery Commander, the Archduke William, who personally and it is universally agreed quite brilliantly, chose the sites for his batteries along the whole front and had emplacements ready dug for them to move into on the evening before the battle. The infantry, too, were dug in along roughly the same line, so that they offered little target for the enemy gunners and none at all to the Needle Gun unless the Prussian infantry could get across the open ground in front of them.

It was, of course, a position out of which Benedek could easily have been manoeuvred, as Maria Theresa's Marshals had so often been out manoeuvred by Frederick the Great. The Prussian Crown Prince was, after all, already on the west bank of the Elbe and had to come back across the river to carry out Moltke's order to move with all his forces to attack the Austrian right flank. But it was also a position from which, if his Corps Commanders faithfully carried out his orders, he could scarcely be dislodged by a frontal attack. To re-direct the Prussian armies on to wide outflanking marches would nevertheless have consumed much time: quite enough, in fact, to enable Benedek to retire peaceably and undisturbed to just such another position further back, whence he would again have to be dislodged by another tedious outflanking manoeuvre. And for political reasons time in 1886, as in 1859, was on the Austrian side. In both campaigns they had, waiting on the sidelines, a powerful potential ally whom the logic of events would eventually force to come in on their side. In 1859 his Imperial pride had driven Francis Joseph to abandon his already shadowy hegemony in Italy rather than owe it to the belated intervention of the despised Prussian army. In 1866 he was fighting for the much more important object of preserving his predominance in Germany; and there was everything to be gained by delaying a decisive military decision until the possibility of an overwhelming increase of Prussia's power and influence in

Germany forced Napoleon III in his own interest to active participation.

Moltke was far more vividly aware of the importance of the time factor than Benedek was. The French government had not yet been plunged into the mood of impotent despondency which followed the Prussian victory at Königgrätz. But the news which had filtered through of the overwhelming Prussian superiority in the opening battles in the last week of June had already warned Napoleon that he had backed the wrong horse. If he was to intervene as mediator with a chance of enforcing a solution of the German problem acceptable to France, he must do so at once before the Austrian army was eliminated as an effective fighting force, thereby forcing him to mobilise on the Rhine an army totally unprepared for the sort of war it would have to fight. On 2 July it was already known at the King of Prussia's Headquarters that the luckless French Ambassador, Count Benedetti, was battling his way forward against every permissible obstacle officialdom could place in his way to lay formal mediation proposals before the King. With the threat of armed mediation behind them such proposals would have been hard to resist while the Austrian army remained in the field, still formidable and undefeated and likely, within a week or so, to be reinforced by the Archduke Albrecht and at least 50,000 of his victorious troops from Italy.

Unless, therefore, he could win a quick and decisive victory, Moltke's own gloomy prediction that an Austro-Prussian war could only result in large gains for France was likely to be fulfilled. Up to 2 July cavalry reconnaissance on both sides had been woefully unadventurous and incompetent. The Crown Prince had lost all touch with Austrian forces and Benedek had no idea where the Crown Prince's army had got to. It was only late that night that a series of daring cavalry patrols suddenly convinced Moltke that Frederick Charles, with von Herwarth's Elbe Army close on his right, had in front of him not merely a rear guard left to defend the Elbe bridges, but the entire massed strength of the Austrian army. The Crown Prince was still near enough to be able to get into the battle by the following afternoon; and he had his chance of fighting the sort of encirclement battle which was always at the back of his mind and winning a decisive victory while Benedetti was still wrestling with the procedural difficulties of getting up to an army headquarters at the crisis of a campaign. He seized the chance with alacrity, though not without a well-concealed trepidation; for there was much which might go wrong.

Benedek had no such clear understanding of his own military predicament or of its political implications. He only knew from a series of sarcastic telegrams from the Emperor's Military Chancery in Vienna and a personal visit from a Colonel von Beck that it would be regarded as a total disgrace to the Empire if he abandoned Bohemia without fighting a major battle. He faced the prospect loyally, but in a mood of gloomy despondency. His long march back from Josefstadt to Königgrätz had degenerated into a semi-mutinous straggle of troops already disillusioned with their weapons, their tactics, and their commanders. It had also revealed the complete incompetence of his staff and his administrative services. Finally, he had been forced to realise that he could not fight against the Needle Gun the sort of battle to which he was accustomed, and after which he still hankered. It was a feat of miraculous leadership to get his army on to the battlefield at all in reasonable order and with its morale entirely restored. But he knew that he had behind him an administrative machine which would break down under the slightest pressure; and he was to fight the sort of battle for which he was temperamentally totally unfitted.

Nevertheless he might just have won the sort of defensive battle which he himself despised, but which would have left him in undisputed possession of the battlefield and free to withdraw in such reasonable order as his administrative services would permit; and he would have left behind a Prussian army which might not have suffered crippling casualties, since their infantry invariably fell back out of range of the devastating Austrian gunfire, but which would certainly have been disheartened, if not actually demoralised by its failure to get to grips with the enemy. He held his main position in the centre with two Army Corps; one commanded by the experienced and imperturbable Gablenz, the other by the Archduke Ernest, one of the few Austrian senior commanders who was prepared to carry out precisely and loyally the orders of a Commander-in-Chief of infinitely lower social status. The most significant tactical lesson of Königgrätz was that these two halted the entire army of Prince Frederick Charles at the forward edge of the Bistritz valley and held it there for over six hours purely by the weight and effectiveness of their artillery fire.

The Prussian infantry was set on the march at two in the morning. By an administrative muddle much more common in their army than its historians will generally admit, they got no breakfast and went into a long day's battle with nothing inside them but a hastily consumed cup of coffee. The only road bridge over the Bistritz, at Sadowa, was from first light under fire, though at extreme range, from the Austrian gunners in the hills; and they had a trying time getting across and deploying along the line of the valley. Their advance through the woods and orchards of the narrow valley was then further hampered and harassed by the Austrian Jaeger battalions which had been sent forward to fight a purely delaying action. These were the only asset of the Austrian reversion to Napoleonic tactics. The vast landed estates and forests of the great nobles provided an almost inexhaustible source of gamekeepers and stalkers, foresters and poachers, whose whole livelihood depended on the brilliant use of cover and the certainty that the first shot would be wasted if it did not hit the mark. Their rifles were weapons of precision and it did not, therefore, much matter that they took some time to reload. Their action in the Bistriz valley could not, of course, be in any way decisive. But one battalion, making skilful use of the ditches and hedges on the edge of the woods, threw a whole Prussian brigade into complete disorder before it retired prudently out of range : and all this helped to demoralise the Prussians when they reached the forward edge of the woods and came under the devastating fire of the Austrian guns on the slopes above. Though repeatedly brought back to the attack, they simply could not face the intensity of the exploding shells, combined as it was with the crashing of branches and tree fragments at the edge of the wood; and for six hours not one battalion could be induced to venture on to the open slopes beyond.

Prince Frederick Charles's gunners were equally unnerved. Few of his Battery Commanders could be induced to risk crossing the narrow Sadowa bridge under fire; and many of them, when they finally made the attempt, found themselves impeded by wagon-loads of wounded and bodies of Prussian infantry falling back out of the battle hungry, exhausted, and demoralised. The King of Prussia, riding up at midday to see how things were going, met a whole Prussian battalion falling back in disorder and by sheer rage drove them back into the battle line. But even when the sappers built them two extra pontoon bridges the gunners were still reluctant to venture into the danger zone of the enemy fire; and even at four o'clock in the afternoon, when the Austrian army finally broke and fled in disorder back to the Elbe, there were still Prussian batteries back behind the Sadowa bridge and out of effective range of the battle area. So Benedek's hope that his guns might so demoralise the Prussian army that even his untrained and incompetent infantry might overwhelm it was not entirely a pipe-dream. But for the disaster on both his flanks he might have pulled it off.

Moltke said that evening that he regretted that Benedek had not launched a massive counter-attack in the centre, since this would have caught the entire army 'in a moustrap'. But this was when he already knew that both Austrian flanks had caved in and that a general advance of the Austrian army would have left the Crown Prince and General von Herwarth free to occupy all the Elbe crossings and cut every possible line of retreat. Moltke, in fact, would have had his Sedan four years earlier, and in his first battle. But the triumph of the Prussian attacks on the Austrian flanks was not at all a foregone conclusion; and Benedek himself cannot fairly be held responsible for either disaster. On the left the Saxon Crown Prince was doing very well until the Austrian vⅢ Corps, which had already been very severely handled at the battle of Skalitz, disintegrated, leaving only one brigade still fighting valiantly on his left flank. Prince Albert perforce disengaged his forces and withdrew with remarkably few casualties in the most orderly – even leisurely fashion, giving General von Herwarth no opportunity whatever to interfere with the main lines of the Austrian retreat. If Moltke's 'mousetrap' had to be closed it could only have been by the Prussian Crown Prince's army on the opposite flank.

Benedek and the Archduke William had designated the positions and dug the gun emplacements for the two Corps which were to cover their right flank with the same care and precision as they had devoted to those of the centre, and there is no reason to suppose that they would not have been just as effective. The Crown Prince's infantry did not get into action until two in the afternoon and, apart from the Guards' Corps, it arrived piecemeal, overmarched, and in no very good order. General von Bonin, for example, although he had ample warning of the impending move back across the Elbe, since the staff officer carrying Moltke's orders to the Crown Prince dropped in at his headquarters on the way to give him the gist of them, got his Corps off to a very confused start and dawdled on his way. He explained afterwards that he had mistaken the din of the Austrian gunfire to the south west for a summer thunder storm in the hills. The two Austrian Corps Commanders concerned, however, the Counts Festetics and Thun, were far too wealthy and well-connected to pay attention to orders which they found idiotic. They decided that the fields of fire of the Archduke's gun emplacements were far too short; and they moved their entire force 1,000 yards forward on to the slightly higher plateau of Maslowed, where they were drawn up in exactly the sort of exposed position which had proved so fatal in the earlier battles.

Much worse was to follow. As General von Fransecky's 7th Prussian Division tried to feel its way round the left of the devastating gunfire in the centre he came in on the now exposed left flank of Count Festetics. The Count at once led the whole of his infantry down the slope to his left and plunged in the thickly forested area of the Swiepwald into exactly the sort of dogfight which Benedek's dispositions had been designed to avoid. Count Thun, feeling that merely to sit on the heights covering the extreme right flank with no enemy in sight was both boring and dishonourable, followed him with a large proportion of his own infantry. The result was precisely what might have been expected. The Jaeger battalions did brilliantly, 'flitting', as one Prussian officer put it, 'like ghosts from tree to tree', never offering a fair target and picking off the enemy with remorseless precision. But they were only a handful. The rest of the Austrian infantry reverted to the forbidden and suicidal massed bayonet charges. Since they outnumbered the enemy by three to one they did occasionally get to hand-to-hand fighting; Fransecky lost 84 officers and 2,036 of his Division in killed and wounded, and was all but forced to fall back from the Swiepwald.

But he had inflicted three times that number of casualties on the enemy and had greatly contributed to the eventual spectacular victory. When the Prussian Guard emerged at two o'clock on the Maslowed plateau it had only to overcome the helplessly exposed Austrian brigades falling back across their front seriously depleted in numbers, totally exhausted and utterly demoralised by their experiences in the Swiepwald. The Guards cut their way through without difficulty and seized the village of Chlum, which was the commanding bastion at the right-hand end of the Austrian centre. Count Thun only made the certainty of a total Austrian disaster more complete and precipitate by immediately ordering his Corps to abandon what positions it still held and get back across the Elbe by the nearest available bridges.

Benedek made many mistakes on that day; and they all sprang from the obsession, dinned into him by the academic Krismanič, that he must first defeat Prince Frederick Charles decisively before turning on the Crown Prince. He remained throughout the morning concentrated on the battle in the centre and totally unaware of events on his right flank. At about noon he was convinced that the victory he wanted was within his grasp : that his gunners had so demoralised the infantry in front that a general assault by his whole main army down the slope would disintegrate and destroy the Prussian 1st Army. He had already turned to one of his staff and said : 'Well, shall we let fly?' when the first news reached him of the disasters in the Swiepwald and of the fact that his right flank was left wide open. It was enough to make him postpone the surge forward which would have put him precisely into Moltke's 'mousetrap'. But he himself stayed where he was and merely sent urgent messages to von Mollinary, who had taken over when Festetics lost a foot, and Thun to disengage immediately and return to the positions originally assigned to them. He would probably have done better to take charge himself on the right and to move his two still-concentrated and undisturbed reserve Army Corps across to the positions which the insubordinate Counts had declined to occupy earlier in the morning. Von Mollinary and Thun could then have been told to disengage as best they could and reconcentrate their troops, in-

cluding the abandoned artillery on the Maslowed heights, somewhere behind the centre where they might have constituted a
substantial, if unreliable, army reserve. The batteries alone, which
had still seen no action, would have been invaluable as replacements for those in the front line which were gradually, as the day
wore on, running out of ammunition.

As it was, the news, brought two hours later by a breathless
staff officer, that Chlum had been occupied by the Prussian
Guard took him so completely by surprise that his immediate
answer was: 'Don't talk such nonsense.' When, after a wild gallop
across the front, he had seen for himself the extent of his disaster,
he merely sacrificed his two reserve Corps in a series of gallant
counter-attacks, many of which he led in person with a characteristic disregard for his own safety, and which served only to
swell the shocking toll taken by the Needle Gun. His main army,
taken in flank and rear, broke and fled, getting across the Elbe
as best it could, saved from total destruction only by the heroism
of its gunners and by the brilliant intervention of the two incomparable reserve divisions of the Austrian heavy cavalry.

So two of the great unanswered 'ifs' of military history remain
unanswerable. Nobody will ever know whether the Crown
Prince's infantry, advancing on to open slopes as it came over the
brow of the Maslowed heights, would have fared any better than
that of Frederick Charles in the Bistritz valley. Nor can it ever be
certain that the Prussian infantry, however reluctant to advance
into the destructive Austrian shellfire, would not have quickly
have recovered its morale and fighting power if the Austrian
massed infantry had charged into the Bistriz valley and come
within range of the deadly Needle Gun. Taken by themselves the
casualty figures give no real estimate of the possible outcome of
the battle. The Austrians and Saxons lost between them in killed,
wounded, missing, and prisoners, over 44,000; the total Prussian
loss was just over 9,000; but there were many factors which made
these figures a disproportionate system of reckoning. An army
which withdraws in disorder from the field must inevitably leave
a high proportion of unwounded prisoners in enemy hands.
Moreover the Austrians, by a bureaucratic oversight, had omitted
to sign the Geneva Convention and their doctors and medical
orderlies, unprotected by the Red Cross were officially combatants

and had to withdraw with the rest. The Prussian field ambulances did their best for the enemy wounded; but naturally enough they saw to their own first, and the vast majority of those listed by the Austrians as 'Missing' were not men who had slipped unnoticed out of the battle, but wounded who had bled to death or died of exposure during the night, before the Prussian doctors could get round to them. Finally it must be remembered that the casualties inflicted by the Needle Gun were at almost muzzle-point and deadly, whereas the Austrian gunners won more by the threat than the infliction of casualties: the Prussian infantry simply declined to move into the deadly dropping zone of the shells.

The only objective evidence which remains for the historian is the reaction of Moltke himself to his own great victory. Throughout the day he had contrived to maintain to his King and to the far more irritating apprehensions of Bismarck the illusion of an imperturbable certainty that the Crown Prince's intervention would be in time and decisive; and he ended up in the evening with a somewhat caustic discourse to his staff on his disappointment that the victory had not been more successfully exploited. With all his qualities, he was not the man to admit, as Wellington had after Waterloo, that 'it had been a damned near-run thing'. But he thereupon collapsed into a raging fever which compelled his staff to take him back to main headquarters at Jitschin in a carriage to recover from the strains which the day had really placed on him; and his long-term reaction was to spend the next four years not on improving his infantry or its weapon, but in re-equipping and reforming the whole tactical doctrine of his artillery. He at least had seen more clearly than *The Times* military correspondent that, though the needle gun had emerged as king, it was the Austrian gunners who had come within an ace of winning the battle.

In this judgement the events of 1870 were to prove Moltke fundamentally correct: and it was this alone which saved him from a disastrous reliance on the excellence of the Needle Gun. For once Napoleon III and his generals thought more quickly and more clearly than he did. Having themselves suffered a major diplomatic and political defeat from the Austrian collapse at Königgrätz, they realised that they would soon have to confront the Prussian army in a straight fight. Like Moltke they appreciated that for any future battlefield they must have a gun even better than the Austrian rifled muzzle-loader. They also perceived that they must have an infantry weapon which would outclass the Dreyse Needle Gun.

On this latter point they were lucky, since they had the answer already to hand. A M. Chassepot, employed in the artillery factory at St Thomas d'Aquain, had after ten years of private experiment produced in 1863 a working model of a rifle which far surpassed the Needle Gun in reliability, range, and rate of fire. The problem of sealing the breech was solved by a rubber ring which, until it became hardened by long use, effectively prevented any escape of gases. An improved bolt mechanism raised the rate of fire; and a reduction in the calibre of the bullet not only enabled it to be sighted to 1,600 yards, as against the Needle Gun's 600, but so lightened the weight of cartridges to be carried as to meet half way the objections of the conservatives who feared that a higher rate of fire would too quickly exhaust their supplies of reserve ammunition. None the less the conservative view, still led in 1863 by the disastrous Marshal Randon, easily prevailed. He and his friends admitted that a further improvement in the morale of French infantry was desirable, but that the victories of 1859 had fully justified both their armament and their tactics.

This complacency, like Napoleon's diplomatic daydreams, was abruptly dissipated by the news of Königgrätz. There could no longer be any question of armed mediation on the Rhine by a French army whose tactics were the same as those of the Austrians, whose weapons were no better, and which had no hope of avoiding the same disastrous fate. Not only was Napoleon left without any bargaining power in negotiations for a radical alteration of the balance of power in central Europe. Until he could rearm his troops and reform his whole military system, France lay virtually at the mercy of a vastly more powerful Prussia. In the matter of an infantry weapon the French War Ministry reacted with an altogether uncharacteristic briskness and efficiency. Before the end of the year M. Chassepot's rifle had been put into mass production and was being issued to the troops. On 3 November 1867, only fifteen months after Königgrätz, General de Failly, who had been sent with a division to save the diminished remnant of the Pope's Temporal Power from being overrun by Garibaldinian irregulars, ended his telegraphic announcement of his victory at Mentana with a sentence which the Italian people never forgot or forgave : *Les fusils Chassepot ont fait merveille.*' By 1870 the French had a million of them and had adjusted their infantry tactics accordingly.[9]

Too much importance should not, of course, be attached to the figures engraved on the sights of pre-1914 rifles. The Lee-Metford issued to British infantry in the 1890s was even sighted up to 2,500 yards. But these figures represented only the daydreams of technicians. Just as the Needle Gun, though sighted up to 600 yards, was effective in battle at ranges of 200 or less, even the most accurate of more modern rifles could not be fired with real effect at over 1,000 yards, and then only if it was offered a dense and massive target. At the outset of the war of 1870, when the Prussians were still advancing in Company columns, they suffered shocking casualties in the long, 800-yard advance before their weapon could effectively engage the enemy infantry on approximately equal terms. In the opening battles, therefore, the Chassepot gave the long-service, professional soldier of the old Imperial army an overwhelming superiority over the Prussian infantry.

Although, tactically, they won every battle until the capitulation of MacMahon at Sedan and the tame surrender of Bazaine at Metz, the Prussians almost invariably suffered the heavier casualties in killed and wounded. At Spicheren they lost in the actual fighting 4,500 against the French 2,000; and even the 2,000 whom the French listed as missing – men who had fallen, wounded or unwounded, into enemy hands in the confusion of the withdrawal at nightfall – did not even the score. At Wörth they did rather better, thanks to MacMahon's out-of-date belief that cavalry could still be used as a shock force in charges across a battlefield dominated by artillery and small-arms fire. But even there they lost 10,500 against the French 11,000; and their triumph in adding a further 200 officers and 9,000 men as unwounded prisoners was due only to the courage with which the French held on to untenable positions until retreat was no longer possible. At Vionville-Mars-la-Tour they lost 15,750 against the French 13,761, though here again they picked up a further 5,400 'missing' – mostly wounded left on the field as the French with-drew. In Bazaine's final and, as it proved, decisive defeat at St Privat and Gravelotte the figures were even more impressive. The Prussian loss was 20,163; the French 12,273. In its frontal attack on St Privat the Prussian Guard alone lost 8,000 men : more than a quarter of its strength. These were the tolls taken by the Chassepot even in battles dominated, in the last resort, by the Prussian artillery.[10]

It is not easy to understand why Moltke allowed the French to gain this important lead over him in infantry fire-power. Even if his Intelligence staff had not already discovered for him its capa-bilities, de Failly's tactless telegram of 1867 informed the world of the excellence of the new French weapon. It is difficult to believe that Prussian inventiveness and efficiency could not have pro-duced within three years a rifle capable of challenging the Chassepot on more or less equal terms. It would seem that he himself was temporarily carried away, like the rest of the world, by the triumph of the Needle Gun in 1866, and that he only realised too late that the 600 yards engraved on the backsight of that rifle meant, in practical terms on the battlefield absolutely nothing. He was in any case far more preoccupied with the pre-dominance established by the Austrian artillery over his own, and better aware than most of the Prussian generals of how lucky he had been at Königgrätz. But for the insubordination of Festetics and Thun the Crown Prince might well have been held to a standstill on his left wing and he would have faced a very difficult situation indeed that evening.

Just as Napoleon had found ready to hand at the critical moment the Chassepot rifle he so badly needed, so Moltke already had Herr Krupp waiting to supply him with any number of the new breech-loaders with which he had begun to re-equip his artillery in 1866. The Essen factory had at last found a method of cooling a flawless steel and had produced a gas-tight, breech-loading all-steel gun with a higher rate of fire and a greater range than any field gun then in use. He also found ready to hand in General von Hindersin an Inspector-General of Artillery of outstanding ability whose new School of Gunnery revolutionised the whole Prussian Field Artillery both technically and tactically. The old doctrine that guns were not to be put at risk was thrown overboard. Battery Commanders were encouraged to push forward as quickly as possible into the thick of the fighting so long as they kept their gunners out of range of the deadly Chassepot. The German generals saw at once that the possession of such a rifle gave the French an overpowering advantage in a defensive battle. They therefore concluded characteristically that they must take the offensive and carry the fight, as the King of Prussia put it, 'to really close quarters,[11] where our rifle and our fire discipline can be fully exploited'. The main task of the Prussian gunners was therefore not merely to keep the enemy artillery at arm's length, but so to hammer the French infantry that the Prussian columns would be able to get across the 800 yards dominated by Chassepot fire to which they themselves had no effective answer.

The best illustration of the extent to which the Austrian artillery performance had impressed the Prussian leaders is perhaps the fact that the old King himself obstinately refused to allow the infantry of his centre to advance for two solid hours after the Prussian Guard had stormed Chlum and virtually won the battle. Only when the last Austrian battery in front of them had diverted its fire northwards to stem the Crown Prince's attack did he let Prince Frederick Charles go and sign the order for 'the pursuit' – the official symbol of victory. It was naturally not an aspect of the battle which the Prussians much cared to publicise; and the rest of the world, including the French General Staff, hypnotised by the performance of the Needle Gun largely overlooked it. Some senior French officers saw in 1867 a demonstration of the new Krupp field gun, which the Belgians were buying for their army, and brought back alarmed reports of its superiority to anything they had in their own army. Krupp was prepared, and indeed anxious to sell them all they needed. But Marshal Leboeuf and his senior colleagues had inherited the old mistrust of steel guns; and, more important still, there was the question of expense. After 1866 the Emperor's health, prestige, and popularity steadily declined and he was forced to concede more and more power to a democratically elected Chamber, including control of the military budget, of which it grudged every penny. Having already spent large sums on the Chassepot, the govern-

The Impact of Technological Advances

ment simply did not dare to ask for what would be needed to
re-equip the artillery.

So the French went into the war of 1870 with the guns of 1859
which, apart from their other obvious shortcomings, fired a shell
much less effective than that of the Prussians, which was loaded
with cordite and exploded on impact. The French shells were
fitted with time fuses which could only be set at ranges of 1,200 or
2,800 yards, and even then were wildly erratic. Their artillery
commanders, moreover, made no attempt to adjust themselves to
the tactical transformation brought about by the Chassepot. They
adhered obstinately to the old Napoleonic tradition of keeping
their batteries concentrated in the rear, waiting to intervene in
close and massive support of the infantry at the crisis of the battle.
In 1870 such moments were rare; and when they got into action
in any effective strength, the issue had generally already been
settled. So the battles of 1870, like those of 1866, became a trial
of strength between the gun and the rifle; in this case between the
Krupp field gun and the Chassepot. This time the field gun won.
But it only did so because the Prussian generals so quickly realised
its potentialities, learned to husband their infantry, and to pin the
enemy down by gunfire alone while they felt their way round his
flanks. Given even moderate leadership the French could, with
the Chassepot and the hitherto undisclosed possibilities of the
Mitrailleuse, quite easily have won at least the opening campaign
of the war.

As it was, the Prussian generals were given time to discover, at
the cost of shocking infantry casualties, that their guns could not
only drive the French artillery more or less out of the battle, but
could pin down the French infantry in defensive positions which
were frontally unassailable while their own troops felt their way
round the enemy flanks and forced a withdrawal. At Wörth, for
example, the battle was opened by the massed artillery of von
Kirchbach's v Corps – some fourteen batteries in all – going into
action against the French centre when the bulk of its own infantry was still moving up behind it. In reply to this the French
were only able to get two batteries into action; and these were
almost immediately ordered to pull out and await a more vulnerable target. On that day MacMahon, outnumbered and outfought, had no chance of victory. His troops fought magnificently

and inflicted very nearly as many casualties as they suffered. It was the Prussian gunfire which prevented him from extricating his army at the end of the day without leaving over 9,000 unwounded prisoners in enemy hands.

At Spicheren, the other opening battle of the main campaign, and fought on the same day, the Prussian gunners achieved no such decisive results. It is true that they early forced the French gunners to withdraw out of range; and the eight guns dragged, with the help of the infantry, up on to the plateaux which had been the original French advance positions effectively frustrated all attempts to counter-attack. But they could not help their infantry to storm the main position on the Spicheren heights nor prevent the French gunners from giving their own infantry excellent support in defence. There was a moment, too, when French guns, installed in unassailable positions, virtually annihilated a regiment of Prussian Hussars moving up a ravine to exploit a local success of their infantry. But it is also true that, thanks to out-of-date thinking, General Frossard at the end of the day still had four batteries which had never been commited at all.

Von Alvensleben at Vionville[12] showed how well he had learnt the lesson of Spicheren. He had seized the vital road junction early in the day by an infantry *coup-de-main*; but he held it, albeit precariously, all day by bringing all fifteen batteries of his Corps into a half circle on the hills south of the main road. Their ammunition supply was a constant source of anxiety; but their contribution to the Prussian victory was largely decisive. Interesting, too, was the skill with which old Canrobert, further along the road to Mars-la-Tour and Verdun, deployed his guns nicely out of reach of the Prussian artillery, but able to give his forward infantry a completely effective defensive support. His success might have been equally important, but for the accident that the Prussians launched the last recorded successful charge of massed heavy cavalry against unbroken infantry and guns. Von Bredow's 'Death Ride' emerged from the dust and smoke of battle only a few hundred yards from Canrobert's guns and moving at a pace which gave the surprised French infantry no time to destroy him. He lost more than half his Brigade; but he created a confusion from which the French never recovered; and Mars-la-Tour fell irretrievably into Prussian hands.

Yet two days later, in the one great set-piece battle of the war between St Privat and Gravelotte, the Prussian Army and Corps Commanders threw overboard every lesson which they should have learnt from Wörth and Spicheren, Vionville and Mars-la-Tour, failed entirely until the very end of the day to make use of their artillery superiority and sacrificed over 20,000 of their best troops in suicidal frontal assaults on a brilliantly selected and prepared position which gave the French gunners as well as the French infantry their ideal target. The inexperienced von Manstein did, indeed, open a battle which Moltke would have preferred to delay by throwing forward the guns of IX Corps, insufficiently supported by infantry, to far too close a range, and a brisk counter-attack by French infantry not only drove them back in disorder, but captured four of their guns. Thereafter the Prussian guns sat back at a more prudent range. They destroyed or set on fire every farm and village along the front and blew to pieces the French wagon- and horse-lines. But they could not reach the well-sited French gun line; and they inflicted only trivial casualties on the dug-in French infantry. From the purely technological point of view the important facts were that tactically the Chassepot and the inferior French artillery dominated the battlefield and inflicted on the Prussians double the number of casualties they suffered themselves. Only at the very end of the day, when Prince Kraft zu Hohenlohe-Ingelfingen, incomparably the ablest of the artillery commanders on either side, got the whole of the Guards' Corps batteries deployed against Canrobert's front and the more methodical genius of the Saxon Crown Prince simultaneously brought all of his into action at right angles beyond the French flank, did the Prussian artillery come back into its own. The French right and centre disintegrated and presented the Germans with a costly victory which was, on the day's fighting, wholly undeserved.

At Sedan the Prussians had at last properly learnt their lesson. There were no more suicidal infantry frontal assaults. Their batteries remorselessly herded MacMahon's army back into the hollow of the little fortress where, under the continuous fire of over 500 guns, the morale both of the French Emperor and his troops finally collapsed; and over 100,000 of France's best troops marched into captivity. But the supreme irony of the campaign lay not in the failure of the French generals to exploit by counter-attack the superiority which the Chassepot almost invariably asserted over the Prussian artillery. It lay in the fact that they had under their hand and failed to use effectively what was to be the war-winner of the future : the only machine gun then in existence.

Napoleon III had counted on the Mitrailleuse to redress the known inferiority of his artillery; and properly handled it might well have done so. It could be fired accurately up to a range of 2,000 yards at a rate of 150 rounds a minute. Used as an infantry weapon in the front line it could not only have made the already devastating fire of the Chassepot invincible in the infantry battle, but have forced the Prussian guns far enough back to allow the French batteries to move close enough to give their infantry over-whelming support. But the French chose to use it as an artillery weapon, organised in batteries and kept well behind the firing line. Its performance was, in consequence, bitterly disappointing. Only Canrobert properly appreciated its potentialities and later lamented that he had not been given them at St Privat where, he reckoned, they could both have completed the destruction of the Prussian Guard and enabled him to thin out his front line to provide a sufficient flank guard to frustrate the Saxon flanking attack which won the battle. So the most important of all the technological military achievements of the period was left entirely unexploited.

5 War Conducted by Amateurs: The American Civil War

The American Civil War does not fit easily into the pattern of the development of the art of warfare in the age of Moltke either chronologically or tactically. In point of time it spanned almost exactly the gap between the Italian War of 1859 and the Austro-Prussian War of 1866, beginning as it did with the bombardment of Fort Sumter on 12 April 1861, and ending with Lee's surrender at Appomattox on 9 April 1865. Thus it was still raging indecisively when Moltke first tried out his new military machine against the Danes in 1864; and there had been no time to study and digest any lessons it had to teach when he launched his victorious campaign against the Austrians in 1866. For the next four years he was not unnaturally preoccupied with learning all he could from his own and his enemies' mistakes in that war, which seemed much more relevant to the problems of the looming struggle with France than anything which had happened in vastly different circumstances on the far side of the Atlantic. He had, moreover, to absorb into his system the populations of the newly acquired territories of the North German Confederation and to organise the adaptation of the armies of the still-independent South German states sufficiently to that system to enable them to collaborate effectively in a campaign against the national hereditary enemy. When that, too, ended in spectacular triumph there seemed no reason to look farther afield for lessons either in strategy or tactics. All the answers were to be found in the organisation, methods, and achievement of the German Army.

Yet in almost every important aspect the American Civil War had produced novel situations and novel solutions to strategic, technical, and tactical problems, all of which deserved close study by the General Staffs and the Admiralties of the European great powers. The Admiralties did, indeed, after some years of muddled experiment, finally study its lessons and apply them. The generals hardly paid any attention at all. Not until the disastrous stalemates of 1914–18 had brought European civilisation to the brink of disintegration did some of the more intelligent thinkers turn back through the pages of history to find in the campaigns of Grant and Lee, Stonewall Jackson and Sherman, some methods of waging modern war less self-destructive than those of their immediate predecessors.

This neglect on the part of the generals was the more surprising because the American Civil War had all the essentials of what the Europeans called *La Grande Guerre.* Though the combatants were theoretically parts of a single great nation, they represented two widely divergent outlooks: almost two distinct civilisations. Each was prepared to fight to the death for what it believed to be the proper American way of life, throwing into the struggle every resource it had : its wealth and every available man and machine. More than any of the European belligerents of the nineteenth century, Federals and Confederates alike conformed most nearly to the Clausewitzian concept of 'the nation at war'; and they fought it out for four long years, demanding almost unprecedented sacrifices of life and wealth from their citizens. By 1865 the Union Army of the North had more than a million men under arms, vastly outnumbering the depleted armies of Lee and Johnston. But they had lost in killed on the battlefield some 360,000; and, in all, their dead as a direct result of the fighting amounted to over half a million. They had spent 3,400,000 dollars – nearly 2·5 million a day – and had put a severe strain on even their enormous resources. The losses in men killed on the Southern side were slightly less though far more serious for their sparser population. Economically the South had thrown in everything it had and was totally ruined.[1]

Both armies were of necessity gigantic improvisations; the regular army of the United States in 1861 numbered only 16,000 men. Most of these were pinned down along the Indian frontier

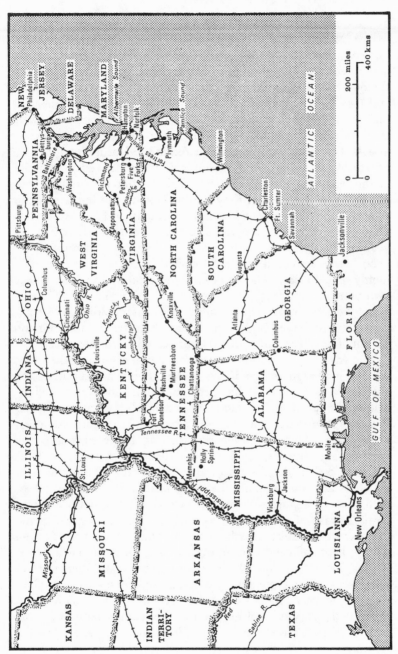

Map 2.   The American Civil War

of the northern states and remained so throughout the war. The troops on both sides were thus, like those of the French revolutionary armies, enthusiastic volunteers who had to be flung into action with the minimum of drill and training. In point of quality the South had the advantage that many of them were horsemen and most knew how to handle a rifle. But both showed the same high courage and endurance; and neither was initially well-enough trained to manoeuvre in the open, whether in defence or attack. This situation was perpetuated in the North by a ludicrous system of recruiting, which was a jealously preserved prerogative of the separate States. Regiments which suffered casualties were not brought up to strength by reinforcements, but left to dwindle slowly out of existence, while new regiments were raised to take their place. Much of the value of the experience gained by the veterans of the early campaigns was thus lost. Nevertheless by 1864 both sides could put into the field largely veteran armies of highly skilled troops who had developed a professionalism of their own which most foreign observers failed to understand. Man for man, the Southerner was certainly the better soldier. Lee could not otherwise have fought out the last year against the immense weight of numbers and material Grant could bring into action.

The vast majority of the senior commanders on the other hand were trained regulars, graduates of West Point; and a remarkably able body they were. It has been said that 'no war in military history produced such a galaxy of generals.'[2] The mere fact that they were without experience in handling large formations enabled them to approach their problems unhampered by accepted theories and traditional doctrines – that professionalism which has been called 'the dry rot of armies'.[3] Of the Commanders-in-Chief, Grant was certainly the most outstanding and could have held his own against any general of the age. Lee never achieved Grant's grasp of a campaign as a whole. He was a great gentleman of a fast vanishing school and perhaps for that very reason seldom kept sufficient control over a battle once he had committed his troops to action. He gave out his orders and thereafter left his often cantankerous and obstinately opinionated Corps Commanders to carry them out as they saw fit. So long as he could delegate the execution of his plans to the original genius of Stonewall Jackson he was nearly invincible; and Jackson's death at

Chancellorsville was probably the worst single disaster suffered by the South in the whole war.

Grant, too, had a lieutenant of outstanding genius in Sherman, and was lucky enough to keep him to the end of the war. What is more, he managed to combine a policy of giving Sherman the maximum freedom and independence in his separate and brilliantly conducted large-scale undertakings with his own more methodical strategy. As Grant closed remorselessly in on Lee at Richmond the decisive factors which broke his enemy's resistance and forced his ultimate surrender were Sherman's advance from Chattanooga in May 1864 to capture the key railway centre of Atlanta and his subsequent devastating marches, first on through Georgia to the coast, and then northward through the Carolinas. These marches, which cut great swathes of ruin through the richest farmlands of the South, were an episode which few civilised nations would wish to celebrate in song : a brutally successful application of the principles of total war. They not only deprived Lee of vital supplies from the prosperous central South, but started a progressive desertion among his troops, who had up to then been fighting back tenaciously against superior numbers and equipment. They were hardened to privation and might have endured the additional hardships imposed by the loss of railway supplies from Atlanta, but the fear that their families were destitute and their farms ruined had a fatal effect on morale. The world for which they were fighting was being systematically destroyed behind them. Desertion had always been a problem for the loosely confederated armies of the South. The devastation of Georgia and the Carolinas turned it into a major factor in their defeat.

Most serious historians are now agreed that Sherman's Atlanta campaign was not only the greatest feat of arms of the Civil War, but the greatest military masterpiece of the whole age which has taken its name from Moltke. But his contemporaries completely overlooked the wholly novel ideas such as the oblique approach on which his strategy was based and the tactical skill with which he applied them. In essence the strategy of the indirect approach was a reversion to the pre-Napoleonic era : to the wars of manoeuvre of the seventeenth and eighteenth centuries. Turenne's proudest moments had been when he had succeeded in overrunning a province without letting the enemy bring him to battle; and Frederick the Great, perpetually aware that he must husband the slender manpower of Prussia, much preferred to prize an enemy out of a position without heavy fighting by threatening his flanks and communications. Only when he either had no time or no room to manoeuvre did he reluctantly resort to what he called 'the emetic of a battle'. Napoleon, often short of time and always of money, aimed at bringing his enemy to battle quickly and on the largest possible scale when, like Moltke at Königgrätz, he could win the war at a single blow. Thanks to Clausewitz, the daydream of victories like Austerlitz and Sedan was to haunt the minds of European generals until long after the age of Moltke had ended. Three-quarters of a century were to elapse before the commonsensical ideas and methods of the Civil War commanders came into their own as a subject of serious study.

Of course the sometimes brilliant tactical innovations of the American generals did not spring merely from the application of exceptionally intelligent minds unhampered by Clausewitz and the preconceived ideas of a powerfully established military hier-archy. They sprang initially partly from circumstances, but mostly from the very limitations of the material out of which they had to build great modern armies. Not original genius but sheer necessity compelled them to become the first to use railways on a large scale' for the transport of troops and supplies. The armies functioned perforce hundreds of miles from their bases and their sources of supply, on fronts which stretched for over a thousand miles from Texas to the Atlantic, and across country where roads were few and primitive. But they were well equipped with trunk-line railways which had already become what they were to re-main for the rest of the century – the spearhead of the westward advance of American civilisation, consolidating the gains of the pioneers and frontiersmen. They were wildly inconvenient for use on a large scale over long distances. The gauge almost invariably changed at every State boundary; and only a single-line track linked the more important junctions. But they were the only means available for the maintenance of the armies and for the swift lateral movements of reinforcements in a fast-moving war. Inevitably the commanders on both sides became dependent on them; and equally inevitably they became major objectives for enemy raids and sabotage. Railways would, of course, remain an important factor in all large-scale operations for a century to come. But, though this was the first occasion on which they were so employed, there would never again be a war in which the plans and movements of both sides depended so completely on them.

There was no new lesson here for European generals. Moltke's Railway Detachment of the Great General Staff was already hard at work on the military adaptation of a far more congested and sophisticated railway system when the American War broke out. The lessons to be learnt from his brilliant exploitation of their labours were obviously far more worthy of study and imitation than the clumsy improvisations imposed on the American generals. They, in turn, once their war was over, saw no reason to study either Moltke's achievements or their own shortcomings. Comfortably isolated within their own continent for the next thirty years with only the Indian, Canadian, and Mexican front-iers to preoccupy them, they relapsed into that apathy which was to land poor General Shafter in such difficulties at Tampa Bay at the end of the century.

The American pioneer use of railways was thus unproductive of any fresh thinking in the United States or anywhere else. It did, however, invite a revolutionary change in cavalry tactics which, if it had been properly studied and understood, might have altered the pattern of all the great wars for the next three-quarters of a century and in so doing have decisively changed the course of history. Two factors combined to force the Civil War generals to rethink their cavalry tactics. One was simply the lack of time to teach the necessary skill at arms for handling lance and sabre and for the elaborate and prolonged drills and exercises needed to train cavalry to move and wheel in closely packed, evenly aligned formations and to control the gallop of the last few hundred yards of a charge so as to strike the enemy in a compact mass. Secondly, even if they had attempted such a task, the cavalry generals would have found that many units on both sides had been equipped with breech-loading rifles more efficient than the Prussian Needle Gun, which had yet to make its appearance on European battlefields. It did not then require much common sense to perceive that to use massed horsemen for shock tactics would be suicidal.

On the other hand both sides had readily available large numbers of men who had been brought up to depend on their own courage and initiative, on their horsemanship and on their skill in handling their rifles for their livelihood, and sometimes for their lives. Even if time had been available, it would have been extremely difficult to impose on such men the severe drills and disciplines needed for old-fashioned cavalry tactics. But they were perfect material out of which to create large formations of irregular cavalry, fast moving and needing little training to fight dismounted as light infantry. It was, in fact, the return to the battlefield of the seventeenth-century Dragoon and of the Hussars from Hungary and Croatia, which the Austrian generals had used in the eighteenth century with brilliant effect, sometimes even against the great Frederick himself. Such formations could be immensely useful for reconnaissance in strength, for large-scale operations against an enemy's flanks and rear, to mask the movements of the main armies, and to seize and hold ground for a short time until guns and infantry could be brought up to relieve them. At the same time, both sides were rich in generals with a natural talent for leading such troops: men like Jeb Stuart and Sheridan, Forrest, Kilpatrick, Morgan and Grierson, all capable of carrying out long-range, independent operations with intelligence and skill; and the long, vulnerable railway supply lines were the most obvious target for such operations.

The decisive effect which such cavalry operations could have on the course of a campaign was well illustrated in the summer of 1862 when the Union government ordered General Buell to advance some two hundred miles eastwards from Mississippi to capture Chattanooga. He was held up for the whole of June by the mere threat of raids on his long supply line running north to his main supply base in Kentucky. The opening up of an alternative line with an advanced supply depot at Nashville, 100 miles north of his line of attack, enabled him to move to within 30 miles of his objective more or less unopposed. But on 9 July Forrest left Chattanooga with 1,400 horse and on 13 July cut the railway line at Murfreesborough 10 miles south of Nashville, capturing the entire enemy garrison of 1,700 men at a cost of only 80 of his own troopers. This halted Buell for a fortnight while the line was repaired. But when he got going again General Morgan rode out with a similar force on a still wider sweep to the north, cutting the railway beyond Nashville, destroying the bridge over the Cumberland River and demolishing a tunnel close beyond it. Buell had to fall hastily back to Murfreesborough. But he was not hasty enough. Bragg, the Confederate Commander at Chattanooga, outmarched and outflanked him and placed himself in a position to threaten simultaneously the two vital bases of Nashville and Louisville. Using less than 3,000 men and at a negligible cost in casualties the cavalry generals had placed Buell at Bragg's mercy; and it was not their fault that Bragg lost his nerve at the critical moment and let his opponent slip past him into the safety of Kentucky.

In December of that same year Forrest again demonstrated his supreme mastery of this kind of cavalry operation. By then the superior numbers available to the Northerners were beginning to tell. Grant moved south with 40,000 men towards Vicksburg against a Confederate army of only 24,000 under Van Doorn, while at the same time Sherman was sent to steam down the Mississippi with another 30,000 for a direct attack on Vicksburg itself, where Pemberton could muster only 12,000 defenders. Van Doorn himself led 3,500 cavalry round Grant's flank on 18 August and on 20 August destroyed his advance supply base at Holly Springs. Simultaneously Forrest, detached by Bragg from in front of Chattanooga, with 2,500 men on a much longer raid, cut the only railway by which Grant could replenish his lost supplies far to the north. The track and all its bridges were systematically destroyed; and Grant, cut off from all communication with the north for over a week, had to abandon his campaign and fall back to his starting point. As an additional bonus Forrest inflicted some 1,500 casualties and kept 20,000 men occupied in vain attempts to intercept him. The counter raid by the Union General Grierson four months later, when he rode with three regiments four hundred miles from north to south in sixteen days and cut all the supply lines to Vicksburg from the east, has been hailed as 'the most successful cavalry raid of the war'.⁴ But it inflicted nothing like the material damage achieved by Forrest, and its chief value was that it distracted and demoralised

Pemberton at the moment when Grant was manoeuvring to get round Vicksburg and invest it from the south.

Twice more, in 1864, when Sherman was advancing on Atlanta in what was to prove the decisive campaign of the war, Forrest showed his outstanding value as a cavalry leader. His mere presence with a few thousand cavalry to the south forced Sherman to leave 80,000 of the 180,000 men he had with him to guard his line of communications to his main supply base at Louisville which lengthened as he advanced to 340 miles. Sherman had insured himself against temporary delays caused by attacks on his advance depots or minor damage to the railway immediately behind him by carrying twenty days' supplies with him close behind his main army. But Forrest, back at Tupelo in Mississippi, was nicely placed for a destructive raid on the northernmost sector of his railway which would cut Sherman off from his main base and in the long run bring his campaign to a halt, as Grant's against Vicksburg had been two years earlier. He therefore detached a mixed force of a further 10,000 under General Sturgis to hunt Forrest out of Tupelo and drive him to the west, out of harm's way. At that very moment Forrest had set out to do just what Sherman most feared; and Sturgis did at least bring him hurrying back to save his base and the troops he had left there. Though outnumbered by more than three to one, Forrest brilliantly concealed his weakness by moving through thickly wooded country, caught Sturgis at Brice's Cross Roads with his infantry and cavalry widely separated and inflicted on him a smashing defeat. As Sturgis fell back to Memphis, he left 2,500 men – a quarter of his army – dead or wounded on the field; and Forrest got back to Tupelo having suffered no more than 500 casualties. Sherman, moreover, when he was just about to mount his decisive manoeuvre to capture Atlanta, had to detach two more precious divisions to bring the force at Memphis up to 15,000, with orders to hunt down Forrest at all costs; and they did at least manage to drive him back into Mississippi to recruit his forces.

He reappeared, for the last time with decisive effect, a fortnight after Sherman had captured Atlanta, and when he was building up his supplies for the daring march into Georgia which would involve cutting loose altogether from his line of supply. Forrest moved suddenly into Tennessee with 4,500 men, terrorised the garrison of Athens into surrender, thereby cutting one of Sherman's important supply lines, and threatening to cut the main one where it would hurt most, close to the main base. He wrecked 80 miles of the subsidiary line, captured or killed 3,000 men, threw Grant into a panic, compelling Sherman to divert no less than three divisions to secure his main supply line. This was too much for Forrest; and he was not given any further opportunity of independent action. As far as long-distance raiding of communications was concerned, none of his contemporary cavalry commanders achieved anything so effective. His senior, 'Fighting Joe' Wheeler made a great name for himself by two great raids, spectacular in their scope and speed of movement but singularly unproductive of decisive results. In the first, having safely arrived on the Cumberland River in January 1863, with orders from Bragg to interrupt the passage of store-ships and transports, he grew bored after two days when nothing fell into his trap. Ignoring Forrest's protests, he mounted a formal assault of Fort Donelson which was bloodily repulsed and returned, having accomplished nothing but some heavy casualties.

His insubordination and his inability to maintain an objective were again displayed in the autumn of the following year, when Sherman was patiently manoeuvring to get the slow-moving, slow-thinking Hood out of Atlanta without a costly frontal assault or the tedium of a siege. Both sides tried the effect of a large-scale raid deep into enemy territory to cut railway communications; and both attempts lamentably failed. Hood sent Wheeler with the bulk of his cavalry north-westwards to cut Sherman's line; and this he successfully did, just south of Jackson and not many miles forward of Chattanooga. He then, however, went off on his own into east Tennessee, where he accomplished nothing; and his railway demolitions were so trivial that they were repaired within a couple of days. A similar fate befell Sherman's attempt at a counter-stroke. His first was a simultaneous raid down both sides of the railway. It was conceived on too small a scale and inflicted little damage, and both wings were caught and badly mauled by Confederate cavalry on their way back. The second, when Kilpatrick was sent with the bulk of the cavalry on a much wider and deeper sweep, achieved more fame than it deserved. Kilpatrick certainly carried out his manoeuvre impeccably, covering in a wide circle some four hundred miles in sixteen days and bringing his whole force back to base intact. But the four miles of damage which he had done to the railway twenty-five miles south-east of Atlanta and which he claimed had put it out of action for at least ten days was, in fact, easily repaired within two. Had a man of Forrest's varied talents been in command the results might have been catastrophic for Hood; and Sherman's army would have been saved several weeks of ponderous manoeuvre.

Forrest and Morgan were the only two generals who right from the start adopted the tactic of using their horses for movement only and fighting on foot. Even on the Southern side most of them only reluctantly accepted the idea that in modern war mounted infantry were a much more useful tool than old-fashioned cavalry. Jeb Stuart, one of the most dashing of them, clung on for as long as he could to the use of the sabre and the massed charge, dismounting his troops only when it was necessary to hold a piece of ground until infantry came up to relieve him. But neither he nor anyone else ever succeeded in using cavalry with any effect in close co-operation with infantry and artillery in the thick of a set-piece battle;[5] and by 1863, when infantry on both sides had formed the settled habit of entrenching themselves, whether in defence or to hold ground gained in attack, even Jeb Stuart had to accept the inevitable. The sabre was retained for the increasingly rare minor engagement against enemy cavalry; and even the troopers learnt to throw up hasty breastworks from behind which they could hold off enemy infantry with their carbines or rifles.

Simultaneously with this development of the use of exclusively mounted forces for long-distance raids, the American generals evolved an entirely new technique for using large masses of cavalry as a component of a lightly equipped force of all arms to operate independently of the main army against an enemy's flank or rear. Speed, surprise and secrecy were the essential elements in such an operation; and all three depended on the intelligent employment of large cavalry formations. They could move fast enough to take the enemy completely by surprise and seize ground which threatened to enfilade his main position or menaced his communications, so compelling him to dissipate his main force in an effort to dislodge them, and could hold it for long enough to let their own infantry come up to take over. Spread out agressively they could mask the size and movements of the force behind them; and, skilfully manoeuvred, they could threaten so many different points simultaneously as to leave the enemy guessing as to the real objective of the movement. These were the conceptions on which were based Stonewall Jackson's long string of brilliant victories in the Shenandoah Valley in May and June of 1862. But Jackson was killed a year later, at a moment when he and Lee might just have been able to force a compromise peace on the war-weary public of the North; and unfortunately for the Confederates, his mantle fell not on one of his own colleagues, but on the Union General Sheridan.

During the first two years of the war the Union cavalry had shown itself vastly inferior in training and morale to that of the Confederates. But by the spring of 1894, when the war reached its final climax, it was easily the equal of its opponents and probably superior as a fighting force to any other cavalry force in the world. It was lucky enough to find itself at this critical moment under the command of a cavalry commander of genius in Sheridan; and they were fortunate to be under the overall command of Grant and Sherman, both of whom had fully grasped the value and the limitations of Cavalry Divisions trained in the tactics of mounted infantry. But for this, Sherman's advance in 1864 down the Atlanta railway and his capture of Atlanta might have been a slow and costly business and his final victory would have come too late to avert a political crisis in the North. In the pending Presidential Election the Democratic candidate, McClellan, threatened to oust Lincoln to the cry that the war had been a mistake from the start and should be ended forthwith. It was upon this that the Southerners, fighting now with their backs to the wall, pinned their last hopes of snatching a reasonable peace. It was Sherman's swift and, at the end, almost bloodless capture of Atlanta which doomed these hopes by sweeping Lincoln back into power on a tide of victorious enthusiasm; and Sherman owed his success very largely to the skill with which he adapted to the needs of large scale manoeuvre the methods of handling cavalry divisions evolved by Jackson and Sheridan on detached operations.

The other decisive influence on the evolution of a new type of both strategy and tactics in this war was the use of entrenchments whenever either infantry or dismounted cavalry were required to hold a piece of ground. This, like the transformation of cavalry into mounted infantry, sprang from the haste with which enthusiastic civilians had to be turned into efficient soldiers. Such men could easily be trained to carry out attacks across open ground with a dash and gallantry at least equal to that of any of the old world's regular infantry. But it was not easy to handle them in a mobile defence, when they were apt to lose both cohesion and nerve. Once entrenched, however, they would fight with the dogged courage and skill of veterans. Their casualties were reduced to a minimum even when subjected to heavy artillery bombardment and there were enough breech loaders in use to make entrenched troops almost invincible. The advantages were so obvious that entrenchment rapidly developed from a temporary expedient into a universal and invariable rule. From the moment that the breech-loading rifle appeared on the battlefield the more intelligent soldiers of all nations had foreseen the enormous advantage it would give to infantry acting on the defensive. The further advantage conferred by the protection of well-sited trenches made the cost of a frontal assault normally prohibitive. In the Civil War neither side could afford to take that risk except in the most desperate circumstances: the South because its reserves of manpower were insufficient; the North because a volatile public opinion was never wholeheartedly convinced of the necessity of the war and, especially after the institution of conscription, liable to be stampeded by heavy casualty lists into a clamour for peace at almost any price. Blundering head-on clashes between large armies after the old-fashioned pattern thus became very rare. Lee, momentarily deprived of his cavalry, and rather than abandon his invasion of Pennsylvania, risked one at Gettysburg in 1863 and suffered a shattering defeat which was probably the turning point of the war. The more flexible-minded generals set themselves to find some other method of dislodging an enemy from his position.

For the habit of entrenchment also had its dangers. An army on the defensive, especially when it was outnumbered, tended to become tied statically to its trenches, abandoning the initiative to the attacker who had in any case far more scope for manoeuvre. If it allowed the enemy to get right round its flanks, cut its communications, and invest it, it was doomed. This was what happened to Pemberton at Vicksburg when Grant moved against him for the second time. Instead of assaulting him, Grant slipped down the Mississippi past his guns and came in from the south, sealing off every avenue of escape. Lee in his last desperate attempt to save Richmond, tried to meet a similar threat by steadily extending his line to his vulnerable right until in the end he over-reached himself, sending General Pickett out to Five Forks with a mixed force in the hope that he, in turn, might get round Grant's left wing. Grant met the threat by sending Sheridan's cavalry divisions to halt the advance of Pickett's infantry and diverting an Infantry Army Corps to support him in his further operations. Dismounted, well entrenched, and with abundant ammunition, Sheridan's cavalry successfully held Pickett's infantry and inflicted heavy casualties on it. The next day, 1 April 1865, in what was to prove the last decisive battle of the campaign at Five Forks, Sheridan gave the most masterly demonstration of the power of a mixed force of all arms when intelligently employed. His dismounted cavalry went over to the offensive and pinned down Pickett's main force, while the infantry prised wide open the gap which had opened between Lee's main army and his detached wing. By the end of the day Pickett's force had been rolled up and dispersed in wild disorder and Lee's main position rendered untenable. He had to abandon Richmond; and it was largely owing to Sheridan's swift pursuit with his cavalry that he was brought to bay in his last entrenched position at Appomattox, cut off from sources of supply, and with no alternative but to surrender.

Forrest had shown that a purely cavalry force, if properly trained and armed for dismounted combat and in the elementary techniques of demolition, could sometimes have a decisive effect on the course of a campaign. Sheridan in turn had demonstrated the much more general utility of a mixed force of all arms, with a strong component of mounted infantry, operating at a distance from the main army but in close co-operation with it. It was Sheridan who showed that large formations of such cavalry could be used as an integral part of the main army, not for shock tactics on the field of battle, but to restore to it the power to manoeuvre and avoid the stalemate threatened by entrenchments and the growing destructiveness of infantry fire-power.

Moltke, foreseeing the dominance of the infantry battlefield by the Needle Gun and the Chassepot, is credited with devising to counter it a combination of the strategic offensive with defensive tactics by seizing ground vital to the enemy, and so throwing on him the dangerous burden of attack.[6] This may well have been his intention. But it is extremely difficult to find a single example of his doing so in his two great campaigns of 1866 and 1870. The history of both was one of continuous offensive, both strategic and tactical. Sherman, on the other hand, had brilliantly demonstrated precisely this method in his victorious advance to the capture of Atlanta in 1864 when Moltke was still learning for the first time the real capabilities of the Needle Gun in his campaign against the Danes.

The general conception underlying Sherman's strategy and the major tactics which went with it was the avoidance at all costs not only of a frontal assault on a dug-in enemy, but also of a direct advance to his main objective along the enemy's main axis. Even if successful, an attack along such lines could only drive an opponent back along his own supply lines, restoring his material losses as he went and replacing his casualties with troops left to guard his communications. Out of this there grew what later historians were to call the Strategy of the Indirect Approach.[7] Its essential elements were secrecy, speed, surprise and bewildering changes of direction. The positions which he took up were selected as far as possible to threaten two or more alternative objectives, so that his opponent was kept continually guessing as to his real intention; and when he was brought to battle it was generally on ground of his own choosing and on the defensive, with all its attendant tactical advantages. He was never able to display the full advantages of this new method of warfare in the grand manner during the Atlanta campaign because he was tied to a single railway line for supplies and reinforcements and the front on which he could manoeuvre was therefore severely limited. In the early stages, moreover, he was confronted by the experienced and wary General Johnston, who had a genius for selecting strong defensive positions coupled with an iron determination not to risk his inferior numbers in futile assaults and an uncanny sense of timing which constantly enabled him to slip out of a trap just before it closed on his line of retreat.

In consequence the opening stages of the Atlanta campaign moved slowly, and both generals found themselves under fire from their political bosses : Sherman because Washington badly wanted a spectacular success before the pending Presidential Election; Johnston because Southern public opinion was exasperated by constant withdrawals unjustified by any defeat in the field. Sherman had Grant to protect him from the politicians. Johnston, whose Fabian tactics might well have delayed the fall of Atlanta for the few vital extra weeks, had no such protection and was superseded by the dull, puzzleheaded Hood – probably the worst of the many military blunders of President Jefferson Davis in the course of the war. The methods by which Sherman used his cavalry divisions to outwit and out-general Hood are perhaps best illustrated by his final manoeuvres, when he had got to within thirty miles of Atlanta, and the Chattahoochee River with its broken bridges was the only natural obstacle between him and his goal. Hood was firmly entrenched on the further bank and Sherman had just been forced to detach two divisions to help contain Forrest's dangerous threats to his communications far to the north. But there was no pause in his operations. One cavalry division was sent downstream to reconnoitre possible crossing points, thereby drawing off the bulk of Hood's cavalry and at the same time screening the movement of infantry formations towards the opposite flank. His other cavalry division Sherman sent twenty miles upstream to cross the river and establish two bridgeheads from which, dismounted and hastily entrenched , they were able to hold off the enemy until the infantry, already on the march, came up to make them good. The whole army was then able to pass round Hood's right flank and force him back to Atlanta.

The capture of Atlanta itself without a costly assault or the long delay of a siege was merely a repetition of the same principle and method. Skilful manoeuvre got him round his opponents' flank and astride their supply line; the city became untenable and was abandoned without a struggle. In his march through Georgia

F*

to the sea he demonstrated another key principle: whenever possible to threaten more than one objective. By seizing Augusta where the railway forked right and left to Savannah and Charleston – both vital ports and nearly a hundred miles apart – he set his outnumbered and demoralised enemies an insoluble problem. They could not defend both, and by concentrating on one they must leave the other at his mercy. There was, of course, nothing fundamentally new in all this. There were few occasions on which Napoleon let himself be manoeuvred into a blundering, head-on clash in what was politically called 'a soldiers' battle'; and it led him to a near disaster at Borodino and a final one at Waterloo. An intelligent general could have gleaned all the essential ideas – Surprise, Deception, Speed of Movement, and continuous Bewilderment of the enemy – from a comparative study of Marlborough's Blenheim campaign and his appallingly costly frontal assault, undertaken for purely political reasons, at Malplaquet. What is surprising is that for more than three-quarters of a century hardly any of them did. Allenby showed something of the same talent in his Palestinian campaign in the First World War, as did his disciple and biographer, Wavell, in the early North African campaigns of the Second. It was not until 1928 that Sherman's strategy of the 'Indirect Approach' was thoroughly analysed and reduced to its first principles by Captain B. H. Liddell Hart;[8] and they were not to be put into practice with ruthless clarity and success until the battle of Alamein.

This was the more surprising because no nineteenth-century war was more closely followed than the American Civil War by observers, both official and unofficial, drawn from every power in the world with any military pretensions. There had been few new and decisive lessons to be learnt from the Crimea, or from the Italian campaign of 1859, and any large-scale war, even if it was conducted largely by amateurs, was a matter of intense interest. Of the technical observers it was the Engineers who came back with most useful information. This was, after all, a sphere in which the amateur was the more professional and could comfortably outmatch the military specialist; and it was a war in which the smashing up of railways, bridges, and tunnels, and their repair bulked particularly large in tactics. They brought back, therefore, especially from watching the Construction Corps of the

Northern army, some remarkable accounts of bridges of record length rebuilt in record time, and much valuable information on the techniques of railway demolition and repair, though in practice none of the European armies save the Russian made much use of it in their subsequent campaigns.[9] They also learnt a lot about the hasty construction of gun emplacements and field fortifications for both infantry and cavalry, all of which might have been of great value in the immediate future if the General Staffs had cared to make use of it.

On the technical side the gunner observers on both sides brought back little that was new. Except for the British, all were broadly agreed already that rifled, breech-loading cannon were the weapon of the future, once the technical construction problems were solved; though it is noteworthy that Robert E. Lee retained to the end a preference for smooth-bore guns for the support of fighting infantry, using them close up after the Napoleonic pattern and putting his faith in good, old-fashioned grape shot instead of shrapnel. But they brought back two lessons potentially immensely valuable. One was the devastating effect of the fire of rifled artillery on old-fashioned permanent fortifications of stone or brick. Two days' bombardment sufficed to destroy the elaborate casemates and gun emplacements of Fort Pulaski in April 1862, leaving the guns nakedly exposed on the crests of scarred and pitted walls; and a year later the walls of Fort Sumter themselves were reduced to piles of rubble. Yet as late as 1914 the Belgians were still staking everything on the belief that the solid fortifications of Liège, Namur, and Antwerp would hold up the Germans for long enough to give their Allies time to come to their relief. The other and opposite lesson was the almost total ineffectiveness of any bombardment, however intense and prolonged, against well-designed and properly dug field entrenchments and earthworks, especially when they were adequately provided with the sand-bagged 'bomb-proofs' which a later age called dug-outs. But this lesson, too, the European armies had to learn the hard way, by bitter experience. Time and again the Russians in the Balkans in 1877 and the British in South Africa in 1899 were to launch infantry assaults against entrenchments which had theoretically been destroyed by intense artillery fire, only to find their men exposed to the increasingly devastating fire-power of modern small arms from defenders who had suffered scarcely even discomfort from their heavy bombardment. Yet by 1914 none of the European General Staffs had digested the lesson, or set themselves to find an intelligent and constructive answer.

As far as infantry and cavalry tactics were concerned, it was the British observers who were most directly concerned and most heavily represented. This was not surprising. When Lee at last threw in his hand Moltke, after all, had already held in Denmark his dress rehearsal for the supreme test of the Austrian war which Bismarck was busily manufacturing out of the Schleswig-Holstein question. In any case, it was scarcely conceivable to a Prussian professional officer that he could have anything to learn from the antics of undisciplined and hastily trained American levies. The French were equally uninterested. Napoleon III, already engaged in his Mexican adventure, toyed with the idea of recognising the Confederate government, but had no intention of getting involved in their war. He was interested only in the prolongation of a struggle which kept the Monroe Doctrine in temporary abeyance while he established a new Emperor in Mexico. The nearest the French came to official representation in the theatre of war was a brief visit to both armies in 1861 by the Emperor's cousin, Prince Napoleon – the *Plon-Plon* of the caricaturists – a man with just enough knowledge and intelligence to make himself a perpetual military and diplomatic nuisance in the European Chancelleries. But he saw no fighting, and returned only with a poor opinion of the recruits on both sides whom he had watched on training exercises, though with a strong bias in favour of the North not wholly welcome to his government. The Prince de Joinville, a son of the deposed Louis Philippe and an ex-Rear Admiral, went out to watch over two nephews who joined the Northern army as volunteers and served in the Potomac campaign until strained relations between Paris and Washington in 1862 made it prudent for all three to return to France. Joinville thus missed the most interesting phase of the naval fighting, on which he might have had something important to say; and his pseudonymous article on the Peninsular Campaign in the *Revue des Deux Mondes* admirably suited the already declared views of the French High Command. Like all the early observers he was contemptuous of Northern staff work and greatly admired the energy and enthusiasm of the men who might, he thought, with proper and prolonged training, have been made first-class soldiers.

But in all essentials he was pedantically obscurantist. Rifled artillery was suited only to open country and at extreme ranges. In woods or at close range he preferred the old smooth bores, 'real fighting guns', firing round shot or 'a good dose of grape'. Cavalry actions fought out with cold steel were all too rare; and he did not believe that the 'costly and capricious amateur soldier who is called a volunteer' could ever match the properly trained professional.[10] All this was re echoed by Prince Napoleon's A.D.C., Lieutenant-Colonel Ferri Pisani, who achieved an undeserved reputation by being one of the first professionals to get into print a full-scale book on the opening stages of the war. He was equally contemptuous of the lack of professionalism of the staffs of both sides and of the quality of their troops. His answer to the question of whether volunteers, however enthusiastic, could compete with regular soldiers was: 'No, a thousand times no.' These judgements suited the French General Staff very well. Solidly entrenched in the glories of the first Napoleon and fresh from their own deceptive 1859 triumphs in Italy, they had deliberately staked their whole national future on the ability of a small army of long-service professionals to defeat even large masses of short-service conscripts and reservists. For them, moreover, the whole concept of the *Levée-en-masse* of revolutionary days was politically unacceptable; and after Sedan, when Gambetta's improvised armies had so unexpectedly and successfully prolonged the war, the French generals saw no reason to look across the Atlantic for lessons which they believed already out of date. For them it became an axiom after 1871 that the best improvised armies the world had ever seen were those of Gambetta; and they saw no reason to look back beyond 1871 for instruction in tactics, training or strategy. It was a mistake which was to lead the *École de Guerre* along many dangerous paths in the years before 1914.

The Austrians and Russians ought to have been more directly interested, since both faced the intractable problems involved in the creation at short notice of hitherto unprovided reserve armies out of the peasant masses who had escaped conscription. Freiherr von Henikstein had been frustrated for years in his ambition to build a volunteer reserve out of this material by the Austrian government's fear of 'arming the masses', and when, in 1866, he had suddenly to form his 'fifth battalions' he faced all the same problems as the American generals in 1861. Unfortunately official Austrian observation of the Civil War had been minimal. Both from the Empire and from South Germany there had been soldiers of fortune serving with both American armies. But no use was made of their potentially invaluable experience of the methods by which an army of that sort could be quickly improvised and protected from sacrificial casualties until it had learnt to fight as well as any body of professionals. Absorbed in the delusion that the secret of success for infantry lay exclusively in the bayonet charge, they ignored the lesson, which the American generals learnt the hard way in 1861 and 1862, that infantry on the defensive must be entrenched to avoid the demoralising casualties inflicted by modern fire-power. Benedek himself had to learn it in a few weeks the same hard way from his disastrous defeats at the Silesian mountain passes; and at Königgrätz he had both infantry and guns sufficiently dug in to defy all the frontal assaults of Prince Frederick Charles.

But Königgrätz was a disaster; and the lesson was again forgotten as the Austrian generals, like everybody else, became hypnotised by Moltke's spectacular successes in France. All tactical thinking became increasingly subservient to the precepts and practice of Berlin; and this tendency was strongly reinforced after 1879, when Bismarck at last achieved his dream of a permanent Dual Alliance between the two great German Empires. By 1914 the Austrian army had virtually become an appanage of the German Empire, and Field-Marshal Conrad von Hötzendorf would take his orders from Berlin. The Russians did a little better since some of their generals clearly profited from a study of the tactical achievements of the great American cavalry leaders like Forrest and Sheridan.[11] But they still paid no attention at all to the problems involved in the organisation of a competent reserve from their bottomless resources of illiterate peasants. Both in 1877 and in 1905 they were to throw these into battle armed and equipped only, and with no drill, training, or preparation for the ordeals which lay before them.

The British, in contrast, were intensely interested in everything they could learn in America. As a result of the shocks of the Crimea and the Mutiny they had committed themselves to providing home defence in the event of a major crisis, and reinforcements for a heavily engaged regular army overseas, to a large body of Volunteer infantry and Yeomanry cavalry for whom there was to be no intensive period of military training at all. Everything had to be learnt in spare time in drill halls; and they badly needed to know the armament and tactics best suited to such a force. A swarm of observers, official and unofficial, visited and accompanied the armies of both sides. The immediate result was a great, but unfortunately short-lived enthusiasm for the novel tactics developed by all arms and the study of the application by fresh minds to fundamental strategic principles which had not altered since the beginning of recorded history. It stimulated during the next twenty-five years a vast literature of books, articles, lectures, and military manuals, all of which drew their inspiration partially, and sometimes wholly, from the events of the American war.

In the resultant cacophony of conflicting observations and conclusions the great majority of those British officers who were able to visit the battlefields came back merely confirmed, and even strengthened in the preconceived ideas and prejudices with which they had set out. Most of them dismissed tactical innovations as the improvisations of generals, themselves inexperienced, who had to build armies out of half-trained volunteers and conscripts. The reports of the official observers sent out by the Gunners and Sappers, some of them extremely shrewd and penetrating, were classified as 'Confidential' and so did not find their way into print. In the end most of them were pigeon-holed in the War Department and forgotten. Then, of course, there were the comments, mostly valueless, of the inevitable sprinkling of amateur strategists and politicians who paid short visits to one or other of the fronts. The most important was Lord Hartington, who might a little unfairly be described as the British equivalent of *Plon-Plon*. He made no serious study of the war and reached no profound conclusions. But he acquired an undeserved reputation for military expertise which was to exercise a dangerous influence on British military operations whenever his social and political eminence landed him in the Cabinet.

Among the diehards, curiously enough in view of his later encouragement of the more enlightened observers, was Garnet Wolseley, the future Commander-in-Chief. He took a couple of months' leave to pay clandestine visits to the Headquarters of both Lee and Stonewall Jackson and returned with a life-long hero-worship for Lee – 'the ablest soldier of my day' and 'a highly cultivated military genius' – views which incidentally, when published years later, infuriated General Sherman. He was, nevertheless, still convinced in 1889 that the judgements of reformers who would transform cavalry into mounted infantry were destructively dangerous and would turn the mounted soldier into a Jack of all trades expert in none of them. At the same time he also expressed the view that trenches encouraged 'a very dangerous tendency to unfit soldiers for all rapid offensive action'. He did gradually modify these opinions under the influence of reformist publications and lectures, but too late to have any effective impact on regimental training and tactics. He was, in any case, mainly preoccupied with the delicate question of the relations of a democratic government with the military commanders in the field. The American generals on both sides were ceaselessly bedevilled by Presidential interference with their plans; and this was the subject of his only published work on the Civil War – an article in the *North American Review* in 1889. It was written with some bitterness, since he, himself, was still smarting from his failure to relieve Gordon at Khartoum in 1884, which he attributed entirely to the 'cant and prejudice' of Gladstone and Hartington which had constantly frustrated his plans. It was in that year, too, that Hartington topped his iniquities by presiding over a Commission which severely curtailed Wolseley's own powers as Commander-in-Chief.[12]

Surprisingly, the effect of all these contemptuous and not very penetrating judgements, as they filtered back to England from 1862 onwards, was to stimulate something of a renaissance in British military thinking. They were avidly studied by men who had not personally been present, and drew quite different conclusions from their records. As early as 1864 Sir Patrick

MacDougall, the first Commandant of the newly formed Staff College at Camberley, was incorporating examples from America in his book, *Modern Warfare as Influenced by Modern Artillery*; and over the years, thanks to the studies and patient experiments of a junior engineer officer as he rose steadily in rank to reach the head of his profession as Sir Thomas Fraser, the new skills developed by the American Sappers, particularly in bridging, were gradually incorporated without fanfare or fuss into the official training manuals. On the other hand the conclusions of the British Sappers on the novel use of railways for supplying armies over great distances were less intelligent. They took the view that a single-track line, if adequately equipped with sidings, could serve very well for an army on the defensive, but would be useless for the nourishment of a great offensive. This was to ignore Sherman's brilliant Atlanta campaign which depended throughout on a long single line of railway. The considerable volume of ephemeral literature on this theme was, however, so swiftly overlaid by the far more sophisticated work of Moltke's railway *Abteilung* in the brilliant offensives of 1866 and 1870 that it almost immediately ceased to be relevant. Like MacDougall and Fraser, General Sir Edward Hamley merely took the American war in his stride when in 1866, after a spell as Professor of Military History at the Staff College, he published his monumental volume, *The Operations of War,* which was to become almost a bible for Staff College graduates for more than fifty years. The operations of Grant and Lee, Sherman and Stonewall Jackson were incorporated among his minute studies of decisive campaigns throughout the ages just as further illustrations of the fact that the art of warfare consisted in the correct application of a few basic and immutable principles to constantly changing tactical and technical situations.

Hamley's doctrine was, of course, profoundly true. But for the cavalry and infantry the correct application of those basic principles to the startling innovations of the American generals was extremely difficult, and on two essentials – the proper use of the cavalry and the importance of field entrenchments to the infantry – bitter controversy was to rage until the disaster of the first World War put a final end to the Age of Moltke. One of the first in the field, in 1867, and by far the most revolutionary was

Major – later General Sir Henry–Havelock, who saw nothing of the Civil War, since he was busy fighting Maoris in New Zealand. He had distinguished himself at Lucknow and won a Victoria Cross at Cawnpore; and in 1858 he was already experimenting successfully in India with the use of cavalry as mounted infantry. The accounts of the exploits of the American cavalry commanders thus merely abundantly confirmed conclusions which he had already reached independently. His final and fanatically held view was that in territory open enough to allow room for manoeuvre and in face of the rising fire-power of modern infantry and artillery 'sabre cavalry' were totally out of date. He preached this conclusion with a fervid intolerance which, though it did no damage to his military career, made them totally suspect to higher authority. His supporters were dubbed by the senior cavalry officers the 'Young Turks', and his practical impact on the British was in consequence in the end almost negligible.

Far more effective in terms of actual achievement were the writings of the Canadian Lieutenant-Colonel George T. Denison, who had already made himself a favourite of Wolseley's by his dashing leadership of cavalry in the Irish disturbances of 1866. He also had the good fortune later to talk at length with several of the defeated Confederate generals who were sulking in Canada after the peace. He was less extremist than Havelock and would have kept a quarter of the cavalry armed and trained on the traditional pattern. But in landscapes similar to those of Canada he was convinced that mounted soldiers should rely mainly on fire-power and use their horses only for mobility. Because his views were more moderately expressed than Havelock's polemics his influence on the future conduct of military operations was far greater. In 1874 he won a prize offered by the Grand Duke Nicholas for an essay on the history of cavalry; and there can be no doubt that his arguments helped to motivate the Russian High Command to train a large number of their Cossack regiments in the tactics of dismounted combat, and a smaller number in the elementary Sapper techniques of effective demolition of railway and telegraph lines, both of which were to play a decisive part in the Balkan War of 1877. What was more important for the future of the British Empire was that not only Canada, but Australia and New Zealand opted for Light Cavalry – the contemporary name for the old-time dragoon – in preference to the traditional Heavy Horse.

A man who had a greater, though unfortunately only a very temporary, influence on British military thinking than either of these was Captain Charles Chesney of the Royal Engineers, who followed Hamley as Professor of Military History at Camberley and who was one of the first to get a major work on the war into print.[13] His two volumes on the fighting in the Eastern States did not suggest that those campaigns revealed any new fundamental principles for the conduct of war. But together with his lectures they brought home to a whole generation of staff officers that the Virginian battles were not just messy encounters between 'armed and dangerous mobs', but serious operations handled in some cases by men of original genius, notably Sherman. More constructive and much more controversial was his conclusion that all strategical and tactical thinking must be adjusted to the fact that the habit of entrenchment, whether in defence or to hold ground gained in attack, had come to stay and was not just a concession to the weaknesses of volunteer soldiers. He agreed with MacDougall that the growing fire-power of modern artillery made it impossible for infantry to survive in the open, however well dispersed, unless they were properly dug in. He, like Denison, had the advantage over Havelock that he stated his views with a studied moderation. In consequence he even won over the highly conservative Commander-in-Chief. Summing up after a lecture of Chesney's to the Royal United Service Institution, the Duke of Cambridge said that what had most struck him was 'that in this war, and, I think, in all future wars, the spade must form a great element in campaigns'. 'Instant entrenchments', he thought, were 'a very great and new element in the features of war' thanks to 'the improvements in arms, both artillery and musketry'.[14]

Unfortunately for the future of the British army this promising period of active and constructive argument was almost immediately brought to an end by a wave of enthusiasm for all things German. Moltke's victories became an exclusive subject of study for all ambitious young officers; and a debased imitation of the *Pickelhaube* even became the standard head-dress for most English regiments. It was a trend which until the late 1880s was well nigh irresistible, though it aroused the irascible Wolseley, always aware that British armies normally confronted climates, enemies, and situations quite remote from those faced by continental generals, to advise Staff College students to 'copy the Germans as regards work and leave their clothes and their methods alone'. But in 1886 Wolseley, then Adjutant-General, discovered a young officer, a Captain G. F. R. Henderson, who had published an anonymous study of *The Campaign of Fredericksburg*. He was so impressed that he promoted Henderson and sent him as an instructor to Sandhurst; and five years later, on the strength of a detailed analysis of the battle of Spicheren which remains a military classic, gave him the key job, as a Lieutenant-Colonel, of Professor of Military History at Camberley.

Henderson was the last, and certainly the most profound of the pre-1914 British military thinkers who sought to apply the lessons of the American Civil War to the problems of the training and tactics best suited to the needs of Great Britain. On the immediate vital and controversial issues which still vexed cavalry and infantry commanders he was only a moderate reformer. He agreed broadly with Chesney about trenches. 'Good infantry', he wrote, 'sufficiently covered is, unshaken by artillery and attacked in front alone, absolutely invincible.' On the subject of cavalry tactics he hedged. Regiments armed, trained, and equipped on the Continental model were, he wrote, 'as obsolete as the Crusaders'. But he still thought there was a place for shock tactics and, perhaps a little inaccurately, judged that Civil War cavalry had 'struck the true balance'. At the same time in a remarkable output of publications and lectures, including his masterpiece on Stonewall Jackson, published in 1898, he covered the whole field of the military art, suggesting that works like Hamley's were too scientific and ignored the factors of morale and discipline, and of the quality of leadership, which were more important than all the theories of strategists and tacticians.

In comparison with the land operations, the naval activities of both sides in the Civil War were on a trivial scale. They occurred, moreover, at a time when all the world's admiralties had been plunged into a total confusion of thought and purpose by a vastly accelerated progress in the techniques of the engineering industry in three important spheres; in manufacture of improved iron and steel plate; the consequent rapid development in the range, calibre, and rate of fire of the guns available to the armed forces; and the evolution of marine engines which would drive ever heavier and larger ships at adequate speeds. The modest success achieved by the French ironclad floating batteries at Sebastopol had been sufficient to convince all but a few die-hard British admirals that the sea-going, ironclad, steam-driven battleship was the weapon of the future. In 1859 the French launched the *Gloire*, prototype of a fleet of such ships; and the British, hard on their heels, were building their first ironclad battleship, the *Warrior*.[15]

In this world of experimentation the US Navy had got left far behind. It was small by European standards and even its best ships were rapidly becoming out of date. Such as it was, almost the whole of it, together with the bulk of the American mercantile fleet, passed immediately into Northern hands. Only the important naval yard at Norfolk in Virginia went to the Confederates, the ships of the powerful squadron stationed there being set on fire and scuttled by their commanders. At sea the North thus had an overwhelming preponderance of force, with the added advantage that the great bulk of the sea-faring population came from Northern ports. Against this the government at Richmond had to improvise what it could out of its meagre industrial resources. Nevertheless this preponderance had far less effect on the outcome of the war than has sometimes been pretended. Even when every merchant ship capable of carrying guns had been fitted out as a cruiser, the fleet was still far too small effectively to blockade the three thousand miles of the Confederate coastline and halt the traffic of the great estuary harbours such as New Orleans and Mobile, Charleston, Savannah and Wilmington through which the South exported its cotton and tobacco and imported almost everything else which it needed.

During the first two years of the war even sailing ships were able to run the blockade; and though the ordinary citizens of the Southern States went short of luxuries such as tea, sugar, and coffee, there was no widespread privation and the armies were adequately supplied with all the weapons, munitions, and military stores which they needed. On the Gulf coast Admiral

Farragut, the one outstanding naval commander thrown up by the war, brilliantly achieved the capture of New Orleans by naval action alone, and so blocked the mouth of the Mississippi, the most important of all the great navigable waterways on which the South normally depended for the bulk of its internal commercial traffic. This also deprived the South of its most important industrial centre. But neither Farragut nor his successors could get control of Mobile and its bay until August 1864. Fast, specially built steamships were able to make substantial profits by blockade running down to the end of that year. It was the army which in the end achieved the strangulation of supplies which more than anything else broke the resistance of the South. By October 1864 all the east coast ports had been occupied except Charleston and Wilmington; and Charleston was closely and effectively blockaded by the fleet. Nevertheless adequate supplies for the army still came in through Wilmington until the end of the year.[16] Then the capture of these two ports combined with the effects of Sherman's devastation of Georgia and Carolina reduced soldiers as well as civilians to the point of near-starvation, desperately short even of bread and meat. The morale of Lee's army broke and the war was over.

With one exception, the naval activities of the Civil War were confined to shallow coastal waters, the great estuaries, and the hundreds of miles of the navigable rivers of the South. Almost the only ocean-going warships on either side were the fast, commerce-destroying cruisers which the Southern government had built by stealth in foreign yards, mostly British, such as the famous *Alabama,* the *Florida* and the *Shenandoah.* In all, nineteen of this class were built and commissioned, and between them they captured more than 200 North American merchant ships.[17] Their immediate effect on the course of the war was negligible. But the US mercantile fleet was virtually destroyed and in the long term their importance was considerable. In 1872 Great Britain was condemned by the Geneva Arbitration Board to pay the US government $15½ million in compensation for the damage they did. But in return she got the restoration for the next fifty years of the near monopoly of the world's carrying trade which she had wrested from the Dutch in the seventeenth century.

The river fighting in the west, on the Cumberland River and the Mississippi was an improvised affair on both sides. Their ships were river steamers and tugboats strengthened with thick oaken planks or iron armour plate, and fitted out as gunboats or rams. Their unconventional battles make a fascinating story of their own, but had no significance for the future of naval design or tactics. They were fought out with great dash and gallantry on both sides, but the Northerners were ultimately victorious, thanks mainly to their vastly superior output of iron and steel. They secured control of the lower reaches of the Cumberland and of a great stretch of the Mississippi, until they were brought to a halt by the batteries of the fortress of Vicksburg, which also halted the advance northwards of squadrons from Farragut's fleet off New Orleans. Insignificant for the remoter future, these operations nevertheless had a disproportionate, and even a decisive effect on the outcome of the whole war. Without this command of the river communications Grant could never have slipped his army across the river and back again to invest Vicksburg from the south and east and force its surrender on 4 July 1863. With that event the war in the far west was won; and from then on the Eastern States of the confederation had to fight it out alone.

In the east coast estuaries of the James and Roanoke Rivers, on the other hand, though there too everything was improvised, there were three episodes of colossal importance for the future of all the world's navies. The first, and by far the most important, was the single-ship action between the *Merrimac* and the *Monitor* – the first clash in all naval history of ironclad steamships and the most often described. After the loss of Norfolk and the Hampton shipyards, and the scuttling of the powerful squadron based there, the Northern navy clung obstinately to what was to become its most important anchorage under the guns of Fortress Monroe at the mouth of the Sound in the hope of closing this vital bolthole for blockade runners. In this they were dangerously successful; and it was Mallory, the very able Confederate Secretary for the Navy, who perceived that only a powerful ironclad fleet could break this strangle-hold. What was more, the first side to get a squadron of such ships afloat would inevitably, he thought, win the war at sea, with incalculable, but almost certainly decisive effect on the final outcome of the war.

He gave orders, accordingly, for the construction of a number of such vessels in the first months of 1862. His main difficulties were purely technological. The rolling mills of Atlanta, which produced the permanent way for the Southern railway lines, could turn out plenty of rail quality iron sheeting from which inferior but temporarily adequate armour plating could be made. But there were none of the trained artificers nor the machines to produce marine engines powerful enough to drive the new, heavy ships he wanted. The weight of armour and guns made converted river steamers painfully slow, and none could make more than five knots. To meet this difficulty he tried raising the powerful steam frigate, *Merrimac,* scuttled by the enemy at Norfolk. Her masts were removed and her top deck was cut away and replaced with a powerfully armed and plated casemate of guns amidships. Over the whole there was a carapace of four-inch railway iron which extended two feet below the water line. Unfortunately he did not know that at the moment when she was abandoned her engines had just been condemned by US Navy inspectors and were due for immediate replacement. Several months under water had not improved them; and the vast weight which had been loaded on to her and her consequently increased draught made her as slow as the tug-boats and almost unmanoeuvrable. It took her over thirty minutes to make a complete turn.

In spite of all this, her appearance in the Sound on 8 March 1862 was dramatically effective. The most powerful units of the US Navy, lying in what had become its principal anchorage, were taken completely by surprise. Their most formidable ship, the *Cumberland,* was rammed and sunk, her shots bouncing ineffectually off the *Merrimac's* armoured shell. The *Congress* was sunk by gunfire and three other ships, scattering in panic, were driven ashore. The *Merrimac* had sustained no damage or casualties, save that she had left her ram broken off and embedded in the hull of the sunken *Cumberland.* She retired across the river for the night to repair the hole in her bows and returned confidently the next morning to finish off the Northern squadron. Two of the casualties of the night before had been refloated; but the *Minnesota* was still fast aground, and the *Merrimac* steamed straight for her, scarcely noticing close alongside her a curious projection above water of a circular structure which was at first thought to be a floating water tank. This was the sublimely propitious moment at which the epoch-making *Monitor* intervened to alter the whole future course of naval history.

It was inevitably impossible to keep secret the reconstruction of the *Merrimac* and the simultaneous adaptation of two equally powerful ships at New Orleans. The Northern government, in panic, invited tenders for a ship which could meet the threat. But when they came to consider three possible designs they were already three months behind in this early armaments race; and there was only one which could possibly be completed in the time available. This was the product of the eccentric Swedish genius, John Ericsson, which outraged every prejudice and principle of the US Navy chiefs, but caught the imagination of President Lincoln. Ericsson, after quarrelling successively with the US, British, and French governments and building a most successful small ship for the Danes,[18] had finally resettled in New York. He now dug out of his files a project for an 'aquatic device' produced thirty years before when he was a young officer in the Swedish Navy. This, furbished up, he now offered as 'an impregnable steam battery of light draught, suitable to navigate the shallow rivers and harbours of the Confederation.'[19] It contained hardly a single conventional feature; and Ericsson acquired more than forty new basic patents from its construction. But it was, in spite of all the embodied novelties, an essentially simple design and easy to build quickly, whereas its most powerful conventional rival, already under construction, was not due for completion until early 1863. This was the factor which decided the issue. Laid down at New York in October 1861, it was launched within 101 days from the signing of the contract, somewhat haphazardly completed by February 1862 and arrived in the James estuary, providentially for the North, on the evening of the *Merrimac*'s first triumphant sortie.

Ericsson christened his new ship the *Monitor* since it was a conscious rebuke to the faulty conceptions underlying the designs of the *Gloire* and the *Warrior*. The hull was a flat, floating platform 172 feet long with a lightly armoured deck less than two feet above the water line; and the deck armour was extended downwards over the sides to provide a canopy of five-inch thick plating protecting the sides and the screw. It was, as a contempor-

ary described it, 'an elongated shallow tin pan' which when finally loaded, drew only ten and a half feet as against the
Merrimac's twenty-two. On this floating platform there were only
two structures : a heavily armoured pilot house forward; and
amidships a revolving turret, protected all round by eight layers
of one-inch thick wrought-iron plates rivetted together, and fitted
with two 11-inch Dahlgren guns smooth-bored to fire solid shot.
There were also two funnels, but these were retracted before
going into action. The conservative Navy Board's stipulation that
there should be masts, spars, sails and rigging Ericsson simply
ignored. Thanks to the essential simplicity of her design and the
fact that she had only two guns to operate, the *Monitor* was
extraordinarily economical in manpower : a total complement of
twelve officers and forty-five seamen, all, incidentally, volunteers,
as against the *Merrimac*'s crew of 320 mostly drafted soldiers.
Even so, their living quarters were appallingly cramped, since so
much complex machinery had been fitted into so small a space.
With her funnels up the *Monitor* could make nine knots to the
Merrimac's five. When they were retracted her speed was halved.
In action she was thus slightly the slower ship but, thanks to her
lighter draught, she was considerably easier to manoeuvre.

The famous four-hour action between these two novel mon-
strosities has been often described and was so devoid of dramatic
incident that it merits no detailed description. Both started with
an accidental handicap. *Merrimac*, expecting to meet wooden
ships only, had restocked her magazines entirely with shell and
carried no solid shot. *Monitor* had the solid shot needed to shatter
armour plate, but its impact was fatally reduced by the timidity
of the Northern gunnery experts who, mistrusting the specific-
ations of the Dahlgren manufacturers, had issued only half-
strength propellant charges. Both, moreover, had scarcely trained
gun crews. In consequence the two circled clumsily, firing very
slowly, sometimes at ranges of only a few yards without inflicting
any visible decisive damage. Not a man was killed in either ship,
and the only serious casualty was the *Monitor*'s Captain, knocked
unconscious and temporarily blinded by a direct hit on the slot in
the pilot house through which he was observing the battle. Many
of the *Merrimac*'s shells missed the small target of the *Monitor*'s
turret altogether, many more glanced off the rounded sides before

exploding, and those which hit it squarely made no impression on the eight-inch armour. Every shot the *Monitor* fired was a hit. But her machinery was so clumsy and her gun crews were so unhandy that she only fired twenty-seven in the whole four hours. In the end the action was broken off by mutual consent and both ships steamed back to their anchorages.

In most histories this famous action is described as 'drawn', or 'indecisive'. In fact it was a great victory for the North and quite decisive. As the *Monitor* hove to again beside the grounded *Minnesota* the frigate's crew cheered themselves hoarse. Lincoln sat beside the wounded Captain's bed that night with tears running down his face and went back to Washington to order the construction of another twenty Monitors. At that moment only the *Merrimac's* officers, sadly surveying broken armour plate and splintered timbers, knew how complete their defeat had been. With her funnel gone and her speed reduced to a crawl, their ship was barely able to regain her berth in the Norfolk yards which she was never again to leave. They reckoned that, had the *Monitor's* guns been given their full propellant charge, her armour would have been shattered and she would have been destroyed. But Lincoln, like the crew of the *Minnesota,* did know that an effective answer had been found to the threat that a squadron of the *Merrimac* type might break the blockade of the Southern ports.

The *Monitor* thus passed her name on not merely to a new class of vessel, but to a wholly new kind of ship which was to remain in useful service for coastal bombardment and defence in the world's navies for the better part of a century.[20] Naturally, as they streamed out from the dockyards, Ericsson steadily improved his designs. All the new ships were more sea-worthy than the original, which very soon foundered in a gale off Cape Hatteras. Some had two turrets instead of one. All had the pilot house moved from the deck to the top of the turret, which gave the guns an all-round field of fire and also made speaking-tube communication between the Captain and the executive officer in the turret much easier; and all had at least one of the 15-inch guns which Ericsson had originally wanted. Some of the later ones were larger and of deeper draught, safely navigable in deeper waters and invaluable for blockade purposes. They could never compose an effective fleet of ocean-going battleships; and they proved useless against coastal forts. But they admirably fulfilled their immediate task. Had Britain or France intervened, as they were much tempted to do, to break the blockade and join the South, a squadron of monitors would almost certainly have been capable of sending their entire navies to the bottom. With the revolving turret, moreover, Ericsson bequeathed to the remoter future what was to become an essential feature of every important warship in the world.

The Confederate government struggled gallantly on, producing improved versions of the *Merrimac* – the *Arkansas* put together in an almost uninhabited swamp by the Yazoo River, and the *Albermarle* rebuilt in a Georgia cornfield. But none had any success against the monitors. In Savannah Sound the *Atlanta* was wrecked and driven aground by five shots at a range of 300 yards from the monitor, *Weehawken.* The *Albermarle,* on the other hand, had a considerable impact on the course of the war. She cleared the Roanoke of Northern gunboats and forced the surrender of the besieged Union garrison at Plymouth; and since the passage over the bar to the extensive Albermarle Sounds was too shallow even for monitors, she had the blockading Northern squadron of wooden ships at her mercy. Before she could complete her task, however, she was sunk by another new device of the utmost significance for the remoter future: an elementary torpedo, indistinguishable in modern terms from a primitive kind of mine, carried on a spar in the bows of a small steam pinnace. A combination of luck and daring enabled Lieutenant Cushing of the US Navy to slip up the Roanoke under cover of darkness and explode his new weapon against the side of the *Albermarle,* sending her to the bottom. He himself was the only survivor of this suicidal enterprise; and he had opened a new chapter in naval history.

In the desperate struggle to break the close blockade of Charleston the South too produced an innovation of incalculable importance: the first submarine which actually functioned successfully. While the *Merrimac* was being built, the North had already experimented with 'submersibles', but without success. Devoted Southerners in Charleston, after many deliberately suicidal atempts, did produce the *David*, a tiny, hand-driven craft submerged by movable side fins, carrying its explosive charge in the snout. They were hermetically sealed, so that even an experimental dive was certain death by asphyxiation for the crew of four. But enough heroes were found to carry through the experiments; and in the end one *David* did succeed in sinking the US *Housatonic,* its crew perishing inevitably in the explosion which destroyed the ironclad. These three devices – the revolving turret, the torpedo, and the submarine – were the Civil War's contribution to the future of naval warfare; and two of them, at least, still plague the naval designers and planners of today.

6 The Aftermath of Moltke's Great Age

Moltke was, of course, a man of genius; and his theories, his methods, and his achievements were to dominate all military thinking for nearly half a century. But the limits within which his genius operated creatively were narrow, though he was much more widely cultivated than his single-minded successor, Schlieffen. Very early in life he had decided that all problems could be solved by mathematics. His original contribution to the science of modern warfare was, in consequence, almost wholly organisational. The Great General Staff and the permeation of the whole army with its officers and its doctrines was his personal creative achievement, and it dominated the battlefields because nobody else had yet thought of it. The inspiration of all the other elements which contributed to his spectacular victories was drawn from an intelligent study of the past. His strategical principles, for example, were derived directly from Napoleon as interpreted by Clausewitz. Later theorists, and in particular the High Command of the German army, were to make much of the thesis that Moltke's central object was the envelopment of the enemy's main army, whereas Napoleon aimed always at its disintegration.[1] Having pinned down the enemy with his main force, Napoleon would use an independent 'mass of manoeuvre' to threaten his flank or rear and so force him to weaken his main position and give the opportunity for a devastating blow which would throw his whole army into confusion. In this the theorists misread their history. Both in 1866 and 1870 Moltke's aim was purely Napoleonic, and at Königgrätz he did in fact achieve an almost pattern Napoleonic victory. The Crown Prince – the 'mass of manoeuvre' – came in on Benedek's right flank in the nick of time and so weakened and demoralised the troops of his centre, hitherto impregnably established on the heights, that they folded up and were only saved from annihilation by the heroism of their gunners and their two divisions of reserve cavalry.

Moltke undoubtedly intended to achieve much the same sort of thing against the French in 1870. He was frustrated by the insubordination of Steinmetz, whose 1st Army was supposed to be the 'mass of manoeuvre', but which got so deeply involved in the unintended battle at Spicheren that it could not be extricated from the main battlefront in Lorraine. Thereafter events moved so fast that there was no time to reformulate a plan of campaign. Bazaine, by his failure to exploit his tactical victories in the opening phases and his reluctance to leave the shelter of the fortress of Metz, virtually forced his own investment and the elimination from the war of France's finest field army. MacMahon, urged on by politically motivated telegrams from the Empress and the War Council in Paris, thrust himself into the trap of Sedan; and with the then overwhelming numbers available to the Germans, it was plain commonsense to besiege Paris rather than risk a costly assault. Envelopment, which was to become an obsession with his successors, was, in fact, not a new strategic concept, but merely a predicament forced on Moltke by the course of events. To say this is in no way to derogate from the brilliant craftsmanship he showed as he methodically remedied the mistakes and exploited the opportunities in the course of the campaign. It is to insist only that his strategic ideas were not new but age-old and entirely sound.

Similarly all the so-called revolutionary changes introduced into the conduct of modern war by Moltke were, in fact, the highly intelligent and systematic application of previous lessons. American generals, for example, had been demonstrating the value of rail communications in military operations for five years before the new Prussian army was launched into its first major war. He found the Needle Gun to hand and brilliantly exploited the opportunities it opened up; but the superiority of the Chassepot took him by surprise at a moment when events were moving too fast for him to adapt his infantry tactics in time to avoid punitive casualties. Yet the essential lesson that the growing fire-power of infantry on the defensive made them virtually invincible to any frontal assault had really been clear since the Minié rifles of the thin red line of the 93rd Highlanders had halted the massive charge of the Russian heavy cavalry at Balaclava. Every battle of the American Civil War had rammed that lesson home, though it was to take the world's general staffs three-quarters of a century to digest and apply it.

The comparative failure of his own artillery in 1866 and the timely provision of all-steel, breech-loading field guns by Herr Krupp enabled Moltke to overcome the shortcomings both of his subordinate commanders and of the tactical training and equipment of his own infantry. It was, indeed, one of his greatest assets that he could learn, in all humility, as much from his own mistakes as from those of others. But, in the sphere of artillery, technical invention was moving at such a pace that any advantage gained was liable to be outdated at any moment by a rival; and the whole science of gunnery was to be an uncertain field of speculation and experiment for many years after 1871. To the two main lessons of the American Civil War – the immense value of cavalry if used not as shock troops, but as mounted infantry, and the greatly increased defensive power of entrenched infantry – Moltke paid no attention at all. Entrenchment had no importance for the sort of war he proposed to fight until his enemy was safely invested; and it does not seem to have occurred to him that Von Rheinbaben's Cavalry Division could have intervened far more decisively on Alvensleben's left flank at Vionville if it had been properly equipped and trained to fight as mounted infantry.

The total effect of all this was that Moltke's personal prestige and the spectacular nature of his great victories tended to have an obscurantist rather than an enlightening effect on the military thinking of succeeding generations, because it overlaid the lessons, much more important for the future, of the American Civil War. There were to be two more wars between major powers before the century ended; and although they taught no new lessons, they rammed home all the old ones. They were conducted by generals who altogether lacked Moltke's skill and adaptability and who were bewildered and baffled by the revolutionary events which, between 1860 and 1871, had altered the whole conception of the part of warfare more fundamentally and irretrievably than even the campaigns of Napoleon I. Since all the campaigns of that period were fought against a background of rapid technical advances, they were all necessarily experimental; and the lessons to be drawn from them were neither so compact nor so complete as to enable a new Clausewitz to summarise clearly the conclusions to be drawn from them and formulate a new doctrine. The full implications of the achievements of the American generals and of Moltke and Roon had still to be worked out. The modern historian can perhaps see the Balkan campaigns of 1877–8 and the American experiences in Cuba ten years later as milestones on a disastrous road which was to lead ultimately to the horrifying concept of the 'war of attrition' brutally defined by von Falkenhayn in 1916, when he proposed to make the French 'bleed to death' in the vital salient at Verdun.[2] Properly regarded, however, the processes which led from 1870 to the indescribably greater horrors of 1914–18 must be treated not as curtain-raisers for the First World War, but as a prolongation of the experimental period of the mid-century – the aftermath, in fact, of the Age of Moltke. In such an analysis the innumerable campaigns of the colonial powers and the internecine conflicts of the emergent Balkan nations are of little account. It was in the major wars of the intervening period that the strategical and tactical lessons of 1860–70 were to be worked out to conclusions which were both illogical and disastrous.

The first of these important conflicts was the Russian attack on Turkey in 1877, which combined both the main aspects of nineteenth-century warfare.[3] It was an attempt to use war simultaneously as an instrument of politics and as means of imperial expansion. It had always been clear that Russia's expansion to the south and south-east could not be the process of comparatively easy erosion by detachments of the standing army such as had won her control of all northern Asia. In the Balkans the turgid nationalism of the already largely autonomous Serbs, Greeks, Roumanians, Montenegrins, and Albanians made any policy of large-scale annexations virtually impossible and certainly inadvisable, quite apart from the fact that it would inevitably arouse the inveterate hostility of Great Britain and Austria, both of whom still considered the integrity of the Ottoman Empire as a vital objective. Even Bulgaria, more rigidly enslaved than the others by its close proximity to Constantinople, would become intractable if denied a large share of Macedonia and free access to the Aegean. A more subtle infiltration was therefore devised, by which Pan-Slavism and the Tsar's claim to be the Protector of all Orthodox Christians might create a number of small states whose mutual jealousies and fears of both Turkey and Austria would compel them to become virtually Russian dependencies. The capture of Constantinople and the domination of the northern shores of the Bosphorus and Dardanelles might then be a practical possibility; and a simultaneous advance from the Caucasus along the southern coast of the Black Sea and through to the Aegean would then at last give Russia the unimpeded access to the Eastern Mediterranean which she had so long desired.

The Balkan insurrections of 1875 and 1876, together with a large-scale massacre of Bulgarians which aroused the horror of the British public and made it impossible for even a Conservative government to come to the help of the Turks, seemed to offer a golden opportunity to achieve all this. Austria was prepared to promise benevolent neutrality in the temporary and wholly mistaken belief that a completely independent Serbia would be a more accommodating neighbour than the Turks and would allow her what she, too, longed for – free access to the Aegean. Bismarck, absorbed in the consolidation of the gains of 1871, had no reason to interfere. The Tsar, therefore, could feel reasonably safe in ordering in November 1876 a tentative and partial mobilisation of his newly reconstituted army; and on 24 April 1877 he announced to the world that, all peaceful means of halting the oppression of his fellow Slavs and co-religionists in the Balkans having been exhausted, he had no alternative but to order his army to cross the Roumanian frontier on to what was still, theoretically, Turkish territory. At the same time he gathered a much smaller force for an assault on the narrow Armenian frontier at the other end of the Black Sea with the aim of seizing the great Turkish fortresses of Kars and Erzerum.

From the point of view of the generals who had planned the great reorganisation in 1874 the diplomatic opportunity came six years too soon. They had based their system on a rough imitation

Map 3. The Balkans, 1878

of the German military *Kreise,* dividing the whole Empire into Military Circumscriptions, though on a geographical pattern much less tidy than that of the Germans owing to the varying density of the populations. They differed, too, from the other great European armies in making the Division rather than the Army Corps the basic formation of their organisation. The generals commanding Circumscriptions had to find the two divisions and the ancillary troops to make up a front-line Corps; but they themselves were only glorified Depot commanders. On mobilisation they had to form the divisions of trained reservists to make up the Reserve Army and to find, on orders from the Ministry of War, the *Ersatz* from the remainder to replace casualties as far as possible in the divisions drawn from their own Districts.

In 1877 they could not possibly have provided the numbers required on paper by the Ukase of 1874. As far as the regular army was concerned, this did not much matter, since Russia's precarious finances, her sketchy transport system and the vast distances involved made it quite impossible to concentrate anything like 900,000 men on one frontier. For the Reserve the situation was far more serious, since there were only three yearly classes available instead of the nine on which the calculations had been based. They scraped together enough to form a Reserve Army of some 200,000 which, in accordance with the fundamental principles of the scheme, had to be kept intact in case of unforeseen emergencies. But there were no trained reservists left for the replacement of casualties. The Tsar was thus forced to call out the first 'Ban' of the Militia – the 180,000 young men who had drawn lucky numbers in the 1874 ballot. These, hastily uniformed, equipped, armed, and given at most a fortnight's drill, were rushed straight into battle to replace the very heavy losses in the front line in the early stages of the war. In the three disastrous assaults on Osman Pasha's army at Plevna there were regiments which lost over 75 per cent of their total strength. From the handful of survivors in each battalion the raw recruits had to learn musketry, tactics, and fieldcraft in the thick of hard-fought battles; and the result, as in the days of the first Napoleon, was a serious falling-off in the fighting efficiency of the infantry.

To make all these largely unavoidable difficulties worse, the Tsar and his advisers seriously underestimated the formidable fighting quality of Turkish infantry on the defensive, and the problems involved in maintaining a field army at the far end of a narrow, 500 mile corridor, exposed to attack from either flank. The distances which the Russian forces had perforce to cover by road were, of course, much longer. Their main column, moving directly on Constantinople from Kishineff on the Roumanian frontier via the Shipka Pass had to march 750 miles. The column protecting their right flank, going by Sofia and Philippopolis, had a march of 970 miles. All this should have been familiar enough to the Russian General Staff, since the same venture had already been undertaken fifty years earlier, when General Debitch had arrived almost within artillery range of Constantinople in 1829, with a striking force so depleted by the need to guard his long line of communications that he dared not risk a final assault. In 1828, moreover, Debitch had the inestimable advantage that the Russian fleet dominated the Black Sea, so that he could advance down the coastal road through Varna with his left flank secure and drawing his supplies and reinforcements by sea from Odessa and Sebastopol. In 1877 the Grand Duke Nicholas had no such advantage. Though the Russians had reasserted in 1871 their right to naval bases and a fleet in the Black Sea, they had not had time to build anything to match the formidable ironclads bought by the Turks, at considerable expense, from Great Britain.

Once across the Danube south of Bucharest the Grand Duke had therefore to move on a route further west than Debitch's with both his flanks exposed. On his left was a Turkish army 50,000 strong concentrated south of the Dobrudja within the quadrangle of the formidable fortresses of Rutchuk, Silistria, Varna, and Shumla. On his right, further away but much more dangerous, there was an army of 60,000 commanded by the only competent general the Turks possessed, Osman Pasha. If they brought in their troops from Egypt, concentrated all the garrisons scattered along the Danube and in the Balkan Mountains, and brought back the crack troops who were more or less permanently engaged in fighting the Montenegrins and Bosnians, the Turks could concentrate another 150,000 men to hold the Shipka Passes which were almost the last effective line of defence before Constantinople. Against such forces it was sheer folly for the Tsar to open the campaign by crossing the Dniester into Roumania with only four Army Corps: 200,000 fighting effectives who were reduced by illness, exhaustion, and the need to drop off detachments all along the line of communications, to some 180,000 when they reached the Danube.

In November 1876 the Tsar had mobilised only the six Army Corps drawn from the circumscriptions nearest to the Roumanian frontier. During the following winter he had brought forward three more from further afield – between 400 and 800 miles distant by rail. But three of these nine were immobilised throughout in defensive positions along the northern Black Sea coast; and of these only one division and one rifle brigade found their way into the theatre of operations. Once the Grand Duke had completed his march down the length of Roumania and forced a crossing of the Danube, he had to drop off two Corps to mask the Quadrilateral fortresses and another three to cover the undisclosed threat to his right flank. He had then only VIII Corps left for his main thrust southwards. Only then did the War Ministry mobilise the Guard and Grenadier Corps and four line divisions – some 120,000 men and 460 guns – and accept the offer of Prince Charles of Roumania to put his army of some 35,000 at their disposal, so bringing their numbers up to what at the outset might have won the war in one swift campaign, before the Great Powers had time for second thoughts and to organise a Congress to rob the Russians of their gains.

The campaign itself is a fascinating subject of study. What is interesting, however, to the student of the art of warfare is the extent to which the commanders on both sides had digested the lessons of Moltke's campaigns and of the American Civil War, and the fallacies in the generally accepted conclusions revealed by their own operations. Every great campaign produces not only valuable lessons for the future, but fallacies and misconceptions which lead the generals and troops of the future to disaster. In the war of 1877–8 the high command on both sides was fumbling and ineffective. Osman Pasha was a clear-headed, commonsensical commander, with a down-to-earth understanding of the capacities of his own troops and armament, and a shrewd appreciation of the limitations of his enemy: what the instructors at the *École de Guerre* in the pre-1914 era used to call, with a slight note of contempt, *'un bon géneral'*. He inflicted in consequence three costly defeats of the Russians at Plevna in the autumn of 1877. But he ended up by surrendering on 10 December an army consisting of 10 Pashas, 130 field-officers, 2,000 company officers, 40,000 foot soldiers and gunners, and 12,000 horsemen, with 77 guns and a mass of spare ammunition, at the end of a battle which cost the Russians only 6,000 casualties. On the Russian side only two comparatively junior generals – Gourko and Skobeleff – showed a brilliant adaptability to the limitations imposed on modern armies by technical progress; and their successes had, of necessity, only a slight impact on the main course of the campaign. The world's great general staffs, obsessed by Moltke's spectacular successes in 1866 and 1870, thus tended to ignore the lessons of this war which, if properly understood, might have saved countless lives between 1914 and 1918.

Both sides in 1877 had clearly understood the importance of the technical development of small arms during the great wars and their tactical implications. The Russians after some experiments with modified muzzle-loaders on Chassepot lines, had re-equipped all their infantry with a reasonably efficient breech-loading rifle – the Krinka – which fired a metal cartridge and was entirely satisfactory until the barrel became dirtied, when the extractor ceased to work and the empty cases had to be pushed out with a ramrod. This was the standard weapon for the infantry of the line in 1877 and it functioned, on the whole, extremely well. They were, however, experimenting with a still better weapon, the Berdan rifle, of smaller calibre and greater range, of which they bought 30,000 from the United States in 1869 for issue to their rifle brigades. In 1870 they had another 30,000 of an improved Berdan manufactured in Birmingham, with the stipulation that all the machine tools used in their manufacture should be handed over to the Russian government on the completion of the contract. In 1877 only the Guard and the Caucasian regiments had been issued with these, though the Cossacks and most of the cavalry had an adapted version with a shortened barrel which made them extremely effective as mounted infantry. It was an admirable weapon which was to become the standard issue for the Russian army; and by 1880 their own factories could turn out on demand 1,000 of them a day.

The Turks, characteristically, waited while the rest of the world experimented and then bought from the Providence Tool Company of Rhode Island 300,000 Peabody-Martini guns of 45 calibre which were reckoned to be the best of all modern breech-loaders. The rest of their numerous but scattered infantry regiments were equipped with the English Snyder ·58, which was at least superior to the Russian Krinka. They acquired, however, another 200,000 Peabody-Martinis during the 1877–8 campaign. Their infantry fire-power was thus greatly superior to that of the Russians; and if they were sufficiently dug in to be immune from artillery fire, they were virtually invincible to any form of frontal assault. This was the factor which inflicted appallingly heavy casualties on the Russians in the course of an eventually victorious campaign; and it effectively disproved the judgements of the pundits after 1871, that henceforth the artillery was 'Queen of the Battlefield'.

In artillery, too, the Turks had a decided advantage in the quality of their guns, all of which were bought from Herr Krupp. Their trouble was that they had too few of them. In Siege-, Field-, and Horse-guns the Russians had weapons greatly inferior in range, accuracy, and rate of fire. Some of their heaviest guns in the siege train and in their fortresses were modern steel pieces. The rest were breech-loading bronze cannon which could not be rifled closely enough to ensure accuracy at long ranges and whose breech mechanism would only stand up to a propellant charge half as powerful as that of the Krupp. Moreover, if used intensively, they were liable to become irreparably damaged by corrosion at the breech. Thus, of the 400 guns which the Russians deployed for a three-day bombardment before their third assault at Plevna, over 60 became permanently useless. In numbers they had an overwhelming preponderance. The four Corps which crossed the Danube initially had, in round figures, 800 guns; and the three Corps later mobilised brought a further reinforcement of 600. Against these the Turks had in the whole European theatre, including those brought from Egypt, only 450 field pieces. But these were enough with their extra 2,000 yards of range to force the Russian artillery back to a point where they could only hit the enemy's forward infantry positions at their maximum range of 5,000 yards; and this imposed a further handicap on the Russian gunners. Thanks to their smaller charge the Russians could only achieve this range by so high a degree of elevation that their high-explosive shells plunged almost vertically into the ground and in consequence they either failed to explode or, when they did, merely threw up harmless quantities of earth.

On the administrative side there were few lessons which either side could profitably learn from Moltke's campaigns. The Turks had few railways they could use to concentrate and supply their armies. For their long march to the Danube the Russians had one which presented almost as many problems as it solved. Down the 300-mile length of Roumania there ran a trunk line from the Galician frontier through Jassy and thence by a winding coastal route to Bucharest and on to the north bank of the Danube. Its deviousness was, indeed, such that, while the distance from Kishineff on the Dniester to Bucharest by main road was 250 miles, by rail it was 425. There were branch lines to the Dobrudja fortresses and the mouth of the Danube which were of little military use. But at Jassy it linked with a branch of the main Russian railway system running back through Kishineff to Odessa.

But the impression that this gave the Russians a direct railway line, even if single track, from Kishineff through Bucharest to the Danube bank was an illusion; and it created for their General Staff a problem which no amount of study of Moltke's use of railways for the Concentration and the Approach March could solve. The extension to Jassy had been constructed during one of the periods when Russia intermittently occupied southern Bessarabia and, naturally enough, on the broad gauge of the Russian system. The Roumanian line was built throughout on the narrower, western European gauge. Thus everything which arrived at Jassy had to be laboriously off-loaded and transferred on to Roumanian trucks before it could be moved south. The Roumanians, moreover, were woefully short of engines and rolling stock and had not yet provided adequate terminal sidings for loading and off-loading at either Jassy or Bucharest. Yet before they could even get into battle the Russians had to transport along the 425 miles of this single track not only the ammunition reserves and supplies for an army of 200,000 men but the siege batteries with their material and ammunition for their own fortresses at Galatz and Braila and those needed for the containment of the Turkish fortresses of Rutchuk, Silistria, and Nikopolis; four pontoon trains for the passage of the Danube, together with a large number of wooden pontoons built at Galatz which further complicated the railway schedule; and, finally, more than twenty-five steam torpedo boats with their torpedoes and

G*

equipment which were to bar off the Turkish fleet from the Danube crossings.[4] Admittedly the Russian staff made things even more difficult for themselves by sending the bulk of IX Corps by rail, instead of letting the troops march the 250 miles of road by easy stages, whereby they could comfortably have arrived long before the necessary equipment. But it was not an easy problem; and it resulted in a delay of ten weeks between the declaration of war and the establishment of the army on the south bank of the Danube on 3 July, at last firmly on enemy territory, but still 80 miles by the direct route from the vital Shipka Pass over the Balkan Mountains, and another 300 from Adrianople and San Stephano on the Sea of Marmora, whence they could closely threaten Constantinople. The column moving on the right flank of the main advance had a march of over 700 miles to reach the same objectives; and it was to take the Russians eight months of hard fighting to get there.

The fighting between the main armies on both flanks and for most of the time on the main front was a drearily repetitive series of battles between incompetent generals commanding, on both sides, troops capable of almost unbelievable courage and endurance. All that is illuminating and instructive in the history of the campaign can be learnt from two comparatively subsidiary episodes which, none the less, largely determined the course and result of the war. One was the advance-guard operation by which the comparatively junior Major-General Gourko, with a mixed detachment of some 8,000 infantry, 4,000 cavalry, and 32 guns, in less than a month after a march of 80 miles from the Danube, turned and captured what should have been the central point of the main Turkish defence at Shipka, more than 3,000 feet above sea-level at the crest of the main pass over the Balkan Mountains. The other was the prolonged battle for Plevna which raged from 20 July to 10 December.

Gourko's campaign, whereby he manoeuvred the whole of his small force over theoretically impassable mountain tracks round the right flank of the Turkish main force at Shipka, leaving it to VIII Corps, moving up the main road behind him to engage them in front while he came up the pass from the south to fall on their rear, was in itself a minor masterpiece. What was chiefly interesting, however, was the way in which he used his cavalry to do the bulk of his fighting. The constitution of his mounted force was in itself instructive, and was clearly based on thorough and intelligent study of the great cavalry sweeps of the American Civil War. It was, moreover, designed not merely in slavish imitation of the operations by which Sheridan, Forrest, Jeb Stuart, and Joe Wheeler harried the communications and sometimes paralysed the movements of whole armies, but also to remedy their deficiencies. Unlike the largely swordless American regiments, Russian cavalry could intervene effectively to exploit an infantry victory and if necessary meet enemy cavalry in hand to hand combat. But the Cossacks were accustomed normally to fight dismounted; and Gourko had a contingent of them trained and equipped as sappers to ensure that any damage done to enemy supply lines would be more permanent than the trivial interruption of the Atlanta rail traffic achieved by Kilpatrick's spectacular raid of August 1864.

Gourko had with him one regular cavalry brigade – two regiments of Dragoons and a horse battery – and a mixed brigade of a Hussar and a Cossack regiment, with a Cossack horse battery, both, oddly enough, commanded by Dukes of Leuchtenberg. But he had also a detachment of mounted pioneers: Cossacks from the Don, the Caucasus, and the Urals, specially trained in engineering techniques, and particularly in the arts of demolition. He had one other final asset. The Russian regular cavalry, though every bit as class-conscious, picturesque, and expensive as that of the other European armies, had alone accepted the fact that it could no longer play an effective part as a shock force in a pitched battle. With their shortened Berdan rifles, to which they could, when necessary, affix bayonets, the Russian cavalry regiments had been trained to function as highly efficient mounted infantry.

It was this last factor which enabled Gourko on the fourth day of his advance from the Danube to turn a reconnaissance in force of the town of Tirnovo, a natural fortress and the vital communications' centre of the whole of northern Bulgaria, into a victorious assault which was to have a decisive effect not only on his own operations, but on the whole course of the campaign. Arrived in front of the town, he at once concluded that it was not held in very great strength. As he emerged from the foot of the western mountain passes the Turks fell back to positions covering the approaches to the town. They had some three thousand infantry, six guns, and four hundred Bashi-Bazouks – irregular cavalry intended to match the Russian Cossacks, but in practice devoted only to plunder and entirely unwilling to become engaged in any serious fighting. Rightly appreciating that the speed of his advance had surprised and unnerved his enemy, Gourko opened fire with the six 4-pounders of his horse battery, brought up four squadrons of Cossacks to work their way round the Turkish flank and harass them from the rear, dismounted and deployed his brigade of regular dragoons and led them into a direct assault. So well did they handle their Berdan rifles that when they fixed bayonets for the final assault the Turks broke and fled. So, with a force of only 1,400 mounted men, outnumbered by more than two to one, Gourko seized the key point of Tirnovo, with enough forage and hard-tack rations to last him for the rest of the campaign. It was to become the Grand Duke's headquarters, and it cost him only two men and eight wounded horses.

Gourko had thus demonstrated one lesson which the rest of the world's armies were very slow to learn : that cavalry still had an enormous potential value in country where there was plenty of room to manoeuvre, provided that they would forget the legendary charges of history, exploit their mobility to the limit, and train themselves to do their fighting on foot. In the course of his subsequent and highly successful operations he was to teach two more. During the great wars of the mid-century the cavalry had failed dismally to carry out what had always been one of its vital functions : the deep and close reconnaissance on which commanders-in-chief were entirely dependent for information of enemy movements and intentions. In 1859 both sides had manoeuvred largely in ignorance of their opponents' dispositions. In 1866 Moltke had been so badly served by his cavalry that he only learnt of the concentration of the whole Austrian army at Königgrätz late at night on the eve of the decisive battle, and Benedek at the same moment had no knowledge of the whereabouts of the powerful army of the Crown Prince away on his right. Again in 1870 Moltke, Bazaine, and MacMahon were for most of the time in almost total ignorance of the movements of their enemies. Gourko's enterprising cavalry patrols deep into enemy territory not only kept him informed of Turkish dispositions on his own immediate front, but enabled him to keep the Grand Duke Nicholas posted on every phase of the concentration of the main Turkish army in Roumelia and its advance to what were to prove the decisive winter battles south of Shipka. None of the other Russian generals made comparable use of their infinitely superior cavalry; and Osman Pasha was able to slip an army of 60,000 men into Plevna, within striking distance of the Danube crossings and the main Russian line of communications with hardly any hint of his movements reaching the Russian high command.

Finally Gourko, alone among the generals of his age, had digested what was, perhaps, the supreme lesson of the American Civil War: the value of powerful cavalry raids deep into the enemy's territory to disrupt their communications and interrupt their supplies. As soon as he was over the main Balkan range he sent out strong patrols, each with its element of Cossack Pioneers, to create the maximum possible havoc in northern Roumelia by demolishing road and railway bridges, blowing up railway stations and telegraph offices, cutting telegraph lines, and tearing up gaps in the railway lines. The already exiguous Turkish road and railway system was thus almost totally disrupted. Moreover, since the Turkish system of command was the worst imaginable, three independent armies being controlled not by a Commander-in-Chief, but by a War Council in Constantinople, the loss of telegraphic communication made it impossible to co-ordinate the army operations. Not until after 1918, when the tracked armoured vehicle had replaced the horse as a means of combining rapid movement with striking power, did the world's general staffs properly grasp the importance of the lessons which Gourko had both learnt and taught.

The fighting round Plevna was far more protracted, more costly to both sides, and far more important strategically than the manoeuvrings of Gourko's little advance guard at Tirnovo; and the lessons which it taught were much more significant for the generals of the future. But, though profound, they were comparatively simple lessons; and no very detailed study of events is necessary for their elucidation. Osman Pasha only occupied the hills around the little town of Plevna because his leading troops were too late to save the fortress of Nikopolis, twenty miles to the north, which fell after a feeble resistance on 16 July to Lieutenant-General Baron Krüdener's IX Corps, which had crossed the Danube less than a week before. Rendered over-confident by this easy success and ignoring reports from Cossack patrols and statements from prisoners that large bodies of Turks were moving down the Danube from the west, the Grand Duke ordered Krüdener simply to 'occupy' Plevna; and Krüdener sent a Brigade Group, without a cavalry advance guard, to blunder into the 25,000 Turks who were already digging themselves in on the hills north of the town. The result was the disaster it deserved to be. The Russians lost nearly two-thirds of their officers and over a third of their troops – nearly 3,000 in all out of a total force of 7,500. The wounded of the rank and file, moreover, were mostly left on the field as the attackers fell back, and were never heard of again.

Ten days later, very reluctantly and only after a sharply repeated order from the Grand Duke, Krüdener tried again. He now had his own depleted IX Corps and a hastily thrown together detachment of about equal strength under the highly incompetent Lieutenant-General Prince Shakofskoi – in all some 30,000 men. Osman Pasha, meanwhile, as his army arrived piecemeal down the road from Wittin, had built up his force to 40,000 and had greatly extended and deepened his redoubts and entrenchments, providing them all with dug-outs which effectively protected his infantry from both shrapnel and high explosive shell fire. He was being steadily supplied with rations and ammunition up the main road from Sofia without interference from the unenterprising Russian cavalry. He therefore awaited a renewal of the assault with fully justified confidence. The battle of 30 July opened with a six-hour artillery duel in which each side knocked out three of the enemy guns and killed a few gunners and inflicted negligible casualties on the infantry. The damage to the Turkish earthworks was also negligible. The Russian infantry assaults in the afternoon were a predictable disaster. They attacked in successive waves, each going in only when its predecessor had been decisively defeated. Here and there, climbing over parapets already paved with corpses,

Russian units captured a redoubt, only to find that the far side was unprotected and that they were trapped and exposed to a merciless rifle fire from prepared positions further back. At nightfall the survivors were withdrawn, while each of the lieutenant-generals bitterly reproached the other for his failure to support him at the critical moment. The Russians lost over 7,000 men – a quarter of their total force and much more than a quarter of their infantry. Turkish losses were estimated at nearly 5,000,[5] mostly sustained in rash counter-attacks which only served to underline the already clear lesson of 1871 : that the modern rifle had made infantry attacks across open country suicidal. The Russian losses were rendered even more serious by the fact that they once again left the vast majority of their wounded on the field to be irretrievably lost.

The Russians had still not learnt their lesson. They called in the 35,000-strong Roumanian army under their Prince Charles – almost the last Hohenzollern actually to command his troops in battle – and a mass of their own reinforcements which brought their total force up to 90,000 with 24 heavy siege guns, 364 field pieces, and 54 of the light horse guns. All this took six weeks, during which Osman continued to dig furiously until he had a complete chain of mutually supporting redoubts and entrenchments round Plevna, while the last of his army marched in to bring his total strength up to 56,000. In this period there were only two incidents of importance to the historian. One was a half-hearted attempt by Osman to take the offensive which merely drove all the old lessons home. After a day of heavy fighting the Turks fell back to their lines losing some 3,000 men and inflicting less than 1,000 casualties on the Russians. The other was one of the rare successful infantry assaults of the campaign, when the Turks were driven out of Lovtchka, a key point on the Russian right flank for their eventual advance on Adrianople. The architect of this victory was the comparatively junior Skobeleff in command of the leading division, who proved himself to be not only one of the bravest, but certainly the most intelligent and at the same time the luckiest general of his time. He had concluded from the previous disasters that a divisional commander must be right forward with the second wave of the assault, ready to lead it into battle at the moment when the front line wavered, but before it broke and retreated. All turned in his opinion on timing this movement correctly and leading it with the *élan* necessary to maintain the momentum of the attack unbroken. On this his appreciation was entirely correct. He had also digested the lessons of Gourko's handling of cavalry. As the Turks broke he threw his large force of mounted Cossacks into the classic operation of 'the pursuit'; and they cut down more than 3,000 of the fleeing enemy, turning their rout into a massacre.

The third Russian assault on Plevna needs no detailed analysis. It was in general merely a dreary repetition of the two previous failures on a vaster scale and with correspondingly vaster losses. The wretched Prince Charles, nominally in overall command, had the Grand Duke and his Headquarters close beside him and, only just behind, the Tsar in person with the whole of his huge military and civilian entourage. His operations, almost certainly foredoomed to failure anyway, were thus rendered even more disastrous by the confusion created by endless Councils of War. The attack on 11 September was preceded by four days of continuous bombardment which achieved practically nothing. As the Turkish batteries one by one fell silent the Russian gunners gleefully congratulated themselves on having knocked out their guns whereas, in point of fact, the Turks had merely, characteristically, run out of ammunition. Turkish infantry casualties were trivial; and the daily damage to their earthworks was mostly easily made good during the following night. Really well constructed entrenchments proved themselves even more indestructible than strong, stone-faced fortifications; thus, in the seven years since Sedan, the artillery had abruptly ceased to be 'Queen of the Battlefield'.

The infantry assault went in in three columns. The right-hand two suffered costly defeats similar to those of Krüdener's earlier attacks. On the far left Skobeleff's eccentric leadership carried his column on to its objectives and he himself led the victorious infantry into the Turkish redoubts. He was by then on foot, his white horse having been killed, and he had with him only one surviving unwounded member of his numerous staff. His position, too, was very precarious, with undamaged and deeply entrenched Turks on both his flanks, and he was in danger of being cut off and completely surrounded. He hung on all day in the desperate hope that somehow IV Corps on his right would find reinforcements for his success. Then he, too, withdrew, leaving just as many dead on the field as his brother column commanders. The Russians committed 60,000 of their available infantry to these attacks and they lost over a quarter of them, some 18,000 in all. The Turks, too, had suffered heavily, losing something between 12,000 and 15,000 men. But they still held Plevna. Then, at last, the Russian high command realised that the place could only be taken by investment. The veteran General Todleben, the Vauban of his age, who twenty years before had so skilfully and obstinately defended Sebastopol, was summoned from his semi-retirement as General ADC to the Tsar. He was given overall command of all the troops round Plevna and he set about his task methodically and inexorably. But he had to wait for over a month before the arrival of the belatedly mobilised Guards' and Grenadier Corps gave him infantry and guns enough for an effective encirclement. Until the last week of October he had to leave it to the large Russian cavalry force to cut the supply routes into Plevna from the west and south. This, under the command of the totally incompetent General Kriloff, it entirely failed to do, so that Osman received no less than 3,000 wagon-loads of vital rations.

Until the Russian Guard had cut his main supply route from Sofia Osman had hung on in the hope that there would be a fourth and still more costly assault on his, by then, almost impregnable positions. He could still have escaped through the narrowing gap to start the whole story over again on the fringe of the mountains further south, with incalculable political and diplomatic consequences. But by then he had received a categorical telegraphic order from Constantinople to hold out to the last man and round. This he did not literally do. But he held out to the last ration. On 10 December, rather than tamely surrender as Bazaine had at Metz, he made a gallant, but costly and hopeless attempt to cut his way out and was forced to capitulate. At least he went down fighting. Against the loss of his army he could set 40,000 Russian casualties, mostly dead, and the fact that his comparatively small force had immobilised the entire Russian army for five solid months. It was a considerable achievement; and he owed it not to any new technological invention, but to one of the oldest implements of warfare – the spade, first exploited on the grand scale of the Persian Emperor Cyrus when he captured Babylon in the fifth century BC. This, apart from the incidental demonstration by Gourko and Skobeleff of the still great potential value of properly trained and well-handled cavalry, was the vital lesson of the campaign of 1877–8; and it was one which the generals of the future were to be surprisingly slow in learning.

One professional observer remarked in his report on the campaign that it was 'the nature of the Russian soldier when he stops for a month to instal himself, in the matter of fortifications, as if he would remain for a day; whereas the Turk, stopping for a day, instals himself as if for a month.' At the outset of the campaign a Russian company had only in its wagons ten shovels and six picks and spades. After Plevna some of their more intelligent divisional commanders like Skobeleff made every soldier carry either a pick or spade slung from his knapsack. They added five pounds to an already heavy load and were highly inconvenient both on the march and when moving through close country under fire. The troops came to value them; but to the end Russian trenches continued to look 'slouchy'[6] in comparison with those of the Turks and too shallow to give effective protection against shrapnel or the weather.

Other armies were sufficiently impressed by Plevna to realise that their infantry must be equipped with some sort of entrenching tool. Shrinking from imposing on their troops a load which the Russian peasant-soldier would carry uncomplainingly as part of the burden of daily life, they experimented first with a trowel-bayonet which had all the faults of dual-purpose weapons. It only made possible the digging of trenches two feet deep, its usefulness as a bayonet was permanently impaired if so used, and it damaged the fire-power of the rifle. By 1880 all the great continental armies had adopted the Linneman spade, a much more useful, short-handled entrenching tool carried on the hip. But that, too, as the Belgian Chief Engineer remarked, had 'all the defects of an implement intended for several uses',[7] since it had an axe- and a saw-edge, both of which were irreparably damaged if it was much used for digging. Proper long-handled spades were carried in company wagons, generally in a proportion of one to every four men, and one pick for every ten.

The final and accurate conclusion of the American Military Attaché was that, while these arrangements would satisfy the general staffs in peacetime, a major war would compel them to accept the lesson of Plevna: that efficient entrenching tools were a 'vital necessity' and that troops would very quickly accept that fact and carry picks and spades 'most cheerfully'. Every improvement in the power and range of artillery was more than matched by the growth of the already formidable defensive strength of properly entrenched infantry behind barbed wire entanglements, equipped with magazine rifles, and closely and heavily supported by modern machine guns. The next great war would not be the greater Sedan of which Schlieffen dreamed in 1900 and which Joffre apprehended in 1914, but Plevna on a continental scale; and central Europe would eventually succumb, like Plevna, not to assault, but to investment. There was, however, an exception to the general rule: the storm of the formidable fortress of Kars, which might easily have become the Plevna of the Armenian front at the other end of the Black Sea.

For his campaign in the Caucasus the Grand Duke Michael had been allotted only 65,000 men. This was, in fact, quite enough to outmatch the field army of the Turks when they had drawn off the necessary forces to garrison Kars and, behind it, the more massively fortified town of Erzerum, which was the key to the control of the whole southern coast of the Black Sea. But the summer was wasted in indecisive fighting by an attempt to bypass Kars and seize Erzerum by a *coup-de-main* with quite inadequate forces. The Grand Duke, having learnt his lesson, then settled down methodically to the capture of these two fortresses. He routed and dispersed into the mountains the enemy field army at the battle of Aladja Dagh, where he caught the Turks before they had time to dig in properly and inflicted on them such heavy casualties by the devastating fire of his artillery's shrapnel that they broke and scattered before the advance of his infantry. By the beginning of November, without venturing an assault, he had completely invested Kars. His Intelligence services, however, informed him, for once accurately, that the

garrison had enough men, guns, food, and ammunition to hold
out for six months. Snugly ensconced in their fortifications and
with the town behind them, the Turks would easily survive the
notoriously harsh winter of those uplands, while his own men
would suffer appallingly in their entrenchments. So he decided
that the place must be taken by storm.

His brilliant success and the reasoning on which it was based
contained more useful lessons for the generals of a future age
than all the campaigns of Moltke, though only Plumer at
Messines and, to a lesser extent, Bying at Vimy Ridge would
show the same ability to distinguish both the limitations and the
opportunities of siege warfare. Firstly he chose as his limited
objectives two fortifications the capture of which would cripple
the enemy defence and lay the whole fortress open to a determined exploitation of success. Secondly he had the courage to
ignore the lesson of all the world's military textbooks that assault
must always be preceded by adequate 'artillery preparation'. He
decided that a preliminary bombardment seldom did any real
damage and served only to alert the enemy and pin-point the
objectives of the impending attack, and that surprise before the
enemy had time to mass reserves behind the threatened points
was far more important. He chose a frosty, moonlit night so as to
have just enough light to avoid chaos in a long advance; and so
well was secrecy and silence preserved that the Turks only
manned their lines when their pickets were suddenly overrun.
The advance began at 8.30 and within an hour the Russian
infantry were fighting a fierce hand-to-hand bayonet battle in
the trenches and covered ways of the forts and the barracks
behind. By dawn they were in the town; and by the middle of
the morning the last of the troops who had broken out to the
south-west had been rounded up by the Cossacks. The Russians
buried 2,500 Turkish dead and took 17,000 unwounded and
5,000 wounded prisoners, with 33 guns and vast quantities of
war materials and hard tack rations. It was one of the most
complete victories of the century.

The American Military Attaché at the headquarters of the
Grand Duke Nicholas rendered to the War Department at
Washington a 500-page, meticulously accurate account of all
these events, with illustrative plates and maps and careful draw-

ings of weapons and equipment, and some fundamental conclusions which were to remain entirely valid for at least thirty
years. They made quite inexcusable the naïveté, ineptitude, and
administrative incompetence of the generals and the antiquated
equipment which were the main characteristics of the United
States' Army when it set out in 1898, on what was virtually a
national crusade, to liberate the Cubans, Puerto Ricans, and
Filippinos from the hated, imperialistic tyranny of Spain. Their
weapons alone were a reproach to a nation which was rapidly
getting ahead of the rest of the world in industrial efficiency and
technology. The bulk of their infantry were armed with the
cumbersome Springfield rifle which fired a quite unnecessarily
large bullet from a heavy cartridge loaded with old-fashioned
black powder which left a puff of white smoke hanging over the
firer every time he discharged his piece. Their 3·2-inch field-
guns were even more out of date. They dated from before the
invention of self-recoil mechanisms, so that every time the gun
was fired the trail leapt out of its trench and it rebounded backwards through two revolutions of the wheels. They, too, used
black powder charges which easily identified their positions to
the enemy. They had few time-fused shells, and therefore little
shrapnel; and they had no instruments for indirect fire and had
to see a target before they could engage it. In terms of the Cuban
landscape this meant that they could normally only come into
action at a range of 1,000 yards or less, when their gunners and
their horse lines would become a sitting target for the deadly
magazine Mauser rifles of the Spanish infantry. They made in
consequence very little contribution to the fighting in front of
Santiago which decided the campaign.

There is, of course, much to be said to excuse the unprepared-
ness of the American senior staff. They had lived for thirty years
in a rigidly isolationist world preoccupied with healing the
wounds of a bitter civil war. Their regular army was only 26,000
strong and was scattered among some forty-six posts on the frontiers of still potentially dangerous, unsubdued Indian tribes.
Their tactical experience was limited to the pursuit of an elusive
mounted enemy who never stood to fight and whose armament
was wholly antique. The Post Commanders got some little battle
experience. Their generals were men who administered a

number of Posts, but could have no experience of commanding a regiment, let alone a brigade or division or army corps. It was, moreover, a rigidly segregationalist army. The 10th (Black) Cavalry did as well as any unit in the Cuban fighting. But it was kept at social arm's length by the white units and, even more remotely, by the largely untrained, but socially prestigious Militia units in the various States. The only senior officers with any experience of warfare on the grand scale were veterans of the Civil War, more than thiry years out of date. 'Fighting Joe Wheeler', for example, had made a great name as a dashing, black-bearded Confederate cavalry commander, and had since been a highly successful Congressman representing the new businessman's South. He reappeared, white haired and bearded, as Commander of the Cavalry Division in General Shafter's Corps, back in the blue uniform in which he had first joined the US Army, with all his qualities of leadership unimpaired. But even in 1863 he had been difficult to control and had made reckless and costly mistakes; and by 1898 he had no knowledge or understanding of the potentialities of contemporary weapons or the tactical thinking which went with them.

More incomprehensibly, in a nation which was already becoming almost morbidly preoccupied with hygiene, the worst administrative failure of all was the breakdown of the army's medical services. There were too few doctors, medical orderlies and ambulances; and the transport officers, like the French in 1859, brought the medical supplies ashore last of all and mostly after the most pressing need for them was past. Even in the great camps in Florida, Virginia and Tennessee where the 180,000 enthusiastic volunteers and the little regular army were concentrated latrine discipline and health precautions generally were so lax that typhoid and other preventable diseases were already rampant before the first expeditionary forces sailed. Half of them never left these camps until they were mustered out at the end of the war; and they suffered casualties from disease comparable to those inflicted on the three divisions which stormed the heights before Santiago at San Juan and El Caney in the one considerable fight of the campaign. At the front things were even worse. 'Sanitation', one recent American historian has written, 'was impossible in the trenches'.[8] But it was just there, in the heart of one of the most fever-ridden territories in South America, that it was most necessary. The troops were even allowed to bathe in and drink unboiled the water of the stagnant pools in the swamps around their lines of approach. In consequence the American army was already half crippled by typhoid, malaria and dysentry even before the great rains at the end of July heralded the season of Yellow Fever, which had once almost destroyed a British expedition in 1741, the history of which Shafter had conscientiously read, unlike Colonel Roosevelt. There were thus no new lessons to be learnt from this war; only the old ones, many of them dating from long before the Age of Moltke. Before leading the Highland Brigade up the heights of the Alma forty years earlier Colin Campbell had warned them that the name of any man seen escorting a wounded comrade out of battle would be posted in his parish porch as a disgrace to his family. Yet, on the day after the San Juan battle, General Wheeler was to report to Shafter that his lines were dangerously thin, 'as so many of the men have gone to the rear with the wounded'. These were, nevertheless, useful lessons for the future for a certain Lieutenant Pershing, who received his baptism of fire on the slopes of San Juan.

The one really new factor in this campaign was the blaze of publicity in which General Shafter was compelled to conduct his operations. In the Crimea Russell of *The Times* had laid a sound foundation for a tradition of responsible, objective, but highly influential reporting; and the more important British campaigns in the following fifty years had been faithfully described by such variously distinguished men as Rudyard Kipling, Winston Churchill, and Conan Doyle. But the army of well-known journalists and, even more dangerously, of professional photographers which settled on Tampa Bay and thereafter clung to the skirts of the Cuban expeditionary force were for General Shafter as formidable an obstacle as all the modern rifles and guns and smokeless powder of the hard-bitten Spanish regular troops in front of him. From the moment that he refused the Press any special arrangements for transportation to Cuba and on top of that forbade any journalist to accompany his leading troops into battle his reputation was doomed. The news-hungry, war-mad, flag-waving people of the United States were given a picture of their gallant boys suffering and fighting heroically under dithering and incompetent leadership. Shafter was no great general. But in spite of his obesity and his gout and his periodical heat-strokes he carried out a very difficult task with skill and great good sense; and in the end, with his troops vociferously demanding to be allowed to assault Santiago and his senior officers demanding instant withdrawal as the deadly Yellow Fever began to spread, he patiently and very cunningly induced the Spaniards to surrender and so got his ungrateful troops clear of the island in the nick of time. His bad press was made much worse by the downright disloyalty of the better-connected and politically minded subordinate commanders who sent a continuous stream of adverse criticism to their friends in the Senate and the State Department. Far the worst of these was Roosevelt, who even gave his own press conferences. Promoted to Brigadier-General, he used the war as the first move in a brilliant publicity campaign which was to carry him in a year to the Governorship of New York, and two years after that to the Presidency of the United States.

Another result of the ubiquitous swarm of newsmen was that a comparatively trivial campaign was so over written-up and so overdramatised that it became in the minds of the American public a major and an epic victory. The picture painted for them was of American youth gallantly advancing uphill, invariably through 'a hail of lead directed by unseen defenders' and 'under a remorseless shower of shrapnel'; and there was always a 'stream of wounded' staggering back down the hill, brilliantly depicted by the press photographers. In point of fact there were only two engagements on the approach march to Santiago. The first was a very minor affair, brought on against the intentions of the Commanders on both sides, by the precipitous advance of Fighting Joe's dismounted Cavalry Division. The Spanish General Linares was hastily withdrawing his army from the ridge at Las Guasimas to the San Juan hills and El Caney immediately in front of Santiago; and Shafter had no desire to interrupt the operation. The Cavalry Division, however, caught a Spanish rearguard of 1,500 men still in position, though eagerly awaiting the order to withdraw. Fighting Joe at once threw 1,000 men of his cavalry, including, of course, Roosevelt's Rough Riders, and sent them up the hill into an entirely successful assault. In spite of the 'hail of lead' the Americans lost only 10 killed and 52 wounded, and the Spaniards left behind them 10 dead and 25 wounded.

The second, when Shafter launched his entire Corps against San Juan and El Caney, was a much more serious affair which could reasonably be described as a battle. Since they had been short of food and sleep for forty-eight hours and were required to advance uphill, in torrid heat and over very difficult ground, the young, untried American infantry did very well indeed; and the Spaniards, outnumbered by more than two to one, fought back skilfully and courageously. The US gunners rashly unlimbered only 500 yards from the enemy, and the hail of lead was at least sufficient to kill a lot of their horses and to send the troops scampering for shelter to abandoned Spanish trenches, whence it proved extremely difficult to dislodge them. But at the end of the day, as the exhausted troops started to dig in on the captured positions, the Corps had lost in killed and wounded less than 1,500. Compared with the 3,000 Krüdener had left on the field after his first Plevna assault or, more strikingly, with the 8,000 lost by the Prussian Guards' Corps in an hour at St Privat, these were not impressive casualties. But to the reporters they were 'appalling'. One of them described the 800 wounded who trickled back into the Corps Field Hospital as 'a great, bloody wave of human agony'. Such stuff was an ill preparation of the American public for the casualty figures twenty years later when their army went into a really major war in the Argonne.

Oddly enough, American historians have perpetuated the exaggerations of the journalists. They remain still appalled by the casualties and sufferings of their troops. One of the most recent even describes as 'the most serious battle of the Puerto Rican campaign' an affair at Coamo in which General Miles's troops lost six men wounded, killed six Spaniards and wounded 'thirty or forty more'.[9] He goes on to tell how the 'Massachusetts and Illinois Regiments won their laurels by charging up a hill and putting to flight a squadron of cavalry' without having a man hit, killing eight Spaniards and wounding 'several'. When it was all over President McKinley addressed the repatriated troops in terms which would have been slightly embarrassing if delivered to the victorious German troops by the King of Prussia in 1871. 'You have come home', he told them, 'after two months of severe campaigning, which has embraced assault and siege and battle, so brilliant in achievement, so far-reaching in results as to command the unstinted praise of all your countrymen'; and John Hay, the US Ambassador in London wrote to Roosevelt: 'It has been a splendid little war; begun with the highest motives, carried on with magnificent intelligence and spirit, favoured by that fortune which loves the brave.' As such it survives in American history. For the historian of the art of warfare it has at least this distinction : that it was in almost all respects a classic example of how things should not be done. The senior officers had not even learnt the lessons of their own war.

7 Epilogue: South Africa and Manchuria

The last two important wars which intervened between 1871 and 1914 had this much in common : neither produced any new creative idea which might have been useful to the commanders of the future. Both the Boer War, which in fact broke out just before the turn of the century, and the land operations of the Russo-Japanese War of 1905 served only to underline, though in vastly different ways, the lessons of the past forty years. They were essentially demonstrations of how much had been learnt and how much forgotten or misunderstood of the experiences of the immediate past; and as such they must be considered rather as the final epilogue to the Age of Moltke, than as precursors or curtain-raisers of the events of 1914.

It must be admitted that the British, when they drifted into war in South Africa in 1899, did not do much better tactically than the Americans had a year before in Cuba. For this they had little excuse. The Staff College, established at Camberley in 1858 largely to remedy the shocking deficiencies revealed in the Crimea, had stimulated throughout the army a profound interest in the lessons to be derived from a study of previous campaigns. By 1870 a distinguished line of Professors of Military History were spreading almost revolutionary views on the proper use of cavalry and of entrenchment mainly derived from close studies of the American Civil War. The events of 1870 in no way diminished the enthusiasm, but concentrated it, disastrously as it turned out, on Moltke's campaigns to the exclusion of all that had gone before. The almost annual publication by Messrs Gale and Polden of Aldershot of learned little monographs on various aspects of battles such as Magenta and Solferino, Sadowa, Spicheren and Wörth, Mars-la-Tour and Gravelotte testified to the assiduity of the strategical and logistical analyses of students and instructors.[1] Almost all had the theoretical knowledge to provide with its necessary supplies and to move by rail or road a division, or even an Army Corps. Almost all of them had had the opportunity in actual warfare to adapt what they had learnt to the special needs of divisional and brigade columns of all arms engaged in remote desert, mountain or jungle campaigns. But if they had assimilated the tactical and technical lessons taught by the major campaigns of other armies, they had entirely failed to disseminate the knowledge among the senior officers at the War Office or in the field. Except for the Sappers, who remained entirely efficient and up to date, but who, through no fault of their own, were seldom present in sufficient numbers at critical moments, the directing staffs of all arms of the British service were gravely at fault. In 1899, ignoring the history of the past fifty years, they sent their troops into what was to prove a major war with antiquated tactics and in some cases inadequate and obsolete weapons.

The Boers certainly presented a wholly new sort of situation for the soldier reared in the age of Moltke. To find a parallel to it the conscientious officer, anxious to base his tactical principles on the lessons of military history, would have had to go back to the campaigns of King Alfred and Edward the Elder. The Huns and the Mongol and Tartar Hordes had, of course, presented all the problems of a completely mounted army which moved with bewildering rapidity. But these also fought as mounted troops and, once brought to battle could be fairly easily defeated by conventional forces. Not since the ninth and tenth centuries, when the 'Great Army' of the Danes harried all northern Europe and all but brought Saxon England to her knees, had western generals had to face an enemy composed entirely of mounted infantry. Gourko's Cossacks, though trained to fight on foot, were also capable of massive charges with their sabres. The Boers, like the Danes, invariably used horses for movement and equally invariably fought on foot. Since most of the Burghers who made up the Commandos, which were the basic formation of the Boer Army, were farmers who spent half their working lives in the saddle, they were born horsemen; and, since most of them also depended on their rifles for a large part of their liveli-hood, they were all trained stalkers and marksmen, used to tak-ing advantage of every scrap of cover among the rocks and mountains of their homeland. Their rifles were the same up-to-date and efficient Mausers as had enabled the Spaniards to take a heavy toll of the enthusiastic American volunteers in Cuba. Finally, they had also provided themselves with about a hundred of the latest Krupp field guns, all horse-drawn and mobile enough to be dispersed among the Commandos, and which they fired with an accuracy scarcely less deadly than that of their Mauser rifles.

The mobilisation of such an army presented no administrative problems. The Presidents of the Transvaal and the Orange Free State had merely to sign decrees to concentrate within a week between 35,000 and 40,000 such men. They kept only scanty muster rolls and they habitually falsified their casualty returns; so there can be no certainty as to the numbers of either. Lord Kitchener, giving evidence before an official enquiry after the war estimated the total Boer numbers at the height of the cam-paign at 95,000. This is generally accepted to be exaggerated, and the true figure was probably around 50,000.[2] But many of these were Dutch rebels from Natal and Cape Colony who were poor fighting stuff compared with the hard-liner frontiersmen from the Republics. What is certain is that it was the cream of this army which fought the opening battles and that they vastly outnumbered the available British forces.

The British army in 1889 was singularly ill-equipped both mentally and materially to deal with such an antagonist. Although both officers and men had in general far more cam-paigning experience than most of their Continental contempor-aries, it was all largely irrelevant to the conditions of a major engagement against a skilled and determined enemy armed with the most modern weapons. Moreover these mountain, desert, and jungle campaigns against tribal forces equipped at best with primitive firearms and only dangerous if allowed to get to close quarters, were regarded by most senior officers as improvisations – which, of course, they mostly were – and therefore exceptions

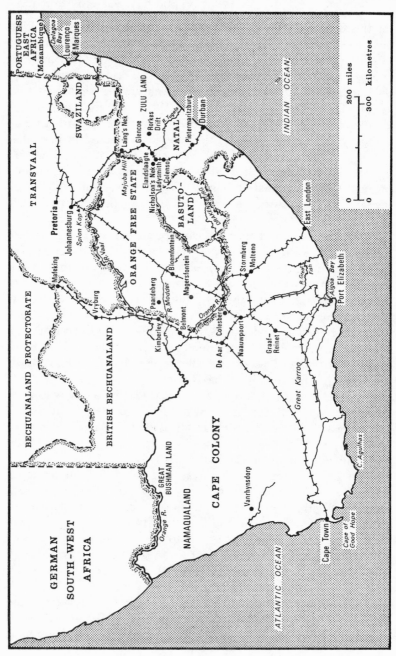

Map 4. South Africa, 1900

to the rule. The rule, as embodied in the training manuals, was established on the drill squares of Aldershot, on the rifle ranges at Bisley, and on the artillery practice areas of Larkhill; and it was annually justified in the Manoeuvres on Salisbury Plain, where the Umpires gave marks for even and tidy alignments and the smartness and precision with which rehearsed drills were reproduced in conditions of mock warfare. Occasionally there would be a scathing comment from the ageing Commander-in-Chief, Lord Wolseley, who still retained the elasticity of mind and shrewdness of appreciation which had won success on battlefields as diverse as the Egyptian desert and the Ashanti jungles. But these went largely unregarded by generals and regimental officers complacently certain that the resistance of a handful of shabby farmers – undrilled 'Irregulars' – would speedily collapse when faced with the disciplined regular regiments of the British army.

The Government and the War Department shared this complacency. On 5 August 1899, when negotiations with President Kruger had almost broken down, there were in South Africa only two British Cavalry Regiments, three field batteries and six and a half infantry battalions – a total of about 6,000 men. 'Protest. Protest', Kruger had scoffed to an emissary from the Colonial Office. 'We have the guns. You have not.' He had perforce to give the British time to reinforce, since he could not launch a war until the great autumn rains had covered the Veldt with lush green grass which would make his Commandos independent of depots and the clutter of forage wagons. Meanwhile troops from India brought the British regular forces available for the defence of Natal and Cape Colony up to 22,000; but even with contingents sent by Australia and New Zealand, the total British force was still outnumbered by nearly two to one. The defence of Natal collapsed in defeat at Glencoe and Ladysmith, leaving Sir George White penned in at Ladysmith with what regular troops remained to him and such of the local loyalist volunteers as could be assembled in time. Pockets of British settlers and local sympathisers similarly established themselves at Mafeking and Kimberley, where they, too, were besieged. To relieve these the British commanders were therefore compelled to offensives which progressively revealed appalling deficiencies in all three of the main arms of the British service, and in the high command itself, which were to make their nominal victories as costly as their more spectacular defeats.

At the centre of power by far the worst offender was that department of the Commander-in-Chief's Headquarters which had replaced the old Board of Ordnance in 1855. By 1870 the whole artillery of the British army had been equipped both at home and in India with rifled, breech-loading Armstrong guns. They were far from perfect and, in the wear and tear of a desert campaign, developed chronic gas leakages. Thus, by 1870, the Royal Artillery was already hankering for a return to the old muzzle-loader, with which nothing much could go wrong, however inferior its rate of fire might be to that of the enemy. Almost unbelievably, after an intensive study of the war of 1870–1, the British authorities decided to rearm all branches of the Royal Artillery with the muzzle-loading cannon long since rejected as obsolete by every other modern army in the world. The overwhelming successes of the Prussian gunners at Spicheren and Mars-la-Tour were put down as exclusively the result of the initiative and skilled tactical handling of the battery commanders; and a vastly disproportionate importance was attached to the revelation that during the course of the campaign some 200 Krupp guns had been withdrawn from service owing to wear on the breech-pieces. Since the German armies had deployed more than 2,000 guns in the course of a war which included the sieges of Metz and Paris, this was not an alarming casualty rate; and the gains had handsomely compensated the loss. Yet, by 1881, there were only two breech-loading batteries left in the British army, both in India; and by 1890 there were none.[3]

This was the period which the gunners of a later age were to name 'the dark years'. But they were not, as the Ordnance Department had hoped, years of peaceful inactivity. Their inventors defeated them by constant improvements in the power of their propellants which enabled larger and larger shells to be fired at ever increasing ranges. Gun barrels had to be lengthened, strengthened, and tapered to fit each stage of progress; and the pace of change was so rapid that between 1860 and 1899 no new modification was ever completed throughout the service before a newer one superseded it.[4] At the same time there was an intense preoccupation, both in and outside the army, with the fear of invasion – odd in a nation which proudly claimed supremacy at sea. As the power and range of the guns mounted on battleships steadily increased the Garrison Artillery in the coastal fortresses had to be re-equipped with weapons to match them; and these in the end became so large that it was not possible to design a casemate sufficiently spacious to allow such guns to be run back far enough to enable the crews to swab them out and reload them from the muzzle. This was the factor which at last forced the Royal Artillery back to the sanity of breech-loading; and fortunately this change was complete throughout the British army and almost complete in India when war broke out in 1899. Even then one muzzle-loading battery of mountain screw-guns from India did find its way to the front in Natal, where it was an infernal nuisance. It could only use black powder charges whose plumes of white smoke brought down heavy fire on its neighbours as well as itself whenever it went into action. Fortunately for the British it passed ingloriously out of history within a week. Detailed to support a two battalion column detached to cover Sir George White's right flank at Nicholson's Nek during the battle of Ladysmith, it lost all its guns, ammunition and transport when its mules stampeded on the night approach march and bolted back to Ladysmith leaving strewn on the road not only their own equipment, but all the column's reserve ammunition and their only heliograph. Unsupported by guns and completely out of touch, two fine battalions of infantry were in consequence forced to surrender and become the first of the Boers' prisoners of war.

In spite of this timely reform the Field Artillery did not acquit itself very well in the opening stages of the war. For this the Ordnance Department of the War Office was primarily to blame. Only when fighting had already begun on the Natal border was it discovered that the Boer Krupps could outrange the British 15-pounder howitzers, also Krupps, and that their fire was devastatingly effective. They also had four enormous Creusot guns which would throw a 96-pound shell a distance of four miles and which they moved about with astonishing rapidity and into positions which professional gunners would have regarded as inaccessible. Finally they had a weapon which the

219

H

British soldiers christened the 'Pom-pom' and dreaded most of all : the Vickers-Maxim one-pounder which delivered its little shells in bursts of about twenty with lethal effect on a gun team or an injudiciously bunched body of infantry. At the Modder River one such burst destroyed the Maxim gun of the Scots Guards and killed its entire crew; and this was a weapon which had been rejected by the Ordnance Department as an unnecessary refinement.

The Navy produced an answer to the heavy howitzers by landing a detachment of long-barrelled, quick-firing, 12-pounders, which had the range of the 'Long Toms'. Their shells were not heavy enough to do any real damage to the enemy guns, but frequently so harried the crews as to force them to withdraw. For the rest the gunners had to do the best they could with their inferior equipment; and thanks to the rigid drills enforced by Woolwich and Larkhill and to a shocking ignorance of recent military history their best was, in fact, not very good. Though they normally deployed far more guns than the Boers, two faults in particular frequently gave the enemy the upper hand. One was a rigid adherence to the Woolwich dictum : 'One gun is no gun.' The Field Artillery brought their guns into action in neat rows of six, spaced only as widely as was necessary to enable the crews to function unhampered by their neighbours. This, which would have delighted the Salisbury Plain Umpires, put them at a triple disadvantage. It was far more difficult to find adequate concealment for six guns than for one; and this disadvantage was accentuated by another factor, unforeseen and probably unforeseeable. In the still air and under the sun of South Africa any gun, even when using smokeless powder, generated above itself a faint haze. The Boers, who had only a hundred field guns for their entire army, dispersed whatever was available for a particular battle singly and cunningly concealed along their whole front. One gun carefully dug in created a haze so slight that it was almost impossible to spot. After a few minutes of rapid fire six guns closely concentrated betrayed their positions unmistakably to the field glasses of the enemy spotters. Thus, while the British fired largely at random, the Boers had the range of the British batteries pinpointed; and they handled their guns with a skill and precision altogether unforeseen. Finally positions where six guns could be evenly and closely aligned tended to be on hard ground on which the Boer high-explosive shells burst with maximum effect; and a lucky hit by a single gun might knock out two gun crews and sometimes their guns as well.

Another factor which made the support given to attacking infantry by the artillery frequently ineffectual was a gross over-estimate of the effectiveness of shrapnel. It was devastating when infantry or gun teams were caught in the open or inadequately dug in, as the Russians had proved twenty years before. But the curving trajectory of the bullets from a shrapnel shell made them virtually harmless against men snugly ensconced behind boulders, or properly entrenched. Time and again in South Africa enemy positions were 'combed' with shrapnel to provide the prescribed 'thorough artillery preparation' for an infantry assault without inflicting a single casualty on the Boer riflemen. But far more disastrous was the tendency to deploy batteries much too far forward in a laudable attempt to give the infantry the closest possible support. Wolseley had commented acidly on this at the manoeuvres of 1898, pointing out that they were exposing gun teams and horse lines dangerously within reach of enemy rifle fire.

In the heat of battle the Commander-in-Chief's warning went unheeded. At the Modder River the 62nd Battery, arriving unexpectedly in the middle of the day and already desperately short of horses, many of which had foundered by the wayside on a forced march of thirty-two miles in eight hours, was pushed so far to the front that the Boer rifles took a heavy toll of gunners and horses before the guns could even be turned round and brought into action. By mid-afternoon Lord Methuen was forced to withdraw all his batteries some 1,400 yards. By then one – the 75th – had lost three out of five officers, nineteen men and twenty-two horses; and all of them had difficulty in mustering enough horses to drag the guns back. General Cronje's disposition of his scanty artillery was in comparison highly scientific. Whether or not he had read Prince Kraft zu Hohenlohe-Ingelfingen's *Thoughts on Artillery*,[5] he appreciated the magnetic attraction for gun layers of a row of prominent buildings or low hills. He had therefore dug his cunningly concealed gun pits two hundred yards forward of the low hills which bounded the broad, flat river valley; and during the early part of the day all the British shells passed harmlessly over their heads. He had, moreover, dug alternative pits to which his guns could move the moment their positions were pinpointed. Sheer weight of numbers in the end prevailed, and the Boer guns were one by one withdrawn to fight another day, leaving only one of their heavies which had been knocked out on the heights.

Far the worst disaster to the Royal Artillery, however, was at Colenso some five weeks later. There Sir Redvers Buller entrusted the artillery support for his main infantry assault on the virtually impregnable Boer position to a Colonel Long, allotting to him two field batteries and six, bullock-drawn naval guns. Long had made a great name for himself in the Sudan, and particularly at Atbara, and had in consequence acquired the habit, as the French did in Algeria, of taking risks quite unjustified in serious warfare. He swept forward with his two batteries, leaving the naval guns far behind and even getting in front of the supporting infantry on his flanks, and unlimbered 1,000 yards from the Boer trenches. The gunners, caught in what was this time a real 'hail of lead' supplemented by the devastating little shells of the 'Pom-poms', fought back with unbelievable gallantry. One only, crazed with fear, cut the traces of a gun horse and rode madly to the rear. The rest fought and died literally to the last man. One lone survivor of a gun team was seen standing to attention beside his gun for a minute or two before he, too, went down. Another, carried back dying to the gully where the surviving horses had been led after the first impact, and where the only surgeon available did what he could, was found to have been hit by no less than sixteen bullets. Four companies of infantry – Devons and Scots Fusiliers detailed for close support – moved up to do what they could and were engulfed in the disaster. The last cry of the mortally wounded Long – 'Abandon be damned. We don't abandon guns' – resulted only in the loss of the remaining horses and many of the surviving gunners in futile attempts to drag at least a gun or two back into safety. Buller's two further attempts with teams drawn from other batteries to bring off the guns succeeded at appalling cost in bringing back only two. The other ten were taken off by the triumphant Boers; and all the surviving gunners and infantry in the gully were made prisoners. The defeat at Colenso was ignominious; but Long's men made it not inglorious. More important, it was a sad lesson on the shortcomings of artillery training methods at home and the dangers of too much battle experience against savage and primitively armed enemies.

For the gunners there had been no clear-cut conclusions to be drawn from the American Civil War, when the transformations of artillery were still in their infancy. They had closely studied the artillery contribution to the battles of 1866, 1870, and 1877 and this had led them to a belated modernisation of their equipment. But there was little they could have learnt that would be tactically useful in 1899 against an unexpectedly formidable enemy in territory vastly different from the already over-crowded battlefields of Europe. For the senior cavalry and infantry officers and for the generals who directed their operations there was no such excuse. In the case of the Regular Cavalry Regiments of the British army their failure to adapt themselves in any way to the conditions of modern warfare was particularly inexcusable.

The British senior cavalry officers proved to have been particularly slow to learn the lessons of the past fifty years. They had misread even the cavalry actions of Moltke's campaigns; and they appeared not to have studied at all Gourko's campaign in 1877. Though they never recognised the fact, the years after 1870 were for them even more 'dark' than they had been for the gunners. The enlightening expositions of American cavalry tactics by men like Chesney, Denison, and Henderson were totally rejected by the mass of cavalry officers who contemptuously nicknamed the rebellious juniors like Henry Havelock the 'Young Turks'. They preferred the judgements of two lieutenant-colonels of Foot Guards,[6] who attributed the fact that there were no cavalry charges at Gettysburg not to elementary prudence, but to the lack of discipline and training of volunteer horsemen. They were therefore prepared to concede that training in dismounted combat might be quite appropriate for the Yeomanry and that in certain types of country these might be very useful. They had to accept the general issue of carbines and bandoliers, though most resented them as adding unnecessary weight and would have preferred revolvers. So they went into South Africa in 1899 nursing wistful memories of von Bredow and dreams of repeating the already legendary charge of the 21st Lancers at Omdurman. Even the Yeomanry obstinately resisted the order to abandon lances and keep swords for ceremonial occasions only. The Northumberland Yeomanry put up such a prolonged resistance to what they felt to be a social degradation that they even managed to get to France in 1914 complete with both swords and lances.

There were periodical efforts at reform. In 1888 the War Department took a tentative step forward by ordering most of the County battalions to form detachments of Mounted Infantry. It was quicker and easier to train selected infantrymen to the minimum standard of horsemanship and horse-management needed to get about the country than to teach a cavalry trooper all his necessary skills; and specialists such as farriers and veterinary sergeants could be borrowed when wanted from the regular cavalry. But it was on a very small scale. Each battalion furnished merely a quarter of a company, so that a brigade commander could by combining them only create a single company of mounted men. In South Africa, however, they were strongly reinforced by the contingents sent by Australia and Canada, both of which found this type of mounted soldier better suited to their needs and temperaments than the more closely drilled formations of old-fashioned cavalry. Combined they provided the more capable generals with an invaluable mobile reserve which could be quickly switched to operate on either flank; and in April 1900, when General Broadwood ran into a destructive ambush on his withdrawal to Bloemfontein, it was the colonial and British mounted infantry who extricated him and then brilliantly covered the retreat of his shattered and exhausted force.

It was particularly tragic for the British that South Africa provided the last great theatre of war where properly trained and equipped mounted troops, imaginatively handled, could exercise a decisive effect on the course of a campaign. There were the wide open spaces in which wide-sweeping cavalry raids after the American pattern could be carried out without serious danger of enemy interference; and both armies depended for their heavier supplies, such as reserve ammunition, on long, vulnerable railway lines, and for their communications on equally vulnerable telegraph lines. The Boer Commandos occasionally exploited their superior mobility in this way : the British hardly ever. Furthermore, the Boer tactics on the battle-field positively invited outflanking movements by cavalry supported by Horse Artillery. They dug themselves in on positions of great natural strength which made them almost invincible by any form of frontal assault. But, mindful of the lessons of Vicksburg and Plevna, they knew that such a force, if it once allowed itself to be enveloped and invested, was doomed. They were thus extremely sensitive to movements which turned and enfiladed their main position and further threatened to surround them completely. In such cases they would slip out of battle, preferably at night, mount their horses, and pull back to another equally formidable defensive position.

In sober fact not even the most romantic cavalry officer can seriously have thought that the entrenched lines of the Boers which had halted, decimated, and sometimes thrown into disordered retreat some of the best infantry in the world could have been breached by a massed cavalry charge; that 'the speed of the horse, the magnetism of the charge and the terror of cold steel'[7] would have disturbed for a moment the aim of a single Boer marksman. Most of them none the less clung nostalgically to the idea that somehow, somewhere, their chance would come. In consequence the troop-horse of the regular cavalry went into the campaign carrying an intolerable burden of equipment and horse-furniture. The Boer farmer, when he rode out to war, loaded his hardy little horse with an old, simple, and workman-like saddle and bridle, his own person, rifle, and bandolier, and a blanket slung across the withers with a rope over it carrying at one end a bag of mealies and biltong, and at the other a bag of spare cartridges. The Argentine horses which, for the sake of economy, were brought across for use by the bulk of British cavalry had to carry not only the heavily accoutred and top-booted trooper, his carbine, ammunition, five-pound sabre, and in some cases a lance, but a mass of saddlery designed for durability and smartness on parade and without regard for weight. Highly polished brass bosses appeared wherever it was possible to put them. Stirrups, bits and curbs were of heavy, burnished steel; and instead of the simple breast strap with which the Russians held the saddle in position there was an elaborate, shiny, metal breastplate. In addition there was a number of small and practically valueless items of equipment such as a satchel for spare shoes, nails, and a hammer which the trooper would rarely be able to use on active service and an elaborately coiled and braided, pipe-clayed watering halter.[8] The total result was that British cavalry moved at a rate on average little better than that of good marching infantry. It remained in fact what Havelock had called it in 1867 : 'a jangling, brilliant, costly, but almost helpless unreality'.[9]

General French's relief of Kimberley with a mounted force of some 5,000 men in February 1900 was widely hailed as a brilliant and imaginative demonstration of the great surviving value of cavalry in modern warfare; and much was made of the 'forced march' of a hundred miles in four days round the flank of the main victorious Boer covering force at Magersfontein which easily broke through the thin enemy lines which were blockading rather than besieging the town. The conception of this wholly successful enterprise reflected the arrival in South Africa of Lord Roberts, with Kitchener as his Chief-of-Staff, to co-ordinate the efforts, hitherto disastrous, of the generals commanding the various columns thrusting northwards to the relief of the beleaguered garrisons of Ladysmith, Kimberley, and Mafeking. It was also significant that Roberts had especially asked for Colonel Henderson as his Chief-of-Intelligence : a man whose enlightened but balanced views on the use of cavalry in modern warfare had caught the eye of Lord Wolseley and earned him rapid promotion. The attention and reserves of the Boers were drawn off to the opposite end of the front by a feint attack of the Highland Brigade, and French was able to gallop his force round a hastily thrown out flanking defence force of Boers on their left flank in open order and with only trivial casualties.

French handled the whole operation extremely competently and fully deserved the credit he won by his successful enterprise. Under the gruelling South African sun it was inevitable that his seven batteries of Royal Horse Artillery should leave a rotting line of dead horses to mark the line of his advance. But the piles of these were vastly swollen by the foundered horses of his regular cavalry regiments: the Carabineers, the composite regiment of Household Cavalry, the Scots Greys, the Inniskillings, the 10th Hussars and the 9th, 12th and 16th Lancers. By the time he reached Kimberley only his two brigades of mounted infantry and his colonial irregular cavalry were still fit and active: the New South Wales Lancers, Rimington's Scouts, and the New Zealand Light Horse, who were the first to penetrate the Boer lines and make contact with the defenders. Many of the troopers of his eight regular cavalry regiments who had not already lost their chargers were dismounted, leading their horses and carrying their heavy saddles on their own shoulders. There could have been no question of mounting a charge, or even of achieving another day of hard marching. Kilpatrick, moving at exactly the same pace in his great raid south of Atlanta in 1864, had covered 400 miles in sixteen days and brought his force back to base practically intact. In their obsession with shock tactics British cavalry had in fact ceased to be in any useful sense mobile.

On the other hand those regiments whose Commanding Officers had taken the trouble to train them properly for dismounted action proved themselves immensely valuable. Perhaps the most decisive was the intervention of Lord Airlie with his 12th Lancers and some detachments of mounted infantry on the right flank at Magersfontein, when a powerful encircling movement by the Boers threatened to turn the disaster which had already overtaken the Highland Brigade into a complete massacre which would also have engulfed the three field batteries and the Horse Artillery battery which had gallantly galloped into dangerously close support. From the early South African dawn until well past midday, with his men dismounted and skilfully posted, Airlie was able to hold off much superior enemy forces until the Coldstream and the Grenadiers arrived to take over, when he could remount his troops and withdraw into reserve. There were, of course, many less important occasions in the scattered encounters which made up such a large part of this confusing campaign when dismounted regular cavalry did every bit as well as the mounted infantry and the Colonial irregulars.

But they did so by courage and improvisation, since they were

H*

themselves, like their horses, wrongly equipped and accoutred for such tasks. Their field boots were too heavy for effective dismounted manoeuvre and their carbines were far less effective than the mounted infantry rifles. Like the Prussian and French cavalry in 1870 and the bulk of the Russians in 1877, they failed most dismally in the opening stages of the war in their elementary task of patrolling and reconnaissance. Whatever their historians may say, the 9th Lancers allowed Lord Methuen to move his whole infantry force in close marching order down the gentle slope of the valley to the near bank of the Modder River with orders only to halt there for breakfast, and totally ignorant that there were superior numbers of Boers beautifully entrenched on both banks of the river, supported by a powerful force of dug-in artillery.

There were, perhaps, some half-dozen occasions in the three years of fighting that the cavalry were given a chance to use their lances and sabres, when small, outmanoeuvred Boer forces were forced to take to their horses and gallop for safety. In most cases they suffered more than the trivial casualties they inflicted; and tragically and ironically the highly intelligent and imaginative Lord Airlie was himself killed in just such an operation at Diamond Hill in June 1900. He led his beloved 12th Lancers in a classic charge against a Boer force which threatened to destroy a dangerously exposed battery, saved the guns, and speared something under twenty of the enemy before they could remount and gallop away again into safety on their less heavily burdened horses. But as the Lancers reformed to withdraw the Boers dismounted and opened fire, knocking out two officers, seventeen men and thirty horses. To the great loss of the army Airlie himself, who had shown himself exceptionally adaptable to the conditions of modern warfare, was one of the last to fall. His last recorded and characteristically courteous words were addressed to a battle-maddened sergeant: 'Pray moderate your language', he said, and dropped with a bullet through his heart.

Still more ironically, it was the Boers who, in the last stages of the war, devised a technique of shock tactics for their mounted troops which was devastatingly effective. When the back of enemy resistance had been broken and the war was virtually won, the British, now in overwhelming numbers, had to spend another exhausting and frustrating year in hunting down and rounding up the elusive, but still highly aggressive die-hard commandos under men like De Wet and Louis Botha. Inevitably the British were scattered in small, partially fortified posts all over South Africa, all of which had to be supplied by equally small and generally weakly escorted convoys of wagons. The new Boer tactic, demonstrated with particular expertise by Botha, was to surprise such detachments by charging in at the gallop from every direction firing rifles from the saddle, Arab-fashion, and catching the defenders before they had time to organise either a dismounted defence or form up for a counter-charge. At Vlaakfontein, Schieper's Nek, Brakenlaagte, and Tweebosch the Boers were able to ride into and over the British, taking prisoner all who were not killed in the first rush. These, whether wounded or unwounded, they generally returned as a tiresome encumbrance. But the supplies they captured kept them going for long, unnecessary, and wearisome months until the last of them were rounded up and the war was really over.

The handling of infantry by the army commanders and the infantry tactics themselves, as developed on Salisbury Plain or on Indian manoeuvres, proved to be almost as antiquated as the ideas of the cavalry commanders. All the careful lessons of the American Civil War, as recorded by Chesney and Henderson at Camberley and endorsed by the Duke of Cambridge, went abruptly by the board. Even the lesson which Moltke had learnt the hard way, that it was impossible to advance in close column of companies, or even half companies, against the concentrated fire of modern rifles was overlooked or discounted. The additional defensive power given to the rifle, and in due course to the machine-gun, by the skilful use of entrenchments, which had been the second great lesson of the American Civil War, and which had since been abundantly confirmed in the Balkans and in Cuba, was similarly ignored. With a complacency equal to that of their cavalry brethren, the infantry commanders within a single week at Magersfontein, Stormberg, and Colenso, launched some of the finest troops in the world into hopeless frontal assaults against carefully prepared positions in formations not much different from those of the Imperial Guard which had suffered disaster under the far less deadly musketry of Wellington's regiments on the slopes of Waterloo. The total casualties, though shattering in their impact on a British public unused for half a century to major warfare, were not by Continental standards large. But in proportion to the numbers engaged they were very heavy indeed. Lord Methuen lost 1,000 in killed, wounded and missing at his so-called victory at the Modder River – more than a tenth of his total force; and ten days later he lost another 1,000 in his much more carefully prepared night assault at Magersfontein. The casualties of the Boers, however understated in their own returns, were certainly by comparison trivial.

The root of these disasters went back to the commentaries of the very large numbers of officers sent out from Britain to report on the operations of both the Federal and Confederate armies in the Civil War. For a brief space, from 1866 to 1876, the views of the enlightened reformers – Chesney, Denison, Henderson, and even the 'Young Turk', Havelock – prevailed, confirmed as they were by the authoritative voice of the Duke of Cambridge. But after 1875 a period set in which was as dark for the infantry as for the gunners and the cavalry. The bulk of the observers were sent out at a moment when the War Department was extremely preoccupied with the problem of suitable training for the amateur army of the Volunteers who were to be Britain's last ditch home defence when the regular army was heavily committed overseas. Their main brief, therefore, was to examine the performance of the enthusiastic but hastily trained amateurs who made up the bulk of both armies in the American War. Unfortunately their judgements were both patronising and shortsighted. They deprecated the habit of the Americans of digging themselves in not only in defence, but in the course of an attack, as being due to their inability to function coherently and effectively in operations in open country. In other words, trenches were just a device for getting the best out of brave and dedicated men who were insufficiently trained to meet regular troops in the open field. Against such troops, it was maintained, a formal and properly conducted assault by fully trained regulars must inevitably prevail. They carried this already faulty reasoning a dangerous stage further by arguing that to train even first class regular infantry to entrench themselves whenever immobilised, either in attack or defence, would encourage a defensive-minded mentality which would sap their morale, deprive them of the spirit of aggression, and by making them dependent on earthworks for protection render them gradually incapable of manoeuvring courageously and competently in the open when necessary. It never occurred to them that the refusal of even Lee's hard-bitten Confederate veterans in 1865 to advance in the open against prepared defences was due not to any lack of training or failure of morale, but to sheer commonsense. In modern conditions it would have been, as Havelock had said of the old-fashioned cavalry charge, 'reckless ineffectual folly'.[10]

The die-hards bolstered these misconceptions of the American Civil War tactics by a series of equally faulty deductions from the history of the major campaigns of the latter part of the century. The French in 1870, incurably defence-minded, had forfeited over and over again chances of significant tactical victories by their reluctance to leave nicely selected positions and risk a counter-attack in the open. The Turks in the Balkans had been imperturbable and almost invincible so long as they remained in their earthworks; but their few attempts to take the offensive had been incompetent, half-hearted, and abortive. The Spaniards in Cuba, experienced regular troops, well-trained and well armed, had been content to sit in their trenches on San Juan hill taking a heavy toll of the American volunteers until numbers and enthusiasm at last forced them back. In every case it had been the defensive-minded army, relying on its positions or its trenches, which had lost the war; and the fact that the Boers never left their entrenchments to move out into the open on foot seemed to confirm both the false conclusions drawn from the American fighting. Here were irregulars, drawn straight from their farms, who naturally could not be expected to display the drill and discipline necessary for ordered movement in the open and were therefore forced to rely on entrenchments and the hypnotic effect of the entrenchments seemed proved by the fact that, when outflanked or successfully assaulted, they immediately withdrew to another entrenched defensive position.

These conclusions left all the relevant facts out of consideration. The French infantry in 1870 had lost none of its traditional fury and *élan* in the attack. It was frustrated only by the ineptitude and lack of self-confidence of its generals. The Turkish regular army was certainly ill-trained and poorly led and in consequence incapable of effective manoeuvre. But Turkish troops were also by nature at their best in a dour defensive; and this was not the result, but the cause of their passion for complex earthworks. They stuck to their trenches because that was where they fought best; and in them they would resist to the last. For the Spaniards heroic resistance to the last extremity was a tradition centuries-old, dating back to the Moorish wars of the Middle Ages, and epitomised in the gouty De Leyva's dogged defiance at Pavia in 1525 of the finest army France could produce; and this enduring characteristic was to show itself again repeatedly in their civil war of the 1930s. Linares' troops at San Juan and El Caney were outnumbered by more than two to one. They were on half rations, with a blockaded and starving city behind them; and in the swampy jungles on their flanks there were swarms of passionately hostile Cuban guerillas. The trenches in which they put up such a gallant, if unavailing resistance were again the consequence and not the cause of their defensive predicament; and the deductions that the failure of the Boers ever to advance on foot in the open against British positions was due either to insufficient training or a lack of aggressiveness induced by dependence on trenches was equally false and, in the light of recent South African history, unforgivable.

Boer tactics were based on a severely practical and commonsensical appreciation of the capacities and limitations both of their own troops and those of the enemy. They had at all times to husband their slender manpower; and they also showed a remarkable ability to adapt their methods quickly to new lessons which could only be learnt on the battlefield. Their passion for careful and complex entrenchment sprang, for example, from the experiences of the first weeks of fighting in Natal, when they found that their habit of concealing themselves among the rocks of ridges and kopjes resulted in heavy casualties under artillery fire from rock splinters which flew in every direction. That they in no way lacked aggressive spirit should have been clear to every British soldier since the surrender of Sir George Colley with his entire force at Majuba Hill in 1881. There Colley, temporarily cut off, had taken refuge in what appeared to him to be an impregnable position : in the large, shallow volcanic crater of a precipitous rocky hill. But the Boers were in sufficient strength to surround him; and the terraced rocks gave them plenty of dead ground and an easy climb to the crest. The slope was so steep that the defenders of the crater ridge had to lean so far out to fire at the advancing enemy that they became sitting targets for the concealed Boers. These were, in consequence, able to reach the outside edge of the ridge and bring the whole inside of the crater under a withering fire which plunged the massed British into confusion and faced Colley with the alternative of surrender or annihilation. They were never offered the chance of victory on the same scale in 1899. But the capture of White's small detached force at Nicholson's Nek in the first week of the war followed exactly the same tactical pattern; and it was to be repeated constantly throughout the war, whenever a small detached force found itself isolated and cut off from water.

It is extremely unlikely that General Cronje, or even his more civilised colleagues like Joubert, Delarey, Botha, and De Wet, had studied the manoeuvres of the American war or Osman Pasha's intricate system of earthworks at Plevna. Cronje was a dark, patriarchal figure, gentle in manner and barbarously ruthless in practice. His military studies were almost certainly restricted to the campaigns of Joshua and the prophetess Deborah. But he brought to the prosecution of modern warfare a flexible intelligence which his British opponents were apt to describe resentfully as a diabolical cunning. He also had the advantage of not being handicapped by the text books and rules of thumb which governed the conduct of operations on Salisbury Plain. The four miles of entrenchments with which he faced Lord Methuen at the Modder River, and again less than a week later at Magersfontein, were a sophisticated masterpiece such as had never been seen on any battlefield and would not be seen again until the construction of the fabled Hindenburg Line. They were not only beautifully concealed, but they cheated on all the known rules. Contrary to all established practice, Cronje dug in his front line on the forward bank of the river, putting in the trenches there with characteristic realism all the less reliable elements of his army : the rebel volunteers from Cape Colony and Natal who knew that if they attempted to fall back across the river they would be massacred by the hard-liner Transvaalers behind them on the near bank. These, moreover, were in three rising tiers of trenches, so that every rifle in the army could open up simultaneously.

The Modder valley was a broad, almost flat plain, in places four miles across, bounded on both sides by craggy hills and with the green line of the river running down the middle. Cronje's trap was rendered all the more effective by the British *idée fixe*, confirmed by recent experience in Natal and by Methuen's two minor preliminary engagements at Belmont and Enslin, that Boers invariably established themselves along the summits of rocky hills or kopjes. It should also be said in extenuation of Methuen's guilelessness that he was vilely badly served by his Intelligence Service and his cavalry patrols. Whatever the 9th Lancers had reported of the presence of Boers along the Modder, they had not pushed their reconnaissance far enough home to give him any inkling that the line was held in force; and he had no idea that the river itself was a formidable obstacle. 'I was given to understand', he wrote afterwards in his Despatch, 'that the Modder was fordable everywhere.' In fact the drifts were few and full of dangerous pot-holes; and in any case nobody knew where they were. At dawn on 27 November the army, not much more than 8,000 strong, set out, after a day's rest, on a five-mile march to the Modder bank where they were to water their horses eat their breakfast, and then to cross the river and form up for an assault on the hills beyond. They moved in close marching order down the hills and across the plain; and such was the Boer discipline that not a shot was fired at them until the Lancer patrols were right up to the Boer trenches and the leading infantry within 500 yards.

The inevitable result was a situation which was to be disastrously repeated over and over again during the early months of the war: British infantry pinned down behind such cover as they could find, anthills and boulders and the like, without a target to aim at, unable to advance and unwilling to retire. Methuen was lucky that he only lost 450 in killed and wounded, more than half of them in the first ten minutes, as the columns were sorted out into some sort of open order. He was luckier still to be able to record an official victory. The Guards' Brigade on his right was hemmed in by another unfordable river and spent the day foodless and waterless, puffing philosophically at their pipes and lying on their rifles to prevent them from becoming too hot to hold. On the other flank the Yorkshire Light Infantry found a feasible crossing place and the Argylls were able to get across and round the Boer trenches. They suffered heavily, contributing a quarter of the total British casualties, mostly from the fire of their own artillery, whose spotters had failed to observe their crossing. Trickles of reinforcements enabled them to hang on until nightfall, and, true to form, once outflanked the Boers slipped away in the night. Cronje had, after all, a far stronger position ready behind him at Magersfontein. Methuen seems to have had no new plan in mind for the next morning save 'a renewal of the assault'. So it was just as well that his advancing troops found the Boer trenches deserted. He told his troops that it had been 'the hardest won victory in our annals of war', and repeated the phrase in his official Despatch. As a comment on a battle in which he had lost less than 500 killed and wounded, it must rank with President McKinley's address to the troops returned from Cuba as one of the great euphoric overstatements of military history.

The sequel to Methuen's Pyrrhic victory was a series of costly defeats which effectively halted the advance of all three columns moving to the relief of Kimberley, Ladysmith, and Mafeking, and which served only to illustrate that British infantry tactics were as antiquated and as unrealistic as the ideas of their commanders. Two of the generals involved had at least learnt the lesson that a daylight advance in the open against prepared Boer positions was suicidal folly; both therefore decided on night approach marches designed to bring their infantry within charging distance of the enemy positions as dawn broke. They reckoned, certainly rightly, that in such circumstances there would be no time for the Boer rifles to take a heavy toll and that the bayonet would easily prevail. Unfortunately, however, neither had given much attention to the problems and difficulties of such a manoeuvre. They may perhaps be forgiven for not having studied the brilliant moonlit operation of the Grand Duke Michael which had placed the great fortress of Kars at his mercy; but they should at least have been familiar with the details of Wolseley's night march in open order across trackless desert to his victory at Tel-el-Kebir.

General Gatacre opened the ball with his attack at Stormberg on the night of 9–10 December. Gatacre was a man as distinguished for his personal courage as he was for his stupidity. He had demonstrated both at Atbara, in the Sudan, when, as general in command of a brigade, he had been the first to reach the enemy zareba and was already tearing it down with his bare hands when his leading troops arrived to help him. He now had a thirty-mile advance to make contact with the position at Stormberg, which had been occupied, mostly by rebel farmers from Cape Colony and Natal. For this he made his plans with such publicity that they were known in detail throughout the army for at least a week in advance, and were actually published in *The Times* the day before he moved. He had only a very attenuated division at his disposal : two infantry battalions, some 250 Mounted Infantry, and two batteries of field guns, in all just under 3,000 men. But it was probably sufficient for the job in hand had it been directed with even reasonable intelligence.

At nine o'clock, in pitch darkness, this whole force moved forward in a single close column from the rail-head at Molteno on what should have been a ten-mile march to the estimated Boer position. They had already spent a long and exhausting day of marching and slow railway-journeying up the twenty-mile line to Molteno, including a three-hour pause when they had sat under the sun in open trucks waiting for somebody to produce the railway engine. After a hasty meal they were required to advance across difficult, boulder-strewn ground towards an objective which had not even been reconnoitred. The general marched in front, on foot and leading his charger. There were no scouts out either in front or on the flanks; and it very soon became clear that the guides had no clear idea of where they were going. The clear South African dawn found them still moving doggedly forward more than seven hours later, when the Boers opened fire from a position which was, in fact, on their right flank and more or less parallel to their line of march. Fortunately for Gatacre the Boers were not Transvaaler marksmen; and their fire, though intense, was wildly inaccurate. Fortunately, too, the Boer artillery which had come down from the north and fired with great accuracy, had been supplied with shells by a fraudulent contractor most of which failed to explode. But the British were famished and exhausted. Many had already fallen asleep on their feet and sunk by the roadside. In the panic and confusion of the opening fusillade nobody gave any coherent orders, and the whole mass surged, to its credit, forward towards the enemy, only to find that the rocky hills had sheer ledges which no troops on earth could scale. The leading men held their ground under the ledges. The rest bolted for cover and then fell back down the line of their advance leaving yet more men asleep and exhausted by the wayside. The gunners, unaware of the gap which had thus opened up between the two bodies of infantry, shelled the forward slope of the hills indiscriminately, thereby completing the demoralisation of those who had clung on under the ledges.

The withdrawal was competently covered by the surviving half-battalion of the Irish Fusiliers, the Mounted Infantry, and the gunners. But the Boers 'gleaned' a large number of unwounded, sleeping prisoners along the way; and those who had clung on to the hillside had no alternative but to surrender. Such was the inaccuracy of the Boer fire that Gatacre's killed and wounded amounted to no more than ninety-four men. It would have been a less dishonourable blow to British pride had they been much higher. For the Boers collected in all over 600 unwounded prisoners and two of the Horse Artillery's guns – more than a fifth of the entire force. The general, unfortunately, survived. Highly esteemed as he was in the higher reaches of the army, he was left in command of his Division until a second disaster four months later at Reddersburg, when five companies of troops under his command were forced to surrender in circumstances which had become impossible. Then, at last, he was recalled and honourably retired.

On the following night, at one in the morning, Methuen launched the Highland Brigade, four battalions strong, on an almost precisely similar but far more disastrous venture : a night assault of the formidable position to which Cronje had retired on the heights at Magersfontein. This time the position had been reconnoitred, though to no purpose. A battery of Horse Artillery and the great Navy 4·7-inch gun, hauled by thirty-two bullocks, had moved up, covered by cavalry, and 'searched' the whole ridge with shrapnel and high explosive without provoking a single answering shot. This was not surprising. Cronje, having observed the immunity of his guns at the Modder, had this time entrenched his riflemen as well some two or three hundred yards forward of the ridge, with a thicket of barbed trip wires loosely hung with tin cans in front. Against this the Highlanders advanced as densely packed as possible in quarter-column to ensure cohesion and direction, the regiments in column with the left guides carrying ropes to preserve perfect alignment. The Brigade had marched up from the Modder and been sent forward, unfed, to lie under a cold drizzle, two men to a blanket, for the first part of the night. When they moved off only General Wauchope, marching in front with the Black Watch, knew what the plan was; and only his guides, a Colonel Benson of the RA and two of Rimington's Scouts, knew the line of deployment.

In fact the order to deploy had just been given when, thanks to Cronje's skilful dispositions, the leading files stumbled into the Boer trip wires some 400 yards forward of his estimated trench line. The first rattling tin can roused a concentration of rifle fire which inflicted 500 casualties within ten minutes and threw the whole Brigade into confusion. The Black Watch, in the lead, suffered worst, losing nearly as many in killed and wounded as they had in the first battle of their history in 1758, when Sir James Abercrombie had led them to disaster at Ticonderoga. They struggled forward to within a few yards of the enemy trenches and small parties even got in temporarily among the Boers with their bayonets, leaving bullet-ridden corpses to be revealed as the sun rose strung like scare-crows on the barbed wire. The rest of the Brigade dispersed and found what cover it could, to spend the rest of the day, as the Argylls already had on the Modder bank, under fire, helpless, foodless, waterless, and tormented by a pitiless sun. By the time that darkness fell and they were extricated with their supporting guns they had lost nearly a quarter of their total numbers. Of the three leading companies of the Black Watch only six men remained on their feet. So Methuen, too, fell back, to his camp on the Modder River. The most fitting comment on the entire episode had already been made by

General Wauchope as he fell, mortally wounded, under the first burst of rifle fire. 'What a pity,' he said.

To these operations the defeats of Sir Redvers Buller at Colenso, Spion Kop, and Vaalkranz furnished only a dismal *coda* devoid of any constructive lesson and illustrating merely the extent of the ignorance of the British High Command of the conditions of modern warfare. Of the commanders in the field Buller was the one most trusted both by the British public and by his own troops. With far the strongest field army, some 21,000 men, he had set out to relieve Ladysmith. He looked pugnacious and had a reputation for bulldog tenacity entirely undeserved by his performance in action. At Colenso he launched a two-pronged frontal assault to force river crossings over the Tugela against unreconnoitred and unidentified Boer positions on the north bank. Almost incredibly, Hart's Irish Brigade advanced in broad daylight into a great loop of the river in the same close packed formation as Wauchope had used three days earlier at Magersfontein to preserve cohesion in the dark. Nobody knew where the only practicable ford was; there were no scouts or skirmishers; and the order to deploy was only given when the Boers had already opened fire from both front and flank. The ford could not be found; and by the time Hart, with great gallantry and skill had extricated and re-formed his Irishmen they had lost almost exactly the same numbers as Wauchope's Highlanders at Magersfontein. The other Brigade, with at least the unmistakable objective of Colenso bridge, and moving more intelligently in open order, might have succeeded, but for the fatal impetuosity of Long's guns. As it was the reputedly tenacious Buller with two virtually uncommitted brigades in hand, threw the game up and withdrew the whole army to his base camp at midday, having suffered some 1,200 casualties and leaving 10 guns and 250 prisoners in enemy hands. At Spion Kop, and later on a smaller scale at Vaalkranz, he re-created, it seemed almost deliberately, the conditions which had led Colley to surrender at Majuba, cramming more and more infantry on to plateaux dominated by Boer rifle fire where every reinforcement served only to swell the casualty list. By the time that he accepted, like Methuen and Gatacre, that he was stalemated, he had lost in all some 5,000 men killed, wounded, and missing.

The arrival of Lord Roberts, Kitchener, and Henderson to give some cohesion and order to the campaign transformed the whole picture. 'Bobs', the legendary hero of Kandahar and Kabul, was accustomed to take his pre-breakfast exercise in singlet and slacks on a round of tent-pegging. But he had no illusions about the function of cavalry in modern war. In 1904, when his office of Commander-in-Chief was abolished, he was to write to his former Chief-of-Staff begging him to continue the abolition of the lance, foreseeing that 'a great struggle will be made to get that weapon re-introduced now that I have left the War Office'.[11] He had equally understood the limitation imposed on infantry tactics by the development of modern fire-power combined with sophisticated entrenchments. He could obviously do nothing immediately about the too heavy equipment of the British cavalry trooper. But it was he who launched French on his well-judged raid to relieve Kimberley; and he followed French up with two infantry brigades to secure the passage thus won round Cronje's flank. Since the Boer position at Magersfontein, like Osman Pasha's at Plevna, was frontally invincible, it must be invested. Cronje fought back viciously, but he was remorselessly herded into Paardeberg, with his back to the Modder River, French coming back from Kimberley just in time to stop the last bolt-hole to the north with his dismounted troopers. It should have been a bloodless victory. Unfortunately, however, Kitchener was in operational command. A brilliant organiser and administrator, he had little understanding of the tactical realities of modern warfare; and he launched a general assault on Cronje's position, which reduced its extent, but chiefly resulted in 1,100 quite unnecessary British casualties. Roberts then took over personal command, suspended all infantry attacks, and by sheer hard pounding with his artillery forced the surrender of the main Boer army and virtually won the war. The way was open to Bloemfontein and Pretoria and there only remained the prolonged and tedious business of rounding up the elusive Commandos of De Wet and Botha. Apart from Roberts, the British generals had totally ignored the lessons of the American Civil War with the results of which Havelock had warned them thirty years before. 'If we neglect its teaching,' he had written, 'then indeed it may be said of us that contemporary military history is enacted before our eyes – in vain.'[12]

The Russo-Japanese War which opened, two days before it was declared, on 8 February 1904, offered, surprisingly enough, fewer lessons for the generals of the future than the Boer War. The South African fighting had rammed home two of the hard facts imposed on modern armies by the technical advances of the latter nineteenth century. One was that, as shock troops, cavalry no longer had any place on a modern battlefield, though when employed as mounted infantry they still had an immense potential value in any theatre of operations where there was plenty of room to manoeuvre. This was perhaps something which might have been exploited, particularly by the Germans, in the opening, mobile phase of 1914 before the Marne battle created the deadlock of trench lines without flanks from the North Sea to the Swiss frontier; and it was exploited in a limited fashion by Allenby in his brilliant Palestinian campaign. But it was already a conclusion from the past which might have been drawn – and indeed was drawn – by the more intelligent observers of the American Civil War forty years before. The second lesson was short and clear: that massive frontal assaults against an adequately entrenched well-armed enemy were massive and suicidal folly. Colenso was, in fact, less an epilogue to the age of Moltke than a prelude to Loos and the Somme.

The Manchurian campaign of 1904–5 jumped back a whole stage in military history. The whole struggle on land separated itself into two closely related, but quite distinct episodes: the siege of Port Arthur; and the manoeuvres and battles of the two great field armies 300 miles to the north on the Yalu River and along the line of the East Chinese extension of the Trans-Siberian railway to Port Arthur. Both looked backwards rather than to the future. Port Arthur was Sebastopol over again, modified only by the increased fire-power of modern weapons; and the great battles of Liao-Yang and Mukden were fought out by armies of comparable size to those of 1870, and modelled on principles and tactics deduced from those of Moltke. Thus they were in no way a curtain-raiser for 1914, but rather the last act of the great drama which had opened at Königgrätz and whose epilogue was to be finally written when the younger Moltke was brought to a halt at the Marne.

The Treaty of Portsmouth in 1905 brought to a decisive halt the last Tsarist phase of Russian imperial expansion. Stalemated by the European Great Powers in the Balkans and by the formidable risks of a direct confrontation with the British-Indian army in the Himalayas, Russia had concentrated all her energy on the seemingly almost effortless advance across northern Asia whose logical end was the control of the whole Pacific coast from the Arctic to the southern tip of Korea. In 1904 this process of erosion seemed to be on the verge of complete and final success. She held on virtually permanent lease the southernmost tip of the Manchurian Peninsula – the isthmus of Liao-tung, with Port Arthur at the extreme end. A fictional joint commercial enterprise with the Chinese had permitted her to extend the Trans-Siberian Railway through Manchuria to Harbin, and from there to both Vladivostock and Port Arthur; and finally she had been able to use the Boxer rising as an excuse for moving a substantial field army into Manchuria which, in spite of constant protests from the European Powers and her own reiterated promises of withdrawal, she successfully maintained in virtually permanent occupation. She thus had a powerful Pacific fleet based on Vladivostock and Port Arthur, and an army little short of 100,000 men grouped round the frontiers of the great coveted Province of Korea. What nobody among the Tsar's advisers realised was that any attempt to pluck the ripened fruit would entail a major war, and one which it would be very difficult to win.

It was a singularly unpropitious moment for Nicholas II to launch a war on any front; and Manchuria was the worst he could have chosen. At home there was a rising tide of industrial discontent in all the great cities of which the revolutionary propagandists were taking full advantage; and a progressive corruption of public life had in the past twenty years spread into the highest circles of the governing class. To the mass of the Russian people the conquest of Korea meant nothing. It was important only to those administrators and army and navy officers who saw in it a chance of self-advancement; to a handful of intellectual imperialist daydreamers; and most of all to a syndicate of financiers, industrialists, and wealthy, highly placed government officials who had heavily invested in a vast project for exploiting the Korean timber resources. The fact that Admiral Alexeieff, the Tsar's Viceroy and Commander-in-Chief of all naval and military forces in Manchuria and Port Arthur, was a large shareholder in this enterprise more than once had a serious influence on local policies.[13] Inevitably, and fatally, this corruption had permeated the lower levels in every branch of the administration.

Thus, of the six projected forts on the rocky hilltops which were the outer perimeter of Port Arthur, only one had been completed, and one half completed when war broke out, though large sums had been available for the development of more profitable, jerry-built commercial structures in the shoddy town which rose rapidly round the newly acquired naval base. The dockyard facilities for the fleet had been almost totally neglected; but large sums had been spent to make the commercial harbour at Dalny, twenty miles further north, entirely adequate and efficient.[14] In the last weeks, when every effort was being made to provision and equip the fortress against a possible siege or assault, the Military Governor, the vain, almost half-witted, and probably corrupt General Stössel, allowed valuable cargoes of flour and grain to leave the port for more profitable markets elsewhere when the owners had already fled for safety to neighbouring neutral ports.[15] The army and navy officers were no better. The ammunition cases of one of the scarce supply trains to reach the port were found to contain nothing but champagne; and an enormous mound of wooden boxes, known locally as the 'Triumphal Arch', contained only vodka. These were some of the handicaps which limited the activities of the Russian field commanders in 1904.

For the Japanese the acquisition of Korea was not just a matter of Imperial prestige, but of dire necessity. Industrialisation and the rapid acquisition of a Western way of life had produced a population explosion which threatened to bring the nation below the subsistence level. The Russian annexation of Sakhalin had closed one obvious outlet; and the conquest of Formosa after the easy victory over China in 1904 had only given a temporary relief, in spite of a massive, organised emigration. The population continued to increase at the rate of 700,000

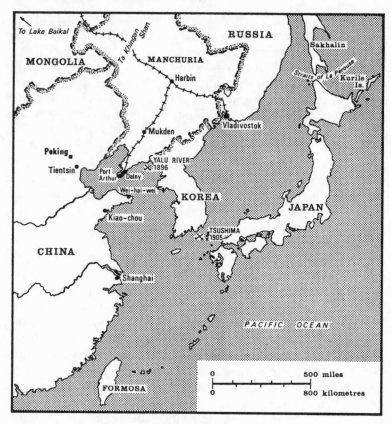

Map 5.   Manchuria and the Far East

a year and had again reached the danger point in 1904. The potentially rich, sparsely peopled, wide spaces of Korea offered the only possible solution. Russia's repeated evasions of promises to evacuate Manchuria, the great timber concessions, and the naval build-up at Port Arthur made it clear that Korea could only be got by risking an army and navy as yet untried in war against any of the established military powers. The only alternative was starvation and ruin.

The land operations of this war were dominated by two factors, neither of which were within the control of the commanders in the field, but which limited and sometimes dictated every decision they made. One was the naval situation; the other the problems involved in building up their forces to a strength sufficient for the tasks assigned to them. For the Japanese the two were closely inter-related. Their armies, their supplies, and their reinforcements had all perforce to come by sea. As a main line of communications it was conveniently short and rapid. But until the Russian Pacific Fleet had been destroyed or totally immobilised it was continuously and dangerously vulnerable; and if it should be completely cut their armies on the mainland were irretrievably doomed. Had Admiral Togo's initial surprise and his subsequent operations been completely successful in penning the Russian main fleet in the harbour of Port Arthur and blocking the entrance channel the problem would have been solved outright. The detached cruiser squadron at Vladivostock could then easily have been contained. But the channel was not effectively blocked; and the Russian fleet, though badly battered, remained a 'fleet in being', safely ensconced behind the hills at the harbour entrance and the coastal batteries where the guns of Togo's battleships could not reach it.[16] It remained a perpetual menace until the Japanese army could get possession of the rocky heights which constituted the outer defences of Port Arthur and bring its guns to bear on the helplessly anchored ships in the harbour; and if the Russians were to succeed in bringing their Baltic Fleet half-way round the world to reinforce it, picking up the so-called Third Pacific Squadron on its way, it could become a force which could, conceivably, win the war at a blow.

That this was not an idle or alarmist calculation by the Japanese high command was proved by the unenterprising, but occasionally successful activity of the Vladivostock cruiser squadron. It sank few transports; but among them, as luck would have it, were four vital ones carrying all the siege guns and ammunition earmarked for the destruction of the Port Arthur forts and the railway engines specially constructed in the USA for the line south to the siege area. All this lent an added and genuine urgency to the frenzied attacks of the Japanese on the outer defences of Port Arthur and the operations of the covering army to push the relieving Russian armies back from the Yalu River, up the railway line towards Harbin and Mukden, and well out of reach of the beleaguered fortress. For, although the build-up of their forces was swift and comparatively uninterrupted, the Japanese started with the disadvantage that at the outset they had to start from scratch. On the mainland they had only a swarm of spies and saboteurs, happily ensconced in the labour force employed in the dockyards and on the fortifications of Port Arthur, thanks to the Russian inability to distinguish between Japanese, Koreans, and Chinese. They had not one single soldier to oppose to the 100,000 men at the disposal of General Kuropatkin when he was abruptly transferred from the Ministry of War to become Commander-in-Chief of all the Russian forces in Manchuria.

But Kuropatkin had even more intransigent problems of supply, and reinforcement imposed, as so often before in recent military history, by the limitations of his railway line. The 5,000-mile long Trans-Siberian Railway was single-track throughout and almost without off-loading bays or sidings at any point. It was, moreover, seriously interrupted at two points. Just beyond Irkutsk in far-eastern Siberia there was Lake Baikal, whose treacherous ice would not carry any but the lightest of loco-motives and temporary track even in mid-winter. The loop line round the south of the lake was still under construction, so that every regiment destined for Manchuria had to undertake a four-to-five day march before it could rejoin the railway. A thousand miles further on there was another hold-up at the line of the Great Kingan Mountains, where the tunnel was still uncom-pleted, and only short and lightly loaded trains could manage the zig-zag ascent to the crest. All in all it was reckoned that it took a Russian regiment anything from four to six weeks to accomplish the journey from Moscow to Harbin. The arrange-ments for their feeding and maintenance on the way were sketchy and haphazard; and it is not surprising that many of them arrived in the theatre of operations exhausted and partially demoralised. The Tsarist government had to retain in the west all its crack regiments – the Guards and the Grenadiers – and the whole of the regular standing army, partly against possible European complications, partly against the perpetual threat of Polish revolt, and as security against the rising tide of industrial and revolutionary unrest in the great cities. Even so, there were still well over a million of trained reservists available for the

Manchurian front – quite enough to overwhelm by sheer weight of numbers what the rickety finances of the Japanese would allow them to mobilise and deploy in the field. The Russian problem was to get them to the front in time to save Port Arthur.

Kuropatkin was certainly on paper the best choice the Tsar could have made as Commander-in-Chief. Without money, birth, or influence, he had come to the top by sheer intellectual capacity and a fine fighting record. He had been the spectacular Skobeleff's Chief-of-Staff in 1877 and its only surviving officer at his general's side when they led the Division into the Turkish front-line trench at the third assault on Plevna. Twenty-five years later he remained the perfect staff officer, enslaved to the book of rules and pre-arranged plans, and without the power of decisive action in a crisis. He was further gravely hampered by the frequently idiotic interference of the Viceroy and the jealousies and disregard of inconvenient orders shown by his better connected subordinates. He started the campaign with one clear principle laid down : that he would not undertake a major offensive until he had built up a numerical superiority which would be overwhelming. To this he obstinately adhered; and the Trans-Siberian Railway failed to give it to him until the war was lost. For the first months it yielded only a trickle of reinforcements – some 20,000 a month. A year later, in March 1905, having been much improved, it was yielding a monthly 100,000. But by then Port Arthur had fallen, the Pacific fleet had been annihilated, Kuropatkin had fought five unsuccessful defensive battles and was in the thick of his last, week-long, and finally fatal fight at Mukden.

There he had managed at last to accumulate 330,000 infantry in the field, as compared with the three Army Corps – some 80,000 – with which he had started a year before. But the Japanese had the reinforcement of the army released by the surrender of Port Arthur, and by throwing in the last available reserve matched him with some 315,000. They got round his flank and cut the railway behind him, forcing him into chaotic retreat westwards where he was able, thanks to the heroism of his infantry and, oddly, of his cooks and bakers, to stabilise his line. He had lost nearly a sixth of his army – some 60,000 men; and he was cut off from all possible reinforcement. But he had inflicted a loss of 53,500 on the enemy; and the Japanese, financially crippled, could not raise another man. To this deadlock the destruction of the Russian Baltic Fleet in the Tsushima Straits in May was merely an aftermath. It enabled President Roosevelt, however, to negotiate a settlement in September which exasperated the Japanese public as much as it did the Tsar. Its essential features were that it put a final end to Tsarist dreams of an ice-free port on the Pacific and gave the Japanese an entry to Korea – less than they had hoped for, but none the less a secure foothold on the Asiatic mainland. Manchuria could wait for a future occasion.

The Japanese army was by European standards small. The principle of universal obligation for military service had been decreed in 1872. But the perpetual financial stringency made it impossible to embody and train more than a tenth of the young men annually available. A few of the untapped remainder were given some sketchy annual training in the hope that they might eventually form a nucleus of a home defence force and an *Ersatz*. But for practical purposes they had in 1904 a front line army of 270,000 men and a trained reserve of suitable age of 530,000. By drawing on the untrained reserves and over-age groups of trained soldiers they were able to muster on paper about 1,100,000 armed troops in the Manchurian theatre by the end of the war. But two-thirds of these were fit only for non-combatant duties and on lines of communication. By September 1904, the Japanese government could not have afforded to raise another regiment; and if it had it could not have found the officers for it.

At the outset of the Japanese *risorgimento* the organisation of a modernised army had been entrusted to the French. After 1870 they prudently transferred the responsibility for supervising the training of their new conscript army to a German Military Mission. The result in 1904 was an almost slavishly precise imitation of the armies and tactical doctrines out of which the great Moltke had built his startling victories. There were, of course, some differences. They dispensed, for example, altogether with the Army Corps as a formation, since, in their constricted space, the Division was the most satisfactory basis for a territorial organisation. In war these were grouped in Armies, each consisting of three Divisions, amounting by European standards to an over-strength Corps – in all some 40,000 men. Moreover, although Japanese infantry were perfectly disciplined, their very nature prevented them from becoming replicas of the over-drilled Prussian soldier. Driven by a fervid, religion-inspired patriotism their ant-like swarms would sacrificially persist in attacking after their precisely aligned formations had, by all the rules, been brought to a decisive halt and would insidiously infiltrate and dislocate theoretically unassailable Russian defensive positions, so snatching victory from defeat. Once they had learnt to avoid the initial mistakes of inexperience such as bunching under rifle fire and adhering too closely to the rigid formations of their first assault, they became a formidable, and to the Russians a wholly disconcerting force on the battlefield.

Unfortunately for them their generals had no comparable ability to adapt their ideas and tactics to situations which did not conform to the rules of 1870. For their Commander-in-Chief, Field-Marshal the Marquis Oyama, such situations simply did not exist. A square, brutal man of outstanding intelligence, with a pedigree stretching back to the eleventh century, he had based all his military theories on a minute study of the writings of Clausewitz and the campaigns of Moltke. Like Schlieffen and his successors on the German General Staff, he dreamt always of a super-Sedan – a great envelopment of the entire enemy army; and in this ambition, though invariably with slightly inferior numbers, he remorselessly persisted to the end of the campaign. He won his battles, and ultimately his campaign simply by the initiative and courage of his own infantry soldiers and the ineptitudes of the opposing commanders. His subordinate generals followed the same reasoning to frequently costly conclusions. Only after his third disastrous assault on the outer defences of Port Arthur did General Baron Nogi accept the fact that open attack in the manner of field manoeuvres against rocky, well-defended, fortified positions were suicidal, and settle belatedly down to the methodical methods of a formal siege.

As far as infantry weapons were concerned the two armies were roughly equally balanced. Both had modern, magazine rifles capable of rapid and accurate fire and good modern machine guns. In the later battles, however, the Russians did have one unforeseen, though not unforeseeable handicap. The war had caught them before the change-over to the new pattern rifle had been completed. The political necessity of keeping the cream of the regular army and the first-line reserves in the west compelled the hasty despatch eastwards of the older age groups of trained reservists to reinforce the East Siberian Divisions. These were men who only knew the obsolete rifle and had to re-learn their musketry with the new one, like the later conscripts of 1878, the hard way, in action. In artillery the Japanese had an unchallengeable superiority. Not only had they a large number of mountain batteries with handy, light, mule-borne guns which got about easily in the rain-soaked countryside of Manchuria in the summer months, and to which the Russians had no answer; their standard field gun was a recoil-less, quick-firing weapon, inferior, perhaps, to the famous '75' which the French were developing, but fitted with the necessary instruments for indirect fire which the Russians wholly lacked. In consequence the Russian guns could only support their infantry from exposed positions where they could see the enemy and were invariably and swiftly silenced by rapid counter-battery fire from Japanese artillery firing from behind cover. The Japanese infantry had continuous close support from their guns. The Russians fought it out, often successfully, unsupported and with the same dogged endurance that their fathers had shown at Shipka.

Cavalry was the one arm in which the Russians had an over-whelming superiority both in numbers and quality. The Japanese cavalry was ill-mounted, poorly led, quite untrained in dis-mounted fighting, unadventurous and ineffective in reconnais-sance, and quite useless on the battlefield. The Russians had little regular cavalry, but masses of Cossacks. Unfortunately they had no Gourko to employ them properly. Time and again Oyama overextended his already outnumbered forces groping round his enemy's flanks in search of the envelopment of which he dreamed; and every time either of his own flanks could have been rolled up by a fast moving Cossack force, fighting dis-mounted and supported only by its own horse artillery. But Kuropatkin was obsessed by the text-book rule that reserves must be husbanded until the decisive moment. Like Bazaine in 1870, he could never make up his mind when the decisive moment came, and at least twice abandoned what could have been a victorious battlefield with large reserve formations still uncommitted. Thus the Cossacks were perpetually held back for a breakthrough which never came and great chances of spectacular victories were lost. It should, however, be recorded that one Cossack regiment was thrown into the thick of the vital battle at Liao-Yang, though in circumstances so bizarre as to be comical. Suddenly issued with lances which it had never learnt to use, it was ordered to charge and disperse a Japanese cavalry regiment. Nothing daunted, the Cossacks looped their reins round their waists and galloped into the enemy using their lances two-handed as quarter-staves and bringing the butt ends down sharply on their opponents' bridle hands. The Japanese broke and fled; and the Cossacks speared some thirty to forty of the luckless dismounted troopers on their leisurely return. These were the only casualties which the cavalry of either side could claim for the *arme blanche* during the entire war.

With two hide-bound commanders manoeuvring faithfully according to an out-of-date book of rules, there was nothing profitable to be learnt by the student of the art of warfare from the field operations in Manchuria. The Japanese infantry did develop a useful technique of digging in quickly on any ground gained during an attack, as security against a counter-attack, and a base for further advance; and this had the germs of a lesson for the future. Otherwise there was nothing. The experiences of General Nogi in his attempts to reduce the fortress of Port Arthur, on the other hand, did offer food for thought to which, unfortunately for the whole world, the generals of 1914 paid far too little attention. The fortress lay at the end of a small peninsula joined to the Manchurian mainland by an isthmus no more than 3,500 yards wide, whose outer edges were impassable by infantry except at low tide, and which was dominated by what could have been the impregnable hill of Nan Shan. At the southern tip was the great anchorage of Port Arthur protected by a line of formidable inner fortifications based on the wall of the old Chinese city, and the outer circle of the Green Hills which dominated the entire countryside and on which an elaborate system of fortifications had been planned, but never built.

The commanders on both sides were handicapped by extraneous pressures quite beyond their own control. A jittery government in Tokio, haunted by the fear that the Baltic Fleet would arrive in time to save the Pacific Fleet and tip the balance of naval power decisively against them, ceaselessly nagged Nogi into premature and costly attacks in open order, against progressively strengthened defences covered by barbed wire and machine gun fire. They had also based all their plans, both from the financial and recruiting point of view, on the assumption of a decisive victory by September 1904 – as events turned out, precisely a year too soon. On the other side the extremely competent General Smirnoff, sent out at the last minute to command the Port Arthur garrison, was continuously hampered by the imbecilities of the Governor-General, Stössel, and by the irresponsibility and disloyalty of many of his subordinates. He did, however, inspire the rank and file of the Russian infantry and sappers with a dedicated enthusiasm which very nearly outmatched the sacrificial patriotism of the Japanese troops.

Nogi won an important initial success on 26 May when, thanks mainly to the incompetence of Stössel's principal toady and right-hand-man, General Fock, he stormed the heights of Nan Shan, thereby gaining control of the isthmus and of the undefended and extremely useful port and railway station of Dalny. After that the operations became Plevna over again, though on a vaster scale. This time, however, investment offered no solution. Port Arthur was amply provisioned to outlast even the slow, accident-plagued voyage of the Baltic Fleet. The place had to be stormed; and from June until the middle of November Nogi strove at appalling cost to do so, and in vain. He launched two major assaults on the fortified hills commanding the harbour. The first, on 7 August, on the north-east corner of the perimeter, suffered from one unforeseen disadvantage, since the Russian fleet for once intervened, sending gunboats up the coast to give the defenders some unusually effective artillery support. At noon the next day the attack was broken off. Some unimportant outlying forts had been carried at the points of the bayonet; and Nogi had lost 1,000 killed and nearly 5,000 wounded. On 19 September he tried again, this time at both ends of the front. He inflicted some 3,000 casualties on the defenders and captured some important outworks which put both the key positions under serious threat. But he lost 15,000 men himself; and he could get no further.

In between these grand assaults there were continuous attacks on a smaller scale, all of them enforcing the same old lesson and ending up the same old way. The infantry on both sides fought heroically; and always the assaults ended up with the Japanese hung up and massacred on the barbed wire or caught in the defence searchlights at their points of debouchment under rifle and machine gun fire so intense that the follow-up troops simply could not climb over the six-foot high piles of corpses in front of them. All through the summer Smirnoff had been steadily improvising with picks and spades, bags of rice, and 1,200,000 sandbags the forts which his inept government had failed to build in the years before; and slowly the lesson dawned on the senior commanders that the best infantry in the world, even when strongly supported by artillery, could not cross 300 yards of open ground against properly constructed and manned defensive positions.

Meanwhile their subordinates, faced with the conditions of what was clearly a good, old-fashioned siege, set themselves doggedly to re-learn techniques which had been far more familiar to the sappers and infantry of the age of Vauban. The Japanese drove saps towards the Russian positions and the Russians started digging counter-saps. The Japanese hewed their way through the rocky soil to place great mines under the Russian forts, and the Russians counter-mined, with listening posts anxiously following the progress of the enemy picks deep underground. As they thus progressed backwards through centuries of military history both sides suffered occasionally from their inexperience. At one point General Smirnoff came up and personally inspected a Russian counter-mine before himself touching off the charge. Unfortunately this had been overestimated. It destroyed the Japanese working party at the head of their tunnel, but it also blew a large hole upwards into one of his own defence works which was briskly and successfully exploited by an enterprising party of Japanese infantry. On another occasion the Japanese failed to tamp sufficiently a large mine under a major enemy position, so that it did no damage to the fort but blew the tamping back, annihilating the assault force assembled in and around the mouth of the tunnel. Once, indeed, in this antiquated warfare, both sides reverted to purely mediaeval methods. The Japanese bridged a ditch in front of a steep rocky fort with fascines of bound corn-stalks, and the Russians deluged them with oil from above and set them on fire with hand grenades.

Nogi was very slow to learn the lesson. Like the bulk of his now very weary troops, he detested this undramatic, underground, and unspectacular fighting. Encouraged by the arrival of 11-inch batteries to replace the siege guns lost at sea five months before, and by a timely reinforcement of 8,000 infantrymen, he launched one last frontal assault on the north-eastern forts, having first saturated them with 150,000 heavy shells, on 27 October, and broke it off after twenty-four hours having lost 1,200 men to no purpose whatever. Then at last he made up his mind to throw in the whole army in a good, old-fashioned storm of the vital hill-top forts at the extreme opposite ends of his front. For a week his sappers toiled to complete the essential mining operations, while the heavy guns blasted the necessary breaches in the defence works. The attack went in on 23 November and, after nearly a fortnight of hard fighting was completely successful. It cost the Russians little more than a thousand casualties and the Japanese something over 20,000. But by 5 December Nogi had outflanked and rendered useless the whole ring of the outer defences and his guns could dominate the harbour and the whole area of the inner defence line. On 8 December his guns opened up on the helpless Russian ships in the harbour and systematically destroyed them.

Nogi had intended this as a birthday present for the Mikado on 3 December. He was five days late; but he had virtually won the war. Stössel was completely unnerved and the morale of the garrison troops at last degenerated. On 29 December there were still in hand rations enough for nearly two months, even without the slaughter of the numerous available horses. There was a formidable 'keep', easily defensible, to which the army could have retired in the south-west corner of the town; and a Council of War of all the senior officers had voted almost unanimously for prolonging a resistance which would at least pin down the

80,000 troops of Nogi's army and give Kuropatkin a chance of restoring the situation by a great victory in front of Mukden. But Stössel had already telegraphed to the Tsar that further resistance was impossible. He furtively opened negotiations with the Japanese for terms of surrender; and once the news that white flags were moving between the armies spread among the troops, not even the stoutest-hearted general could believe that he could rally his men to renew the battle.

There were still to come the forlorn end of the Baltic Fleet, deprived of refuge at Port Arthur and forced to run the gauntlet of the Tsushima Straits in the hope of reaching Vladivostock, and the fumbling end of Kuropatkin's manoeuvres round Mukden. But these were the last struggles of two Powers both at the end of their resources. The surrender of Port Arthur had given the Japanese, apart from the mass of stores, ammunition, and guns, 873 officers, 23,251 troops and 8,956 seamen as prisoners of war; and the defenders had already lost in killed, wounded and missing 31,306. The Japanese had lost in action 57,780 and 33,769 sick, most of them victims of beri-beri. This was the event which, on a note of high drama, as was suitable, brought the age of Moltke to an end. It had brought into world politics a new nation which was seriously to disturb the carefully preserved Balance of Power of the nineteenth century; and it had brought into existence new problems of techniques and tactics which the commanders of the future were to take nearly forty years to solve.

8 *The World's Navies in the Age of Moltke*

The bewilderingly rapid industrial and technological developments of the latter half of the nineteenth century had posed
serious and difficult problems to the army commanders and had
resulted at times in a fumbling uncertainty of leadership as they
groped their way into a modernised world with the increasingly
massive forces at their disposal. Among the world's navies it
produced a demented and acrimonious chaos which was to last
from 1860 until 1890, when at last something like a pattern of
design for the warships of the future began to take shape; though
even then the ideas of many of the admirals on how to handle
their new ships in battle were often archaic. Over the whole
period there raged a prolonged battle between inventors and
constructors, often men of genius, but often, too, overambitious
and overconfident, and die-hard admirals who fought bitterly
for a way of life they had always known which was sanctified by
centuries of tradition. There was this much to be said in defence
of the admirals : the naval lessons of the American Civil War
were less clear-cut, though far more decisive and revolutionary,
than anything the generals were required to learn from the land
fighting. Wellington could easily have recognised all the com-
ponents of a British army on the march in 1900 and would not
have needed a great deal of technical instruction to adapt his
tactical ideas to the handling of it in battle. Nelson, confronted
with a fleet of the same period, would have found that it shared
with his Trafalgar line of battle only two features : it floated, and
it carried guns. Even a man of his genius would have needed a

lifetime of technical instruction and practical experience to learn how to handle it, in or out of battle.

There was another disadvantage under which all the world's admiralties suffered in their experiments. From the battle of Lissa between the Austrians and Italians in 1866, when the American Civil War had only just ended, and the Yalu River battle in the Sino-Japanese War of 1894 there was no major clash of steam-driven, ironclad fleets on the high seas. The impact on large-scale operations in open water of the tentative inventions which had proved so effective in the shallow, enclosed estuaries of the James River and the Mississippi could only be guessed, by both the inventors and the commanders who would have to take their products into action. Lissa was, moreover, a highly misleading battle – the last of the pell-mell fights so dear to Nelson's heart. Admiral von Tegetthof, indeed, actually used, for the last time, the Nelsonic tactic of breaking the enemy line. It was fought, too, at a moment when the techniques of the manufacturers of armour plate had far outstripped those of the ordnance factories. The vital parts of every ironclad present were so heavily protected as to be impenetrable by the heaviest guns, even at ranges of a few hundred yards. Battleships could thus batter away at each other for hours without the remotest chance of sinking an opponent by gunfire, or even of inflicting serious casualties on his crew. The only hope was that a chance hit might start a fire in the mass of inflammable material carried inside the armour plate by every ship of the period. If such a fire spread to the magazine, the ship would then blow herself to pieces; and this was in fact the fate of the *Palestro* at Lissa, though she was one of the most modern Italian battleships with a hull built entirely of iron.

The battle of Lissa, fought on 20 July 1866, had no strategic significance for either side. It resulted only from their diplomatic necessities in the preliminary peace negotiations which had already opened. The Italians, humiliated at Custoza, wished to avoid appearing at the final conference as the poorest of poor relations, owing the acquisition of Venetia to Prussian victories in Bohemia and the benevolence of Napoleon III, who had secured the cession of the Province as a possible bargaining counter in a situation which had passed beyond his control, and whose powerful fleet was already on its way to Venice. Francis Joseph was equally standing on a point of honour. For prestige reasons he wished to make it clear to the world that his concessions of territory in Italy owed nothing to the efforts of the Italians themselves. So both admirals were sent to sea on what was purely a point of honour; and the result of their encounter would not in fact have the slightest effect on the conditions of the ultimate peace settlement, which would be dictated in severely realistic terms by the clear-headed Bismarck.

The Italian Commander-in-Chief, Admiral Persano, was a man with a distinguished career behind him who found himself completely overwhelmed by the responsibilities suddenly thrust upon him. At the outset of the war he had already a powerful superiority both in numbers and in armament. He had eleven armoured battleships, four of them with hulls constructed throughout of iron, as against the seven Austrians, all wooden ships coated with armour plate. Both fleets were constructed on antiquated lines, with large numbers of guns housed only for firing broadsides. But Persano's guns were up-to-date 6-inch rifled muzzle-loaders which could comfortably outrange the Austrian smooth-bores; and his ships were by a knot or two the faster. His most cherished asset, however, was a twelfth battleship, the *Affondatore,* which only joined him after the outbreak of war. Built by the British at Millwall, she was a 'turreted ram', her main armament two 300-pr. muzzle-loaders mounted in turrets pointing fore and aft and, as an offensive weapon, a sharp ram twenty-six feet long. Until her crew had shaken down and learnt, more or less, how to handle her, Persano obstinately refused to stir far enough from port to risk a general engagement; and she was still not quite ready when his exasperated government gave him a direct order to bombard and capture the island harbour of Lissa off the Dalmatian coast.

All through 18 and 19 July the Lissa forts were hammered by a bombardment which, as was usual with such operations, made a great deal of mess and did very little real damage. Persano gave no apparent thought to the fact that the Austrian fleet was based only seventeen miles away to the north, even when an intercepted message informed him that it had left port. The *Affondatore* had joined him on 19 July, and this seems to have set his mind completely at rest. Though the *Formidabile* had been badly damaged by fortress fire, he sent the *Terribile* off to bombard a neighbouring island; and he was preparing at leisure to cover the landing of his marines from his squadron of wooden ships when the solitary scout he had sent out signalled that the whole Austrian fleet was coming down fast from the north-west. His immediate reactions were sensible enough and showed no sign of panic. He formed his nine original ironclads in three squadrons in a curving line ahead, with himself in the centre in the *Re d'Italia,* and *Affondatore* on his starboard quarter in reserve, with a roving commission to intervene whenever she saw an opportunity to use her formidable ram. With all his broadsides bearing, he counted on his Armstrong guns to hold the enemy at arm's length until he had so battered them that he could safely risk moving in to close quarters.

Tegetthof had no intention of fighting the sort of battle which would put him at a disadvantage right from the start. His two newest and most powerful ships, the flagship *Erzherzog Ferdinand Max* and the *Habsburg,* had never received the heavy Krupp breech-loaders ordered for them before the war; and he knew that, even when he had run the inevitable gauntlet of 1,000 yards or so when he would be under fire and unable to reply, he would still be gravely handicapped in a gun fight. His orders to all his ships were therefore to close at once and force a mêlée in which they would use their short, blunt, iron rams as their principal weapon. He led every ship he could lay his hands on into battle in three closely packed wedges one behind the other at intervals of 1,000 yards. In front were the ironclads; next were the seven wooden ships led by the ancient *Kaiser* of ninety-four guns, already condemned to the scrap yard, but reprieved for the duration, with orders to get into the thick of the battle and do what they could. Finally there were eleven light craft, mostly gunboats, with three steam yachts fitted out with what guns could be found, which were merely to harry the enemy with intensive, if ineffective, gunfire to distract their gunners and create the maximum possible confusion.

This totally unexpected assault took Persano entirely by surprise and seems to have unnerved him. He immediately transformed himself, though not unfortunately his flag, from the *Re d'Italia* at which Tegetthof had aimed his leading wedge, to his beloved *Affondatore*. In her locker, however, there was nothing better than a Vice-Admiral's flag, so that the signals by which he tried to regain control of his fleet merely bewildered his subordinates. But in any case the confusion created by Tegetthof's plunge into the Italian centre was such that all control ceased to be possible. The whole area of the mêlée, moreover, was quickly obscured by the clouds of smoke belching from the funnels and thrown up by the black powder charges of nearly 1,300 guns, so that visibility was reduced to little over 200 yards. In this dense obscurity the ships churned around for over an hour, the black-painted Austrians seeking to implement Tegetthof's last signal to 'ram everything grey', the Italians dodging them without much difficulty, while the guns pounded away ineffectually at the armoured hulls of their opponents. Not even those present could give a coherent account of what took place, and the historian can only seize on the occasional vivid episodes which illustrate the limitations of the ironclad of 1866 and its potentialities for the future.[1]

Certain facts emerge clearly and vividly, as do the conclusions which could be drawn from them. The battle sorted itself out right from the start into three separate actions, each of which was fought out independently of the others. The leading Italian division, engaged by three of Tegetthof's ironclads, fought an entirely indecisive battle in which both sides expended much ammunition to no purpose whatever : damage and casualties on both sides were negligible, and there was no successful attempt to ram. At the other end of the line Commodore von Petch in *Kaiser* gallantly led all the wooden ships in what should have been a suicidal, but was in fact entirely successful attempt to keep the enemy rear division out of the main battle. He even managed to divert and hold in play the formidable *Affondatore,* and got off in the end without losing a ship. Persano had sudden last-minute doubts about the long, thin ram of his new flagship. It dawned on him that, while it would certainly sink any ship it struck, it might either break off, leaving a gaping hole in his own bows, or take so long to withdraw that he would be dragged down and swamped along with his enemy. So he decided that it would be more prudent to try it out first on the towering bulk of the wooden *Kaiser*. He did manage to hit her amidships with one of his powerful turret guns, doing considerable damage. But he missed both his attempts to ram, the second of them carrying him so fast past his target that it took him nine minutes to get turned round and back. At that moment it seemed to him that he was on the edge of a glorious victory. In dodging the *Affondatore*'s ram the *Kaiser* had placed herself right across the bows of the *Re di Portogallo*. Petch avoided immediate destruction by turning almost head-on into a collision in which *Kaiser* inflicted little damage and herself suffered heavily, all the upper works of her bow being stove in and her foremast thrown back on to the funnel, where it caught fire. Dodging one last ramming attempt by the *Maria Pia*, the *Kaiser*, by now well ablaze, drew off towards Lissa shepherded by the whole Austrian squadron of wooden ships.

The sight of the burning *Kaiser* and the whole of her squadron in apparent flight sent Persano steaming along the line frantically signalling to all his ships to pull out of the mêlée and rejoin him. The *Terribile*, steering for the sound of the guns, had just come up and he expected to be able to re-form an overwhelmingly powerful battle line for the *coup-de-grace*. Only as they one by one emerged and the smoke slowly cleared did he realise that, while he had been footling about with the *Kaiser*, the central division which he had abandoned had been decisively defeated. In spite of having four ships to the enemy's three, the Austrians had for an hour been completely frustrated in their repeated attempts to ram, all of which either missed altogether or struck only glancing and ineffectual blows. Their gunners, meanwhile, firing more slowly than the Italians, but with much greater care and accuracy, had dominated the fire-fight; and they deserved the four lucky shells which gave Tegetthof his victory. One burst in a mass of inflammable material on the afterdeck of the *San Martino* and set her whole stern ablaze. Another, fired by the *Ferdinand Max* just as she missed her second ramming attack on the *Palestro,* exploded in the wardroom which adjoined the powder-chamber and started a much more serious fire amidships. Most important of all, two shells put the steering gear of the *Re d'Italia* out of action just as she was passing straight ahead of the *Ferdinand Max*, emerging from her last duel with the *Palestro*. The Austrian Flag Captain, exasperated by the frustrations of the past hour, charged ahead at full speed, ignoring the usual precaution of stopping his engines well before impact. This threw the Italian captain into a panic in which he ordered full speed ahead, changed his mind and reversed his engines, and so lay helpless and practically motionless when the *Ferdinand Max* struck him amidships with a shock which threw every one of her own officers and men to the deck.

The Austrian flagship damaged her ram and forward armour plating so badly that she could not risk another such manoeuvre. But she backed safely enough out of the twenty-foot gash she had torn in her enemy's side. Within three minutes the *Re d'Italia* had sunk, taking with her two-thirds of her crew. One gallant officer with a handful of men fought off a panic rush by the crew to haul down her flag. So she went down with colours flying; and her captain drew his revolver and blew out his brains before she disappeared. The realisation of her loss threw Persano into a fresh state of indecision, which was prolonged by the sight of the *San Martino,* her fire extinguished, steaming briskly off towards Ancona flying a signal that she was 'unfit for further action'. At that moment the *Palestro* blew up in full view of both fleets and sank, taking with her most of her crew, who had gallantly volunteered to stay with their captain to fight the fire. This settled the issue. The Italian fleet turned to follow the *San Martino*;[2] and Tegetthof, only four of whose ships were fast enough to pursue, decided to leave it at that, and took his fleet into Lissa, where he found the *Kaiser*, her fire safely extinguished, getting herself repaired so rapidly that by the next morning she was able to report herself as fit for action. He had, after all, won the victory which his Emperor had demanded of him without losing a ship, and there was nothing to be gained by further action. He had also added a large slice to naval history.

Three clear lessons emerged from Lissa, though it was to take the world's admiralties the better part of thirty years to accept and apply them. The first was that five-inch armour was impenetrable by any naval gun then in use. After an hour and a half of intense gunfire at ranges of 200 yards or less not one ship on either side had suffered the slightest damage to their armoured hulls. The casualty figures told the same tale. The Italians lost some 630 officers and men in the *Re d'Italia* and *Palestro*. Apart from those they had only 5 killed and 39 wounded. The Austrians had 38 killed and 138 wounded; but 99 of these were in the wooden-walled *Kaiser* and mostly resulted from the single direct hit from the *Affondatore*'s big gun. Clearly new, better, and bigger guns were needed, and ships must be radically altered in design so as to mount them and use them effectively.

Secondly it was clear that the greatest danger to a battleship under fire lay in the clutter of inflammable material on the decks and between decks, and in the wooden hulls and decks themselves which were the base on which the armour was mounted. But it was to be forty years before the older-fashioned navies applied this lesson, and even the more up-to-date ones were very slow to accept the absolute necessity of building ships entirely of steel. Elaborate scroll-work and ornamentation in wood, and superstructures which recalled the glorious days of sail were very dear to senior officers and the older school of designers, and the reformers had the greatest difficulty in getting rid of them.

The third lesson of Lissa was perhaps the most obvious; that the ram had been obsolete for centuries and should never have been reincorporated into naval design. Lissa demonstrated over and over again that no ship which had not already been partially disabled need have any difficulty in dodging out of the way of a ram. The dramatic climax of the battle caught the world's imagination and entirely obscured the fact that it was essentially the disablement of the *Re d'Italia*'s steering gear which gave Tegetthof his opportunity. For the next thirty years all but the smallest warships were invariably equipped with rams; and in 1915 both British and French navies had still on active service in the Mediterranean battleships of the 1895 era fitted with rams. When Sir Edward Reed retired from the post of Chief Constructor in the British navy in 1870 he gave it as his considered opinion that the gun was rapidly becoming obsolete as a naval weapon, save for secondary armament. The battleship of the future, with her ram, would herself be the projectile which would destroy the enemy. This view was encouraged by the fact that in the following years no less than seven ships, including three British battleships, were accidentally sunk on manoeuvres by the rams of their sister ships; and the Chilean sloop, *Esmeralda*, was sunk by the ram of the Peruvian *Huascar* in an actual battle.

This, however, was only one of the many acrimoniously bitter controversies which bedevilled all naval thinking for nearly thirty years after 1866, and during which no nation developed a settled pattern of ship design and therefore no coherent tactical doctrine. None of the admiralties had any clear conception of what might happen if their fleets became involved in a serious engagement. Incredible though it may seem, a preliminary and prolonged battle had to be fought out with conservatives who would have preferred to reject steam power for battleships altogether and stick to sail. For them engine rooms and stoke-holds were messy, dirty, and dangerous, and engineer officers a lower form of social being. They were able to fight a protracted rearguard action because for a long time it was not possible for a heavily armed ship to store enough coal for a long voyage, so that all ocean-going warships had perforce to be fully rigged and to use steam as an auxiliary and only in emergencies. But the habit of providing battleships with three fully rigged masts persisted long after the problem of finding room to bunker enough coal for an extended sea passage had been solved. There was then a shorter secondary struggle between the engineers and the advocates of the paddle steamer, who refused to believe that a ship driven by a single screw could be properly steered, though the Americans had done so with ease in 1863.

Of course, innumerable minor controversies arose, all conducted with the same bitter acrimony. There were endless arguments on the different material and thicknesses of armour plate and on the merits of a solid wooden base for hulls, which tended to crack and warp under the increasing weight of armour and added enormously to the inflammable material in the interior of a battleship. Brooding over all of them and ultimately dominating all of them by its very importance was the problem of finding a more effective naval gun and of so mounting it that it could fire fore and aft as well as in broadsides. A square rig necessitated jibs and mizzens which prevented the mounting of any guns in turrets on the bow and stern; and even guns mounted in projected barbettes or sponsons along the sides endangered the shrouds and spars of the sail rigging. Yet effective fire forwards was an absolute necessity for a ship of any size which hoped to get within ramming range of an enemy. In its search for the right type of gun the British navy, in particular, went through even darker years than the army and went back even further in history, reverting at one period to smooth-bore muzzle-loaders, since solid round shot was found to be more effective against wrought-iron armour than the cylindrical projectiles of the rifled gun. In the end sanity prevailed, and the Royal Arsenal at Woolwich was induced to produce the types of powerful, breech-loading guns of all calibres to meet the needs of both services. This in turn at last forced the conservatives to abandon the conception of the battleship fully rigged for sail. The British did indeed produce the *Temeraire* in 1877, fully rigged and with powerful guns distributed in barbettes along her hollowed out sides which could fire fore and aft, but left the gun crews mercilessly exposed. But she was long out-of-date even before she was launched.

The British *Devastation*, commissioned in 1873, set a pattern for the future development of the battleship so decisively that even the revolutionary and famous *Dreadnought* of 1906 was only a final extension of the principles which she embodied. *Devastation* had a single central mast with spars and halyards for signalling purposes only. She had, of course, a powerful ram; and her sides were heavily armoured against a ramming attack. But she also had enough bunkering space to store coal for an extended voyage, and her four 35-ton rifled guns were mounted in turrets fore and aft, giving her in effect an all round arc of fire and enough fire-power forwards to enable her to batter her way to close quarters and use her ram. Her hull was also divided into watertight compartments. From 1882 onwards all battleships broadly conformed to this pattern, with their big guns mounted fore and aft. The revolving turret disappeared, but the word was taken over to describe the later barbettes with armoured hoods which protected the crews and revolved with the guns. They had a higher freeboard than the *Devastation*, and they mounted progressively more powerful secondary batteries on the main deck between the turrets. These were an answer to the new threat posed by Mr Whitehead's self-propelled torpedo, which he had perfected in 1868 while in the service of the Austrian government at Fiume, and which was to have wide repercussions. The first torpedo boats were small and their torpedoes could only be fired accurately at ranges of a few hundred yards. Against these machine guns which could sweep their open decks provided an adequate secondary armament; and in the development of this weapon the navies were far ahead of the armies. As torpedoes improved and torpedo boats grew larger the American Hotchkiss machine gun, which fired a 1½-pound shell, was added. But torpedo boats went on getting larger, developing into the prototypes of the destroyers of the First World War.

For a time Nordenfeldt and Hotchkiss quick-firers, delivering 3- and 6-pound shells at a rate of 15 a minute met the need. But gyroscopic control and improved propelling mechanism gradually increased the accuracy and extended the effective range of the torpedo to 1,000 yards, and a much more substantial weapon was needed. By 1886 the Ellswick firm was producing a 4·7-inch gun which fired 10 aimed rounds in 47 seconds; and this was quickly followed by a similar 6-inch, which could fire with devastating accuracy up to two miles. These rapidly became not only the standard secondary armament of the battleship, but produced a whole new element in the battlefleet – the fighting cruiser. Hitherto cruisers had been unarmoured, used occasionally as scouts, but chiefly regarded as commerce raiders. There now emerged two new and quite distinctive types: the Light Cruiser, fast and lightly armoured and equipped with 6- and 4·7-inch guns; and the slower Protected, or Armoured Cruiser, with an armoured deck and two or more heavier guns in addition to the 6-inch. These last were the forerunners of the Battle Cruiser of the Dreadnought era, capable for a time of taking their place in a battleline, though by 1914 they were totally obsolete.

The chief rivalry throughout this period was between the French and the British. For a time the Russians competed, and their designers and senior officers showed considerable ingenuity and initiative. This was particularly well illustrated in the Balkan War of 1877. The Russians were already experts at transporting ships by rail, since for years they built even their big ships in Baltic yards and then transported them in pieces to the Black Sea, where they were reassembled and fitted out. The rickety Roumanian railway line, already over-burdened by army transport, could scarcely have carried even a dismantled torpedo boat, and in any case time was too precious for such a tedious enterprise. The army needed quickly a crossing over the Danube completely protected from the powerful Turkish flotillas of armoured monitors and gunboats which patrolled as far upstream as Nikopolis. The sailors had therefore first to clear of all Turkish warships a stretch of river long enough to put the crossing point out of range of the powerful guns of the Turkish monitors, both upstream and downstream, and then seal it off by strings of torpedoes – a word which was then used indiscriminately to describe both White-head's invention and what would soon be called the sea mine.

All this had to be carried out from the river bank, since Turkish supremacy in the Black Sea was undisputed. Theoretically Turkish dominance of the Danube waters up to the Iron Gates was equally indisputable, and they should have been able to defeat any attempt by the Russians to cross the river and invade the Balkans. They had in the lower river and around its mouths a fleet of 8 large ironclads with four-inch armour plating and between them some 30 guns of varying calibre; up-river there was a squadron of lighter draught ships: some light-draught monitors, 7 more thinly plated gunboats, and 18 wooden ships mounting in all about 60 rather smaller guns. Even when the Russian artillery appeared in strength on the north bank, making the navigation of the smaller vessels in narrow waterways extremely hazardous, they could only bring into action the 24-pounders of their siege batteries, while the larger Turkish monitors each carried 150-pound Armstrong guns. Enterprisingly handled the Turkish flotillas should have been able to make the construction of pontoon bridges and the passage of a large army with all its necessary supplies not only costly, but impossible.

At the very outset the Russians had a stroke of luck when a 6-inch mortar bomb from the first siege battery hastily rushed to the north bank of the Pruth, landed on the deck of one of the most powerful Turkish monitors, the *Lufti-Djelil*, and exploded her powder magazine, so that she sank with the total loss of her complement of 17 officers and 200 men. Since they had no base within torpedo boat range of the Danube mouths, the Russian senior naval officers had perforce to improvise. But clearly they had studied the naval operations of the American Civil War as carefully as Gourko had studied the great cavalry raids of Forrest and Joe Wheeler. With the twenty-five launches and lavish supplies of torpedo equipment brought down among the first train loads they proposed to revert completely, though with somewhat more sophisticated weapons, to the spar-rigged torpedo and the tactics used so brilliantly by Lieutenant Cushing against the *Albermarle*. Within a fortnight of the declaration of war and while the Turks were still recovering their nerve after the disaster to the *Lufti-Djelil* the first essential task had been completed, long before their army appeared in any strength south of Bucharest. The only two approaches from the sea to the main stream of the Danube were effectively blocked by double rows of mines strung across the rivers which would explode on impact and could also be detonated electrically from the bank. No attempt was made to interfere with this operation; and thereafter powerful batteries on the north bank prevented the Turkish light craft from sweeping passages through these barriers. Thus the Turkish down-river squadron, which might have disrupted the whole campaign, was pinned to the estuary. Its demoralisation was completed by a Russian attack from the seaward side which, though unsuccessful, confirmed its determination to stay firmly anchored under the protection of the fortress guns at the mouths of the river. This attack, though it sank only one ship, served also to emphasise the total ineffectiveness of the main Turkish fleet. Its commander, an ex-officer of the British Navy, called Hobart Pasha, had at his disposal 15 up-to-date sea-going ironclads and nearly 120 smaller vessels, mostly wooden. But no attempt was made to interrupt the Russian coastal traffic from the Crimean ports and Odessa, and his only aggressive action was the bombardment of some strategically insignificant villages on the Caucasian coast. In consequence the steamer *Constantine* was able to tow six torpedo launches from Odessa to strike at the main Turkish naval base at Sulina. The torpedo nets of the Turkish monitors saved all but one, which ventured out and sank after striking an underwater mine. The

Russians lost one boat; and the effect was to pin the whole powerful down-river fleet under the guns of Sulina for the rest of the war.

Successful aggressive action also forced the rather more enterprising Turkish up-river fleet back under the guns of Nikopolis, far up-stream and well out of range of the Russian crossing points. The operation which virtually decided the issue was a daring attack by four Russian torpedo launches from Braila on a detached Turkish squadron of three ships; and it well illustrated the strengths and limitations of the naval weapons and armament available at that period. Under the cover of darkness the leading torpedo-boat got within striking distance of the light-draught, but powerfully armoured monitor *Seifé* and under a hail of musketry fire successfully planted her torpedo under the enemy's port quarter. She was herself swamped by the explosion and no visibly decisive damage had been done, so the second boat went in and exploded her torpedo under the enemy's stern, whereupon the *Seifé* sank within minutes, taking with her her complement of over 120 officers and men. The second boat had also been immobilised by enemy wreckage tangled round her propeller; and the third had been disabled on the run-in by a shell. The undamaged fourth, however, was able to extricate all three under fire; and the flotilla got back to base complete and without having a single man hit.

The effects of this miniature action were out of all proportion to the effort expended on it. The demoralised Turkish up-river squadron retired far up-stream to the shelter of the guns of Nikopolis where it, too, was barred off by double lines of torpedoes. Their monitors made two abortive attempts to interrupt these operations, but were so spiritedly met by torpedo boats supported by shore batteries that they withdrew into total inactivity. In the end the whole squadron, including two powerfully armed monitors, tamely surrendered when the Russian army captured Nikopolis two months later. Finally, in October, when the Russians captured Sulina, the Turkish fleet withdrew altogether, losing another large sea-going ironclad on a mine in the process. The significance of these comparatively trivial operations lay not in the defeat of the Turkish navy, which deplorable leadership and low morale made almost inevitable : it was the demonstration that in the naval warfare of the future the decisive factors would ultimately be neither the ram nor the heavy gun of the battleship but the mine and the torpedo – until, of course, the advent of Air Power upset all the calculations over again.

After 1878 the Russian Navy gradually succumbed to the lethargic disillusionment which spread throughout the nation during the next thirty years and corrupted every branch of the national service. On paper, and at enormous expense, the government created a fleet in the Baltic and Pacific which was formidable only in size. Like almost everybody else in Russia, the designers, too, seem to have lost heart for a variety of reasons which could make by themselves a separate chapter in Russian social history. The plain fact was that their battleships produced between 1890 and 1904 were towering monsters, over-gunned and over-weighted above the water-line, slow and cumbersome, and presenting an enormous target to a well-equipped enemy. From 1880 onwards the United States began to build a powerful fleet along eccentric lines which were not to prove in action altogether satisfactory; and the Austrians and Italians were each staging a renaissance, though only on a small scale. The vital new development was the accumulation by Japan of a fleet modelled entirely on the British, built in British yards or under British supervision, and trained by British officers. They had the luck to start late, when both British and French fleets were ceasing to be 'collections of samples';[3] and the Japanese were by nature a tidy-minded race. Everywhere else progress was still 'by guess and by God'; a series of reactions to new threats of unpredictable importance.

All of them lived in a cloud-cuckoo land dominated by a picture of battleship actions at ranges of less than 2,000 yards culminating in a ramming attack, and even ranged close alongside each other, firing their turret guns down on an opponent's decks.[4] A short story in 1891 described a single-ship duel between thinly disguised British and French battleships in which fire was opened at two miles – considered excessive by the experts – and which ended with the Briton, understandably battered by the fire of 12-inch guns at 300 yards, triumphantly ramming the equally battered Frenchman. This was hailed by a

Captain in the US Navy as coming very near 'the seaman's idea of what the future sea fight will be';[5] and his opinion was shared by the senior officers of every great navy. Three years later at the Yalu River, the Japanese were to give them their first glimpse of the true facts.

When the Japanese set out to acquire *Lebensraum* in Korea nobody doubted that they would easily defeat the Chinese army, in spite of their mushroom growth. But the Chinese fleet, built entirely in foreign yards and still with French and German officers serving aboard, was expected to give a good account of itself. No allowance was made for the corrupt inefficiency of China's administration, or for the ignorance and idleness of her senior naval officers. They were, for example, so unaccustomed to attend gunnery practices that Admiral Ting and his entire staff were thrown to the bridge deck by the first discharge of the 12-inch guns of his flagship, the Battleship *Ting Yuen*, the admiral being knocked unconscious. Since he had no second-in-command, his fleet was thus left leaderless. The Japanese Admiral Ito and his staff, on the other hand, unhampered by prejudice and centuries of tradition, brought a very clear understanding to their quite novel problems. The battle of the Yalu on 16 September 1894, was to show up with devastating clarity how little the sailors of the West had learnt from Lissa, and how much in the past thirty years they had misunderstood. It should be added, that, apart from a few gunnery experts, they paid little attention to the lessons of the Yalu battle either.

Ting took his fleet – twelve ships in all – into action in line abreast, his two 12-inch gun Battleships, elderly, but by no means obsolete, in the centre with his four heavier cruisers, and the Light Cruisers on the flanks. All his cruisers were old and some of them quite out-of-date. Clearly he was seeking to force the sort of mêlée which had given Tegetthof the chance to get his rams into action at Lissa. But Ito had no intention of fighting that sort of battle. He had only a cruiser fleet, though his four Armoured Cruisers were powerfully armed, three of them mounting a 12·5 inch Canet gun which threw a far heavier shell than the antiquated Krupps of the Chinese Battleships and outranged them. His four fast, modern Light Cruisers, all armed with quick-firing 4·7- or 6-inch guns, he formed into a separate

Flying Squadron. His weaknesses were the thin armour plate of even his heavy cruisers, easily penetrable by 12-inch and even 8-inch shells, and the four aged, useless ships wished on him by his high command to make numbers even. His strength, which was to prove overwhelming, lay in his quick-firing lighter guns with a range of 3,000 yards, of which he had sixty-six as against the Chinese two. The Chinese 8-inch and 10-inch guns could not fire much faster than the 12-inch heavies; and these at that period were slow to load and difficult to aim at a moving target.

Ito advanced against the centre of the Chinese line with his squadrons abreast in line ahead, leaving the old ships in the rear. At 3,000 yards he swung to port, bringing his eight cruisers into line, and circled fast round the Chinese right flank, gradually reducing the range to 1,000 yards, and deluging the enemy cruisers with such a hail of shells as had never been seen. Japanese gunnery was less good than had been expected, but the volume of fire was so intense that there was inevitably a large number of hits, and as the range decreased these became more frequent. Thanks to the Chinese passion for paint and lacquer, all their crews spent a large part of the three-hour battle fighting fires. They returned to the fight gallantly enough as often as they could, but it was not long before all but the heaviest of their cruisers had been sunk or driven off in flames. The battle thereafter became very confused. The Japanese were using very bad coal; and only one ship present had guns fitted for smokeless charges. The result was a dense fog almost as thick as that of Lissa, and no coherent account of the later stages of the battle survives. Ito sent his Light Squadron off independently on the task for which it had been designed – the hunting down and destruction of the dispersed enemy cruisers, while he, with his four heavier ships, set himself to eliminate the Chinese battleships and the three heavy cruisers which had stayed with them.

The over-all results were, however, clear enough. Of the Chinese cruisers, four were sunk by gunfire. One, after a collision as she tried to escape, was run ashore and later destroyed. Two managed to slip away. But in the main battle between Ito's Heavy Squadron and the surviving Chinese heavy ships honours were more even. When Ting, having run out of all but solid, armour-piercing shells, made off for Port Arthur with the two battleships and three of his heavy cruisers, one cruiser had been completely gutted by fire, all had been badly damaged, and the Battleship *Chen Yuen* had fought and subdued no less than eight fires. But, though repeatedly hit, even by the Japanese heavy guns, neither of the battleships had suffered damage to any of their heavily armoured vital installations. The Japanese had fired no torpedoes, because they regarded this still as a weapon for use at night only. The Chinese big ships fired a lot, not with any hope of scoring hits, but to reduce the danger to themselves of an underwater explosion. The plain answer was that it was still, as it had been at Lissa, very difficult to sink an armoured battleship by gunfire. Ito, equally, had suffered severely by exposing his thinly armoured cruisers to the fire of heavy guns. A 10-inch shell had pierced his deck early in the action and might have sunk it, had it not been loaded with concrete; and a 12-inch shell which struck him amidships later on demolished his port battery, dismounted one 4·7-inch gun, and killed or wounded over a hundred officers and men. Had the Chinese gunnery been better, all his heavy cruisers must have been destroyed. The essential lessons were still the lessons of Lissa; but it was to take two more naval campaigns to drive them home.

The land fighting in the Spanish-American War of 1898 had produced no new lessons for the commanders of the future. It had merely underlined those, some of them age-old, of previous campaigns. The war at sea, however, which eliminated Spain for good as a naval power, though it resulted only in two almost bloodless victories of no great tactical significance for the Americans, did, like the Russo-Turk operations in the Danube estuary of 1877, illustrate a new factor which was to play an increasingly important part in the naval warfare of the future. Lissa was almost, though not quite, the last occasion on which two fleets roughly equal in numbers, speed and armament, confronted each other in conditions where victory would go to the ships which were better fought and better handled. Rapid progress in the design both of ships and guns was already beginning to make even quite recently built ships obsolete and virtually defenceless, as the Japanese had shown at the Yalu, against still newer ships which could both out-steam and out-range them. Quality rather than quantity became the all-important factor in the accelerating naval armaments' race from 1890 onwards; progressively the admirals were to be placed at the mercy of their designers and naval constructors and the strategists in the Admiralties. It was a factor which did not become fully decisive until 1914, when Von Spee successively found Craddock's cruisers at his mercy at Coronel and himself went down in turn against Studee's Battle Cruisers at the Falkland Islands.

The fighting of 1898 took place at the beginning of the transitional period, when the admirals had not yet fully digested the impact of this tactical revolution and largely failed to exploit it. It did, none the less, herald a new kind of naval warfare. In spite of laboratory tests and speed trials and target practices, the designers could not know with any certainty how the armour plating and guns and engines of their new ships would stand up to the test of battle against a reasonably well-armed enemy. Furthermore, admirals and captains were still unsure of the potentialities of the new weapons placed at their disposal and had formulated no clear tactical doctrines for their proper exploitation. None the less the US naval operations in 1898 clearly looked forwards rather than backwards and, both in the Pacific and the Atlantic, gave clear indications of future trends in naval warfare. For over seven months before President McKinley made up his mind to ask Congressional support for a declaration of war on Spain, the Navy Department at Washington, stimulated by the zeal of Assistant Secretary Roosevelt, had been steadily building up the strength of the Asiatic Squadron to the point at which it could be reasonably certain of destroying the antiquated Spanish fleet in the Philippines.

At that period, blissfully unaware of the rising threat of Japan, the naval powers maintained in the Far East only Cruiser Squadrons, mostly painted an elegent white and designed mainly to 'show the flag' in the Oceanic Archipelago and in the pirate-infested water of the China Sea. By the time that war began to seem inevitable Commodore Dewey had assembled in Hong Kong a thoroughly up-to-date squadron of five ships. His flagship, *Olympia*, was a 'Protected Cruiser', heavily armoured, reasonably fast and equipped with modern 8-inch guns in each of her forward turrets. His four Light Cruisers were as fast and as well-equipped as any of their class afloat; and he had for reconnaissance purposes two fast armed Revenue Cutters. In the nick of time, just two days before the formal declaration of war forced him to leave the neutral port, he also received the valuable reinforcement of the Armoured Cruiser, *Baltimore,* less heavily armed, but faster than *Olympia,* and carrying a welcome cargo of extra ammunition for the whole squadron. He had already repainted his ships a workmanlike battleship grey and had put ashore all the clutter of wooden and canvas equipment designed for peacetime comfort, but dangerously inflammable in action. Within the available forty-eight hours heroic efforts by her crew and the willing co-operation of the British dockyard authorities got *Baltimore's* bottom scraped, all her surplus gear removed, and the whole ship repainted in time to sail; and after a short pause at sea to distribute *Baltimore's* ammunition cargo, Dewey made straight for Manila. His orders, received two months before, were to pin the Spanish squadron to the Asiatic coast 'and then to start offensive operations in the Philippine Islands'.[6]

The British at Hong Kong had clearly no very high opinion of Dewey and his ships. It was impossible in the clubs to lay a bet, even at the longest odds, on an American success; and an officer of a regiment which had entertained some American officers at a guest night was heard to remark as he saw them off: 'A fine set of fellows, but unhappily we shall never see them again.'[7] Equally clearly the British were inadequately informed about the constitution and condition of Rear-Admiral Patricio Montojo y Passaron's fleet in the Philippines. He was, like all his brother Spanish commanders, naval or military, immensely brave, but so pessimistic as to be incapable of any aggressive initiative. He had under command seven ships. Two of them, the *Reina Cristina* and the *Castilla* were rated as Armoured Cruisers, First Class, but all of them were totally out of date. Their very appearance, with their high prows elaborately decorated with wooden scrollwork and their massively inflammable top-hamper, conjured up a bygone age. Some of the smaller cruisers were even fitted out with masts and spars for auxiliary sail. All but the *Castilla* had been repainted a drab brown for the occasion, but they still presented a ridiculously vulnerable target to the superior American armament. Their admiral, gloomily aware that much of his ammunition was defective and that he could not risk a running fight in open waters, took refuge under the guns of the battery and dockyard of Cavite, across the harbour from Manila, and there fatalistically awaited his doom.

Dewey took one bold decision when he refused to risk preliminary damage to his ships by engaging the powerful batteries covering the channel into Manila Bay. Instead he ran the passage, blacked out, at night. His luck held, as it was to do throughout the following day. For the smoke-stack of *McCulloch,* the Revenue Cutter, twice caught fire and sent up a pillar of flame. But the Spanish gunners on Corregidor failed to realise the significance of the soaring beacon and not a shot was fired until, at first light, he emerged into the open waters of the bay. From then on the scene, as watched by an officer in *Petrel's* foretop, seemed less like a battle than a 'performance that had been very carefully rehearsed'. For nearly three hours the US squadron, in line ahead, steamed at a stately six knots, six times to and fro along a course of two and a half miles, delivering broadsides slowly and deliberately at ranges which steadily decreased from three miles to less than one. Two of the Spanish ships remained at anchor. The rest steamed about aimlessly, masking each other's fire with their smoke, and making occasional futile dashes to get within torpedo or ramming range. Towards the end the flagship *Reina Cristina,* making an exceptionally gallant sortie, was hard hit and set on fire fore and aft and, as she turned back, a third and lucky shell fell through the gaping hole in her stern to burst in her boiler room. With a jet of steam added to the columns of flame and smoke she grounded, a flaming wreck, under the guns of Cavite Battery. Shortly afterwards the *Duero* suffered a similar fate, while the *Castillo,* whose gleaming white paint attracted concentrated fire, had every gun out of action. At 7.30 a.m. Dewey broke off the action and ordered all hands to breakfast.

The resumed battle in the middle of the morning was in the nature of a mopping-up operation. *Baltimore* forged ahead round Cavite Mole and in ten spectacular minutes showed the devastating effect 8-inch shells from modern naval guns could have on even massive earthworks backed by boiler plate. The parapets were blown back on top of guns and gunners. The survivors hastily hoisted a white flag and withdrew in an ambulance to the main fort at Sangley which in turn capitulated under the concentrated fire of the whole squadron. The light-draught *Petrel* steamed into the Arsenal where all the gunboats hastened to haul down their colours, and soon the white flags had gone up everywhere. The only serious and very gallant resistance was put up by the surviving cruiser, *Antonio de Ulloa*. Moored behind the Mole she fought it out until she was entirely disabled. Then the crew dived and swam for the shore while she slowly turned over and sank, and the victory was complete. It was, indeed, one of the few complete victories of modern naval history. The Spaniards had lost every single ship and nearly four hundred men. The Americans suffered negligible damage and had a few men injured. Their only real casualties were from heat stroke and exhaustion among the stokers, engineers, and the men working below decks in the ammunition hoists. That evening the squadron anchored peaceably and undisturbed off the city of Manila. At sundown the bands played in the wardroom messes and there were the usual concerts between decks. There were a good many officers present who felt that the whole scene was a little unreal and, indeed, embarrassing.

Dewey, nevertheless, became overnight the national hero of the over-excited American public. Photographs of him appeared in almost every home, and city corporations eagerly commissioned sculptured busts. Within a week of the declaration of war he had won a resounding victory and apparently conquered the Philippines. He alone of the commanders on land or sea was given the full honours of a ceremonial reception on his return. He was paraded on Fifth Avenue under an enormous plaster triumphal arch in the Roman manner; and in front of the Capitol was presented formally by the President with a sword of honour voted to him by Congress and blessed by Cardinal Gibbons. But a disillusionment almost equally dramatic very soon followed. Philippine patriots who had regarded the American troops as liberators did not think annexation by a paternalist American government as at all the same thing; and the US army had to fight a wearisome and frustrating guerilla war to establish its supremacy. The triumphal arch, which was to have been replaced in marble, slowly disintegrated, its centre space filled with advertisements by an enterprising tobacconist, until it was finally demolished; and the photographs came down off the walls.

Admiral Dewey had, in fact, done a competent job; but he had not fully or imaginatively exploited the immense technical superiority of his ships. Instead of lying off beyond the reach of the Spanish guns he had closed to what was, in effect, point-blank range and given the Spanish gunners an equal chance with his own. The Spanish fire was much more rapid and not much less accurate than that of the Americans; and all Dewey's ships were hit repeatedly. When his crews came up for breakfast they found the sides of their ships 'blistered' and 'flame-scarred'; and all their ships had suffered considerable superficial damage. *Raleigh* had all her boats shot away; and of the three direct hits on *Olympia* one shell had ploughed a furrow across her decks which might well, had the luck been running for the Spaniards that day, have started a lethal fire. Part of Dewey's immunity was due to his own prudence in jettisoning all surplus inflammable stuff at Hong Kong. But fundamentally it was the fact that the ineffective Spanish shells could not penetrate the American armour plate. The inescapable lesson, which was to hold for the next fifty years and probably still holds good, was that the more powerful and up-to-date ships, even if out-numbered, will win against an inferior enemy, however bravely and skilfully he may fight.

The other great American naval victory of the war, off the south coast of Cuba two months later, proved nothing except that an overwhelmingly powerful fleet, however ineptly handled, will almost inevitably win a battle. As Shafter's lines closed inexorably round starving Santiago the Spanish Admiral Cervera, after weeks of indecision, made up his mind to make a dash for freedom rather than tamely surrender to the US army. Had the bottoms of his ships – four armoured cruisers and two torpedo boats – not been fouled by weeks of inactivity in Santiago harbour, he might well have slipped past the blockading fleet which was caught at a singularly inopportune moment. Not only were two powerful ships away on routine coaling, but the Commander, Admiral Sampson, had departed in his fastest ship, the *New York*, with two escort vessels to Daiquiri for a conference ashore with the generals. Rear-Admiral Schley in the modern Armoured Cruiser, *Brooklyn*, had therefore under command only four battleships of the Atlantic fleet and two converted steam yachts, *Vixen* and *Gloucester* – in private life J. P. Morgan's luxury cruising yacht, *Corsair* – which were intended to frustrate any attack by enemy torpedo boats. The battleships, moreover, after weeks of monotonous blockade, were cruising with many of their engines unhooked from the driving shafts and their furnaces cold, in order, quite unnecessarily, to save coal. Even so, the 12-inch and 13-inch guns of the battleships were enough to annihilate the Spaniards as they emerged from the harbour without any risk of damage to themselves.

Instead the American captains, ignoring all the lessons of recent history, plunged into an action at close quarters in which they attempted to reproduce the tactics of Lissa, and in doing so created by their gunfire and the thick columns of black smoke from their hastily restoked furnaces such obscurity and confusion that they came near to destroying themselves. *Brooklyn* missed by only six feet a collision with *Texas* which would have sent both to the bottom; and *Gloucester,* on a foray against the enemy torpedo boats, narrowly escaped destruction by the guns of her own fleet. Only when it was clear that they had not the speed to ram the enemy ships did the battleship captains settle down to their systematic destruction by gunfire, which with their overwhelming weight of metal, they easily accomplished. Moreover, had the two Spanish torpedo boats launched their extremely gallant attack early in the battle instead of right at the end, when they had much further to go and brought upon themselves the concentrated fire of all the American ships, they could hardly have failed to find a target. Schley had ordered 'close action', which meant a range of a little over a thousand yards. That was enough to put his ships out of range of the underwater torpedo tubes of the enemy cruisers; but in the milling confusion prevailing at the start of the action the torpedo boats could scarcely have failed to cover undamaged the few hundred yards they needed to get within comfortable range, with unpredictable, but almost certainly devastating effect.

For the admirals and designers of the future there were two useful general lessons to be learnt from the battles of Manila and

Santiago. The first and more obvious was that the ram was already a totally obsolete weapon. The advent of the Whitehead torpedo alone made a repetition of the scene at Lissa virtually impossible; improvements in torpedo design in the early 1900s which increased its range from 1,000 to 4,000 yards made it unimaginable. The lesson took a long time to sink in. For a time the development in large numbers of efficient submarines prolonged the usefulness of the ram for destroyers and other small craft pending the evolution of other more efficient methods of anti-submarine warfare. But for larger ships they had become cumbersome and useless pieces of equipment. The other lesson, scarcely less obvious, was that newer and more powerful vessels forfeited all the advantages of their speed and armament if they closed to within the enemy's range. Sturdee was to have this experience at the Falkland Islands and immediately and prudently corrected his mistake. The destruction of an enemy at extreme range was inevitably slow; but it was more or less certain and avoided all risk.

For the Navy Department at Washington there were more serious lessons to be learnt; for both battles had revealed alarming defects in the construction and armament of even their newest ships. At Manila, for example, every time *Olympia* fired a broadside the concussion and vibration were such that the half-naked stokers were showered with soot, cinders, and splashes of scalding water. Even more alarming defects were revealed during the battle of Santiago. Towards the end of the action the Spanish cruiser *Almirante Oquendo* defended herself so well in an unequal duel with the 12-inch gunned battleship *Texas* that the accuracy of her fire compelled Captain Philip of the *Texas* to evacuate the upper bridge and move his staff down to the lower bridge around the conning-tower. While the last of them were still on the ladders a 6-inch shell exploded in the pilot-house above them where it would certainly have killed them all. Minutes later another shell landed just under the lower bridge, throwing them all to the ground; and it was only luck that their solitary casualty was a Midshipman with a split eardrum. A third direct hit immediately afterwards came very near destroying the battleship altogether. It landed, as Captain Philip wrote in his report, 'forward of the ash-hoist, and, after passing through the outer plating of hammock-berthing, exploded, the mass of pieces penetrating the bulkhead and casing of the starboard smoke-pipe'.[8] It set on fire the stored hammocks and sailors' clothing and sent a shower of shell fragments, pieces of burning cloth, and clouds of smoke down into the stokehold. There was no panic and the fire was eventually brought under control. Had it spread it might well have caused a fatal explosion.

The misgivings of the Navy Department when the reports of the various commanders had been studied were increased by the findings of a special board sent out after the war to examine the wrecks of the four Spanish ships. It found evidence of only 122 direct hits. The American fleet had fired a total of 9,433 shells, mostly at ranges of little over 1,000 yards. The fourteen 13- and 12-inch guns had fired over 300 rounds and scored only two hits. Even if the board had made a gross underestimate, it was still not an impressive performance. Both among the professionals and in the public at large disillusionment rapidly dispelled the first enthusiasm over these too-easy successes. The atmosphere was further soured by an unseemly dispute between the admirals for the credit of the Santiago victory. Sampson in *New York* had turned back when he saw the first puff of gunsmoke off the harbour mouth and spent the morning chasing the battle, still in the boots and spurs he had donned for his journey to meet the generals, and had arrived just as the last shots were fired. To Schley's signal: 'A glorious victory has been achieved. Details later', he vouchsafed no reply. To a second signal: 'This is a glorious day for our country', he only answered: 'Report casualties.' Schley laconically reported one dead and two wounded and, seeing how the wind blew, went below to compose a telegram to Washington announcing his victory. One of Sampson's staff, however, got to the cable office at Siboney in time to cancel Schley's despatch and substitute the pompous and somewhat misleading message, dated 3 July: 'The fleet under my command offers the nation, as a Fourth of July present, the whole of Cervera's fleet.'

There were no triumphal arches for either admiral; and the rather squalid dispute dragged on after the war, culminating in a formal Naval Court of Enquiry five years later. The Navy

Department, more realistically, briskly set about rebuilding, enlarging, and modernising the whole US Fleet. In 1917 it would take its place with legitimate pride beside the Grand Fleet in Scapa Flow; and by 1921 it had established its claim to parity with the British and a five-to-three superiority over the Japanese. This was the real and important result of the battles of Manila Bay and Santiago.

Towards the end of 1903, when it became clear that Russia and Japan were headed inevitably to a major struggle for Korea and Manchuria, Admiral Alexeieff in his capacity of Viceroy and Commander-in-Chief of all naval and military forces in the Far East laid it down as an axiom on which all planning was to be based that the Russian Pacific Fleet could in no circumstances be defeated by the Japanese. All the military preparations for the defence of Port Arthur and the Manchurian campaign had been based on this assumption; and he persisted in this view long after it had clearly become untenable and until he was providentially recalled and the generals and admirals were free to face the real facts of the situation. Even then the conviction remained as strongly held in the navy as in the army that, in spite of the Yalu victory, the Japanese were 'just yellow apes, with a lust to kill'. The Japanese soldier or sailor was 'nothing but a mosquito' in whom they proposed to 'stick a pin and send home in a letter'.

On paper the rival Pacific Fleets at the outbreak of war appeared to be fairly evenly matched. The Russians had seven first-class battleships to the Japanese six, and nine first-class cruisers to six. But the Japanese ships were nearly all more recently built, all but one in foreign yards, and all under British supervision. Indeed, two of their best cruisers only arrived at their base a week after the opening of hostilities, from Argentina, where they had been built as a speculation and offered in the first place to the Russians, who had contemptuously rejected them. In consequence the speed of their ships, class for class, exceeded that of the Russians by at least two knots; and they could bring to bear a heavier weight of armament with every calibre of gun than the Russian total. In smaller vessels, light cruisers, destroyers, torpedo boats, gunboats, mine sweepers and the like the Japanese had, as was natural in their home waters, a large preponderance which was easily maintained, since their own yards were by then capable of building the lighter craft. They also had the better seamen. Their long island seaboard provided a large reserve of sea-faring man-power. The Russians had to man their ships mostly with illiterate peasant farmers who took years to adapt themselves to a life at sea, and to whom the problems presented by simple navigational and gun-laying instruments were permanently insoluble. They were brave enough and might in time have been made into good seamen. But far too little time was spent in peace on manoeuvres and gunnery practice; and when war came it was too late. On the other hand in the matter of naval training, as in so much else, the Japanese had tried to do too much too fast; and in battle the shooting on both sides, except at extremely short ranges, was extremely erratic.

Finally the Japanese had the advantage of four well-defended dockyard bases in the Tsushima Straits, with excellent repair facilities for capital ships. Port Arthur, on the other hand, apart from its great advantage in being ice-free all the year round, was a most unsatisfactory naval base. The great anchorage had only one exit channel between high hills which was too shallow for battleships except at the top of the tide; and even then it was difficult to navigate. At the outset it was, moreover, undefended save for the coastal batteries on the cliffs whose angle of fire could not be sufficiently depressed to cover the harbour mouth. Financial stringency and lethargic irresponsibility and corruption in high places had left the dockyard facilities of the new town incomplete and without a dry dock large enough for even an Armoured Cruiser. For major underwater damage the Russian battleships were dependent on British or German bases in the Treaty Ports which were automatically banned to them on the outbreak of war.

In their contempt for upstart Asiatics the Russian admirals had given little thought to these problems and difficulties. Admiral Togo on the other hand, though he had not, like many of his senior military colleagues, started his fighting career in plate armour and wielding a two-handed broadsword, was a thoroughly realistic and ruthless exponent of the Samurai code. He had taken to heart Admiral Fisher's bombastic overstatement that 'Rashness in war is prudence; prudence in war is imbecili-ty.' But he was by nature and by the exigencies of his strategic situation a prudent man. As Churchill was to say of Jellicoe in a later era, he 'could lose the war in an afternoon' if he suffered losses heavy enough to expose the supply lines of the Japanese army to the Russian cruisers. In consequence, though he occa-sionally plunged into rash attacks, he was always inclined to pull his punches and so forfeit the decisive victory which he constant-ly sought.

This was well illustrated in the night torpedo attacks on 8 February with which he opened the war. The Japanese ambas-sador at St Petersburg had demanded absolutely clear-cut under-takings from the Russians by 4 February, which had not been forthcoming. The demand had not, however, been couched as a formal ultimatum so that technically the two nations were still at peace. But this should at least have put the Port Arthur fleet and garrison on the alert. More strangely still, on 7 February the Japanese landed a substantial army advance guard under cruiser escort at Chemulpo on the Korean coast opposite Port Arthur, destroying in the process an unarmoured gunboat and an old cruiser which they found in the harbour; yet there was still no whisper of alarm. On the night of 8 February Port Arthur was brightly lit and the restaurants and cabarets were crammed with officers of both services. The fleet, also fully illuminated, lay at anchor in the roadstead outside the harbour entrance largely without officers, since Vice-Admiral Starck, the commander, was giving a gigantic birthday party ashore. Only one precaution had been taken : all the ships had their torpedo nets in position.

At this period the torpedo had acquired a new improvement; and the Japanese torpedoes were fitted with a net-cutting device in the snout. That night it largely failed to function. The next morning the battleship *Tsarevitch* picked no less than four un-exploded torpedoes out of her nets. In her largely officerless state, she had done well, sinking one Japanese destroyer with her secondary armament and damaging several others. But one torpedo had got through all the same, hitting her astern; and in struggling to get through the entrance channel on a falling tide she had run aground. Two others of the seven Russian battle-ships had also been hit and had also run aground – the *Retvisan*

with a gaping hole in her bows right at the mouth of the
harbour, where she slowly settled down on the bottom to become
for a month or two, until she was pumped out and refloated,
nothing but a useful powerful battery at the channel entrance.
Togo had achieved all this with only about a quarter of the
torpedo force which he might have sent in; and he had kept his
battle fleet well out of range, so that it could not move in quickly
enough to administer the *coup-de-grace* which might have eliminated the Russian Pacific Fleet altogether as a factor in the
campaign. Had he thrown in everything he had there is little
doubt that enough torpedoes would have cut their way through
to inflict much greater damage and leave the whole Russian fleet
at the mercy of the guns of his battleships and cruisers before it
could get back to the shelter of the hills surrounding the harbour.
As it was it remained, somewhat miraculously, 'a fleet in being';
and it was to cost the Japanese some months of tedious and
costly fighting before it was finally bottled up and powerless. A
surprise blow of the kind delivered by Togo in defiance of all the
normal rules of war needs to be overwhelming and decisive – a
lesson which was not lost on his successors when they planned
their attack on Pearl Harbour.

Having missed his best chance of destroying the Pacific Fleet
at a single blow, Togo fell back on his second-best : an attempt to
force it to come out so that he might destroy or at least cripple it
in open battle. At ten the next morning he brought up his whole
fleet and opened fire on the town and harbour at extreme range.
The Russians, less their three damaged battleships, were lying in
the outer harbour with steam up and they did come out, though
only after a long delay, since Starck was detained at the Viceroy's Headquarters receiving 'final instructions'. An exasperated
Chief-of-Staff eventually got it on the move and the Admiral
had to chase after his flagship in a steam launch. So Togo got his
battle, but only for forty minutes and at extreme range, since he
would not risk his precious ships within reach of the plunging fire
of the coastal batteries on the cliffs. On that one morning as it
happened, he might safely have done so, since, in the milling
confusion of the night before, no live ammunition had been sent
up to most of the batteries, which were firing blanks, presumably
as a deterrent. The Russians admitted defeat and returned to

port badly hammered. But they had suffered no irreparable damage, and Togo had again failed through over-caution to achieve his main object. Falling back on his third possibility he made three night attempts, all very gallantly executed, to sink block ships in the fairway of the entrance of the outer harbour. But by then the Russian defences had been vastly improved. A few block ships did penetrate, but none was sunk in a position where it constituted more than a navigational nuisance. On 22 March Togo made one last attempt to subdue Port Arthur by naval action alone. But by then Starck had been superseded by one of the few really competent senior officers in the Russian navy, Vice-Admiral Makharoff, who had also that rare ability to inspire loyalty and gallantry among the officers and men of an entire fleet. He won with ease a defensive battle in which the firing on both sides was wildly inaccurate.

So Togo had to settle to the tedium of a prolonged blockade which kept his whole fleet permanently afloat in the Korean Gulf and allowed him only to detach a thin cruiser screen to frustrate the raids of the adventurous Russian cruiser squadron in Vladivostock. This managed to sink not only the four vital ships carrying the railway locomotives and the heavy guns, but also a number of transports, drowning or making prisoner all the troops they were carrying to the Yalu River. Under Makharoff, moreover, the Port Arthur fleet remained very much 'in being'. On 13 April he brought it out to challenge Togo's blockading fleet once again in the open. But he had the misfortune to run into one of the large minefields which both sides had begun to lay somewhat indiscriminately in the battle area; and his flagship, the *Petropalovsk*, blew up and sank within two minutes, taking with her the Admiral and most of her complement of 900 men. At same time another battleship, the *Pobeida,* suffered underwater damage from a mine. The now leaderless Russian fleet turned back in panic-stricken flight, firing wildly in every direction in the mistaken belief that it was being attacked by submarines. The loss of the battleship mattered far less than that of the Admiral and was, in fact, more than counterbalanced a fortnight later when the ineffectual Rear-Admiral Witgeft took his surviving ships out on another tentative sortie. This time the Japanese ran into a minefield and two of Togo's six irreplaceable battleships and one of his cruisers were sunk. Witgeft lacked the initiative to take any advantage of the opportunity; and since two of the Japanese ships sank out of sight of the Russians, their loss was successfully kept secret for months, so that, as far as Russian calculations were concerned, they remained in being. In actual fact, thanks to brilliant improvisation by a large body of Baltic artificers, deep-sea divers, and salvage engineers who had been disembarked by accident on their way to Dalny, all the disabled Russian ships were refloated and made more or less seaworthy before the siege ended, so that on balance the paper superiority of the Russians over Togo was not diminished but increased by these months of indecisive fighting.

The Pacific Fleet, however, was none the less finally immobilised and rendered impotent, not by Togo, but by its own Commander-in-Chief, Alexeieff. When the news arrived of General Nogi's large-scale landings on 4 May the Viceroy scuttled north to Mukden on a heavily marked hospital train – almost the last to get through – leaving behind him a fatal directive which was to be known among embittered Russian naval officers as 'The Edict of Renunciation'. It laid down that the Pacific Ocean Squadron was no longer capable of active enterprise, and that therefore 'all its means must be utilised for the defence of Port Arthur until better times come round again.' This meant that, in spite of the miracles of repair being wrought by the salvage squads, the fleet lay rotting at anchor in the shelter of the hills, its effectiveness and morale steadily degenerating, as gradually the secondary armament of the larger ships was dismantled, so that the guns could thicken up the artillery of the forts, and large drafts of officers and seamen were drawn off to replace the infantry of the garrison.

As a general rule there is not a great deal to be learnt from military or naval operations in which one side is inadequately armed and ineptly led. The fleet actions off Port Arthur between February and May of 1904 are, however, an exception, and are worthy of serious study because they demonstrated much that was important for the development of naval policies and tactics. They took place at the moment when the big battleship was just coming into its own as the dominating factor in naval warfare; and those four months had already shown the limitations which were to make its dominance so brief and evanescent. Togo was certainly the best and most successful fighting admiral of his generation. He had a faster, more heavily armed, and altogether more efficient fleet than his opponents. Yet he was held at arm's length, constantly deprived of the Nelsonic victory of which he dreamed, and forced in the end to leave the destruction of his enemy to the guns of the Japanese army. This fact alone was deeply significant for the future.

Two paradoxical trends were already to be observed in the evolution and employment of the battleship and both were to persist until the development of modern air power put an end to the story. On the one hand it was becoming almost impossible to sink a battleship by gunfire, and very difficult by any other means; and this was even more so when Britain within a year launched into the world the new type of dreadnought. Ever-thickening armour plating and a multiplicity of water-tight compartments defied the armour piercing shell and even made it unlikely that a single mine or torpedo would send them to the bottom. All the three ships hit by Togo's first torpedo attack got safely back into port and were eventually sufficiently repaired to resume their place in the battle line. The *Pobeida,* which struck a mine in the battle of 13 April, got safely home. The *Petropalovsk* perished because the mine she struck detonated an explosion in her magazine which blew her apart. It is probable that the Japanese *Hatsuse* struck more than one mine; the *Yashima* very nearly got home and took thirty-six hours to sink.

On the other hand the destructive power of both mines and torpedoes would also increase as the years went on. The coastal minefields widely laid by both sides in 1904 would become larger and more formidable and would seriously restrict the movements of battle fleets when they moved out from their bases into open waters; and they were precluded from closing with an enemy for fear of a massive torpedo attack by destroyers or concealed submarines, since nobody knew how many torpedo hits would defeat even the dreadnought's watertight arrangements. They could only move in and out of port when preceded by a swarm of minesweepers and only cruise on the high seas under the protection of destroyer flotillas and light cruiser squadrons powerful enough to frustrate an attack by the enemy's light craft. Thus, while they became the essential base for any large-scale naval operation such as a blockade or a major raid, they were essentially a defensive base. Properly screened and manoeuvred with caution they were virtually indestructible. Otherwise they became extremely vulnerable; and there was little chance in the future of battleships being able to close into what Nelson called 'a pell-mell battle'.

All the portents for this future were made clear even in the pathetic last effort of the Russian Pacific Fleet to escape from its inevitable doom in Port Arthur. At the beginning of August when it became clear that the land defences of the fortress were collapsing Alexeieff, aware that he was liable to be recalled in disgrace, sent the wretched Witgeft a suggestion rather than an order that it might be best to break out to Vladivostock. It was phrased with a beautiful ambiguity which would give the Viceroy all the credit for a bold decision if it was successful. If it failed or was not attempted, all the blame could be thrown on the Rear-Admiral. For two days Witgeft hesitated. With luck all his ships could be got to sea. But few of them were seaworthy, let alone battle-worthy. The battleships had almost all been deprived of their 6-inch guns to help out the land defences and all his crews had been depleted. After three months enforced immobility in harbour nobody knew how the engines and other mechanical gear would function; and two of his battleships were veterans, capable at the best of times of a speed of 14 knots as compared with the 16·3 of his better ships and the 18·3 of the Japanese. But throughout those two days his ships were being repeatedly hit by indirect and unobserved but intermittently effective fire from Japanese land batteries; and he himself was wounded in the leg by a shell splinter. He decided that any action was better than accepting the certain doom of staying where he was. Rejecting all compromise schemes for sacrificial actions by the two old battleships and the less seaworthy small craft which might tempt Togo to divide his force and give the better ships a chance of getting through, he threw the responsibility firmly back to Alexeieff, where it belonged. 'My orders are to go to Vladivostock with the whole squadron', he said, 'and that I shall do.'

At 4.41 on the morning of 10 August – twenty-four hours late because the Captain of the *Pobeida* had not been feeling well – the little cruiser *Novik*, whose guns had opened the war, led Witgeft's forlorn hope out through the now very tricky entrance channel. Miraculously all got through without mishap, including the battered old *Retvisan,* her bows clumsily patched and 400 tons of water still sloshing about in her holds. The whole fleet was there, the six battleships in the van, followed by the three armoured cruisers and the destroyer and torpedo-boat flotillas. They were held up twice by engine room failures in *Tsarevitch* and *Pobeida,* but they steamed doggedly on for eight hours before, having narrowly dodged a floating minefield, they came into contact with the Japanese fleet, spread out to the south to cut them off both from the British port of Wei-hai-wei and the southern tip of Korea which they must round before turning north for Vladivostock. Togo fought his usual cautious battle, with his torpedo craft out in front supported by the armoured cruisers, and his four precious battleships within range of the enemy, but well out of immediate danger. It was not his plan to win a dramatic victory on the high seas, but merely to force the Russians back on their tracks. He had laid a large new minefield the night before on the southern approaches to Port Arthur; and on to this he proposed to drive the whole Russian fleet by torpedo attacks during the following night as they struggled home.

The battle has come down in history as a Japanese victory, as it ought to have been, since their ships could by then heavily outgun and outsteam their opponents and were in much better condition. Yet, after nearly four hours of fighting, the Russian fleet was still steaming doggedly on its course and had suffered no decisive damage. The Russian battleships had defended themselves manfully, using, in default of their lesser armament, their 12-inch guns at almost point-blank range, and the badly battered Japanese torpedo craft had fallen back having scored only one hit – again on the luckless *Retvisan*. A direct hit had destroyed the conning tower of *Tsarevitch* killing everybody in it, including Admiral Witgeft, and another had carried away the mainmast of the *Peresviet*. Otherwise there was only superficial damage. Even when Togo concentrated the fire of his whole fleet on the three Russian cruisers they were knocked about by shell splinters, but suffered no direct hit and not a single casualty.

When disaster struck the Russians it was mechanical. The steering gear of *Tsarevitch* broke down completely and she gyrated helplessly at the head of the line throwing the whole fleet into confusion. The flag-captain, who had so far omitted to inform the fleet of the death of its commander, hoisted a despairing signal : 'The Admiral hands over command.' But since Prince Utomsky on whom the command devolved had lost all his signal halyards along with *Peresviet*'s mainmast, he could give no orders and the individual captains scattered to make their own best way out of the battle. Togo flung in his torpedo craft again for a final killing; but a last signal from *Tsarevitch* ordered the Russian light craft forward to cover the withdrawal, and this they successfully did.

Four of the Russian battleships and all their small craft got back into Port Arthur, including the battered *Retvisan. Tsarevitch,* steering erratically by her engines, got to Kiao-chou and only the aged *Sebastopol* fouled Togo's minefield. Even she, however, struggled to anchor under the coastal guns, fought off torpedo attacks all night, and made her way safely home the next morning. The cruisers all got away. *Askold* fetched up at Shanghai; *Pallada* rejoined the fleet in Port Arthur; *Diana,* badly knocked about, steamed twelve hundred miles to Saigon; and the heroic little *Novik* would have made Vladivostock had not the cruiser squadron there been annihilated by the Japanese just as she arrived. So ended the active career of the Russian Pacific Fleet. It is a story only worth the telling because it illustrates so well how difficult it already was in 1905 for an efficient, up-to-date, well-handled fleet to destroy in battle even a not very well matched opponent.

It might seem that the total destruction of the Russian Baltic Fleet, renamed the Second and Third Pacific Squadrons, in the Tsushima Straits nine months later falsified this conclusion; and it did indeed provide powerful ammunition for the many advocates in all the world's navies for larger fleets of even bigger battleships. In fact it proved nothing except that a fleet cannot be improvised in a few months, particularly when the crews have to be drawn from a largely non-seafaring population and at a period when technical advances demand many new kinds of expertise other than seamanship. The cream of both officers and

K*

seamen available had already been drafted to the Pacific. Vice-Admiral Roshestvensky was given three months to hammer into shape crews half drawn from illiterate peasants straight from their farms, half from ageing reservists who had learnt all their techniques on ships long out-of-date. Both halves were permeated with Marxist propagandists who regarded the defeat of the fleet as a necessary first stage in the coming revolution; and the vast majority of his officers were rich, irresponsible aristocrats more preoccupied with their own champagne supplies than with the comfort or efficiency of the men they commanded.

His ships were equally inadequate for their task. On paper he had a decisive superiority over Togo's depleted fleet, even if he was too late to be reinforced by the ships at Port Arthur. The fighting core of his fleet was a battle squadron consisting of his flagship, *Suvaroff*, and her three sister ships, *Orel, Borodino,* and *Alexander III*. So fresh from the dockyards that they had scarcely completed their working-up trials, these were the most modern battleships afloat. They carried two pairs of 12-inch guns in turrets fore and aft and as secondary armament twelve 6-inch and forty-six smaller guns; and their designed speed was over eighteen knots. Their weakness was that this massive secondary armament necessitated an uncomfortably lofty superstructure; and this had been accentuated by intrigues and alarms at the Admiralty while they were building which added large extra accommodation for officers' quarters and heavier armour on the top deck, so that they rolled excessively in rough weather and presented enormous targets to the enemy. There were also four brand-new fast light cruisers as good as anything of their class afloat. Roshestvensky would have preferred to take these eight ships only, and his nine fast torpedo boats, with the necessary supply ships and transports, for the sake of a uniform high speed both on the long journey out and in battle. But the High Command insisted on adding to his fleet a number of older and slower ships which were merely a liability in battle or out of it.

There was a Second Battle Squadron under Admiral von Felzerkam in *Oslyabya*, a comparatively new ship, but a designer's freak. She had only 10-inch guns for main armament and so many smaller guns that they had to be fitted into three superimposed tiers. In consequence her towering hull made her

slow and scarcely seaworthy; and the lowest tier of guns was so
near the water-line that the gunports had to be closed if there
was anything of a sea running. With her were two ancient battleships designed for coastal defence, both very slow and prodigious
burners of coal, with inadequate armour and obsolete guns. A
further heterogeneous mass of freaks were added to the cruiser
fleet – the oldest of them, the *Donskoy*, dating from 1870 and
originally designed as an armoured frigate rigged for sail. Finally, they were all grossly overloaded. Great Britain had been
Japan's ally since 1902 and her many coaling stations on which
the world's sea-borne traffic mainly depended were inexorably
closed to Roshestvensky. Everything the Russians might need to
fight their way past Togo into Port Arthur or Vladivostock had
therefore to be carried with them. The big ships were in consequence so low in the water that only two feet of their belt of
armour plate extended above the water-line and they dared not
risk the passage of the Suez Canal. They therefore faced a
voyage of 18,000 miles round Africa and across the Indian
Ocean with only a few German and French harbours where the
neutrality laws might be stretched a little in their favour. Coaling
had to be done the hard way, at sea, from a fleet of attendant
colliers hired from the *Hamburg-Amerika* line; and they would
need in all 500,000 tons of coal.

The seven-month voyage of the Baltic Fleet, from its farcical
opening engagement with the British North Sea herring fleet to
its heroic and hopeless doom at Tsushima on 28 May 1905, has
been described often and recently enough and in sufficient detail
to make it clear that the very few tactical deductions which
could be drawn from the final battle were misleading.[9]
Roshestvensky's ships went into action with coal sacks piled on
their decks and stuffed into every available cranny below; and
none of this could be jettisoned before battle, since without it
they could not hope to reach Vladivostock. Their bottoms had
accumulated on the way a foot of tropical seaweed showing even
at the water-line. These two factors alone had reduced the cruising speed of even his newest ships by a third. He was even
further slowed up by the higher strategists at St Petersburg, who
compelled him, under protest, to wait in a bay off Saigon for
Rear-Admiral Nebogatov in the totally obsolete battleship

Nicholas I and the rest of the newly created Third Pacific Squadron : two ancient coastal defence battleships and four flat, shallow-draught batteries armed with 10-inch guns, but designed exclusively for operations in the shelving waters of the Baltic, which were to be christened the 'goloshes' by the fleet's seamen. The Russian fleet therefore sailed on its final dash for Vladivostock in three divisions, none of which was capable of any but the simplest manoeuvre. But this mattered little, since Roshestvensky himself had no tactical experience and had formulated no ideas of how he proposed to fight his battle. In a mood compounded of hysterical rage with the incompetence of his subordinates and a fatalistic acceptance of certain failure, he drove doggedly into the Tsushima Straits in the hope that at least his more powerful and faster ships might batter their way through to a shelter where they might be cleaned and refitted to harry Japanese communications with the mainland. He had already told his government that the fall of Port Arthur ended all hope of sweeping the Japanese from the seas and dominating the waters off Korea and Manchuria.

Togo, who had constantly forfeited decisive success off Port Arthur by excessive caution, opened the battle of Tsushima with a recklessly daring manoeuvre which might have proved fatal. In spite of a thick fog, he knew precisely where the enemy was, thanks to the insubordination of the Captain of Roshestvensky's hospital ship who had kept all his lights blazing as he entered the Straits the night before; and he had received massive reports from spies and observers of the ineptitude of Russian seamanship and gunnery. He therefore steamed boldly across the head of the Russian line as it emerged into open waters the following afternoon, turned south to place himself between the Russians and Vladivostock, and then turned his battle line of eleven ships about in succession as they came abreast of *Suvaroff*. This brought each of them in turn nicely within range, at 9,000 yards, of the whole Russian fleet; and the excellence of the Russian shooting took Togo completely by surprise. Roshestvensky owed his promotion to his performance as senior gunnery officer of the fleet; and for the first half-hour of the battle his gunners fully justified his rigorous training methods. By the time the Japanese line had straightened out on a parallel course the flagship, *Mikasa*, had been hit fifteen times. Two of Togo's other three battleships were hard hit, *Yakumo*'s fore-turret being knocked out, and *Asama*'s steering gear so badly jammed by a shell from Nebogatov's despised *Nicholas I* that she wobbled out of the line. Almost all Togo's heavy cruisers were badly damaged and one was disabled. Russian gunfire completely dominated the battle and even the despised 'goloshes' were scoring hits with their 10-inch guns.

Then, however, the slower ships at the rear of the Russian line dropped hopelessly behind and, as Togo shortened the range to a little over a mile, the deluge of contact-fused shells from nearly five hundred guns bewildered and demoralised the Russian gunners, as it had the Chinese at the Yalu. They could not penetrate armour plate. But a hit on a turret or conning-tower sent steel splinters flying inside; and on those coal-packed decks the smallest shell was liable to start a fire. Within twenty minutes of completing their dangerous turn the surviving ten ships in Togo's battle line established an overwhelming superiority. Russian fire, though still rapid, became wildly inaccurate. Using his superior speed, Togo constantly threatened to cross the Russian T again, this time at devastatingly close range, so forcing Roshestvensky steadily eastwards and away from Vladivostock. The Russian Second and Third Squadrons were left far behind and clean out of the fight. Only the four *Suvaroff*-class battleships and the gigantic *Oslyabya* remained in the line; and it was not long before all five were ablaze from stem to stern. When Togo switched from contact-fuses to armour-piercing shell the results were catastrophic. *Oslyabya* was the first to go. So overloaded that her whole belt of armour plate was submerged and her lowest tier of guns permanently useless, she was virtually unprotected. One hit on the water-line from a 12-inch shell was enough. She heeled rapidly over, capsized, and sank.

A few minutes later *Suvarov* reeled out of the line and came to a halt, her steering gear jammed and only one 75 cm. quick-firing gun left in action; and soon after *Alexander III* suffered a similar fate. Finally, towards sundown, as Togo pulled away to give his torpedo craft a clear field for the kill, a single 12-inch shell from *Fuji* crashed through *Borodino*'s deck amidships and blew her apart, leaving one naked seaman clinging to a lifeboat mast to be picked up the next morning as her sole survivor. *Orel,* with only two small guns left in action, slipped away to join Admiral Nebogatov's ancient ships still cruising doggedly at their best speed towards Vladivostock. Roshestvensky had been twice seriously wounded and was only intermittently conscious when disaster overtook his flagship. His over-zealous staff, anxious only to save his life, got him transferred – and, incidentally, them-selves – to a destroyer,[10] leaving *Suvaroff* under command of the indomitable Midshipman von Kursel who refused to accom-pany them, with all her wounded and perhaps a hundred still able-bodied seamen to fight her fires and keep the remaining gun in action; and this they did magnificently, fighting off two attacks by massed torpedo-craft until, at last light, the simulta-neous explosion of four torpedoes sent her to the bottom, to be followed almost immediately by her sister-ship, *Alexander III.*

There were no useful tactical lessons to be learnt from the rest of the battle. Of all the Russian senior officers the tubby, un-impressive Admiral Nebogatov really did best. Japanese light cruisers scattered his old cruisers, his 'goloshes' and his transports in confusion; and Admiral Enkvist prudently took his three fast modern cruisers, which were supposed to be the fighting core of his Squadron, out of the battle to take refuge in neutral intern-ment at Manila. The main body steamed on through the night towards Vladivostock, using even their heavy guns to beat off the swarming Japanese torpedo-craft. They survived mainly because Nebogatov had trained them to fight at night without search-lights and because *Orel* had no working lights left. But dawn found him still three hundred miles short of his objective with only five ships left: his own three ancient ironclads, the useless *Orel,* and the fast, still undamaged cruiser, *Irzumrud.* Within an hour he was surrounded by the entire Japanese fleet, being shelled accurately at a range of 12,000 yards, which was 1,000 yards beyond the reach of any gun left to him. So – with some difficulty, since the Japanese signal book did not include the international code word for 'Surrender' – he hauled down his colours to save his men's lives. *Irzumrud* slipped away at twenty-four knots and when she ran out of coal was beached and systematically destroyed by her Captain before he marched his crew into captivity. Only the derided, thirty-year-old converted frigate, *Donskoy,* really covered herself with glory. Crammed with *Oslyabya*'s survivors, she fought off four Japanese cruisers, sank two torpedo-boats – the only ships, incidentally, the Japanese lost – until she finally foundered in a Korean cove with not a single unwounded man aboard her.

Broadly speaking, the Russian fleet was annihilated. By burning every bit of wooden structure two fast destroyers got to Vladivostock; and the old cruiser, *Almaz,* driven early out of the fight, made it with help from a collier sent out to meet her. A few remnants found refuge, like Enkvist, in neutral ports. Otherwise no ships and hardly a man survived. It was a victory even more dramatic and complete than Trafalgar, and with equally conclusive results. Togo, somewhat undeservedly, was dubbed the 'greatest naval commander of the age'. His personal courage, his efficiency, and his generosity to a beaten enemy were beyond praise. But he was not a tactical genius. He never faced a properly led first-class fleet; and the dramatic completeness of his victory at Tsushima created an illusion which was to haunt both the admirals and the public of the world's naval powers for the next forty years.

What could not be realised in 1905, and has perhaps been insufficiently emphasised by historians ever since, was that, while the *Oslyabya* and *Borodino* were the first powerfully armoured battleships to be sunk by gunfire alone, they were also the last. For a brief period the *Dreadnought*-type battleship, launched by the British in 1906, was to dominate the naval scene as the essential basis of 'the fleet in being'. Within forty years the mine, the torpedo, the submarine and, ultimately the aerial bomb were to render it an obsolete nuisance. But for that period Tsushima was to remain for fighting admirals and armchair tacticians an unattainable ideal. Neither the British public nor most historians have ever quite forgiven Jellicoe for failing to reproduce at Jutland Togo's triumph in the Yellow Sea ten years before. Only Pearl Harbour, the destruction of the *Prince of Wales* off Malaya, and the prolonged agony of the *Bismarck* would convince the theorists and the designers that they had for fifty years been backing the wrong horse. Tsushima, in fact, perpetuated as many illusions as Lissa had for an earlier generation; but with far more disastrous results.

9 The Legacy of Moltke

The legacy of Moltke was, rather surprisingly, entirely disastrous to the generals and military thinkers of the succeeding age. He himself had inherited from Clausewitz his General Staff and along with it his careful analysis of the fundamental principles of war as demonstrated in the campaigns of Napoleon. Cautious conservative as he was, Moltke agreed with Sir Edward Hamley that those principles were few and in all circumstances unchanging; and his own original contribution was the brilliant application of these same principles in a period of social and technological revolution. With overwhelming success he exploited them in terms of the Needle Gun, the progressive inventions of Herr Krupp, the achievements of the railway engineers, and of the expanded forces made available to him by the army reforms of von Roon and King William. He was so able to take full advantage of the political opportunities opened for him by the far greater creative genius of Bismarck. Under his guidance an enlarged and dedicated General Staff combined all these factors to build one of the most formidable fighting machines the world has ever seen. But its triumphs were too easy and spectacular, and were won over opponents who, however brave, had no comparable instrument to match it. However unintentionally, Moltke in the years after 1871 laid on his own army – and derivatively on every other army in Europe – a hand as dead as that laid by Wellington on the British army in the years after Waterloo.

Of course, assiduous students at the *Kriegsakademie*, the *Ecole de Guerre* and the Camberly Staff College, mulling over the events of 1866 and 1870, could see for themselves the immense superiority of Prussian military organisation, weapons, training, and tactics over those of the Austrians and French. It did not need any very detailed study of the campaigns in Bohemia and northern France to learn how wretchedly badly Benedek and Bazaine were served by their staffs. Austrian staff officers were either plodding, slow-witted, desk-bound students of Clausewitz, like General Krismaniç, or light-hearted, irresponsible aristocrats, accustomed to living in a sort of perpetual eve of Waterloo ball, who shared Count Berchtold's view that, whereas in other countries situations were often described as 'serious, but not desperate', in Austria they were 'always desperate, but never serious'. The contrast between these and the equally aristocratic, but conscientious and hard-working Prussians can perhaps best be illustrated by two episodes in the preliminary manoeuvres leading up to Königgrätz. Only at midnight on 2 July did Moltke sign the short, decisive order which was to bring the Crown Prince's army on to the Austrian right flank the following afternoon. One copy went by a safe but roundabout route through Prince Frederick Charles's Headquarters, and was bound to arrive dangerously late. A second was therefore entrusted to one of the King's ADCs, Lieutenant-Colonel Count Finckenstein, to be carried across country on tracks which would bring him dangerously close to the Austrian outposts. For a good horseman it was a two-hour ride; and if luck was with him he would enable the Crown Prince to get his whole army on the move by daybreak.

Finckenstein refused to wait for his cavalry escort to get booted and saddled and galloped off with only his groom. He was completely informed of the contents and importance of the order which he carried and he made such good time that he was even able to drop into von Bonin's Corps Headquarters on the way to give him a warning to prepare to move. Three days earlier the Austrian Major Count Sternberg set off at eight in the morning on a comparable, though entirely safe ride, carrying an equally vital despatch from Benedek to Crown Prince Albert of Saxony. The Prince was not to stand and fight with his two Corps, as planned, at Jitschin, but to fall back at once to the new position on which Benedek was now proposing to stage the decisive battle. Towards midday Sternberg dropped in on some friends at the castle of Milicowes for rest and refreshment. Learning that they were expecting the Crown Prince and his staff there that evening, he decided that it would be pleasanter to await him there. The Crown Prince had spent a tormenting morning, since he had had no recent orders of any kind and the Prussian advance guards were closing up on him. At two o'clock his doubts were ended by a telegram from Benedek confirming the original order, and he confidently accepted a general engagement in the expectation that the main army would be arriving before nightfall in his support. The telegram had been held up for over two days by a breakdown of the service; but it was reasonable to suppose that he would have been urgently informed of any change of plan.

It was not until six p.m. that a breathless Count Sternberg, roused from his pleasant afternoon by the thunder of guns to the north, arrived with the true facts. The Crown Prince successfully disengaged his army before dark. But in the face of a greatly superior enemy it was not easy; and the Austrian Corps of Count Clam-Gallas broke under the strain, sending its wagon train galloping in wild panic down the road to Sadowa to spread alarm and despondency in the main army. The whole episode was a quite unnecessary disaster which had its effect at König-grätz. As far as staff work was concerned the lesson was clear enough; and it could have been underlined a dozen times from the ambiguous orders and clumsy staff work of the French in 1870. For the whole military world it became an axiom that the Great General Staff was invincible unless opposed by the same methods and the same disciplines. All thinking after 1871 was oriented towards the German army, its achievements, its procedures and its intentions as decisively as it had been towards France in the first half of the century; and, as before, the political and diplomatic situation accentuated this tendency.

In 1879 Bismarck got the virtually permanent alliance with Austria which had always been his aim once he had secured Prussia's predominance in Germany. In this Alliance Italy became an uneasy third, abandoning for the time being her long-standing ambition to round off the *Risorgimento* by the annexation of the South Tyrol, in the hope of support against the French intrusion into what she regarded as her sphere of influence in North Africa. It was a bad bargain since there was nothing effective the Central Powers could do to help her, and she risked involvement in European issues which were of no importance to her. But it meant that Bismarck had created a power bloc comprising the central, the most populous, and the most prosperous areas of Europe from the Baltic to the Mediterranean, which inevitably posed a threat to every nation on the fringes of the Continent. Not even he could for long reproduce the forty years of Metternichian calm, when all the powers had been united in fearing a revival of Napoleonic ambitions in France. Personal prestige and sheer diplomatic skill enabled him to postpone any crisis by expedients such as the League of the Three Emperors and his secret Reinsurance Treaties with Russia. None of his successors had the necessary juggler's skill. However disparate the ambitions of France and Russia might be in different parts of the world, they were perforce thrown together, if only to ensure that neither should be left isolated by the defeat of the other. The loudly publicised creation of a German fleet at the turn of the century so designed that it could only be a threat to British predominance in the North Sea forced Great Britain in her turn to abandon an isolation which had never really been 'splendid' and which, as Lord Salisbury had said, was not a policy, but a predicament. Reluctantly, and with many reservations, Britain by 1906 had become a partner in the Triple Entente which replaced the Dual Alliance.[1]

It has been a common oversimplification to regard the outbreak of war in 1914 as merely the inevitable consequence of the division of Europe into two armed camps and the resulting armaments race. But both the opposed alliances were weakened and divided by reservations and mutual hostilities which cut across these groupings. For more than a century Britain had been accustomed to regard Russian ambitions in the Balkans as a threat to her imperial communications. Russia's restless activity beyond the western Himalayas had given the British public the 'Russian Bogey'; and British Liberal opinion intensely disliked any condonation of the brutal military autocracy which alone kept Nicholas II on his throne. French statesmen had always insisted that their support could not be invoked if Russia became involved in a Balkan war; and there were surviving tensions between France and Britain over Egypt and the Sudan which made their arrangements for mutual support extremely tentative. On the other side Italy, as her colonial dreams gradually evaporated, was increasingly doubtful of the value of an alliance which meant a perpetual abandonment of her ambitions in the Trentino – of *Italia Irridenta*. The Italians, anyway, were, as always, chiefly concerned to be sure that if they went to war it would be on the winning side; an ambition they successfully achieved until Mussolini made his fatal miscalculation in 1940. Finally German statesmen remained quite clear that the Austrian alliance was vital to them, but had no more wish than the French to be dragged into Balkan squabbles. But in the last analysis, of course, they had no choice. If the Russian 'steam-roller' ground the Austrians into the dust the emancipation of the Balkan Slavs would inevitably disintegrate the Austro-Hungarian Empire, leaving Germany in total isolation: at last really exposed, as the German public hysterically believed her to be, to 'encirclement' by hostile powers.

For the General Staffs, on the other hand, the problems of the future resolved themselves with a stark and uncompromising simplicity. However diplomats might hesitate, the generals saw clearly that Germany must intervene if Austria found herself involved single-handed against Russia. In that case France, too, was bound to intervene or face destruction later, and alone. What the British and Italians might do was for the Germans of no immediate importance. Both sides were inclined to dismiss the Italians as a negligible factor. Only the Austrians, as it turned out rightly, took their army seriously; and one senior British admiral was heard to say that in a Mediterranean war he would regard the collaboration of the Italian fleet as a liability, rather than an asset. The British Expeditionary Force was dismissed by both French and Germans as 'contemptible', though only Kaiser Wilhelm II was rude enough to say so in public; and it was difficult to see how a British fleet could intervene effectively in the short, swift struggle which everybody envisaged.

Thus, whether they liked it or not, Moltke and his successors found themselves faced with Bismarck's haunting nightmare of a war on two fronts; and this was the strategic background against which the new German army sedulously prepared for what seemed likely to be a final trial of strength. They were handicapped by the fact that nobody was more impressed by the victories of 1866 and 1870 than they were themselves. As has been authoritatively pointed out,[2] one of Moltke's greatest assets as a leader was his capacity for self-criticism; and this habit of mind he ceaselessly inculcated in his staff. On the evening of even a spectacular victory like Königgrätz he liked to assemble his personal entourage and expound the mistakes which had been made and point out things which could have been better done. But even Moltke had his little vanities to which, as time went on, he tended to succumb. He liked the popular image of himself sitting back at General Headquarters, the spider at the centre of his web, sensitive to every movement at the far-away front, and deftly controlling the movements of his armies. He would never, for example, admit that there was any moment in the Bohemian campaign when he was not in a position to unite his widely scattered armies before one of them could be defeated in detail, though there were plenty of expert military historians prepared to demonstrate that this was not always true. This tendency became even more noticeable in the official staff history of 1870–1, which he himself supervised. The battle of Spicheren was fought on the south side of the Saar by the inextricably entangled advanced formations of 1st and 2nd Armies at a moment when they should have been clearly separated and both were strictly forbidden without direct authority from General Headquarters to cross the river, which did not in fact reach them until the following morning. Moreover, it threw Moltke's carefully prepared strategic offensive completely out of gear by involving 1st Army in the thick of the frontal advance through Lorraine. But it was none the less an important victory; and Moltke was not prepared to admit that he had not been its architect. The actions of the leading commanders – so ran the official account – 'nevertheless fulfilled the intentions of the higher command, although the order issued to this effect had not yet been received'.[3]

This could, perhaps, be discounted as the harmless conceit of an ageing and immensely successful general. But it underlined an attitude of mind which would colour all his decisions for the seventeen years during which he continued in office after 1871;

and it was to condition the outlook of the Great General Staff until 1914. They were the first to be dazzled by their own demonstrable excellence and invincibility; and they became the prisoners of their own too-rigid efficiency. Any useful lessons which might have been learnt from the American Civil War were overlaid by their own triumphs. The reports of their observers in the Balkan War of 1877–8 and on the Manchurian front in 1904 were studied only in strategic terms to see how far the manoeuvres of the generals concerned conformed to the rules and principles which had governed their own victorious campaigns. The land fighting in Cuba in 1898 was ignored, since they could expect to learn nothing from the antics of half-trained American volunteers or the lethargic dispositions of the effete and disheartened regular army of Spain. The tactics and operations of both sides in the South African War were so patently amateurish that they were dismissed as altogether unworthy of study.

Hammered into the Prussian pattern, the senior officers and staffs of the new German army remained, of course, supremely efficient and self-confident. The new divisions made available to them by growth of the population were tidily incorporated into their organisation and provided for in the incessantly revised mobilisation plans. Railway extensions were duly noted and exploited. New and improved guns, small arms, and equipment replaced the obsolete as they became available. Most important of all, they alone among the European Staffs appreciated the force of old Canrobert's lament that he had not had a couple of batteries of Mitrailleuses in his infantry front lines at Gravelotte to turn the costly attack of the Prussian Guard into a massacre and at the same time leave him with enough spare infantry to protect his vulnerable right flank. It was the lavish provision of machine guns to their infantry regiments which was to give the Germans their nearly decisive tactical superiority in 1914. But the war which they were planning to win remained always an extended version of 1870, with enlarged and improved armies operating in the traditional frontier areas of Alsace-Lorraine and Poland and East Prussia. The problems of war on two fronts were complicated by the French construction of a new and formidable fortified line from Verdun to Belfort, resting on both flanks on diplomatically inviolable frontiers. Moltke planned to allow them to batter their army to pieces against an equally powerful fortified line from Metz to Strasbourg, where comparatively few divisions would suffice to fend them off from the vital industrial area of the Rhineland, while he used the bulk of his army to destroy the massive Russian forces as they moved slowly but inexorably across a frontier dangerously close to Berlin. Overwhelming forces could then be brought back to breach the French fortified zone and repeat the triumphs of 1870 in the west.

There was a brief interlude when Moltke at last retired. Waldersee soon found that this was the one post at Berlin which could not be held down merely by vanity, intrigue and flattery.[4] So the great inheritance passed in 1892 to Count Schlieffen: a dedicated product of the General Staff tradition, brilliantly clearheaded, but only within the severe limits of his own military problems. Nothing else held any interest for him.[5] For ten years he accepted Moltke's plan and was content to polish and elaborate it. But in 1902 he changed his mind, with disastrous results for the future. He decided that, even with the extra numbers provided by the new army law and the phenomenal growth of the German population, he would still be unable to eliminate the Russian army in a single swift campaign. With the French in no danger, the Russians would be able to fall back through their eastern wastes, playing their well-tried game of selling space for time and so eluding decisive defeat.

Strategically his decision was undoubtedly correct. He reckoned that the skeleton defence which was all that he could spare either in the east or west could not hold out for much more than six weeks. Whether he accepted the risk of a Russian army at the gates of Berlin or that of a triumphant French army storming across the Rhine to disrupt German industry and dislocate his communications, he had to have an overwhelming victory on one of his fronts within that time limit. On the Polish borders that was out of the question. But prolonged and meticulous studies convinced him that it was possible to break through on the Vosges and round up the whole French army in a sort of combined Metz and Sedan in not much more than six weeks. The Russians could then be dealt with at leisure. All this made sound military sense. But it deprived German statesmen of all freedom of manoeuvre. Bismarck had carefully preserved control of the delicate machinery of the European Balance of Power. With his Reinsurance Treaties and the rest he retained the option of keeping Germany and France neutral if a Balkan crisis provoked an Austro-Russian confrontation. He could, moreover, restrain Austria by withholding German support, and Russia by the threat to mobilise on the eastern frontier only. Once the Schlieffen thesis was accepted, that a defeat of France was an essential preliminary to any action against Russia, all these options disappeared. Berlin could no longer control European developments or localise a Balkan conflict. In fairness to Schlieffen it should be added that by 1902 there was no politician in Berlin clear-headed enough to make such a control effective. Henceforth the soldiers rather than the diplomats were the final arbiters of the fate of Europe, as 1914 would show.[6]

In fact the German decision meant that no politician anywhere had any longer the power to prevent the most trivial conflict, however remote, from plunging all five European Great Powers into a catastrophe. As the Schlieffen Plan developed into the form later familiar to all newspaper readers in the west, it further ensured that a much wider world than Europe would become involved. As the French strengthened their fortified zone they ended Schlieffen's hope of a quick break-through in that confined space. He would have to go round. The final Plan is such familiar territory that it needs no detailed elucidation: an 'enticing defensive' on the Rhine; a massive mobilisation along the frontiers of both Holland and Belgium; and finally the heavily weighted right hook which was to move down the Channel coast before wheeling eastwards south of Paris. The fortresses, including Paris, were to be masked only by reserve divisions; and the French army, folded back round Verdun on its own fortified line, to be there hammered into surrender. The timings had been carefully cut to a minimum to ensure that within six weeks the troop trains would be rolling the victorious army back across Germany to the Polish frontier. Further, the crossing of the neutral frontiers was to be delayed to the last possible minute in the hope that the looming threat would break the French nerve and tempt them to move up to the line of the Meuse – so much more defensible than their flat northern frontier. The onus of violating Belgian neutrality would then fall on them, and the British might hesitate until it was too late to intervene effectively. But in any case none of the Continental soldiers thought that the two Army Corps of the Expeditionary Force could affect the issue either way.

Schlieffen died, adjuring those around his death bed only to 'keep the right strong'. The younger Moltke, who succeeded him largely because of the Kaiser's superstitious reverence for his name, never grasped the ideas underlying the Plan; and he had no advisers more competent than himself. In the years before 1914 the project was truncated. Dutch neutrality was to be left undisturbed so that Germany might have a 'lung' open for trade with the outer world. The shortened line brought the right hook far short of the Channel coast, so that it passed east instead of west of Paris and exposed the Germans, in the event, to defeat on the Marne. Moltke's nervousness further led him not only to use all the new divisions which became available to him after 1906 to strengthen his forces on the Rhine and in Prussia, both of which Schlieffen had deliberately left weak, but also to substitute regular divisions from the right flank for the reserves which were to have sealed off the Belgian fortresses. So the whole initial plan went wrong and the First World War bogged down in trench lines behind barbed wire.

For the student of warfare Schlieffen's plan has a double fascination. On the one hand it embodied all the strategic principles of Sherman's Atlanta campaign : surprise and deception, secrecy, and the preservation to the last possible moment of as many alternative objectives as were available. The French were to be kept guessing and the British kept out of the war altogether until it was too late for effective intervention. But tactically it was doomed to failure because all its thought was based on the assumption that the new war would be a renewal, on the old battlefields, of the war of 1870, though on a larger scale and with greater numbers involved. With Schlieffen in command and the enemy on the run, he might just have pulled off the gigantic Sedan which he had planned. But if his enemy got a breathing space in which to dig himself in, the chance had gone. All the ignored experiences of the Americans in the Civil

War and in Cuba, of the Balkan campaigns of 1877–8, and the Boer War made that clear. Almost inevitably the war in the west – and later to a lesser extent in the east – was to settle down to the sort of siege conditions which had characterised the fighting round Richmond in 1865, around Plevna and Shipka in 1877, before Santiago in 1898, and in the operations at Port Arthur in 1905. For such a contingency neither Schlieffen nor any of his colleagues had made any plans at all.

It is hard to excuse the German generals for their failure in 1914 to implement lessons which could easily have been learnt from the reports plentifully available to them from 1865 onwards. Moltke's restricted sweep through Belgium and northern France opened up dazzling possibilities for his cavalry at a moment when the war was still entirely mobile in the wide spaces between the right of von Klück's army and the coast : a cavalry commander of Forrest's ability could have created total havoc in and around the Channel ports. A few properly trained and equipped divisions could have disrupted the British disembarkation as far south as Étaples. The 'old contemptibles', in fact, would never have got to Mons at all. But the legend of von Bredow's improbable triumph at Mars-la-Tour still haunted the German cavalry which remained in 1914 the same 'jangling, expensive nuisance' as it had been in 1870. It was not even efficient in its elementary duty of reconnaissance. When the generals faced the problems presented by enemy infantry in properly dug earthworks, adequately armed, and protected by barbed wire, this was nothing new. Admittedly, when the front stretched from the North Sea to the Swiss frontier, there was no flank to be turned and an investment could not be achieved by military means on land. But the fundamental lesson had long been entirely clear : a large-scale assault frontally on such a position was merely a form of mass suicide. A condition of siege warfare had to be accepted as a fact.

The German General Staff thus remained spell-bound in contemplation of its own excellencies until it was actually engulfed in a new war, when it was too late for any fundamental rethinking. At the same time, towards the turn of the century, Prussian society and with it the old army suffered some degeneration as it was merged into a newly rich German Empire under a new

Emperor, both self-consciously aggressive and self-assertive. Both in international politics, and in the Imperial Court and social world of Berlin elder statesmen and senior diplomats from Vienna, St Petersburg, and London were increasingly aware of a decay of manners: a touchy, combative arrogance, and a vulgar parade of new wealth and new power which suggested the *parvenu* and the *nouveau riche*. New wealth permeated even the old Corps of Officers; and foreign guests at the Adlon Hotel were apt to be offended by noisy parties of young men who drank with loud insolence to *Der Tag* – the day when Germany would break out of her encirclement and rule the world. Monocled and well-connected officers from crack cavalry regiments appeared at every important western social function and hunted periodically for a season with one of the Leicestershire packs. It was all a far cry from the frugal, stiffly correct, and strictly Lutheran General Staff of old Moltke's day. The atmosphere of monastic dedication which still surrounded Schlieffen disappeared with his death. Professional efficiency survived to a remarkable degree. But the old iron self-discipline and the solidly based, imperturbable self-confidence of the age of Moltke had perished. Ludendorff, the last man of genius to sit in Moltke's seat, lapsed into hysterical self-pity when Haig's well-timed offensive brought Imperial Germany face to face with its final crisis in 1918.

This was the background on which the German generals performed, on an unprecedented scale, the classic operation of planning victory not in the next war, but in the last. They were to come, nevertheless, very near to success; and their opponents vastly helped by enthusiastically doing the same thing in reverse. A whole generation of French officers, like General Bonnal, made their reputations lecturing to the *École de Guerre* on how a sound application of Napoleonic principles could have defeated Moltke over and over again both in 1866 and 1870. Thus they played right into Schlieffen's hands; and the disastrous Plan XVII which Joffre inherited was designed to win the next campaign of Metz and Sedan by the methods which Bazaine and MacMahon had so neglected. Both their strategy and their tactics were based on dangerously loose and sweeping generalisations. Napoleon's dictum that the moral was to the physical as two is to one bulked large in all their calculations. By extending their period of military service from two to three years they were just able to match the increased strength of the German army created by Schlieffen's new Army Law. But this enlargement was bought at the expense of the future. Thanks to their static population they must very soon find themselves drawing for reserves and replacements on a well very much shallower than that of the Germans. Thus, even more decisively than the Germans, they committed themselves to a quick victory in northern France. But from the very start the theoretical French superiority of morale was going to have to outbalance the German material advantages; and out of that in turn grew an even more dangerous fallacy : a fixed belief that only in the attack did the French soldier show his true quality. The army of 1914 was to revive the glories of the *furia francese* of the fifteenth and sixteenth centuries and the irresistible enthusiasm and momentum of the Revolutionary column. As to the material aspect, they counted on their new and incomparable field gun – the 75 – to counter the known predominance of the German machine guns. The official doctrine became that of the *offensive-à-outrance* : the golden rule for all commanders at all levels was that in all circumstances they should keep their troops on the attack.

That the German military chiefs should have failed altogether to digest the lessons of the age throughout which they had lived and which had created all the fundamental problems which were to confront them in 1914 is understandable, though scarcely forgivable. They had not been well served by their observers of the American Civil War. After 1871 they had no direct experience of active operations, save for a brutally punitive expedition against helpless tribesmen in East Africa and their participation in the international force which moved up the Pai-Ho to take over the protection of the Legations at Pekin from the Japanese. The Austrians were similarly without battle experience since 1866; and after 1879 their army became progressively a mere appendix to that of the Germans, conforming in its tactical doctrine, and gradually even in its strategic decisions to the precepts of Potsdam. Not even the most light-hearted Austrian officer could believe it possible to beat the Russians in a straight fight, with a nominal and totally unpredictable Italian ally waiting beyond the Brenner to see which way the cat would jump. The mere survival of the Austrian Empire in peacetime was an annually repeated miracle. There was thus no stimulus for new thinking or tactical innovation, as Austrian generals and statesmen gradually reached the conclusion that war was the least of the apparent evils confronting the Dual Monarchy. The aged Francis Joseph voiced this fatalism in a characteristic phrase when he reluctantly initialled the ultimatum to Serbia at the Crown Council in 1914 which precipitated Europe into war. If the Empire was to perish, he observed, it might as well do so 'with honour'. That his armies would remain in the field for the next three years, fighting with dogged courage and endurance, was the last and least expected of the miracles which preserved the Empire throughout its long decline. The military organisation of Germany's nominal other ally, Italy, had always conformed to the Prussian territorial pattern, and there was little that her soldiers could learn from their own recent military history, even if they had been capable of logically applying their conclusions. The massacre at Adowa and the too-easy successes against the Turks in Tripolitania were no basis on which to plan a major campaign against either the Austrians or the French on the Alps. Clearly their army needed a competent and conscientious staff corps and better leadership at all levels. But these they were unable to contrive; and in the military, as in the naval sphere they remained in 1914 what they had long been – a liability rather than an asset to the power to which they finally decided to attach themselves.

On the other side, nothing serious could be expected in the way of creative thinking from the Russians. Their humiliating experiences in Manchuria overlaid all the promising features of the Balkan campaign of 1877. The brilliant adaptation of American Civil War tactics to the Bulgarian theatre by Gourko's Cossack units and their trained demolition squads was forgotten or neglected at the one moment on the northern Polish frontier when large Cossack formations might conceivably have achieved results as spectacular as those of Forrest's great raids in thickly forested, almost trackless country. General von Prittwitz had lost his nerve. The two generals who were to restore the German

situation – Hindenburg and his Chief-of-Staff, Ludendorff –
and thereby make their enormous reputations, together with the
divisions which they needed from the western front, had all to
come by a railway line which at its Prussian end became increasingly tenuous and vulnerable and was far too long to be effectively protected. Equally no attention was paid to the methods
by which Skobeloff had occasionally mastered the problems presented by the fire-power of infantry on the defensive properly
entrenched behind barbed wire.

On the Prussian front in 1914 a distracted and incompetent
Russian administration, haunted by the fear of imminent revolution, and so corrupt that even Grand Dukes were taking their
rake-off from armaments contracts with the USA, was to launch
two vast armies of peasant conscripts, scarcely trained, half-
armed, and inadequately supplied across the marshy Polish
wastes which were to have been bridged by the strategic railway
network due for completion in 1915. In the following three
years, until Lenin's revolution finally closed down the eastern
front, the only Russian commander who gave any sign of having
studied the history of their own war of 1877 was the Grand
Duke Nicholas in Armenia. In the last twilight of the Tsarist
regime he achieved the objective of that earlier Grand Duke,
Michael, and stormed Erzerum by a brilliantly executed *coup-
de-main* in a manner highly reminiscent in its planning and
techniques of the storm of Kars nearly forty years before. It
would not, of course, have been reasonable to expect the two
Army Commanders in Poland in 1914, Generals Samsomov and
Rennenkampf, to lead their reserve divisions into action at the
decisive moment mounted on white horses and wearing spectacular white cloaks as a rallying point for the troops, in the manner
in which Skobeleff had led his Army Corps in 1878. That sort of
leadership from the top was already out of date when Benedek
had gallantly tried to lead his Hungarian troops into a forlorn-
hope counter-attack on his disintegrated right flank.

So both the lessons of 1870 and those of Bulgaria were to be
ignored. The Russian armies in 1914 merely rolled westward
with Berlin as the general objective, to fend for themselves as
best they could. The only man in that campaign to win a prize
for intelligent application of the lessons of military history was

von Prittwitz's Chief-of-Staff, Hoffmann, who had ready for Hindenburg and Ludendorff on their arrival the blueprint for the impressive victory of Tannenberg which gave the vastly out-numbered Germans 90,000 unwounded prisoners and inflicted twice as many casualties in killed and wounded. Hoffmann based his plan on a personal memory of a scene on Mukden railway station in 1905 when, as an official observer with the Russians, he had seen General Samsomov slap the face of General Rennenkampf. It was a wild gamble. But in the event Rennenkampf remained impervious to frenzied appeals for help from his colleague, the last of them a personal letter sent by aeroplane. So Hindenburg and Ludendorff sailed to supreme command, with Hoffmann in their train; and Samsomov, riding back with his staff through the wooded wastes of the Prpet Marshes, fell aside and out of sight to blow out his brains.

Worst of all in their repudiation of the lessons of the past were the British and the French. Of the two, the British were far the more blameworthy. Their senior soldiers all had the advantage of having been immensely well-taught at the Staff college by instructors of the calibre of Chesney and Henderson, who had made their studies of the Civil War a basis, only, for remarkably accurate forecasts of future trends in the conduct of warfare. They had won over to their essentially moderate views – they were not, after all, Young Turks – the last two Commanders-in-Chief, Wolseley and Roberts, both highly distinguished and experienced field commanders; and they had even convinced the Duke of Cambridge of the importance of entrenchment in any future war and of the value of what he called 'a handy body of light horse', by which he meant Mounted Infantry. HRH was a traditionalist and would have retained two-thirds of the avail-able numbers as heavy cavalry, armed, mounted and equipped on the old pattern. Wolseley tentatively, and Roberts after his South African experiences, absolutely, rejected the whole con-ception of heavy cavalry as being a total anachronism in the conditions of modern war.

After all, apart from colonial wars on the fringes of empire, which had their own peculiar dangers and special rules, every major campaign in the era of Moltke between forces similarly armed and reasonably well-trained had the same lessons to teach; and these were few, simple, and so obvious as to be in-escapable. From Vicksburg and Richmond to Plevna and San-tiago, in South Africa and in Manchuria in 1905 they remained unchanged and were steadily reinforced. As infantry fire-power increased and guns and gunnery improved so that shrapnel became devastatingly effective against troops in the open, it was clear that infantry on the defensive, even in one of the *positions magnifiques* beloved of the statically-minded French generals of 1870, needed earthworks and ultimately barbed wire to avoid heavy and unnecessary casualties. Equally, when on the attack even well-trained and well-dispersed infantry had little or no hope of getting to grips with such an entrenched position. Still more obviously, a massed cavalry charge in such conditions could only result in mass suicide. Even the most die-hard British cavalry commanders in South Africa never dared to suggest charging Cronje's lines at Magersfontein or Paardeberg.

What is astonishing is that in the closing years of the age of Moltke – the years immediately preceding the outbreak of the 1914 war – an issue so clearly settled and dead as the role of heavy cavalry in modern war should have become the subject of embittered controversy among the senior generals and the histo-rians at the staff colleges and in the military periodicals of western Europe. For any intelligent student it was not in any way a new issue. For two centuries at the close of the Middle Ages, from Crécy to Solway Moss, the accuracy, range, and rate of fire of the English archer had dominated every battlefield on which he appeared and totally eclipsed the dominance of the heavily armed feudal cavalry. In tactical essentials there was no difference between the disaster which overtook the flower of the French aristocracy when the Constable of France led them in close order against Henry v's outnumbered bowmen at Agin-court, and that suffered by Lord Cardigan's Light Brigade at Balaclava. It was the general independability, short range, and inaccuracy of the musket as compared with the long bow which alone allowed heavy cavalry to reappear as an occasionally deci-sive factor in the pitched battles of the seventeenth and eigh-teenth centuries and in the Napoleonic age. The period ended at Balaclava, when the marginal superiority of the Minié rifle over

Brown Bess enabled the 93rd Highlanders to halt the massed Russian cavalry with their Thin Red Line. After the total failure of both Russian and Japanese cavalry in Manchuria the whole question should have been as dead as mutton. Only the Japanese sensibly decided that they could find neither the sort of horse nor the type of man needed to ride it to produce an old-fashioned body of shock troops. The Russians continued to embody large formations of both regular cavalry and Cossack divisions without giving much thought to their training or the use which might be made of them. Austrian officers, basking contentedly in the reputation won for them so spectacularly by the two divisions which had saved Benedek's army from total destruction at Königgrätz, were not again asked to give any serious consideration to the role they might play in future warfare. Beautifully uniformed, socially entertaining and of impeccable ancestry, they waltzed to tunes by Strauss and Lehar in a sort of perpetual eve of Waterloo ball. Italian cavalry, elegantly corseted and booted even into the age of Mussolini, had no contribution to make to the military problems of the twentieth century. Social prestige similarly enabled the German cavalry regiments to survive, though no practical use was ever to be found for them.

There was far less excuse for the British, with their Boer War experiences still fresh in mind to reinforce the two important lessons brought back by the more intelligent observers of the American war forty years before. Sir John French, Commander-in-Chief designate of the Expeditionary Force designed to help the French, had made his reputation by clever handling of cavalry at Elandslaagte and elsewhere. He cannot have forgotten that at the end of his celebrated march on Kimberley his crack cavalry regiments were virtually immobilised by the exhaustion of their horses, and that only his colonial Light Horse had cohesion and energy enough left to penetrate the Boer lines and make contact with the besieged garrison. His far more intelligent Chief-of-Staff and ultimate successor, Douglas Haig, had shared in this experience and had even written a memorandum in November 1899 on the 'greatly increased power of cavalry, now that it is armed with a good carbine'.[7] He is, moreover on record as holding the opinion that General Forrest was 'one of the greatest

L

English-speaking commanders of mounted troops'. Yet in 1908 he wrote that : 'it is not the weapon carried but the moral factor of an apparently irresistible force, coming on at highest speed in spite of rifle fire, which affects the nerve and aim of the rapidly dismounted rifleman.' In such circumstances, he thought, the advent of the magazine rifle would merely mean the waste of ammunition in wild and inaccurate shooting. Such conditions had not in his opinion 'really so very much changed the conditions of thirty years ago'.[8] French joined him in the view 'that only the old knee to knee cavalry charge with lance or sword' would decide the wars of the future.[9] The prevalence of this view resulted in two old-fashioned cavalry divisions being included in the BEF – nearly a quarter of the fighting strength earmarked for France – for which no use would ever be found by either general until the men were at last reluctantly separated from their horses and sent to supplement the depleted infantry in the front line. It was in any case unlikely that the German rifleman's self-confidence would be much endangered when he was ensconced in a trench behind barbed wire, and the fire of his magazine rifle was supplemented by the cross-fire of machine-guns which could be mounted on fixed lines, and had no nerves.

The controversy between cavalry and mounted infantry advocates was not in the long run of any great practical importance, since the conditions of the coming war quickly made it clear that in the shell-pitted mud of the battle zone there was no place for a horseman, however trained and equipped, since he could not even move across it as fast as the infantry. But it illustrated the complete failure of the British generals to grapple imaginatively with the problems of a future large-scale war. It also indicated how little thought they had devoted to the factor of trench warfare, when armies would be immobilised in front of each other, deprived of all power of manoeuvre on the flanks, and doomed to prohibitive casualties if thrown into a frontal assault : a situation which was to repeat itself with disastrous frequency after September 1914. But, once the beneficent influence of Lord Roberts was withdrawn, the useless slaughter of Colenso, Magersfontein, and Paardeberg was forgotten and the old die-hards reasserted their views. In the teeth of all the evidence all the old, obscurantist doctrines prevailed : trenches were the refuge of amateur volunteer or conscript armies, or those which lacked the training and morale for skilled manoeuvre in the open; and any encouragement of the techniques of entrenchment was held liable to demoralise regular soldiers and deprive them of the essential offensive spirit. The champions of this logic could point triumphantly to the fact that neither the Turks in Bulgaria, nor the Spaniards in Cuba, nor the Boers had ever staged a convincing counter-attack from their entrenchments. But the logic was faulty, since it left altogether out of account the native shortcomings of the defending troops and, more importantly, the shocking casualties sustained by the Russians at Plevna, by the Americans before Santiago, and by the Highland Brigade at Magersfontein and in Kitchener's entirely unnecessary battle at Paardeberg.

The French military thinkers reached almost exactly the same conclusions, though by a very different chain of reasoning. To guide them they had no direct experience of major war since 1871, and only the reports on events elsewhere in the world by their expert professional observers who were equally geared to the business of defeating Moltke in a war of movement. More than any other of the European armies, the French of the Third Republic lived in a romanticised Napoleonic past. In an age when most others had evolved for war inconspicuous uniforms of field grey or dull browns, and the British appeared in a hideously drab khaki, the Zouaves were to plunge into action in 1914 in all the glory of baggy scarlet breeches and dark blue coats; and the Cadets of St Cyr, the cream of their officer potential for the immediate future, went into battle as an infantry battalion with their swords and their white gloves and their white-cockaded képis. It was in this spirit that the senior instructors at the *École de Guerre* formulated a theory of cavalry tactics which almost precisely conformed to Haig's considered judgement of 1908. Colonel Cordonnier, a sometime *Professeur*, summed it up in his history of the land fighting in the Russo-Japanese war, published in 1911 :

> Certain military writers [he wrote] proclaim the bankruptcy of cavalry, and, arguing from the smallness of its services in Manchuria, demand the reduction, if not the practical aboli-

tion of this costly arm. .... If cavalry is only to be used for fighting on foot, and we have to convert it into mounted rifles, it can with advantage be replaced by infantry on ponies. But let these infantrymen on ponies once collide with cavalry that gallops and uses the sword, and they will soon be destroyed.[10]

This, of course, begged the whole question of cavalry operations against modern infantry; and in the same spirit French writers deplored the instruction of the infantry in the techniques of entrenchment, not on any practical grounds, but because it would discourage the traditional *élan* and the offensive instinct of the French infantryman. So both the western Allies were taken as completely by surprise as the Germans by the deadlock of October 1914, when the trench lines stretched from the Alps to the coast of Flanders. There were no flanks to be turned; and there seemed to be no opportunity of applying the three age-old principles of war of surprise, secrecy, and deception, as redefined by Sherman. Four years later both sides were still equally baffled and bewildered by the situation.

Even on the Russian front the troops became bogged down in the same conditions of what was essentially siege warfare; and in due course, when the Italians at last made up their minds to come in on the Allied side, they and the Austrians conformed to the same dreary pattern in the foothills of the southern Alps. Strictly these developments are the province of the historian of a later age. But they were the direct consequence in the military sphere of events from Balaclava to the retreat from Mons – the legacy, in fact, of the Age of Moltke. Ironically, the actual campaigns of Moltke himself in 1866 and 1871 strongly suggest that he was fully aware of the difficulties and dangers attending attacks on entrenched positions. He routed out Benedek from his *position magnifique* at Königgrätz by operating against his vulnerable flanks, and did his best to prevent the impetuous Frederick Charles from turning what was meant to be a holding attack into an all-out frontal assault. There was no attempt to storm Metz or Paris. Bombardment and starvation were his weapons, and he preferred to leave it to the *Gardes Mobiles* to splinter themselves in heroic but futile assaults on his own trench lines. Neither his successors nor their opponents had given any thought to what would happen if the quick victory for which both sides hoped in the opening months eluded them. When the stalemate came none of them had any coherent answer to the problems which it presented.

Yet this situation was not only foreseeable, but had long been foreseen. As early as 1895 Captain L. Auger of the French Engineers published a profound history of the Civil War.[11] He found little that might be useful for French officers in the strategy of the American generals since they operated in such different country and without the swollen numbers which were likely to overcrowd the European battlefields of the future. His important conclusions were all tactical, and they challenged root and branch the basic principles on which French military thinking was based. While conceding that the West Point preoccupation with the problems of engineering and gunnery, and the natural tendency for inexperienced troops to fight more happily and efficiently from cover, Auger insisted that the main reason for the domination of American battlefields by entrenchments was the mere fact that the growing fire-power of modern weapons had made all movement in the open increasingly costly and unrewarding. Since 1865, he pointed out, this situation had been immensely intensified by new inventions and the massive output of modern armaments factories; and he drew a grim and all too accurate picture of the European fronts of the future : congested armies in shell-torn countrysides, crowded into trench lines which would become continuous. The French commanders, moreover, would find themselves, like Lee, outnumbered and dependent on diminishing sources of reserves. Lee in these circumstances had for a long time held his own by letting the enemy batter themselves to pieces against a strong defensive position before he went cautiously over to the attack, manoeuvring for preference round their flanks. Auger's conclusion was that the defensive was 'the true method of combat of the future'. It was even the only one possible in face of the 'probable hecatomb' of the next European war; and when the opportunity came for attack, it would not be an affair of 'numbers and *élan*', but slow and cautious, with every gain immediately and powerfully consolidated. There would still be plenty of opportunity for *élan*, as there had been for Lee's and Grant's troops in 1865. But it would be wise to allot much more time to training French infantry in field engineering.

Auger was just an exceptionally able military historian who correctly applied the lessons of his studies to his own army in the immediate future. Nobody was to notice that his judgements were proved to be prophetic until long after 1918; and all circumstance combined to prevent him from becoming the prophet of a vociferous and rebellious school of thought, as Havelock had in England twenty years before. His book appeared at the very moment when the school of thought which purported to derive from Napoleon the doctrines of the *élan* and of the *offensive-à-outrance* achieved a complete and paralysing dominance in the French army. In the years immediately after 1870 the official thinking of the *École de Guerre* had tended towards a balanced answer to the fatal defensive-mindedness of Bazaine and his contemporaries : a combination of a preliminary defensive to be followed by a swift offensive when the edge of the enemy attack had been blunted. But in the 1890s the Napoleonic school swept all before them. On the theoretical side men like General Bonnal, as Commandant of the *École de Guerre,* and, still more importantly, Foch who followed him there some years later, imposed on the senior officers who were to lead the French army in 1914 their own somewhat rhetorical version of Clausewitz's methodical and essentially Prussian attempt to confine the erratic genius of Napoleon within sweeping and absolute generalised rules which the great man himself would scarcely have recognised. At the same time, on the practical side and lower down the scale, there was a romanticisation of Napoleonic tactical methods which flowered in the new Infantry Regulations in the very year in which Auger published his book. Here was a precise formulation of the rules governing the movements of an infantry regiment when putting into practice the doctrines of the *offensive-à-outrance*; 400 metres from the enemy the leading battalion would pause, fix bayonets and open 'individual fire of the greatest intensity' while the reserve battalion moved up to thicken the line. The whole was then to advance 'by fire and movement' in short rushes to within 150 metres, where 'magazine fire' would be opened and every available man closed up for the assault. Finally : 'at a signal from the Colonel the drums beat, the bugles sound the advance and the entire line charges forward with cries of *"en avant, à la baionette".'* Precisely this was what the French infantry would try to do against German machine-guns in 1914.

In Germany and in Great Britain solitary voices also cried, like Auger's, in the wilderness that not Napoleonic tactics but the machine-gun and the trench would be the dominant factors in the next war. As a *Kriegsakademie* lecturer and an accepted authority, Baron von Freytag-Loringhoven carried much bigger guns than Captain Auger. Between 1901 and 1911 he published a number of articles and books on various aspects of contemporary warfare, drawing predominately on examples from the American War. He was an intelligent commentator and on most controversial topics his opinions strikingly coincided with those preached by Henderson at Camberley and at the Royal United Services Institution. He was, however, essentially of the 'establishment' and most of his views conformed to the official teaching of the General Staff. Only on the subject of entrenchments did he venture into occasional eccentricity. The lesson that there was no real difference between 'field' and 'fortress' fortification was, he claimed, one which had been entirely overlooked in Germany. In attack or defence the rules governing both were the same; and all field commanders should be taught what they were. When all had been said to derogate from the training and discipline of the Americans, their troops were fairly matched; and entrenched infantry on the defensive, however exhausted and outnumbered, would always prevail 'despite the tenacious energy of the High Command and the commendable sacrificial courage' of the attackers. He further held that, though solid fortifications resisted better, field fortifications were preferable. They were cheaper, easier to construct and in unpredictable situations would be where they were wanted.[12] Even this mild heresy was decisively rejected by the General Staff on the grounds that the improvement of heavy howitzers and mortars since 1865 had greatly reduced the value of earthworks – a view which was not confirmed by recent British experiences in South Africa.[13] The American Civil War never found a place in the syllabus of the *Kriegsakademie*.

The lone voice which cried in the British wilderness was that of Lieutenant-Colonel J. E. Edmonds, a Sapper, and as such professionally interested in the technique of field fortification and its effectiveness. He was also a first-class military historian who later, as Brigadier-General Sir James Edmonds, was to edit the official history of the 1914–18 war. In 1905, in collaboration with a volunteer officer, he published a two-volume history of the Civil War[14] which, subsequently abbreviated and constantly republished, remains to this day the best English history of the war. He strongly supported Henderson's tentative suggestion that the Wilderness campaign in Northern Virginia in 1864–5 forecast the shape of wars to come; and he reinforced his arguments in articles in the *Journals* of the Royal Artillery and Royal Engineers demonstrating that the Russo-Japanese War had closely followed the same pattern: 'the battles of many days' duration; the continued use of night operations; the universal use of the spade both in the attack and the defence, making the war one of what may be called siege operations in the field; and the employment of all available troops in the front line without retaining a general reserve.' It was not a bad forecast of the tactical situation of the future. But it fell on totally deaf ears.[15]

In the naval sphere the rapid technical advances of the Moltke era left the admirals in a situation as frustrating as that of the generals. Progress, instead of opening new vistas of decisive and destructive action, more and more hampered freedom of movement and prevented the application of the old tactical principles. The fleet commanders, like the army commanders, found themselves in a world where there was a steadily shrinking opportunity for displays of initiative and the achievement of spectacular victories. As on land, the important new discoveries – the mine and the torpedo – were calculated progressively to restrict the sea-room available for manoeuvre, even in the comparatively wide waters of the North Sea. For naval tacticians in 1914 the practical lessons were to be learnt not from Tsushima, which was already an anachronism when it was fought, though it inevitably caught the public imagination both in Britain and Germany and raised hopes and ambitions which it was quite impossible to satisfy. Only in the remoteness of the South Pacific and the South Atlantic were the cruiser admirals able to fight a good, old-fashioned sort of battle, undisturbed by fears of minefields and ambushes by massed submarines. The real lessons were thus to be learnt from the earlier operations of the Russian and Japanese fleets off Port Arthur, when all the major losses had resulted from torpedo attacks or from the accidental straying of capital ships on to mines.

Between 1905 and 1914 the factor which dominated the plans and fears of politicians as well as admirals was the threat embodied in the accelerated German naval building programme and the massive British response to it. What was also clear to the naval experts, though perhaps not always to the politicians, was that the nature of the fleet which the Germans were building made it certain that, in the event of a general European war, the decisive naval theatre would be confined to the North Sea and the Channel. For propaganda purposes the Germans loudly proclaimed that the colonial empire which they had acquired demanded a fleet to protect its trade routes. But the ships which they built for their High Seas Fleet were quite incapable of doing anything of the sort. It was universally accepted doctrine that cruisers, whether they were policing their own trade routes or hounding the enemy merchant commerce off the seas, depended wherever they were on the solid base of a battle fleet – the 'fleet in being'[16] – as indispensable in the twentieth century as it had been two hundred years before.

The new German ships, and particularly their capital ships, were designed purely as highly efficient fighting machines, with a multiplicity of water-tight compartments which made them very hard to sink; and everything was sacrificed to the provision of heavy armour, at the expense of fuel capacity and of even the most meagre comforts for officers and crews. Since Germany, furthermore, altogether lacked the widely dispersed, protected coaling stations which alone made operations possible on the far side of the world, their big ships had not the cruising range necessary for remote ocean stations; and the cramped discomfort of the living accommodation for the ship's company was endurable only for a week or so in northern waters provided that the crew could rest and recuperate in comfortable barracks on getting back to port. In such ships the most devotedly patriotic seaman would quickly have become demoralised, and even mutinous, on a tropical station where the bulk of his time would be spent afloat under a relentless sun.

Moreover the North German coast needed no seaborne defence : there was no possibility of a new Copenhagen. Thus the High Seas Fleet could only be an aggressive weapon designed against Britain alone, to whittle down her supremacy in home waters, expose her coasts to invasion, and disrupt the cruiser blockade which was in the long run her best weapon for winning the war by sealing off the commerce of the German ports. The British would have been criminally negligent if they had not reacted violently to these implied threats. They set themselves doggedly to outbuild the Germans year by year; and, when the *Entente Cordiale* became a going concern in 1906, they arranged for the French to take over responsibility for dealing with the Austrians and, if necessary, the Italians in the Mediterranean, while they took over the task of protecting the coasts of both powers in northern waters. This in itself was one more cumulative factor in making British intervention in a general war almost inevitable. With their far flung commitments in mind the British could not build a battle fleet which, ship for ship, was a match for the Germans. At Jutland Hipper's outnumbered battle-cruisers were to prove more than a match for Beatty's ships; and no one will ever know 'if Jellicoe's dreadnoughts could have achieved the Tsushima he sought had luck allowed him to be placed the next morning between the High Seas Fleet and its bases with a whole day of good light in front of him. But it must be remembered that no German battle cruiser could have carried enough fuel to make the dash which Sturdee made with *Invincible* and *Inflexible* to destroy von Spee's victorious squadron at the Falkland Islands. In the last analysis the sober calculations of the British naval authorities in the uncertain years before 1914 were wholly justified. The High Seas Fleet was to be penned to its harbours; the much more serious threat of the U-Boats was frustrated; and the remorselessly enforced blockade was the ultimate factor in breaking the German will to resistance. This was the conclusive demonstration of the lesson, continuously enforced outside the dramatic battlefields of Europe in the age of Moltke, that an entrenched enemy who cannot be dislodged by frontal assault and whose flanks are invulnerable can only be defeated by investment and starvation.

There was one other, and entirely novel factor which the war ministries of 1914 would have to face as part of their inheritance from the preceding era: the emergence of air power and its potential value in war on land and sea. At the outbreak of war the activities of aeronauts were still embryonic and their potential military contribution was problematical. Balloons had, of course, been in practical use for some time. Gambetta's journeys in and out of Paris had roused great enthusiasm, but had no tactical significance. The Japanese had used them in a more direct military context and to some slight purpose for artillery spotting at the siege of Port Arthur. Before that the US forward troops in Cuba had moved continuously under a balloon in the hope that it might give them some knowledge of enemy positions in the dense jungle in front of them. This it failed to do; and it proved in fact a serious liability, since it gave the Spanish gunners a precise knowledge of their progress and an aiming mark for a destructive fire on their leading infantry.[17] Balloons were abandoned; but dirigibles still had some practical value. Count Zeppelin was to immortalise his name with the airships which occasionally brought the drama of war to the citizens of London and did some useful reconnaissance work with the German fleet. Their impact was, by modern standards, very modest; and they were too vulnerable for use in war. The US Navy was making tentative experiments with heavier-than-air flying machines, but had not yet constructed a ship with a long enough flight deck to enable them to return once they had taken off. The British had a Fleet Seaplane Carrier – the *Hermes*; and all the armies had aeroplanes on the western front in August 1914, for reconnaissance purposes, some of whose reports were valuable. Already the observers in their two-man crews were fighting duels with their revolvers in the air – the forerunners of the heroic single combats of more sophisticated aircraft later in the war. The British were slightly in the lead with this new weapon, and the French very slow to realise its possibilities. General Foch remarked at the end of a display in 1910 that it was good sport, 'but for the army it is of no value'.[18]

The Age of Moltke had a disastrous general effect on the

future, in that it created vast and cumbrous military machines
which the generals themselves could not control once they had
been set in motion, so that in any crisis politicians striving for
peace found themselves paralysed by panic-stricken soldiers fearful that any hesitation would enable the enemy to steal a march
on them; and western civilisation in the last decade of peace
survived perpetually on the edge of a catastrophe. Its influence
on the art and practice of warfare was equally disastrous.
Clausewitz passed on to Moltke and his contemporaries an
inspiring inheritance derived from his study of the campaigns of
Napoleon; and Moltke himself made such brilliant use of it that
he enabled Bismarck and Cavour between them to reconstruct
the map of Europe. In the opening years, thanks to the smooth
efficiency of the Prussian military machine, which was mostly his
own creation, Moltke was able to keep control of events and
achieve glittering military and political results in a series of swift,
economical campaigns which caused the minimum of disruption
of civilised life among the communities involved. At the same
time, although there were ugly incidents in France in 1870–1,
war itself seemed to contemporaries to be becoming a more
gentlemanly or, as far as possible, a less uncivilised affair than
before. The Geneva Convention did much to mitigate the sufferings of its victims; and with few exceptions those involved
accepted and applied what had come to be regarded as its rules.
Whether or not the humanisation of war – it itself a barbarous
practice – represented an advance is, of course, endlessly debat-
able. It certainly appeared so to most civilised Europeans in the
decade before 1914, who were to be deeply shocked by Belgian
'atrocities' which were not wholly an invention of Allied propaganda. The ruthless destruction of Louvain, 'unrestricted' submarine warfare, poison gas, and air raids on undefended cities
which could not possibly be classified as fortresses were inescapable realities which indicated the beginnings of a reversion to the
vicious inhumanities of the sixteenth- and seventeenth-century
Wars of Religion.

Pacifist idealists would reject such reasoning altogether. But
humanity has not yet found an answer other than the use of
force in situations where embittered feelings have frustrated all
attempts at rational, peaceful solution. So long as this is so,

wars – civil, international, religious, racial, or ideological – will continue to be the final arbiters; and military historians will need no justification for studying the methods by which they may be settled quickly, decisively, and with a minimum of human suffering. Judged by these standards the Age of Moltke must be considered retrogressive. However promising and exciting its beginnings, it was always an implementation of the Prussian doctrine that might was right. In military terms its final consequence was to bring the armies from the horrors of a Russian winter in the trenches in front of Sebastopol to the squalid, meaningless endurance test in mud of 1914–18 which all but destroyed a whole generation of the young men on whom the future of civilisation depended. This has to be the ultimate judgement of history on the Age of Moltke.

Appendix: SIEGES

| Fortress | Duration | Numbers engaged at surrender | | | | Casualties, including sickness and prisoners | |
| | | Attackers | | Defenders | | | |
		Troops	Guns	Troops	Guns	Attackers	Defenders
Vicksburg	165 days	71,000	248	32,000	172	9,000	17,000
Richmond	340 days	121,000	408	60,000	273	87,000	60,000
Metz	72 days	197,000	658	173,000	694	47,000	38,000
Paris	133 days	200,000	788	400,000	744	15,000	25,000
Plevna	142 days	110,000	500	40,000	77	40,000	30,000
Kars	14 days	35,000	144	25,000	303	2,300	24,000
Port Arthur	216 days	100,000	420	41,000	400*	91,500	64,300

*Total uncertain. No figures for the small armament loaded from the battleships.

Notes

Chapter 1: The Legacy of Napoleon

1 Raoul Girardet, *La Société militaire dans la France contemporaine 1815–1939* (Paris 1953).

2 The Spanish Civil War of the 1930s, when Germany and Russia experimented both with armoured forces and in the air, might be considered an exception.

3 For this campaign see especially David Chandler, *The Campaigns of Napoleon* (London 1967: Weidenfeld and Nicolson) pp. 667 *et seq.*

4 The best description of the disintegration of the head of a column under effective fire-power is the frequently quoted account in Marshal T. R. Bugeaud, *Aperçus sur quelques détails de la guerre* (Paris 1846).

5 The most recent authoritative account of Napoleon's army is in G. Lefebvre, *Napoleon* 5th ed. (Presses Universitaires de France 1965; English translation London 1969: Routledge and Kegan Paul) pp. 214–31.

6 See Lefebvre, *Napoleon,* p. 230.

7 Antoine Henri (Baron) de Jomini, *Essais sur la Tactique* (Paris 1836).

8 Wolfe did the same thing at Quebec in 1759 to eke out numbers, and his example was frequently followed in America.

9 The division, as a formation, was not a standard part of Austrian army organisation (see page 49).

10 W. H. Russell, Malta, 17 March 1854, *The Times Despatches* (London 1855: Routledge), p. 8.

11 Russell, *The Times Despatches,* p. 227.

Chapter 2: War as an Instrument of Policy: The Armies of the Continental Powers

1 This was the ration strength which could give an approximate total of 240,000 combatant troops. For this and for the Russian forces see Friedjung, *The Struggle for Supremacy in Germany*, translated by A. J. P. Taylor and W. L. McElwee (New York 1966), p. 236.

2 It was fixed at seven years in 1832 and so remained until Marshal Niel's reforms of 1868.

3 For 1859 see G. A. Bonnal, *Le Haut Commandement français au début de chacune des guerres de 1859 et de 1870* (Paris 1905) *passim*. For 1870 see especially Michael Howard, *The Franco-Prussian War* (London 1961: Rupert Hart-Davis), pp. 16–17.

4 Bonnal, *Le Haut Commandement français au début de chacune des guerres de 1859 et de 1870*, part II, 'Le désastre de Metz', p. 128 *et seq*.

5 Bonnal, *Le Haut Commandement français au début de chacune des guerres de 1859 et de 1870*, p. 12.

6 Ibid.

7 Ibid., p. 30.

8 Ibid., p. 32.

9 Ibid.

10 H. C. Wylly, *The Campaign of Magenta and Solferino, 1859* (London 1907).

11 Depôt de la Guerre, *Campagne de Napoleon Trois en Italie*, (Paris 1860). Canrobert, equally prudently, preserved his own papers. See Constant Germain Bapst, *Le Maréchal Canrobert*, six vols (Paris 1898–1913), and Bonnal, *Le Haut Commandement Français au début de chacune des guerres de 1859 et de 1870*. pp. 7–8.

12 Howard, *The Franco-Prussian War*, p. 39.

13 See above, p. 3 n. 1

14 Most English accounts of the war of 1859, including those published under the aegis of the War Office, were based mainly on French narratives which grossly exaggerated the Austrian numbers engaged, e.g. Wylly, *The Campaign of Magenta and Solferino, 1859*. The true figures were only published in 1916 when Friedjung had had access to the archives of the Kriegs-

ministerium. Italian historians confirm Friedjung's figures. See
B. Pieri, *Storia Militare del Risorgimento* (Turin 1962), and
Friedjung, *The Struggle for Supremacy in Germany*.
15 Since no Crown Council minutes were kept, Buol later stated
that it had not been consulted. This has since been disproved.
See Heinrich von Srbik, *Metternich* (Vienna 1925), vol. 2, p.
506, and Friedjung, *The Struggle for Supremacy in Germany*,
p. 13n.
16 Made verbally and in secret when the two met, strictly
incognito, at Plombières in July 1858 to arrange their joint
reconstruction of Italy. The terms were embodied in a military
treaty in January 1859.
17 Memorandum to the King, February 1860.
18 Historical section of the Great General Staff, *The Franco-
Prussian War*, German ed. (Berlin 1872) vol. 1, p. 357.
19 Great General Staff, *Kriegsgeschictliche Einzelschriften
Heft 18, Das Generalkommando des III Armee Korps bei
Spicheren und Vionville* (Berlin 1895).

Chapter 3: War as a Means of Imperial Expansion
1 See Wilhelm Treue, *Invasionen 1066–1944, Eine Studie zur
Geschichte des amphibischen Krieges* (Darmstadt 1955). The
naval strengths and policies of the powers are discussed in
chapter 8.
2 Lieutenant-General W. H. Goodenough and Lieutenant-
Colonel J. C. Dalton, *The Army Book for the British Empire*
(London 1893: HMSO).
3 W. H. Russell, *The Times Despatches*, p. 227.
4 Brian Bond, ed., *Victorian Military Campaigns* (London
1967: Hutchinson), Appendix 1.
5 Quoted in Goodenough and Dalton, *The Army Book for the
British Empire*, p. 31.
6 Bond, *Victorian Military Campaigns*, p. 80 (John Selby, 'The
Third China War').
7 Ibid., pp. 121–3. (D. C. Chandler, 'The Expedition to
Abyssinia 1867–68').
8 Ibid. p. 257 (Dr M. J. Williams, 'The Egyptian Campaign of
1882').

9 Goodenough and Dalton, *The Army Book for the British Empire*, p. 37.
10 John Pemble, *The Invasion of Nepal* (London 1971: OUP), p. 347.
11 Goodenough and Dalton, *The Army Book for the British Empire*, p. 55.
12 Cardwell delivered a particularly trenchant speech to the House of Commons on this subject on 3 March 1870; see Hansard.
13 Table of 'terms of engagement', War Office, 1 January 1892.
14 See above, p. 83.
15 Particularly well depicted in Rudyard Kipling's novel *Kim*.
16 The Intelligence Branch of the Quartermaster-General's department published a complete translation (London 1875: Horse Guards). It is, however, very adequately summarised in F. V. Greene, *The Russian Army and its Campaign in Turkey in 1877–8*, 2nd ed. (London 1880: W. H. Allen), pp. 4–18.
17 The Cossacks of the Don Basin were fairly quickly absorbed into the mainstream of Russian life, and their cavalry regiments were not treated as irregulars but absorbed into the light cavalry of the regular army. See Greene, *The Russian Army and its Campaign in Turkey in 1877–8*, pp. 46–8.
18 This is brilliantly summarised in A. J. P. Taylor's *Germany's First Bid for Colonies 1884–1885* (London 1938: Macmillan).
19 Goodenough and Dalton, writing in 1893, describe it as 'peculiar' and 'by no means a model for general imitation': *The Army Book for the British Empire*, p. 84.

Chapter 4: The Impact of Technological Advances on Strategy and Tactics
1 Herbert Rosinski, *The German Army* (London 1939: Hogarth Press), p. 136 *et seq.*
2 William Dinwiddie. Report in the *Washington Star*, quoted by Frank Freidel in *The Splendid Little War* (Bramhall House 1958: Clarkson N. Potter).
3 Ibid., p.61.
4 Ibid., p. 70.
5 For this subject nobody save the post-graduate student assidu-

ously seeking a topic for a monograph need look further than the opening pages of Howard, *The Franco-Prussian War*.

6 For example, Benedek's all-important despatch to Crown Prince Albert of Saxony at Jitschin on 29 June: and Moltke's order to the Crown Prince the night before Königgrätz which virtually decided the campaign. See below, ch. 9, p. 299.

7 It is however to be noted that shortage of infantry ammunition was a contributory reason for General Frossard's withdrawal from his commanding position at Spicheren.

8 Lord Wavell, *Generals and Generalship* (Cambridge 1938: CUP).

9 Howard, *The Franco-Prussian War*, p. 35.

10 The official figures for both sides are neither of them wholly reliable. I have throughout accepted as final the calculations of Howard, *The Franco-Prussian War*.

11 'Dicht auf den Leib' in the original German, quoted in Howard, *The Franco-Prussian War*, p. 7, from the *Memoirs* of Alfred Graf von Waldersee in a passage omitted from the abbreviated English translation of that tedius work.

12 See above, chapter 2, p. 66.

Chapter 5: War Conducted by Amateurs: The American Civil War

1 Dodge, quoted in W. Birkbeck Wood and Brigadier-General Sir James E. Edmonds, *The Civil War in the United States* (London 1937: Methuen).

2 John F. C. Fuller, *Generalship; its Diseases and their Cure: A Study of the Personal Factor in Command* (London 1933: Faber and Faber), p. 39.

3 Fuller, quoted in J. Luvaas, *The Military Legacy of the Civil War* (Chicago 1959: University of Chicago Press) p. 215.

4 Wood & Edmonds, *The Civil War in the United States*, p. 57.

5 Captain B. H. Liddell Hart, quoted in Luvaas, *The Military Legacy of The Civil War*, p. 243.

6 Howard, *The Franco-Prussian War*.

7 B. H. Liddell Hart, *The Remaking of Modern Armies* (London 1927).

8 B. H. Liddell Hart, *Reputations* (London 1928). The underlying ideas were to be developed by the author in a whole series of publications, all of them extensively quoted in Luvaas, *The Military Legacy of the Civil War*, ch. 9.

9 Luvaas, for linguistic reasons, gives no account of the reports of Russian observers, but the facts of Gourko's campaign in Bulgaria in 1877 speak for themselves.

10 Both of these extensively quoted in Luvaas, *The Military Legacy of the Civil War*, pp. 80–7.

11 See below, ch. 6 *passim*.

12 Wolseley's views and influences are also given comprehensively in Luvaas, *The Military Legacy of the Civil War*.

13 Charles Chesney, *Campaigns in Virginia* (London 1864), revised and enlarged edition (London 1865).

14 Quoted by Luvaas, *The Military Legacy of the Civil War*, p. 107.

15 Oscar Parkes, *British Battleships, 'Warrior' 1860 to 'Vanguard' 1950* (London 1957: Seeley).

16 Wood and Edmonds, *The Civil War in the United States*, p. 278n.

17 Russell B. Nye and J. Eric Morpurgo, *History of the United States* (London 1955: Penguin) vol. 2, p. 500.

18 The *Rolf Krake* which singlehanded held off the antiquated Prussian fleet in 1864; see Douglas G. Browne, *The Floating Bulwark* (London 1963 : Cassell).

19 Quoted in Wood & Edmonds, *The Civil War in the United States*, p. 266.

20 There were monitors in commission in the British Navy as late as 1939.

Chapter 6:   The Aftermath of Moltke's Great Age

1 The German word for this is *Zersplitterung*. I have racked my brains in vain to find an equally expressive English equivalent.

2 A. J. P. Taylor, *The Struggle for Mastery in Europe* (London 1954: OUP) p. 549 *et seq.*

3 The best account of this remains the report of the American Military Attaché at Russian headquarters, F. V. Greene, which he published more or less complete as *The Russian Army and its Campaigns in Turkey in 1877–1878* (New York 1879: D. Appleton).

4 For the naval actions on the Danube, see chapter 8, pp. 266–70.

5 Greene, *The Russian Army and its Campaign in Turkey 1877–8*. The Turks published no official casualty lists.

6 Greene, *The Russian Army and its Campaign in Turkey 1877–8*, p. 433.

7 Lieutenant-General A. Brialmont, *La Fortification du Champ de Bataille* (Brussels 1879), ch. 3.

8 Freidel, *The Splendid Little War*, p. 249.

9 Ibid., p. 275.

Chapter 7: Epilogue: South Africa and Manchuria

1 By 1907 this firm had in stock over half a million books on military history.

2 See, *inter alia*, Conan Doyle, *The Great Boer War*, 16th ed. (London 1903: Nelson), p. 550. He puts the true figure as 75,000, which is almost certainly an exaggeration.

3 Major-General Sir C. Callwell and Major-General Sir J. Headlam, *The History of the Royal Artillery from the Indian Mutiny to the Great War* (Woolwich 1931), vol. I, table in appendix C.

4 Ibid., p. 161n.

5 Prince Kraft von Hohenlohe-Ingelfingen, *Thoughts on Artillery*, English translation, 2nd ed. (London 1890).

6 H. C. Fletcher of the Scots Guards and J. A. R. Fremantle of the Coldstream Guards; Luvaas, *The Military Legacy of the Civil War*, pp. 17 and 21.

7 Erskine Childers, writing satirically in *War and the Arme Blanche* (London 1910) p. 3.

8 See, for example, Kipling's fictitious but undoubtedly accurate picture in *Soldiers Three*, Service ed. (London 1914: Macmillan), p. 140 *et seq.*

9 Quoted in Luvaas, *The Military Legacy of the Civil War*, p. 111.

10 Ibid., pp. 110–11.

11 Ibid., p. 196.

12 Henry Havelock, *Three Main Military Questions of the Day* (London 1897).

13 Reginald Hargreaves, *Red Sun Rising: The Siege of Port Arthur* (London 1963: Weidenfeld and Nicolson), p. 28.
14 Ibid.
15 Ibid., p. 24.
16 The details of the naval fighting are dealt with in the next chapter.

Chapter 8: The World's Navies in the Age of Moltke
1 There is a good short account of the battle and its lessons in D. G. Browne, *The Floating Bulwark*, pp. 161–6. The best detailed objective account remains that in Friedjung, *The Struggle for Supremacy in Germany,* vol. 2, pp. 454–513.
2 Persano still had a decided preponderance in ships and guns; and he was subsequently court-martialled and cashiered for his successive failures of nerve.
3 Parkes, *British Battleships, 1860–1950*; quoted in Browne, *The Floating Bulwark*, p. 182.
4 Browne, *The Floating Bulwark*, p. 202.
5 Ibid., p. 205.
6 Fiedel, *The Splendid Little War*, p. 14.
7 Ibid.
8 Quoted in Freidel, *The Splendid Little War*, pp. 107–8.
9 Notably Richard Hough, *The Fleet that had to Die* (London 1958: Hamish Hamilton), and Noel F. Busch, *The Emperor's Sword* (Liverpool 1969: Gallery Press).
10 As torpedo-boats were enlarged and strengthened, there emerged a new class named initially torpedo-boat destroyers. The two classes became amalgamated and in most navies they came to be known simply as destroyers.

Chapter 9: The Legacy of Moltke
1 The conflicting rivalries and ambitions of the powers are analysed in lucid detail in A. J. P. Taylor's *The Struggle for Mastery in Europe*, chs 15–20.
2 Howard, *The Franco-Prussian War, passim.*
3 Howard, *The Franco-Prussian War*, vol. 1, p. 377.
4 See above, p. 142.
5 It is related that, when his attention was drawn to a particularly grandiose Bavarian landscape visible through a carriage

window, he only remarked after a cursory glance that the river
was not an obstacle and that the country was not adapted for a
defensive position.

6 For a lucid analysis of the diplomatic consequences of
Schlieffen's plan see Taylor, *The Struggle for Mastery in
Europe*, pp. 330–42.

7 Printed in full in Duff Cooper, *Haig* (London 1935), vol. 1
pp. 377 *et seq.*

8 Luvaas, *The Military Legacy of the Civil War*, p. 198.

9 Ibid., p. 199.

10 Colonel E. L. V. Cordonnier, *The Japanese in Manchuria
1904*, English translation by Captain C. F. Atkinson (London
1912), vol. 1, p. 238.

11 Captain L. Auger, *La Guerre de sécession* (Paris 1895).

12 Freytag-Loringhoven, *Studien über Kriegführiung auf
Grundlage des nordamerikanischen Sezessionskrieges* (Berlin
1901–3), vol. 3, pp. 60 and 104.

13 Freytag-Loringhoven, *Studien zur Kriegsgeschichte und
Taktik* (Berlin 1905), vol. 4.

14 Wood and Edmonds, *The Civil War in the United States*.

15 All these writers are extensively quoted in Luvaas, *The Military Legacy of the Civil War, passim*.

16 Admiral A. T. Mahan, *The Influence of Sea Power upon
History* (London 1890).

17 It is an interesting and rare example of history repeating
itself that the barrage balloons over the British beach at Ouistre-
ham on D-Day 1944 had to be cut adrift because they gave the
German heavy guns, out of sight at Le Havre, a perfect aiming
mark.

18 B. H. Liddell Hart, *Foch, Man of Orléans* (London 1937;
Penguin) vol. 1, p. 58.

Index

Index

Index

Index

Index

Togoland, 96
Tonkin, 97–8
Trafalgar, battle of, 5, 71, 256, 297
Transvaal, 215
Trautenau, battle of, 127–8
Trentino, 98, 110, 301
Tripoli, 97, 100, 311
Trieste, 51, 110
Trochu, Gen Louis-Jules, 40
Tsarevitch, Russian battleship, 284, 290–1
Tchernaya, battle of the, 12, 68
Tsushima, battle of, 248, 255, 283, 291, 293–7, 322, 324
Tuareg, the, 95
Tunis, 95, 100
Turenne, Marshal Henri de la Tour d'Auvergne, Vicomte de, 151
Turkestan, 88–9
Turkey, 88–9, 91, 95, 100, 187–8
Tuyen-Quan, 98
Tweebosch, 229

Ukase of 1874, 88, 91–5, 190
Utomsky, Admiral Prince, 291
Ulm, battle of, 15, 27
Ural Mts, 88, 197

Vaalkranz, 239
Vaillant, Marshal Philibert, 39, 41
Vauban, Marshal Sebastien le Prestre, Seigneur de, 203, 253
Van Doorn, Earl, Confederate General, 155
Varna, 191
Venetia, 11, 33, 51, 53, 69, 257
Verdun, 66, 103, 111, 118, 144, 187, 304, 306

Vickers-Maxim gun, 220, 222
Vicksburg, 155–6, 161, 177, 225, 314
Victor Emmanuel II of Italy, 7, 40, 68
Victoria, Queen, 75
Vienna, 8, 28, 40, 48, 53, 56, 110, 132, 309
Vienna, Congress of, 1, 3, 7, 12, 22, 70, 106
Villafranca, Armistice of, 37
Vimy Ridge, battle of, 206
Vionville, battle of, 66–7, 140, 144–5, 186
Virginia, 208
Vixen, USS, 279
Vlaakfontein, 229
Vladivostock, 89, 90, 242, 245, 286, 289–91, 293–7
Volunteer Movement, 78, 82–3

Wagram, battle of, 15, 20, 25, 27, 49, 53, 57
Waldersee, F-M Graf von, 305
Walewski, Alexandre, Comte, 8
Warrior, HMS, 175, 179
Washington, DC, 7, 163, 166, 181, 206, 280–1
Waterloo, battle of, 3–5, 7, 15–16, 19, 20, 30, 71, 73, 95, 124, 138, 164, 230, 298–9, 315
Wauchope, Gen, 238–9
Wavell, Archibald, F-M Lord, 120, 164
Weehawken, USS, 182
Wei-hai-wei, 290
Wellington, Arthur Wellesley, Duke of, 4, 15–16, 19, 20, 23–5, 72, 81, 138, 229–30, 256, 298
Westphalia, 63

West Point, 150, 319
Wheeler, Gen Joe, 157, 197, 208–9, 218
White, Gen Sir George, 217, 219, 233
Whitehall, 72, 75, 77
Whitehead Torpedo, 266, 280
White Mutiny, 74, 76
William I, German Emperor, 6, 34, 58–63, 107–8, 131, 134, 138, 142, 298
William II, German Emperor, 5, 70, 104, 109, 302, 307
Wilmington, 175–6
Wimpffen, F-M Graf, 49–50, 124, 126
Wyndham, 80
Windischgrätz, Prince, 28
Witgeft, Rear-Admiral, 286–7, 289–90
Wolseley, F-M Sir Garnet late Lord, 24, 77, 120, 172–4, 217, 221, 226, 298
Wolfe, Gen James, 329
Woolwich, 113, 220–1
Wörth, battle of, 46, 94, 111, 140, 143, 145, 214
Wrangel, Gen von, 28, 68, 127
Wylly, Lt Col H. C., 330

Yakumo, Japanese battleship, 295
Yalu River, 241, 245, 257, 271–3, 282, 286, 295
Yashima, Japanese battleship, 288
York, F-M, HRH Prince Frederick, Duke of, 17, 84

Zastrow, Lt-Gen von, 66
Zeppelin airships, 325
Zula, 77, 113
Zulus, 24, 101